Studies in Modern History

General Editor: **J. C. D. Clark**, Joyce and Elizabeth Hall Distinguished Professor of British History, University of Kansas

Titles include:

Bernard Cottret (*editor*)
BOLINGBROKE'S POLITICAL WRITINGS
The Conservative Enlightenment

Richard R. Follett
EVANGELICALISM, PENAL THEORY AND THE POLITICS OF CRIMINAL LAW REFORM IN ENGLAND, 1808–30

Philip Hicks
NEOCLASSICAL HISTORY AND ENGLISH CULTURE
From Clarendon to Hume

William M. Kuhn
DEMOCRATIC ROYALISM
The Transformation of the British Monarchy, 1861–1914

Kim Lawes
PATERNALISM AND POLITICS
The Revival of Paternalism in Early Nineteenth-Century Britain

Nancy D. LoPatin
POLITICAL UNIONS, POPULAR POLITICS AND THE GREAT REFORM ACT OF 1832

Marjorie Morgan
NATIONAL IDENTITIES AND TRAVEL IN VICTORIAN BRITAIN

James Muldoon
EMPIRE AND ORDER
The Concept of Empire, 800–1800

W. D. Rubinstein and Hilary Rubinstein
PHILOSEMITISM
Admiration and Support for Jews in the English-Speaking World, 1840–1939

Lynne Taylor
BETWEEN RESISTANCE AND COLLABORATION
Popular Protest in Northern France, 1940–45

Studies in Modern History
Series Standing Order ISBN 0-333-79328-5
(*outside North America only*)

You can receive future titles in this series as they are published by placing a standing order. Please contact your bookseller or, in case of difficulty, write to us at the address below with your name and address, the title of the series and the ISBN quoted above.

Customer Services Department, Macmillan Distribution Ltd, Houndmills, Basingstoke, Hampshire RG21 6XS, England

National Identities and Travel in Victorian Britain

Marjorie Morgan
Associate Professor of History
Southern Illinois University
Carbondale
Illinois

© Marjorie Morgan 2001

All rights reserved. No reproduction, copy or transmission of this publication may be made without written permission.

No paragraph of this publication may be reproduced, copied or transmitted save with written permission or in accordance with the provisions of the Copyright, Designs and Patents Act 1988, or under the terms of any licence permitting limited copying issued by the Copyright Licensing Agency, 90 Tottenham Court Road, London W1P 0LP.

Any person who does any unauthorised act in relation to this publication may be liable to criminal prosecution and civil claims for damages.

The author has asserted her right to be identified as the author of this work in accordance with the Copyright, Designs and Patents Act 1988.

First published 2001 by
PALGRAVE
Houndmills, Basingstoke, Hampshire RG21 6XS and
175 Fifth Avenue, New York, N.Y. 10010
Companies and representatives throughout the world

PALGRAVE is the new global academic imprint of
St. Martin's Press LLC Scholarly and Reference Division and
Palgrave Publishers Ltd (formerly Macmillan Press Ltd).

ISBN 0-333-71999-9

This book is printed on paper suitable for recycling and made from fully managed and sustained forest sources.

A catalogue record for this book is available from the British Library.

Library of Congress Cataloging-in-Publication Data
Morgan, Marjorie.
   National identities and travel in Victorian Britain / Marjorie Morgan.
   p. cm.
Includes bibliographical references and index.
ISBN 0-333-71999-9
   1. National characteristics, British—History—19th century. 2. British-
-Travel—Europe—History—19th century. 3. Travelers—Great Britain-
-History—19th century. 4. Great Britain—History—Victoria,
1837-1901. 5. Great Britain—Civilization—19th century. 6. Great
Britain—Description and travel. 7. Europe—Description and travel. I.
Title.
DA533 .M75 2000
941.081—dc21

00-041511

10 9 8 7 6 5 4 3 2 1
10 09 08 07 06 05 04 03 02 01

Printed and bound in Great Britain by
Antony Rowe Ltd, Chippenham, Wiltshire

*In memory of my father,
Leonard S. Lustick*

Contents

Acknowledgements	ix
Introduction	1
1 The Meaning and Mechanics of Travel in the Victorian Age	9
2 Landscape and Climate	46
3 Religion	83
4 Customs, Comfort and Class	119
5 Liberty, Language and History	155
6 The Discourse of National Identity among Victorian Travellers	195
Conclusion	217
Appendix: Biographical Information on Travellers	220
Notes	230
Bibliography	255
Index	265

Acknowledgements

My parents instilled a love of travel in me and my siblings even before we were old enough for schooling. They took us by train, plane and car on annual family vacations to various regions of the United States, sometimes to visit family, but more often to see new sites. Our most memorable trip was a coast-to-coast ride by train when I was ten years old. I watched with amazement the balancing acts by dining car waiters, was often found perched on a raised seat in the glass dome car so as not to miss any noteworthy scenery and fulminated against rattling toilets that kept me awake much of the night. Despite the discomforts, I did not want the ride to end, and thus did my best to immortalize it and the rest of the trip by compiling a scrapbook of carefully captioned and pasted brochures, postcards, tickets and other travel ephemera. To this day, I am happiest when on the road or rail, camera across my shoulder, journal in hand.

This affection for travelling no doubt had something to do with my becoming an historian. After all, historians are by profession travellers, at least with respect to time. I am thankful to be part of a profession that enables me to combine one of my loves or hobbies – travel – with my work as a researcher. In this book, I travel back in time to explore the meaning and mechanics of travel, and their significance for national identities in Victorian Britain. The project involved a number of trips to and around Britain, and I want to thank Southern Illinois University for a Summer Research Fellowship that helped make these trips possible.

The librarians and staff of the following institutions provided invaluable assistance locating sources and sometimes even offered coffee and snacks during those frustrating slump periods of the day: Barnet Local Studies and Archive Centre, London, British Library, Brompton Oratory Archives, Friends House, London, Guildhall Library, Greater London Record Office, National Library of Scotland, National Library of Wales, Public Record Office, Kew, Thomas Cook Archive and University College Library, London. Their assistance is much appreciated.

I owe special thanks to those individuals who either read or heard parts of the book and helped me to think through various issues during the course of the project. Michael Batinski read several chapters and offered many helpful suggestions for improvement. Questions and challenges from graduate students in my 'Travel and Cultural Identity' colloquium/seminar and from audiences at sessions of the Midwest Conference on British Studies and North American Conference on British Studies meetings encouraged me to refine and sharpen many of the ideas presented here.

I have relied on the good adivce, support and patience of my editors. Jonathan Clark and Maike Bohn helped to facilitate the production process, and Ruth Willats saved me from numerous semantic and stylistic errors.

Any traveller is most appreciative of comfortable accommodations. The staff of William Goodenough House and London House provided me, summer after summer, with a most friendly and supportive place to live in London. They created just the sort of stimulating, stress-free community that allows a researcher to thrive. A very special thanks to staff member and fellow traveller Valerie Martin whose encouragement throughout this entire project was unfailing.

I am most indebted to my parents who taught me the joys of travelling in the first place. More importantly, they encouraged me to be pained by my own ignorance and never failed to support my interests and studies. My father, in particular, showed me with his words and deeds that there are no closed doors in life. I am grateful for his example and his love, and dedicate this book to his memory.

Introduction

In 1984, when I turned 30, I still did not really understand what it meant to identify with a place or a people. Perhaps this was because I had called a number of places 'home' by that time. I was born in Michigan, 'got tall' in Southern California, attended high school in New Orleans, college in Houston, and graduate school back in New Orleans. Michigan was much clearer on my birth certificate than in my memory, but the other places I had come to know well, and even felt affection for Southern California and, especially, for New Orleans. Given my love of fine food, drink-in-hand conversations, river sounds and rocking-chair porch life, New Orleans was undoubtedly the most suitable place of the three for me. But I never identified with the city in the sense of feeling as if I were from or rooted there. In fact, when asked where I was from, I mostly fidgeted, trying to find a simple way of saying that I didn't know. My fidgets and feelings of rootlessness continued until the autumn of 1984 when I left the United States for the first time. Only then did an identity with respect to place begin to come clear in my mind.

I had crossed the Atlantic for a year-plus stay in Britain to gather material for my dissertation. But I also looked forward to collecting impressions of British sites, landscapes, foods and peoples so that I could enhance my history courses with first-hand accounts of the places and peoples we were studying. The famous sites were exciting to see, but everything from flushing gadgetry to fashionable boutiques seemed fascinating and worthy of a journal entry. I walked for at least eight hours every Sunday, took occasional day trips and sampled dozens of pubs and plays, always making sure that a Ryman's journal – my most constant companion – received my impressions. I was surprised by many things I encountered, such as the British penchant for picnicking on hill tops in the fiercest of winds. But I was perhaps most surprised by my own journals, which gradually filled with as many comments about the US as about the Britain I was experiencing while writing. The constant confrontation with things foreign made me think, for the first time in my life, about what it meant to be an American. I actually began to *feel* American, and to recognize that I had roots in a particular place and culture. My concepts of what was scenic, humorous or polite, which I had always assumed were natural or human, suddenly became identified as American in my mind. It was not yet fashionable to talk about the 'Other', but I certainly had discovered how crucially important such a frame of reference was for crystallizing personal and collective identity.

It was this discovery and the experience of perusing my 15 journal volumes on the plane back to the US in November 1985 that suggested a book project to follow my dissertation. What I knew by the time the plane touched down in St. Louis was that I wanted to explore collective identities in Victorian Britain by looking at Britons' encounters with the 'Other', though which other(s) was not clear at the time. I also knew that travel writing would be the main source I would draw on for the project. It seemed the ideal source for several reasons. First, reading travel literature and writing about my own travels had always been much loved hobbies. Instructors told me over and over again, and I now tell my students, to write about what really interests you. Second, travelling removes people from their familiar milieux and confronts them with the other, or the foreign. This confrontation – as I learned from my own travel experience – forces them to reflect on the familiar, making them more aware of how it defines them individually and collectively. Accounts of such confrontations thus seemed an excellent vehicle for examining identities, particularly national identities, in Victorian Britain. Finally, in the mid-1980s, travel writing was still a largely untapped source, especially among historians.[1]

Writing and revising the dissertation kept me busy for several years, so it was not until the early 1990s that I was able to conceptualize the project on travel and identity. At that time, several trends in the scholarly and political worlds influenced how my project took shape. The study of nationalism and national identity had become an academic growth industry dominating many conferences and press catalogues. Although the topic was not new, it was being approached in new and exciting ways.[2] Instead of assuming that nations were natural communities that emerged as states due to such forces as industrialization or the decline of religion as a primary social and cultural bond, scholars were emphasizing that nations were cultural constructs, and thus subject to continual analysis, debate and change.[3] To put it another way, the focus in nation studies came to be on change, construction, imagination and invention, rather than on naturalness and time immemorial. Furthermore, scholars were giving less attention to nations in the abstract, and more to the processes by which individual nations were made and remade by means of such things as language, myth, symbols and ceremonies.

Even British historians got on the nation studies bandwagon. I say 'even', because until the mid- to late 1980s, scholars studying Britain had completely ignored the topic of nationalism and national identity.[4] They had been influenced by the English themselves, who have tended to see nationalism, like rabies, as something that never made it across the Channel where the nation had existed for so long as to seem unproblematic.[5] The rise in the 1980s of a less English-centred approach to the history of the British Isles shifted focus to the interaction of peoples and cultures.[6] With this shift and the new approaches to studying nations mentioned above, it was no longer possible to take for granted a single nation or national culture. The nation-state-making process involving the creation and re-creation of multiple cultures that continually negotiate and renegotiate their relative positions became of central interest to many historians of Britain.[7]

Outside the academy, the early 1990s was a time when the growing integration of Europe was often front-page news. More to the point, 1992 was the year when the process of incorporating Britain into a more united Europe was to begin. It seemed to me that from that point on, scholars and the general public would be increasingly interested in Britons' perception of themselves vis-à-vis the Continent and the history of that perception. Thus I was not surprised when *History Today* started the year with a lead article by Bernard Porter entitled 'The Victorians and Europe'.[8]

These developments in the early 1990s scholarly and political worlds helped me to settle more clearly on my book project. Its aim became, and still is, to use travel writing (published and non-published) about trips to the Continent *and* around Britain to explore components of national identity imagined by middle- and upper-middle-class men and women from England, Scotland and Wales during Victoria's reign (1837–1901).[9] Their journals are full of details about local eating habits, sense of humour, religious practices, and so forth, as well as speculation on the implications of these and other details for the national groups being observed. But such discussions also prompted these travellers to compare and to comment on their own habits and attitudes, which resulted in their drawing conclusions about their national identities. My goal is to reveal what travellers from each of the main regions of Britain had in mind when they used such terms as 'British', 'English', 'Scotch' and 'Welsh' to imagine and describe themselves collectively.

My choice of Europe as a travel destination is related, in part, to my belief that an interest in the history of Britain's relationship with Europe will continue to increase during the next decade and beyond. I chose travel within Britain as a focus for study as well because I wanted to explore the degree to which context, particularly geographic context, affected national imagining. In other words, I wanted to examine how the 'us', or national group imagined, depended on the 'them', or the Other, encountered by travellers at any given time. I did not want to confine the study to travel within Britain, because I believe, like Maura O'Connor, that nations are forged both from within and from outside national borders, and thus 'crossing national boundaries should be at the heart of our study of nation making'.[10] Regarding time-frame, the length of a monarch's reign may seem an arbitrary period to choose for a study. This period is significant, however, with respect to the history of travel. It was in the mid- and late nineteenth century that large numbers of middle-class men and women began to travel to Europe and other lands outside of Britain. Focusing on this time-frame thus allowed me to go beyond looking at a small number of aristocrats, to examine how a much larger group of middle-class Britons collectively imagined themselves.

I argue three main points in this book. First, the images and material goods of everyday experience and ritual were important contributors to people's sense of national belonging, or identity, in the Victorian period. They included such things as landscape, religious ritual, food and drink, manners, recreational rituals, methods of hierarchical ordering, and so forth. These things were as or more important to feelings of national belonging as were state-sponsored ceremonies, pageantry and propaganda, which people experienced more sporadically.

Second, context is key for understanding national identity. Despite the existence of passports and other legal documents proclaiming a certainty about Victorians being 'British subjects', travellers' actual perceptions reveal a much more interesting ambiguity and slipperiness regarding their national identity. Individual men and women from Britain displayed multiple and varying national identities, depending on such things as geographic context, gender or whether the context was governmental/abstract or cultural/emotional. For example, they were more likely to identify with a sense of Britishness when on the Continent or when referring to governmental matters, but with a distinct form of Englishness, Scottishness or Welshness when travelling around Britain itself or when defining themselves culturally. My study thus suggests that we are dealing with four nations when we talk of Great Britain proper in the Victorian period, and very likely at least five if we consider the whole British Isles and thus include Ireland.[11]

Finally, I argue that the process of national imagining is not simply a matter of continually inventing new images and traditions. Recent scholarship tends to stress how nations and national identity are inventions constructed at particular moments in time, rather than givens existing since time immemorial. This view has made us more aware of the creative, protean nature of national identity and tradition, but it has blinded us to the continuities shaping national identity.[12] My study argues for a blending of old and new, by showing how national identities rest on age-old stereotypes continually invested with new meanings.

The arguments and focus here engage with recent scholarship on national identity and travel in other ways as well. Most studies of national identity in Britain explore how the nation has been forged or constructed by the State and institutions of the cultural elite. Discussions typically focus on such things as royal pageantry, censuses, national museums and biographies, school textbooks, government propaganda, laws, and military paraphernalia and policies. Very little attention has been given to how ordinary people internalize and imagine the nation.[13] Thus we have models of how the state and elites tried to fashion a sense of Britishness or Englishness – what we might call 'official nationalism' – but very little understanding of the many qualities ordinary people had in mind when they used these terms to refer to themselves. My study attempts to enhance this understanding by exploring the components of national identities rather than their means of construction.

In that I highlight the flexible repertoire of national identities in Victorian Britain rather than the dominance of one, I depart from some key existing studies. Colley, for example, gave a passing nod to the persistence of traditional identities including Englishness, Scottishness, and Welshness, but then devoted her entire book *Britons* to documenting the emergence of a new *British* identity in the eighteenth century. Similarly, Newman explored the rise of English nationalism to the exclusion of other nationalisms. Some scholars such as Eric Evans have argued against the existence of multiple identities on a national scale. Speaking of the period from 1790 to 1870, Evans declared:

The quest for a distinctively *English*, as opposed to a *British*, identity in this period is, in fact, one that will prove fruitless. 'British' is the dominant descriptor of patriotic identification; and at any level more local than that of 'Britain', the English were more likely to identify with their own regions and localities than with the whole country of England *per se*.[14]

A few scholars *have* emphasized the plurality of identities in Britain, including Britishness and the traditional national identities, especially in the area of religion. D.W. Bebbington recognized that Scotland and Wales had distinct religious identities that coexisted with an overarching British religious identity grounded in Evangelicalism.[15] But no study to date has documented, as I do here, the existence and constitutive elements of distinct English, Welsh, Scots *and* British identities in ordinary people's imaginations by shifting the geographic contexts in which imagining took place and by analysing patterns of discourse about national identity. What emerges from this study is the conclusion that there were four national identities in Great Britain (excluding Ireland) during the Victorian period. Depending on circumstances, the similarities between Englishness, Scottishness, and Welshness seemed paramount, resulting in a shared sense of Britishness; in other cases the differences seemed most obvious, making a plurality of nations most evident. The survival of Britain as a state as compared to the former Yugoslavia suggests that perhaps this combination of an overarching national identity and more narrowly focused regional ones is essential if a state composed of multiple nationalities and cultures is to remain intact.

By adopting Britain and Europe as geographic contexts for my study, I am somewhat out of step with most other scholars interested in the relationship between travel and identity. These scholars have tended to emphasize travel to non-European areas with an eye to revealing the imperial mentality.[16] In their view, it is not possible to understand Britain or Europe outside the imperial context, because key values were forged outside Europe during the course of interactions with non-European peoples. In other words, outside influences are key, and some scholars go so far as to argue that the nation is not, therefore, a meaningful subject for study.[17] I have already explained my choice of Europe as a travel destination – a geographic place which I believe functioned very much as an 'outside influence' with respect to Britain. I do not mean to suggest by this choice that Empire is unimportant, but much of what we are now terming 'colonial' existed within Europe itself before there were any overseas colonies. In the case of Britain, the most long-lasting discourse of the sort we call 'colonial' was not Orientalism, but rather anti-Catholicism. Furthermore, the imperial experience began in Britain itself with an English empire. Rather than privileging empire as a context, it seems more meaningful to view empire as one of many contexts in which people from Britain framed their identity.

The book begins with an overview of the Victorian world of travel, particularly of its commercialization. This was the age of the first standardized travel guidebooks, packaged tours and travellers' cheques – all things helping to make foreign travel possible for the middle, in some cases even the working, classes. I discuss the meaning, methods and paraphernalia of nineteenth-century travel, but also entertaining tidbits such as optimum solutions for flea-filled beds, seasickness and scorching rays from the sun. Modern-day readers will no doubt heave a sigh of relief when they read here about the implications of political conditions for travel, particularly on the Continent before unification of nation-states minimized hassles from endless currency exchanges and meddlesome customs officials. These combined with lumbering conveyances, made foreign travel in the Victorian period a very time-consuming and vexatious endeavour. In our age of global tourism and technology, which have nearly annihilated time and space, it seems important to point out that it took weeks to travel from Le Havre to Marseilles in the mid-nineteenth century. The chapter thus transports readers back to the nineteenth century, while at the same time offering them some understanding of the context that generated the travel writing analysed in the book.

The next four chapters focus on components of identity imagined by travellers from Britain. Their journals suggest that images, material goods and rituals to do with landscape, religion, food and drink, manners, recreation, comfort, liberty and government contributed most strongly to Victorian Britons' (meaning people from Britain) sense of national belonging. These chapters document various ways that context, especially geographic context, influenced the form national imagining took. They also call into question the view that travel worked primarily to reinforce Europeans' (including Britons) sense of superiority. It did sometimes do this, but travel also made many people more critical of their culture. Thus in some cases travel confirmed what people already perceived to be true about their home culture; in others, it modified their perceptions.

The final chapter explores patterns of discourse, or use of terminology, with respect to national identity. There were many times in the

Victorian period, as now, when English and British were used interchangeably. But a careful reading of nearly 100 travel books suggests that usage fell into patterns, with travellers being most likely to use British in certain contexts, and English in others. By patterns, I do not mean precision. Usage was often technically inaccurate, as when people used England to mean England and Wales, or all of Britain. But the inaccuracy could be one of exclusion as well. To some travellers, England meant only southern England, and Scotland those areas not populated mostly by Gaels. This chapter, like the others, reinforces the notion that nations are imagined and, therefore, much more ambiguous than maps or passports would suggest. If this were not the case, I would never have wanted to spend several years studying national identity in Britain or anywhere else.

1
The Meaning and Mechanics of Travel in the Victorian Age

In 1870, the writer and loyal Londoner Edmund Gosse travelled with a companion as far north in Scotland as Stornoway. Though critical of most lowland Scottish people he met, Gosse thought the people of Stornoway were very Norse in their looks and among the finest 'race of men'. With their nicely chiselled features and burnt flesh tints reminiscent of Titian, the lounging Stornoway fishermen seemed like 'handsome giants'. The women, too, appeared comely and taller even than 'Scotch lassies', who seemed more universally towering than English ones. In this extreme northwest area of Scotland, Gosse felt more remote from his beloved London than he would have if he had been in southern Italy or northern Turkey. Tourists were a rarity in Stornoway, and Gosse seemed as strange and unfamiliar to the locals as they did to him. The misunderstandings and lapses in communication between Gosse and the native population were so great as to be amusing. As he explained it, '[T]here was a general puzzlement as to what on earth we had come for.' The puzzlement reached a climax when he asked at his inn for oatcakes, a sample of the local fare. The landlady expressed wonder and dismay. Knowing him to be a gentleman from the South, she had prepared a steamer-like meal – what one might have received in Glasgow. It was impossible for her to believe that he wanted to sample the everyday 'productions' of Stornoway. Her perplexed look seemed to say, 'Could gentlefolk really prefer oatcake to the bread from the south!'[1]

The encounter between Gosse and the Stornoway landlady was one between strangers, but strangers who had preconceptions about each other that formed a basis for expectations about desires and behaviour, and about how the encounter would unfold. As is often the case when strangers encounter each other, the expectations turned out to be wrong, causing puzzlement and dismay. Such encounters between strangers and moments of puzzlement characterize the travel experience and have significance for personal and collective identity. For it is such jarring puzzlements that make travellers and those 'strangers', or 'others', they encounter ponder the meaning and value of who they are. Put another way, individual and collective identities move more sharply into focus as a result of cross-cultural contact, or contact with others. As the travel scholar Eric Leed argued, 'The transformations of social being in travel suggest that there is no self without an other; and that, at bottom, identity is done with mirrors.'[2] The Stornoway landlady confronted Gosse with a mirror reflecting the southern gentleman he was imagined to be, and he flashed back an image of Stornoway that very likely caused the landlady to reassess the value of her everyday Stornoway 'productions' and culture. The *meaning* of travel and its implications for collective self-awareness will become clearer if we think of travel as doing four things, particularly to travellers, but sometimes to those they encounter as well: estranging, transforming, liberating and unsettling.

The initial stage of travel involves departure from a routine social and cultural milieu, and it thus *estranges* the traveller from what is familiar.[3] Travellers literally step outside their identity-forming environment and are, therefore, better able to observe and evaluate that environment objectively. The experience sharpens and can even alter their perception of the familiar. For example, what once was taken for granted at home as being natural and universal suddenly becomes, upon comparison with 'others', categorized as uniquely English, Lowland Scots or some other regionally or nationally specific identity. Furthermore, departing puts one's own identity temporarily in limbo by estranging one from oneself. The traveller becomes more free to fashion any identity he or she chooses, a freedom in which Samuel Johnson's biographer, James Boswell, revelled.[4] Boswell was a most accomplished self-fashioner. During his travels, he changed from being lord and courtier to philosopher, lover, diplomat and merchant as easily as if he were changing clothing. The eventual arrival in some new and distant land is also estranging – the traveller is perceived by others as a stranger, and thus intriguing, threatening and exploitable. He or she must be on guard in a way that is *transforming*.

Being on guard involves heightening one's perceptive, imaginative, emotional and sensory powers. Travellers are thus transformed into keen observers of their own and others' cultures. 'In travelling...our sight is on the alert,' said one traveller.[5] Journals suggest that travellers believed many other sorts of transformations occurred during journeys as well. Some emphasized the various improvements afforded by travel – improvement of mind, heart, body, character and/or social prestige. Travelling was thought to enhance knowledge of human nature and, therefore, to civilize and liberalize the mind. Alexander Graham Dunlop noted how acute the mind and sight were when travelling so that, in his words, 'We improve and... Our prejudices leave us one by one... Our benevolence extends itself with our knowledge.'[6] Others travelled for *re*creation of mind and body in order to renew their spirits and thus make the trammels of routine easier to endure. Thus Charles Lucey took an extended tour of Wales 'amid new and uncommon scenes which should invigorate both body and mind and strengthen them for renewed exertions'.[7] Learned men often travelled, particularly to Greece and Italy, to validate their education by standing among the ruins of the classical civilizations that formed the core of their formal studies. But travels to the Mediterranean for men and women frequently had as much to do with improving their physical as mental health. Britain's damp and dreary winter days drove those with coughs, fevers and a sufficient bank account to Europe's more balmy southern climate, where they colonized the Mediterranean coast and dozens of strategically located inland spa towns, such as Pau.

For other travellers, transforming character and social status was more the goal than convalescing. They believed that making one's way in a foreign country fostered habits of self-reliance and a heightened awareness of one's ignorance and limitations that would strengthen character. A desire to boost social value and prestige also sent people to the Continent. That is, they crossed the Channel to acquire the manners, dancing steps and foreign phrases for shining in polite society at home. Many went as well to tick off the sights, so they could score social points at home by saying at advantageous moments that they had seen such and such, usually something starred in a guidebook. Several travellers confessed to doing undesirable, even agonising, things simply because they were fashionable or guaranteed to impress. For example, social pressure sent one woman across all the famous Alpine passes. One wonders how much scenery she admired, as she insisted on knitting her way over every foot of the mountain terrain to assuage her guilt about wasting time. Gosse and his travelling companion took a dip while touring the Isle of Skye 'inspired more by the desire of saying that [they] swam in a Skye Loch, than by the glamour of the water, which was yellow, or the bottom which was mud.'[8]

In addition to being estranging and transforming, travel is very *liberating*, in that it permits one to engage with the 'Other' and to forsake the strictures of home. Protestant British travellers, for example, who never felt at liberty to enter a Catholic Church in their own country, found themselves walking down the aisles and attending Mass in dozens on the Continent. They could easily justify the visits because they felt obliged to see the art, architecture and religiosity of the foreign cultures they were encountering. Such visits confronted travellers with their own religious prejudices, in some cases reinforcing and in others softening them, as we will see in chapter 3. Women felt emboldened enough once outside their country to venture out in public alone, and the experience heightened their awareness of how their own culture was stifling to liberty. Male travellers also noted the freedom afforded by travel. In the canoe paddler John MacGregor's case, he emphasized the freedom from such trappings of polite society as the hat, braces, razor and umbrella.

Other travellers revelled in the freedom from the familiar – whether work, boredom, cares or general routine – found on the road, where they felt suspended between the past and the future, and thus free wholly to experience and enjoy the present. Jemima Morrell, for example, said of her tour of Switzerland, 'It was an entire change; the usual routine of life was gone. All memory of times and seasons faded away and we lived only in the enjoyment of the present.'[9] Even the shackles of time and age disappeared for some such as Gosse, who noted how a remote part of Scotland, more distant from his London residence than Belgrade, afforded a much-appreciated freedom from the clock. New places and sites enabled Dunlop to escape temporarily his years and feel himself a child again, full of energy and eagerness tempered by only the most momentary of cares.

The myriad of new stimuli offered by travel – whether of sights, sounds, tastes, coins or ideas – was no doubt exciting and liberating, but also *unsettling*. Constant exposure to the unfamiliar was disorienting and often made travellers feel vulnerable. For a start, travelling was physically disturbing to the stomach, bowels and skin. But it also challenged travellers' basic beliefs and assaulted their daily rituals in a way that not only made them more acutely aware of those beliefs and rituals, but also caused them to question and sometimes to be less satisfied with them. Furthermore, foreigners often imposed an identity on travellers, taking the very core of their being out of their control, as when Europeans insisted that Scots and all other peoples from the British Isles were English. Such jolts to the body, senses and imagination prompted travellers to seek protectors in the form of medicines and powders, guidebooks, tour guides, English hotels, and English and Scottish churches.

The protectors travellers chose and the things they shielded themselves from say something about their values, and highlight once again the connection between travel and collective self-awareness, or national identity. Furthermore, these protectors remind us that travel is a quest both for the new and unfamiliar *and* for a shielding from them. Although the bulk of this book focuses on the components of national identity revealed in travel journals, the remainder of chapter 1 explores the *mechanics* of travel in the Victorian period in order to help recreate an important context in which increasing numbers of people from Britain framed their personal and collective identities.

Queen Victoria's reign (1837–1901) coincided with such a dramatic transformation in travel that a tourist in the mid-century would have found little useful information in the two-volume *Traveller's Oracle* published ten years before Victoria came to the throne.[10] Its pages talk of carriages – their sizes, wheels and speeds – and dwell even more on details of horse care so essential for travelling by road. The first 30 years of the nineteenth century were the most enthusiastic years of road travel and, until the craze for motor cars emerged in the early twentieth, the last. In between, rails replaced roads as popular thoroughfares, bringing a steam-powered, speedy form of travel within the budget of even a working-class family. The democratization of travel made possible by the railway caused many to conclude that the Victorian age was, more than anything else, a 'travelling age'.

In this 'travelling age', likely destinations changed as dramatically as methods of transport. Before the mid-nineteenth century, only a percentage of the aristocratic elite set their sights beyond the British Isles when they formulated travel plans. Thus *The Traveller's Oracle* devoted only one chapter of its two volumes to advice on travel in foreign countries. By 1841, however, when Thomas Cook organized his first cheap excursion, increasing numbers of middle-class travellers were clutching guidebooks for the Continent as they experienced their first cross-Channel passage. Even some workers were taking short trips to Paris or cheap packaged tours to the Continent by the end of the nineteenth century. When Victoria died in 1901, travel to the Continent had become so *passé* and taken for granted among the aristocracy and middle class that it did not warrant even a mention in a retrospective on the late Queen's reign. *The Illustrated London News* had a review of the reign composed of 3–4-page sections on every topic from art to imperial policy. The section on travel ignored tourism on the Continent, concentrating instead on exploration of more distant lands such as Africa, the Americas, Asia and Antarctica. For its author, F.C. Selous, travel was synonymous with exploring the unknown and uncharted. He boasted of how the unexplored half of the globe's surface existing when Victoria came to the throne had been mapped and trod by her subjects before she died. In short, the world of global travel and tourism was emerging.[11]

Clarification regarding terminology and sources is important before proceeding. Recent scholars tend to stress the dichotomy between travel and tourism, viewing it as an integral part of modern tourism itself. James Buzard, for example, argued that the commercialization of touring in the nineteenth century caused members of the middle and upper classes to seek cultural authenticity by positioning themselves as 'travellers' in relation to the mass of mere 'tourists'. That is, self-proclaimed 'travellers' distanced themselves from and denigrated 'tourists' by depicting them as passive, dependent followers of the beaten track laid for them by rail companies, guidebooks and entrepreneurs such as Thomas Cook. They saw themselves, on the other hand, as aesthetically sensitive, independent spirits, bent on avoiding well-trodden paths and thus experiencing other places and peoples in an original, authentic way. While such posturing and protests against tourists occur in many travel accounts, most of my sources use the terms 'tourist/traveller' and 'tourism/travel' interchangeably, and thus I do the same. Even Murray's Handbooks, those trailblazers aimed at tourists wanting to be told what was worth seeing in a given place, were titled Handbooks 'For Travellers'. The linguistic distinction that seems more prominent in my sources is that made between 'travel' or 'tourism' and 'exploration'. The first two terms suggested trips to familiar, well-mapped places, while the latter implied treks to distant, unfamiliar, 'exotic' and uncharted lands – Africa and Antarctica, for example. In that I take travellers no further than the Continent, the term 'exploration' is, for the most part, inappropriate and therefore not used. Although the subsequent chapters on national identity draw on accounts of travels around the Continent and Britain, this chapter uses evidence primarily from journals of tours to the Continent. These journals tend to include more specifics on the mechanics of travel itself in this so-called 'travelling age', which is the rest of the chapter's focus.

The burgeoning of foreign travel during Victoria's reign is evident when looking at numbers of and comments about travellers. In the 1830s, roughly 50,000 people a year embarked from Britain's Channel ports; by 1913 the number had risen to 660,000.[12] So many sightseers from England in particular trekked around Europe that the English came to be characterized by the locals and by themselves as a nation of travellers. This penchant for travelling disgusted elitist Englishmen such as George Gissing (just the sort who would have imagined himself a 'traveller') who longed for the days when only the well-to-do wandered. While in Rome at the end of the century, he complained of the swarms of 'vulgar' English offending his highly cultured ears and wondered in dismay, 'How in heaven's name do they get enough money to come here?... What business have these gross animals in such places?'[13] Even fifty years earlier the number of journal-writing English tourists had increased sufficiently to prompt complaints in *Blackwood's Edinburgh Magazine* about assaults on the reading public. In a discussion of railways and steamboats the magazine noted:

> They have afflicted our generation with one desperate evil; they have covered Europe with Tourists, all pen in hand, all determined not to let a henroost remain undescribed, all portfolioed, all handbooked, all 'getting up a Journal,' and all pouring their busy nothings on the 'reading public,' without compassion of conscience.[14]

This touring frenzy affected not only the reading public, but also the landscape in Europe's and Britain's towns and countryside. In this sense, travel transformed not only travellers themselves, but also the places they visited. Restaurants opened, for example, in hundreds of towns and cities – one even appeared half-way up the tower of Utrecht Cathedral – to cater to the growing tourist traffic. And the inevitable mountain-peak restaurant resulted from local entrepreneurs capitalizing on the passion for peak views typical among nineteenth-century tourists from Britain. Even summits like Snowdon's, which were not spacious enough to support a proper restaurant, had a cabin or two where weary climbers could rest and sip beverages.

Although tourists trekking to the top of Mount Snowdon were not rewarded with edible delights, they were offered many species of ferns. Filling bags and cases with ferns carefully plucked from the mountain became the goal of every tourist, so much so that Snowdon ferns became, according to one despondent traveller, 'almost extinct, every bit having been pulled up by tourists'.[15] While some travellers regretted the depletion of plant life brought about by tourism, others bemoaned the cropping up of crowd-drawing buildings. A Scottish aristocrat, for example, was greatly saddened by a trip he took in the late nineteenth century to a village near Genoa where he had visited his grandfather's villa nearly 50 years before. As he stood by the villa remembering the quiet, cosy place he romped around as a boy, he noted, 'The whole village... has been entirely transformed. Hotels, pensions, and villas having grown up everywhere – overrun by tourists, and the charm of the place as I recollect it quite destroyed.'[16]

The burgeoning of travel was both cause and effect of the growth of a highly commercialized touring industry in the Victorian period. It was this industry that created those often denigrated 'tourists' – conventional market creatures dependent on 'experts' in the business to tell them how to travel, where to go, what to see, how to see, and so forth. Some Victorians may have styled themselves as 'travellers' in search of authentic experiences and untrodden paths, but, as Buzard noted, nearly everyone was a tourist by the mid-nineteenth century in that they took trains and resorted to guidebooks when they travelled.[17] Thus sightseeing became, for all, more standardized, predictable and quantifiable according to time. Unabashed tourists boasted that they 'did Turin this morning' or 'did Milan today'. A sarcastic participant in the Toynbee Travellers Club tour to Florence in 1888 poked fun at the whole touring phenomenon:

> On the whole I much enjoyed my tour. In the fortnight I did Antwerp, Brussels, Lucerne, Milan, Florence, Pisa, Genoa, Rome and Naples *thoroughly*. I might have got to Venice, Verona and some other places besides but it is better to do a few things well than to half do a much greater number.[18]

Time was not the only thing measured. Quantification is at the heart of the commercialization process, and it affected how guidebooks presented sights and how tourists saw and interpreted them. In many instances, sightseeing became a statistical rather than a personal experience. Thus instead of recording her own impressions of St. Peter's in Rome, Sophia Holworthy recorded that it took 176 years to build, 350 to perfect, all during the lives of 43 popes, costing £10 million to build and £360 a year to keep in repair; it covers 8 acres, has a nave 607 ft. long, a dome 448 ft. high, 46 altars, 400 statues, 208 staircases, 4422 rooms and 20 courts. She added, finally, that it was one of 370 churces in Rome.[19] Statistics also dominated W.A. Stephenson's rendition of the Forth Railway Bridge, which he considered the greatest engineering feat of the age. Four pages of his journal contain numerical information about the bridge such as:

> The extreme height, above water is 370 ft. The height from the rocky bottom, on which the loftiest pier is built is 452 ft. 21,000 tons of cement, 700,000 cubic feet of granite, 11,700 cubic yards of masonry,

and 44 miles of steel plates having been used. There were 4000 men employed, of which 56 lost their lives, during the 7 years.[20]

Even human beings are quantified objects in this description which was probably lifted from a guidebook. Both these journals reveal the degree to which sites were packaged statistically by a commercialized travel industry and consumed by eager, impressionable, in-a-hurry tourists. Such tourists very likely resorted to statistics because they felt overwhelmed by what they saw and thus at a loss for words. Numbers were safe and convenient.

The growing commercialization of travel can best be seen by examining travel paraphernalia, guidebooks and Cook's Tours. The early Murray travel guides published in the 1840s contain few travel-related adverts, but from 1850 on the advertisement sections grew to booklet length. Although hotel adverts predominate, the travel shop and all its specialized items are puffed and promoted as well. An 1875 guide announces the following:

Est. 1832
Lee & Carter
W. Strand – opposite Charing Cross Hotel
The Original Guide and Travellers' Depot,
also Passport Agency[21]

The advert goes on to list some select items for purchase including: knapsacks, foreign dictionaries, travel journals, railway rugs, travellers chess, portable closet seats, door fasteners and insect powder. These items and more (30 kg allowed free of charge on European trains) would be carried in bags, portmanteaux (suitcases and trunks) and medicine chests, all sold in shops specializing in luggage.

Advertisers and advice writers considered some items more essential for the traveller than others. Some sort of port-a-loo, or 'Inodorous Standard Pail', was advisable, especially for ladies, in order to make them independent of hotel lobbies *and* those foreign cabinets, which often displayed unrefined writing or pictures on the panels. Travellers from Britain tended to find Continental graffiti an assault on respectability from which women in particular needed shielding. Stopping in Godesburg on their trip along the Rhine, the Scottish phrenologist George Combe and his wife took a bedroom in the best inn in town. The room was fine, except for the French wallpaper depicting Italian landscapes. Some 'brute' with a pencil had 'rendered all the female figures indecent' and had put spectacles on the men and the women. The inn staff had tried to erase the 'abominations', but had been unsuccessful. Apparently, even more offensive images confronted the visitor in need of the facilities. Combe explained: 'On the door of the water closet...which Ladies were under the necessity of frequenting, was a drawing in pencil, too abominable to be named.'[22] Port-a-loo pails can thus be seen not only as travelling gear for bodily functions, but also as part of the respectable armour Britons used in waging war against and in protecting themselves from Continental immorality.

An array of powders, chemicals and spirits clearly was essential for doing battle with the unnerving European entomological world and for dealing with medical matters. For coping with flea-ridden beds, many travellers left home armed with oil of lavendar, though the remedy was not always effective. Keating filled the need for a more general insect repellant with his Persian Insect Destroying Powder. According to one advert, it was 'indispensable to Travellers by Rail or Steamboat, and Visitors to the Seaside, for protecting Bedding and Cabins from FLEAS, BUGS, COCKROACHES, MOTHS and MOSQUITOES.'[23] Beds and their occupants were also shielded from mosquitoes by netting. There apparently was no nineteenth-century version of 'Off', or insect repellant for the body. Terrace conversations and outdoor walks resulted in numerous insect bites and journal outbursts. During her tour of Switzerland, Mary Dundas took *Frankenstein* on to a terrace, hoping for a 'blood-curdling' story. The book did not meet her expectations, and she explained her disappointment by suggesting, 'It may be that I had no blood left in me to be curdled – for the mosquitoes and other venomous beasts were devouring me bodily.'[24]

In addition to insect repellants, travellers' medicine chests would have contained various remedies for physical ailments. Essence of tar might have been packed to prevent seasickness (oranges were used by some), methylated spirits or brandy for nerves, lemon juice for mosquito bites and glycerine tablets to protect the skin from sun or snow. In the interest of healthy skin, advertisements urged travellers to pack Rowland's Kalydor for effective protection against the sun's scorching rays. The adverts guaranteed that a generous application of the product would prevent freckles, tan, spots, pimples, flushes and any other discoloration so as to preserve a complexion of 'delicate clearness, with the glow of beauty and bloom'.[25] Maintaining healthy bowels could be achieved in a variety of ways, according to the guidebooks. There was a hierarchy of treatment for diarrhoea, depending on the severity of the case. Travellers were advised that an incipient case could sometimes be checked by a 'good pull of brandy', a remedy suggested for many ailments and situations (a flask was an indispensable piece of travelling gear). For more than mild cases (such cases being considered beneficial), chlorodyne was considered the most convenient medicine to carry. Persistent bouts required a more complicated mixture of 15 grains of prepared chalk, bismuth and charcoal, added to water. If this drink did not bring a return to normality, travellers were told to add laudanum (tincture of opium) to the chalky concoction. A future Welsh MP took this advice to heart. To stave off severe diarrhoea so he could get comfortably from Boulogne to a Paris meeting regarding the Congress on Peace, he pumped himself full of 'chalk medicine, laudanum and brandy'.[26] One wonders if he later had need of rhubarb or quinine pills, the accepted treatments for constipation.

A new item appeared in many travellers' luggage during the 1890s – the Kodak. Until that time, travellers sat for photographs and bought them, but rarely took their own. As late as 1885, *The Illustrated London News* contained no camera adverts. By 1890, however, the magazine was advertising New Kodaks in eight sizes with over 20,000 in use. Seven years later summer issues announced, 'A KODAK is a POSITIVE NECESSITY during the JUBILEE WEEK'. They could be purchased for £1. A more expensive (£2 10s) folding pocket Kodak appeared in 1901 and was billed as suitable for ladies, cyclists and tourists. Travellers' journals begin to mention Kodaks in the 1890s, and some even include photographs taken by the author.[27]

The most indispensable item in travelling gear was the guidebook, or handbook, as it was often termed. In 1836 John Murray published the first volume of what became the most popular series of travel handbooks until eclipsed by Baedekers towards the end of the century. Before Murray's handbooks appeared, individual authors wrote one- or two-volume guides based on their travels, but no one attempted to produce a series methodically covering whole countries and continents. Murray wrote the initial series volumes himself, but subsequently hired as writers other travel devotees including Augustus Hare, Richard Ford, Sir Francis Palgrave and Sir George Bowen. Murray instructed his authors to base their guides on personal travel experience or, if this was lacking, the experience of friends. The guides were to be standardized dispensers of useful information devoid of the authors' personal tastes and sentiments, much to the annoyance of writers like Hare, who preferred more emotionally charged prose. When first employed by Murray in 1859 Hare stated his authorial frustrations:

The style of my writing was to be as hard, dry, and incisive as my taskmaster. It was to be a mere catalogue of facts and dates, mingled with measurements of, buildings, and irritating details as to the 'E.E.,' 'Dec.,' or 'Perp.' architecture even of the most insignificant churches.... No sentiment, no expression of opinion were ever to be allowed; all description was to be reduced to its barest bones, dusty, dead, and colourless. In fact, I was to produce a book which I knew to be utterly unreadable, though correct and useful for reference.[28]

No wonder Sophia Holworthy, when reflecting on St. Peter's, thought of nothing but listable numbers.

Although Murrays may not have been scintillating reading, the rank and file of British tourism poured into Europe with the guides in hand. Demand for their advice was so great that the print-run for a handbook of a single country was between 500,000 and 700,000 in the nineteenth century.[29] The guides satisfied a need expressed by Horace Francis who toured Wales the year after the first Murray guide appeared. He and his companion went from place to place inquiring immediately upon arrival at an intended destination, 'What is there to be seen of interest to strangers?'[30] Murray guides answered the question in straightforward fashion. They were easy-to-carry cultural authorities dictating the sights to see and the zig-zagged terraces, crowns, slopes, ravines, valleys and summit points to trek. As if without any opinions and travel plans of their own, tourists deferred entirely to their Murrays, termed 'silent and precious guides' by one sightseer. When intrigued by a scene not mentioned in Murray, tourists obediently abandoned their personal interest in order to follow the guide. Thus Jemima Morrell steered herself and friends away from admiring some beautiful crockery saying, 'We cannot spare time to study the willow or any other pattern on mine host's crockery, when within one hundred yards is that view which Murray says is worth the cost of a journey from London to see.'[31]

The power exerted first by Murray and then by Baedeker guides could sometimes be oppressive. Tourists frequently sacrificed sleep in an effort to tick off every sight in a handbook. After spending three months in Florence dutifully working her way through Murray, Nona Bellairs felt rushed to finish at the end of her stay admitting, 'Is not Murray the most tiresome book in England... we cannot get on without them, but yet how they torment us!' Such guides tyrannized over businesses as well. In 1906, E.V. Lucas spoke of a hotel in the Hague that had fallen on hard times since he was first in the area seven years before. He explained that the hotel had suffered 'the greatest misfortune that can come upon an hotel-keeper...Baedeker had excised their star!'[32] Hotels desiring business from the English had to be listed in the guidebooks. On his trip through the German states, Combe discovered that new hotels not yet included in Murray's handbooks were cheaper than those that were listed. They were so, he explained, because the English – who frequently complained about being charged more than everyone else for things on the Continent – were not to be found among their patrons. The guides did make a special effort to point out hotels, eating places, and churches catering to the English, and can therefore be seen as both protectors from the foreign as well as invitations to new and exciting sites.

In their journals, travellers sometimes pointed out that Murray was wrong about a particular point. Sir Henry Campbell-Bannerman, for example, discovered that Murray was mistaken in recommending Puerto de Santa Maria as preferable to Cadiz as a place to visit. For Campbell-Bannerman, Puerto was undesirable in every respect, especially in its overpowering smells. Similarly, F.W. Faber challenged Murray's comments about all Hungarian inns being filthy. He stayed in many out-of-the-way *auberges* as well as peasant cottages in Hungary and was struck by 'the scrupulous Dutch-like cleanliness that reigned within'. One traveller expressed downright hostility towards guidebooks for the deceptive descriptions and incorrect opinions they dispensed. He devoted two pages of his journal to taking issue with a guidebook's preference for Glencoe over Glencroe, saying that if tourists to Glencoe 'are to be crammed with the *lying jargon* of guide books, they will be mightily disappointed'. Such challenges did not, however, shake travellers' faith in their Murrays. In fact, even when tourists saw with their own eyes something that called Murray into question they tended to believe the guide. While setting up house in Pau, Elizabeth Carne took an amateurish interest in the local geology. Her attempts to identify rocks were frustrated at times because lichens and weather stains totally obscured rock formations. At the Pont d'Enfer she simply abandoned trust in what was before her eyes and relied on Murray, noting, 'Murray says that...granite supersedes limestone. I take it for granted that he is correct.'[33] The above discussion suggests that women were more apt than men to take Murray's accuracy for granted, though both genders deferred to the guidebooks when travelling. In general and in keeping with society's expectations for women, female travellers tended to be more reverent to travel authorities (mostly male), whether Murray books or tour organizers/guides such as Thomas Cook.

The publication of standardized guidebooks for all parts of the world had a transforming effect on the journals travellers wrote, whether for private use or publication. Prior to Murrays' appearance, travel journals tended to focus on information about places and peoples seen and about the mechanics of travel, including transport, accommodations, cost, and so forth. They read more like guidebooks than personal accounts. Once Murray began dispensing the practical information and descriptions, travellers devoted their journals more to detailing personal impressions, or how they were *affected* by what they saw. A Scotsman travelling in Italy for health reasons wrote during his trip to Pompeii, 'The Guide Books are so minute in their descriptions that little can be added. The impressions made on the mind are most remarkable.'[34] He thus went on to write about these. Other travellers refrained from providing their own descriptions and information, including instead page numbers or quotes from guidebooks. Why struggle to find adjectives to describe a summit view when Murray put a list at your disposal? Admiring the view from the top of Llanberis Pass, Samuel Linder consulted his guidebook and then wrote, 'We find such terms as exquisite, charming, lovely, sublime, grand, terrific. We think therefore we may be excused for not attempting its description.'[35] We might relate this shift from information packed to impressionistic travel journals to a similar shift occurring in painting. Before the invention of the camera, painters were occupied primarily with drawing, or describing, what they actually saw. Once such 'realistic' scenes could be produced at the press of a button, painters turned more to depicting their impressions. The guidebook and the camera thus had similar effects, albeit on different forms of expression. At any rate, the popularity of books on travel was second only to that of novels in nineteenth-century Britain.[36]

In addition to affecting the nature of travel journals, Murray and other travel guides influenced ways of imagining countries and continents simply by means of their coverage and titles. Two popular guides to Europe, for example, created 'mental maps' reflecting a hierarchy of value accorded to the various European countries.[37] The percentage of total pages that each volume devoted to specific countries signalled to travellers that the British Isles, Switzerland and Italy were most worthy of a visit. In general, the guides conveyed the message that the western portion of Europe was much more highly valued as a travel destination than anything east of Germany and Austria. In fact, many areas in eastern Europe received hardly any mention at all in the guides.

The Murray guide series in particular predisposed travellers to imagine geographic and collective identities within the British Isles in certain ways. No guide for Britain as a whole was ever published during the nineteenth century. Instead, Murray handbook titles encouraged travellers to think of the British Isles as being divided into three main parts: Scotland (*Handbook for Travellers in Scotland*, 1867), England and Wales (*Handbook for England and Wales*, 1878) and Ireland (*Handbook for Travellers in Ireland*, 1864). Although no single handbook for all of Wales appeared in the Victorian period, the guides did work somewhat subtly to set Wales apart in people's minds as a community separate from England. This perceptual separation is evident when looking at the guides for specific regions within England and Wales. Murray guides define regions in England according to counties, with guides for Wiltshire and Dorset, Kent and Sussex, Westmorland and Cumberland, and so forth. In the case of Wales, however, the guides partition the area, as if it were a community in its own right, into South Wales (*A Handbook for Travellers in South Wales and its Borders, including the River Wye*, 1860) and North Wales (*A Handbook for Travellers in North Wales*, 1861). There are no guides for counties in Wales, suggesting different forms of imagining for England and Wales. Thus these portable cultural authorities served to reduce the idea of a British identity, and to reinforce English, Scottish, Welsh and Irish identities.

Murray was not the only authority to whom Victorian tourists willingly deferred. In the second half of the nineteenth century, all those in the market for untroubled travel put their faith in Thomas Cook, the pioneer of packaged touring.[38] For Cook, travel was an aid to cultural and moral improvement. Combined with temperance, train travel would, according to Cook, overcome intolerance, promote benevolence and diminish the number of tavern sippers. Thus it is no surprise that his first cheap train excursion took 570 people from Leicester to Loughborough for a Temperance rally at a price of 1 shilling per person. Cook accompanied the group and took personal responsibility for the practical details involving transport, food and entertainment. Such excursions designed to distract workers from drink proved so popular that Cook began to tap the more lucrative holiday travel market, adding profit to his goals of cultural and moral improvement. In 1845 he organized a trip for first- and second-class passengers to Liverpool, with supplementary excursions to Caernarvon and Mount Snowdon. After negotiating smooth connections and low-cost fares with several railway companies as well as arrangements with hotels and inns, Cook headed for Liverpool with 350 eager tourists all carrying his handbook of trip details. The tour was such a success that Cook offered a repeat journey two weeks later.

Always expanding his travel and business sights, Cook soon began organizing excursions to Scotland. By 1860 he had made arrangements for at least 50,000 tourists to explore lands north of the Tweed. Jealous of the money going to Cook as middleman between railway barons and excursionists, Scottish rail companies took over the task of organizing excursions in 1862, forcing Cook out of the market. He promptly turned the financial blow into an opportunity by directing his entrepreneurial skills across the Channel. As in Britain, Cook blazed touring trails on the Continent, negotiating agreements for reasonable transport and accommodation of future customers. In 1863 several hundred eager customers accompanied him on a three-week tour of Switzerland at about £16 per person. They crossed the Channel from Newhaven to Dieppe, spent a night in Paris and passed through Dijon, Macon and Lyons on their way to Switzerland. Nine years later his travel sights obviously were no longer country- or Continent-bound. He conducted 14 travellers on the first 'round-the-world' tour.

Thomas Cook's son John joined the firm in 1865 and was largely responsible for transforming a successful but haphazardly run business into a 'commercial empire'.[39] As the scope and volume of business increased, impersonal services such as handling passports, carrying out foreign exchange transactions, dispensing inclusive tourist tickets and providing circular notes (similar to modern travellers' cheques) came to predominate over personally conducted tours. Using tourist tickets afforded travellers slightly more independence than taking a tour with personal guide. The tickets were inclusive, covering transport, accommodation and meals for a tour designed by Cook, and travellers could use them as and when they wished. Murray guidebooks preferred such 'ticket tours' to guided ones because they gave more scope to travellers' autonomy. Of the personally guided, or packaged, tour, the guidebook to Switzerland said, 'This is an arrangement suited only for those who would otherwise be altogether excluded from the advantages of foreign travel, many of which, however, are necessarily lost by such a system.'[40]

Whether travelling with tickets or personal guide, Cook's services relieved the tourist of all responsibility for the vexatious and sometimes bewildering practical details of travelling. Women in particular felt emboldened to embark for foreign shores because of the assistance and protection provided by Cook. Letters of appreciation addressed to Cook fill the *Excursionist*, a magazine launched in 1851 to promote Cook's travel services, though not all Cook's customers were as satisfied as these letter writers. At the end of a Cook tour to Palestine and Syria in 1871, the participants thanked God, not Mr Cook, for the positive experiences they had. Regarding Cook's contribution to the tour, they adopted several resolutions to send to the travel organizer:

> That whereas it would have been a great source of pleasure, if the party could have expressed their unqualified approval of the organization and management of this portion of the tour, a sense of duty compels them to record their regret that they have been subjected to many inconveniences, discomforts and dangers which they cannot but feel might have been avoided by a more competent and efficient management...
>
> that the damage and destruction of baggage are due to a carelessness...
>
> that, while led to expect from the prospectus that many advantages would accrue to the party from being personally conducted, we regret that Mr. Cook did not retain in his own hands some portion of the authority committed to the dragoman.[41]

As was the case with Murray, the occasional dissatisfaction with and challenge to Cook did not diminish faith in his travel services. These services greatly eased the burdens and fear of travelling, leaving tourists free to relax and enjoy the sights.

The burdensome and bewildering aspects of travelling in the Victorian period began with passport particulars before tourists left Britain's shores. Rules regarding these documents varied from country to country and changed whimsically until the adoption of more formal and standardized procedures after 1914. Before the 1860s, most European countries required British travellers to carry a passport with appropriate *visé*, though not necessarily a British passport. British passports issued by the Foreign Office (FO) were considered expensive at £2 7s 6d., especially when passports issued by foreign ministers in London were granted to British subjects free of charge. Thus prior to passport fee reforms in 1851, Murray's handbooks did not advise obtaining an FO passport and only a minority of British travellers to the Continent bothered to secure one. In 1847, for example, the Foreign Office issued 785 passports, while the French, Prussian and Belgian ministers in London issued 10,168, 758 and 2,550 of their passports respectively.[42]

Four years later the Foreign Office adopted reforms making its passport cheaper and easier to obtain. The fee was reduced to 7s 6d. on 22 February 1851. During the year before the reform the largest number of FO passports granted on any single day was 14; the comparable number for the following year was 76.[43] To obtain an FO passport a prospective traveller had either to be known by the Secretary of State, to present a letter of introduction from a banking firm in the United Kingdom, or to produce a Certificate of Identity signed by any mayor, magistrate, justice of the peace, minister of religion, physician, surgeon, solicitor or notary, resident in the United Kingdom. These worthies had to vouch for the applicant's identity, because British passports were issued only to British-born subjects, Ionians or such foreigners as had become naturalized either by Act of Parliament or by a Certificate of Naturalization. They also had to vouch for an applicant's general character entitling him or her to the British Government's protection abroad. Passports were either sent to applicants by post, or issued at the Foreign Office between the hours of noon and 4 o'clock on the day following that on which the application was received.

During the second half of the nineteenth century, guidebooks and officials emphasized the importance of carrying a British passport. From 1854 on Murray's *Handbook for Travellers in France* recommended that travellers procure such a passport and have it countersigned, or *viséd*, before leaving London by the authorities of the countries they intended to visit. The handbook assured those about to leave Britain that an FO passport was 'the best certificate of nationality which an Englishman can carry abroad'. The Foreign Secretary, Lord Palmerston, concurred, arguing in Parliament, 'A passport is a *bona fide* indication of the nationality of the bearer.'[44] Provided it was signed by the authorities of the countries to which the bearer was travelling, it was also a grant of permission to travel freely through those countries. Even at the end of the century when most European countries no longer required such grants or passports, ministers and guidebooks still recommended that travellers not leave Britain without the FO document. They argued that foreigners on the Continent could at any time be asked to certify their nationality and the British passport was the easiest means of doing so. Furthermore, it was useful: in destabilizing conditions such as war, epidemics or political turmoil within countries when a passport might be demanded; at Post Offices when applying for payment of money orders; in claiming letters at the *poste restante*; in passing through Customs; and for ensuring civility from public officials. The British passport was of no use, however, in Britain itself. In 1855 Frederick Calland wrote to the Foreign Office inquiring whether he could use his FO passport to gain admission to the British Library. The Foreign Office responded:

> Passports are issued by the British Government to British Subjects solely for the purpose of travel, and with the view of enabling

Travellers to fulfil formalities which are requisite, according to the existing Laws and Regulations of different States, before foreigners are allowed to enter, travel, or reside in such states: But Passports, as such, can never be considered as of any use whatever, directly or indirectly, to an Englishman in his own country.[45]

British travellers were not even required to present British passports on leaving and entering their own country until after 1914.

A typical FO passport requested, in the name of Her Majesty, that all those concerned allow the named traveller or travellers to pass freely through designated areas. The traveller's name, national identity as 'British Subject' or 'Naturalized British Subject', and destination were written by hand and were the only identity indicators on the passport. Personal information such as age or profession was not part of the Victorian FO passport, and photos did not appear on passports until after 1914. Passports often entitled more than one person to travel freely abroad. A married man travelling with his family, for example, usually carried one passport listing all family members, including servants, governesses, and so forth. Women travelling with children could and did do the same. Occasionally two or more unrelated adults had their names on a single passport, but this was not common practice, unless the passport was a Cook's party one on which men were named and women numbered.

As the above passport definitions and format reveal, passports directly linked travel and national identity, and I shall have more to say about their significance in this respect later in the book. For now, I want to emphasize how vexatious they were to British tourists who were used to travelling throughout their native islands without the need to present documents to officials.[46] On the Continent by contrast, travellers faced a barrage of patience-taxing checkpoints where officials either cast an eye over passports or confiscated them for more detailed police inspection. Checkpoints were particularly numerous before German and Italian unification when the various small states each confronted travellers with tiresome border rituals. A central travel authority like Cook eventually helped to make travellers aware of the ever-changing rules regarding passports. Without such knowledge, travel plans might be frustrated. Travellers bound for Greece in 1851 and armed with FO passports issued in London needed to know, for example, that the Greek government had recently imposed a new regulation on those entering Greece: they had to have passports *viséd* by the Greek consul in the city where the passport was issued.

Having secured a passport and necessary signatures, luggage-laden tourists then had to cope with decisions and discomforts to do with the Channel. A Frenchman in a hydrogen balloon made the first successful aerial Channel crossing in 1785, a feat not repeated until over a century later in 1909 when an aeroplane made the journey in 37 minutes. During the intervening years, steamers carried passengers across the Channel, the first such service being established between Brighton and Le Havre in 1816. Five years later the Dover-to-Calais route opened, taking passengers across in three hours for 8–10 shillings per person. By 1840 travellers could choose between at least six cross-Channel routes if they were going from London to Paris. For fastest overall trip time from London to Paris, the Brighton to Dieppe route was the best choice, with the nearly straight-line route taking only 20 hours 45 minutes (7 hours 30 minutes steamer time). But if least steamer time was the traveller's object, then Dover to Calais was the route to choose, though the overall trip time was 32 hours.

The significance of steamer time was likely to increase in direct proportion to the number of times a traveller had been tossed around by the Channel. According to Agnes Twining who took annual trips to the Continent during the five years prior to her marriage in 1872, the odds favoured one bad and one good Channel crossing per tour. She confessed, 'It was more than I ever dared to hope to have two calm crossings in one year!'[47] Despite recourse to oranges and essence of tar, many travellers ended up clutching the 'suspicious looking white basins' which would emerge on rough crossings. Deck scenes could be most distressing, as was the case when Eliza Anne Salvin endured the 15–hour journey from Le Havre to Southampton. Of her fellow passengers she stated with some exasperation, 'They were all ill on the deck, & oh! on each other also – I never saw anything to equal it!' Experienced travellers sometimes adopted a more matter-of-course attitude towards the discomforts of steamer travel. Lt.-Col. Edward H. Legge, for example, noted nonchalantly, 'Had a meal on arrival at Folkestone, but lost it again during passage across channel.'[48] Some seasoned passengers even took pride in the way they managed to lose their meal. While steaming from Ireland to Bristol, Charles Lucey noted the mess created by seasick travellers. But of his own hearty dinner he said boastfully, 'When I found that it would not settle quietly [I] made a transfer of it over side for the benefit of the fishes, an operation which did not last two minutes or leave any unpleasant symptoms behind.'[49]

Upon arriving at the intended Continental Channel port, people, horses and carriages pressed their way out of the steamer to face an array of bewildering, sometimes intimidating, officials. They were met first by *gens d'armes* who seemed very foreign and disconcerting to British travellers. On his first trip to the Continent, the Scotsman James Smith did not enjoy the 'welcoming' rituals at Calais. Immediately after vacating the steamer for the passport office, he confessed, 'Truly I found myself a foreigner. Imagine a narrow door and a Soldier and a musket in the very entry... I was quite sure that I would not be bayonetted – But truly I did not like the musket and my nose kissing each other.'[50] Such an initial encounter made Smith and other British travellers aware of how different their attitude towards officialdom was, as we will see in Chapter 5.

Once passport formalities were completed, travellers then encountered meddlesome *douaniers*, or customs officials, poised to rummage through luggage in search of tea, tobacco, biscuits, buns, and other dutiable items. Some of them used their noses as well. At the customs in Boulogne, sponge-bags were sniffed for tobacco, much to Eliza Salvin's surprise. One *douanier* looked suspiciously at pockets bulging with *petits cadeaux*, but let them pass with no duty to pay. Another examined, with particular attention, a drawing box containing papers and drawings as if there were something sinister about it. This concern may be attributed to Europeans' lack of familiarity with sketching as a hobby. The British, on the other hand, were passionate sketchers, and their pencils and pads sometimes caused a stir. When two of Rev. Trench's companions began sketching in Pamplona, interested and amazed crowds gathered in such numbers that the mayor sent two policemen so no nuisance would befall the sketchers.

Having successfully negotiated the customs inspection, travellers entered a customs house anteroom crammed with pushy shopkeepers, inn touters and rail agents redolent of onion. Personal couriers or Cook guides served to shield travellers from such importunate creatures. If travelling without such assistance, guidebooks advised travellers to write ahead to a desired hotel so a commissionaire would be waiting at the customs house when they arrived. They had only to proclaim the hotel's name at the customs checkpoint and the hotel commissionaire would come forward to meet them and receive the luggage keys. He would clear the bags through customs before transporting them and their owners to the hotel.

Travellers on the Continent could never wander very far without a customs encounter.[51] Officials were stationed at all border crossings and sometimes at points within states as well. In France, for example, people entering city gates had to pay a local tax, the *octroi*, on oil, wine and other items brought in from outside the town, in order to help maintain the country's regional character. Experiences at Continental customs checks varied widely. Some travellers were waived through without even the slightest rummage or sniff, particularly those carrying small-sized bags. But the best way to ensure smooth sailing through customs was to travel with a generous bribing budget, or else be willing to share certain choice items like tobacco. Just as officials in Dieppe discovered cigars in William Merry's trunk, he purposely spilled some snuff from a carefully packed canister. A powder-pinching frenzy ensued until snuff boxes were filled and their owners suddenly 'quite sure that Monsieur had nothing contraband among his luggage'.[52] Officials were sometimes brash enough to demand such handouts. At a French *douane* Frederick Fryer noted, 'A woman who could speak English pretty well, was very active in getting our things examined and when we were passed asked for a present as she had got us so nicely through.'[53] Other travellers were not so lucky. On reaching Civita Vecchia from Leghorn, Lt.-Col. Legge suffered interminable delays and steep fees before being reunited with his luggage. He described the four-hour ordeal which ruined his travel arrangements:

> First of all, all the passengers are counted over.... This is repeated no less than three times. The luggage is then got up from below... police come one by one with receipts for our passports, and by 3 p.m. we and our baggage are making for the shore, but there are fresh delays – fees and payments endless – luggage receipts and customs; baggage examined, and everything turned inside out, newspapers read, and time wasted to such an extent, that we don't leave the custom house for the station before 20 minutes to 4 p.m....[54]

Fryer and his brother-in-law were delayed so long that they missed the last train by five minutes and were unable to proceed to Rome that night as planned.

Another challenge for British tourists on the Continent was keeping abreast of the many currency changes.[55] They needed to pay bills with francs in France, florins in Bavaria, thalers in Prussia, kreutzers in Nuremberg, florins and zwanzigers in Austria, sovereigns in Belgium, guilders in Holland and lire in Italy. Furthermore, currency with the same name often had different value depending on the country. For example, the florin in Austria was worth 2 English shillings while the Bavarian florin equalled 1s 8d. Before 1850, Switzerland had the most complicated currency. Each canton had its own, and pieces legal in one canton were not legal in another. A Diet decree at mid-century legalized French currency throughout nearly all cantons, much to the relief of travellers. The establishment of a unified German Empire in 1871 also worked to simplify money matters, as the new state adopted a uniform decimal monetary system with marks and pfennigs as the principal units. In contrast to currency types, exchange rates changed very little or not at all. For example, the pound sterling was equivalent to 25 French francs for the whole Victorian period. Gold coins were the only international currency, and they along with Bank of England notes could be exchanged for the local currency anywhere in Europe.

Cook greatly simplified currency transactions for tourists going abroad. After being robbed of his gold in Jerusalem, he decided that travellers should not carry gold coins. Thus in the late 1860s he persuaded Continental hoteliers to accept his hotel coupons for which they would be reimbursed by Cook's firm. Before leaving home, travellers could purchase the coupons to cover bedroom, breakfast, as well as *table d'hôte* lunch and dinner. In 1874, Cook started a precursor to modern travellers' cheques known as 'circular notes'. On presentation of these notes issued by Cook in pound sterling denominations, foreign banks would pay out in the local currency the current exchange rate value. For travellers taking Cook's packaged tours, nearly all costs were paid in advance, thus minimizing currency transactions on the Continent. A seven-day Cook tour down the Rhine cost £5 5s. in 1900. That included fare for second-class travel, a saloon on the Rhine steamer, accommodations and full board. The only things not included were meals *en route* and the omnibus from Briebrich to Wiesbaden and back. The same fee bought a six-day tour to Lucerne which included a travel ticket to Switzerland and back, second-class travel on the Continent, accommodation of bedroom, lights and service, breakfast, dinner and the services of a conductor.

These trips and any others on the Continent involved using varied methods of transport, and Cook's inclusive tickets and tours saved tourists from having to research fares and make choices about conveyance. Aggressive railway construction did not get underway in Europe until the mid-nineteenth century, so Victorian tourists had to rely on roads and horse power for much of the time. Travel writers in the early nineteenth century noted some improvements in road travel. Bridges replaced many ferry boats, rough and mountainous roads were made smooth, and many new roads were being built. To meet his military needs, Napoleon had roads built across the Simplon and Mont Cenis passes over the Alps. The Simplon road begun in 1800 took 30,000 men six years to build at a cost of £5,000 a mile. Despite these and other improvements, road travel remained slow, with travellers able to expect to cover 40–50 miles a day at best. Furthermore, road quality varied from area to area. French roads were divided into three classes and tended to be well maintained. *Routes impériale* were maintained by central government, *départementales* fell under the jurisdiction of specific departments, and *chemins vicinaux* belonging to communes or parishes were maintained by local support. In the German territories, on the other hand, roads often ran along jurisdictional cracks, as Sir John Barrow discovered while making his way from Hamburgh to Lubeck. Although only a 30-mile journey, the trip seemed interminable because he had to inch along at 3 m.p.h. on a road of uneven stones atop a sandy foundation. He explained that the road was shared by three states and so cared for by none.[56] Even in France, roads could be treacherous. On his trip to Rouvray, Merry noted that posting laws forced him to travel with an extra horse because the roads were so bad. He thought an artillery wagon the only vehicle appropriate for the route.[57]

A variety of vehicles and methods of transport were available for travelling Europe's roads. In France the range of road conveyances extended from the heavily-laden *roulage*, or merchant's baggage van, to the fast, light phaeton for the fashionable. The *char à banc* with its rows of crosswise seating and fitted canopy was strong and light and considered ideal for negotiating mountain roads appropriate for wheeled traffic. In describing this mountain vehicle for two or three persons, Murray guides compared it to a four-poster bedstead on wheels. If enamoured of the open air, travellers might ride in a calash, the precursor of the modern convertible. Its low-wheeled body was equipped with a removable folding hood. Such a hood topped the German and Eastern European *britzska*, popular with ambassadors and diplomats. Seating was crosswise or in a rumble seat, and the interior could be converted into a sleeper for two. In the most northerly climes *carrioles* were common. Drawn by one horse, these small, two-wheeled vehicles in turn pulled a sleigh-like cab for sitting with outstretched legs.

Well-to-do British travellers intent on comfortable rides and no shoulder-touching with strangers took their own carriages across the Channel, hiring horses and drivers *en route*. Comfort and privacy could also be had by contracting with a *voiturin* (French) or *vetturino* (Italian). These entrepreneurs owned a carriage and horses and agreed to transport travellers to a desired destination and provide food and lodging along the way, all for a fixed sum. Although not to be beaten for comfort and exclusivity, these forms of travel were slow. Horses were not changed and so needed frequent rests, making 35 miles a day the maximum to be expected.

Posting was faster and provided a similar shielding from strangers. Travellers hired carriages, horses and a postillion or two from government postmasters stationed at roughly equidistant points along a route. This method was faster because horses could be changed regularly at stations. It did not always provide, however, carriages to inspire confidence. To go from Marseilles to Toulon, Nona Bellairs and her companions hired a carriage and four horses. As they creaked along, she exclaimed:

> Behold us! four lean wretched horses, tied with old ropes, and harness[ed] at random.... The carriage, a landau, a huge, untidy, ill-shapen machine, but very roomy and comfortable, tied up with old string where time had dealt severely with it... off we go – dragging, tearing, jolting, jingling, crackling along the dusty roads.[58]

By this method, they managed to achieve 30 miles in nine hours.

In Italy, particularly before unification, travellers sometimes opted for the *vetturino* rather than the posting method of travel because, though slower, it was much simpler. At a time when each Italian state had different posting regulations and different currency, contracting with and paying a driver in advance for everything eliminated the hassles of posting stations and currency transactions. The other main disadvantage of travelling post was the necessity of sometimes changing carriages as well as horses, making the loading and reloading of luggage necessary.

Less well-off travellers had to rely on public transport, the most common type on the Continent being the 'diligence'. Weighing several tons, this dinosaur of a vehicle lumbered along carrying between 15 and 30 passengers at no more than 6 or 7 miles an hour. The diligence was composed of a *coupé* in front, an *intérieur* behind composing the body, and a *banquette*, or outside seat, on top. The *coupé* was the favoured spot because inside and holding only three or four people. Seats in the *intérieur* were more plentiful, but tended to leave British travellers gasping from garlic and tobacco fumes. Fresh air and unobstructed views could be had from the *banquette*, but this outside perch had its obvious disadvantages in bad weather. Places in the diligence were numbered and assigned to passengers in the order in which they booked, with corner seats given out first. Murray advised corner seats for comfort, but British travellers' comments suggest they were not impressed with the comfort or with any other aspect of public conveyances on the Continent. Sarah Ellis drew conclusions about national character based on her experiences of such conveyances:

> If anyone should be disposed to doubt the real difference of national character between the French and the English, they need only look at such public conveyances, to be convinced in a moment, that there is something radically dissimilar in their modes of thinking and feeling.... Polite as we all allow them to be, and celebrated as they justly are for their good taste, the French look every day without a smile, or a wish for improvement, upon some of the most outlandish machines that ever were constructed for the conveyance of passengers; and which, if they were driven along the streets of London, would unquestionably attract a mob.[59]

The Scotsman John Dunlop likened the diligence to a railway carriage, but noted:

> even in a railway carriage, horrid tho the noises be, they cannot compare with those heard in the Diligence. What with the continual cracking of whips, and shouting of the driver, mingled with the hollow rumbling of the huge vehicle... I think any person of quiet disposition and retired manners would find himself quite out of his element here.[60]

These Continental conveyances were also sometimes anxiety producing for the inexperienced traveller from Britain. Guidebooks warned that horses hauling a diligence slowed to a walk with the slightest elevation of terrain, but that on the descents they often went quite fast, appearing to be out of control. In discussing the diligence on downhill slopes, Murray's handbook for Switzerland warned, 'To those who have not become hardened by use it is rather a nervous thing to see the heavy diligence turn round the corners of the zigzags in the face of precipices, with the reins flying lose, and the horses apparently under no control.'[61] The guidebook tried to reassure readers by saying that the horses knew the roads and thus accidents seldom occurred.

Before railways covered the Continent, travellers often opted for water travel where possible. On rivers and canals, it certainly afforded a tranquillity of mind and body not to be had in bone-shaking road vehicles. And keeping a detailed journal was no doubt easier from a deck perch than from inside a cramped diligence. While gliding past river banks, Sir John Forbes felt 'inspired by the open daylight and free air of nature.... In no other situation, has the traveller such convenience and facility of taking notes of the things he sees on the very spot, and at the very time he sees them.'[62] Such note-taking would have been especially easy when travelling leisurely by *trekschuit*. Popular in Holland where canals were as numerous as roads in other countries, this horse-drawn canal barge offered elevated seats for viewing the passing countryside. Its main disadvantages were a slow speed of 4 miles per hour and a tendency to stop at the outskirts of towns, leaving passengers with a mile or more trek to an inn.

In other parts of the Continent, river steamers were common by the 1830s. Steaming down the Rhine became a popular way of proceeding to Switzerland and Italy, and travellers frequently switched from the road to the Rhône as they headed south in France. William Boxall explained the switch by pointing out, 'The Rhône is so rapid that the boat performs in one day what it takes by diligence two days and two nights.'[63] Steamers plied Europe's principal lakes, with those on Lakes Lucerne, Geneva and the Italian Lakes offering comfortable upper decks and good restaurants. Coastal steamers were also much used, especially in the Mediterranean, to go from the French Riviera to Italy where the land route was mountainous. The 160-mile trip from Nice to Genoa was likely to take a week by *voiturin* carriage because of steep mountains. Coasting the length of Italy was also popular, especially for those in a hurry and determined to avoid bad inns and imposing postmasters. Excursion steamers could also be booked between Britain and the Scandinavian countries, and considerable coasting traffic plied Norway's fjords. Steamers became popular even within Britain, especially if one's destination was the Western Isles or the Highlands of Scotland, where there was many gaps in the road and rail networks. Expansion of the canal and coastal steamship network in these two areas made them much more accessible by the mid-nineteenth century when rail lines existed only in central and eastern Scotland and extended north only as far as Aberdeen.[64] One could also secure steamship service to Scotland from London and Liverpool.

Despite the advantages of water transport and the prevalence of road travel, the railway eclipsed both over the course of the nineteenth century. Passenger rail travel on a large scale began first in Britain in 1830 with the opening of the Liverpool and Manchester Railway. During its first year of operation, the line carried four times as many people as could have been transported by all the coaches running between the two cities.[65] By mid-century the 5,000 miles of track criss-crossing the United Kingdom had driven most horse-drawn conveyances off the principal roads of England, Scotland and Wales. Travelling a turnpike road in the Manchester area in 1846, Reverend Francis Trench noted, 'For mile after mile no carriage, cart, or even traveller of any class passed us. The railroad is so extremely cheap...and offers so many stations...that the labouring population avail themselves of this mode of locomotion.'[66] For 1d per mile, third-class rail travellers could cross the countryside averaging 30 miles per hour, five times the number of miles possible by coach travel. At mid-century, James Smith drew time/cost comparisons between diligence and railway travel in Switzerland. In 1855, it took him nine hours and cost 7s 6d to go by diligence the 54-mile stretch between Basle and Zurich. Had there been an express train, the same trip would have taken 1 hour 36 minutes and cost 4 shillings.

Bradshaw's *Railway Timetables* were first published in Britain in 1839 and expanded to include Continental trains in 1847. By that date, aggressive railway construction had begun on the Continent, particularly in the German *länder* and in France. At mid-century when the United Kingdom had 5,000 miles of track in operation, the Germanic *länder*, together with Denmark and Holland, had 4,542 miles, and France 1,722 miles open for business. Other areas were much slower in laying track, with Belgium, Russia and Italy having, at mid-century, only 457, 200, and 170 miles of track respectively. In Greece, as late as 1880, the only train service was from Athens to Piraeus. Switzerland was also slow in constructing rail lines (only after 1855) due more to jealousies between cantons and legal difficulties in procuring land than to obstacles presented by the mountainous terrain. Even in states such as France where rail travel was relatively extensive, it remained intermittent on most routes until the end of the century. The 1892 edition of Murray's handbook for France was the first to declare, 'Posting has nearly become a thing of the past.' Thus when on land, most Victorian tourists had to combine road and rail travel, as did Fanny Kemble on her journey from Dieppe to Paris in 1847. She had to endure the discomforts of diligence travelling as far as Rouen's railway station where her lumbering vehicle was lifted off its wheels and placed, passengers, luggage and all, onto a wheeled platform attached to the train. Travelling between states often involved changing from rail to mountainous road travel until late in the century. The Mont Cenis Tunnel did not link France and Italy by rail until 1871, and tracks did not cross the border between Switzerland and Italy until 1882.

The British edge on the Continent with respect to railway development did not apply to comfort. In 1847 when Kemble and diligence rode the Rouen to Paris line through windy, sleety weather, she criticized the open second-class carriages. By 1870, however, Murray admitted that French railway carriages were much cleaner and more comfortable than British ones. Praising the heat from hot-water footstools provided in first-class French carriages, Murray went on to say that second-class carriages in France were often as good as the first-class ones on British lines. Travellers from Britain were also very impressed with trains running in Belgium. Travelling in a first-class carriage out of Brussels, James Smith could not help but compare the vehicle to its counterpart back home:

> It was luxurious – far beyond any first class carriage in Britain. It was large. The seats wide, softly stuffed at bottom and sides – and covered with elegant claret coloured leather. A brilliant lamp hung from the roof fixed in the ordinary way, and a good thick carpet was under our feet. We travelled like Princes.[67]

He went on to speculate as to why rail carriages and stations were so much more magnificent in Belgium. In his view, the explanation had to do with the lie of the land and line. Glances out the carriage window revealed scarcely a railway bridge, hardly any cuttings and no viaducts. He thus concluded that railway construction in Belgium cost much less per mile than it did in Britain, leaving more funds for carriages and stations.

It was the Belgians rather than the British who pioneered the railway sleeping car, though there were no sleeping or dining cars on Continental trains until the last quarter of the century. Before they were equipped with rolling restaurants, trains halted at certain intervals for 10–30 minutes to allow passengers time either to purchase provisions or to dine at a *table d'hôte* or a refreshment room known in France as a 'buffet'. On a train bound for Epernay, Eliza Salvin noted how the guard asked how many planned to dine at the *table d'hôte*. He then telegraphed the number to the chef in Epernay so the food would be ready when they arrived.

Although Victorian travellers forsook traditional methods of transport for trains, they expressed mixed feelings about the steam-powered vehicles. Beatrix Potter confessed that, unlike some people, she saw more to trains than smoke trails and dividends. For her, simply the sight of a locomotive in motion was exhilarating. Addressing those who could see no sentiment or beauty in a railway she said,

To my mind there is scarcely a more splendid beast in the world than a large Locomotive: if it loses something of mystery through being the work of man, it surely gains in a corresponding degree the pride of possession. I cannot imagine a finer sight than the Express, with two engines, rushing down this incline at the edge of dusk.[68]

Looking at the sights inside a railway carriage, Nona Bellairs was struck by the entertaining aspects of train travel. She noted the main amusement in railway travelling which was lost in posting:

> The watching your neighbours trying to make themselves comfortable; the ingenious devices for putting everything nowhere; the cases of water, and cases of wine, the brushes and combs, and salt and Bologna sausage and cheese, and travelling caps, that all come out of a little bag no size at all.[69]

In contrast to praising the railway, many travellers fulminated against it for a variety of reasons. Some were of what one traveller termed the 'anti-go-ahead-and-set-your-face-against-improvement' school and thus constantly looked back nostalgically to the 'good old times' when travel by stagecoach was the rage. Others complained of 'railway speed' which hurtled them through fields, over high roads and under canals with a swiftness that reduced countryside details to a blur. Most frequently, they lamented that the high speeds, predetermined routes and closed carriages insulated passengers from their surroundings and deprived them of the freedom spontaneously to pursue untrammelled paths. Walking and posting were, they argued, far superior methods of transport because they did not monotonously shunt people across the countryside like so much merchandise. Although Bellairs found the rail carriage community amusing, she nevertheless despised the shackles of train travelling. When writing of her rail journey through the Apennines she confessed:

> I have always hated the railways, and then more than ever when I longed to pry into the secret nooks, and corners of those mountain-passes, longed to say, 'God speed!' to the labourers as they looked round at the vulgar, incongruous train, as it went rushing on in its heedless impertinent manner, dragging unwilling travellers onwards, without one moment's respite.[70]

For Katharine Harris, the speed and suddenness of rail travel took the romance out of travelling. On rolling into Venice she exclaimed with some dismay, 'We found ourselves arrived at Venice without being even aware of it – Now in all this the romance of the thing is entirely done away with, the idea of entering Venice by a railroad...instead of smoothly gliding along the canals into the town fresh upon you by degrees.' The compiler of the Toynbee Travellers Club logbook of an expedition to Florence would have agreed, noting that 'the certainty of railway journeying and faith in Cook's Hotel Coupons have robbed travel of the romance which commended it to the chivalrous knights of old.'[71]

One of the most hostile diatribes against the railways came from a commercial traveller, Throne Crick. He argued that the new form of transport was undermining the commercial community, particularly that found in the commercial rooms of hotels and inns. Those rooms had been, in his view, sanctums of propriety and gentlemanly behaviour until the coming of the railway when they were invaded by swarms of 'architects and attorneys, engineers, civil and otherwise, surveyors, and levellers' whose vulgar language and dirty overalls rendered the rooms more like fairs or beer gardens. Regarding the railways he branded them 'from starting point to terminus, as one universal epidemic, which... will prove more fatal than any visitation that man...has ever before sought out to afflict our world.'[72] Another traveller went so far as to suggest that the publishing world would be compromised by railway travel. Because he found train journeys to be monotonous and without incident, Hugh Miller predicted confidently, 'There will be an end, surely, to all works of travels, when the railway system of the world shall be completed.' He also believed the number of novels would diminish in comparison to the late eighteenth century when authors like Henry Fielding and Tobias Smollett transformed travels and tours into novel form. As he explained it, 'It would be rather a difficult matter in these later times to make a novel out of an English tour. The country, measured by days' journeys, has grown nine-tenths smaller than it was in the times of Fielding and Smollett.'[73]

Although mistaken about the decline of travel books and novels, Miller was correct about railways diminishing time and space. By 1871 when the Mont Cenis Tunnel was completed, it was possible to enter a railway carriage in Calais and not leave it again until arriving in Rome. The trip took 60 hours, the same amount of time it had taken to go from Paris to Calais a century before and from Paris to Lyons by diligence in 1840. The Simplon Tunnel was a great time-saver as well. Instead of taking ten or eleven hours to cross the pass from Brieg to Domodossola by diligence, trains went from town to town in 50 minutes. Travelling the length of France became a matter of hours rather than days or weeks. At mid-century it took Fanny Kemble nearly three weeks to go from Le Havre to Marseilles. Murray guides at the time were more optimistic, indicating a four-day travel time for a London to Marseilles trip. By 1892 Murray listed a 26-hour travel time for the same journey. One could thus travel the length of France at the end of the century in about the same time it had taken to go from Paris to Calais in the 1830s. To put the change in more global terms, it was possible at the opening of the twentieth century to go from London to Japan in less time than it had taken Kemble to travel from one end of France to the other half a century earlier.

As Fanny Kemble and other travellers discovered, guidebook times for a journey did not always correspond to reality. Low tide, high water, missed diligence connections, hazardous travelling conditions, lack of sunlight, unreturned passports and many other unforeseen events worked to foil the most meticulously planned itineraries. Before the relaxing of rules regarding passports, document delays were at times most annoying. Police in Geneva told Sanderson Walker that he could not return to Paris via Lyons as planned, because he was coming from Italy and thus needed a French ambassador's permission. Obtaining the required permission meant travelling to Turin or Berne, as no French ambassador resided in Geneva. Walker's only other choice was to return to England via Germany. An equally frustrating encounter with officialdom occurred earlier when he was on his way to Italy. At the border between Austria and the Papal Territories, Walker and a friend were stopped because they did not have a bill of health from Venice. Officials informed them that they could not cross the border without first spending twelve days in quarantine, a common precaution for controlling the spread of cholera. The order to this effect had just reached the border and would only reach Venice that same day, so Walker and his friend could not have known of it ahead of time.

Even at the end of the century when rules about documents were less stringent and one could supposedly count on 'the certainty of railway journeying', delays were common. Journals are full of stories about the delaying tactics of entrepreneurial innkeepers. Travellers were told at their inn, for example, that they should wait for an omnibus rather than walk to the train station because the distance was too great. As they waited, they typically partook of some refreshment, much to the delight of the innkeeper. When the omnibus finally arrived and whisked them to the station, they realized it was only minutes away. Nature could be as irksome as innkeepers. In winter, trains were sometimes blocked by telegraph wires and poles lying across the track, brought down by the weight of snow. Avalanches burying rail lines caused lengthier delays, as when luggage-laden Toynbee Travellers had to sledge their way across one to a train on the other side. The same group encountered a broken bridge near Bologna and had to walk over a temporary bridge and up a steep embankment to an omnibus which took them to another train. On her first journey around Italy, Catherine Braithwaite was two hours late arriving in Naples. Her train had encountered a landslip on the way, and passengers had to haul bags and mail over a stony stretch of line to reach a train sent from Naples on the other side.

Such delays are only one example of the many routine annoyances confronting Victorian travellers. Travel journals are full of complaints about such things as canal stench, garlic breath, vibrating steamers, dust-filled carriages and German pipe-smokers. Railway lines typically contained a smoking carriage, but it was permissible to smoke in any carriage provided no one objected. Travellers from Britain felt awkward about objecting, and thus had to suffer the fumes or even worse consequences. James Smith applied 'Blue Preserver' to his eye when it got irritated by burning cigar ash blown his way in a rail carriage.

One of the most common gripes among travellers concerned insects, particularly fleas, mosquitoes and flies. Many a night's sleep was lost due to beds filled with fleas, despite a generous dousing with oil of lavendar. In the Mediterranean mosquitoes were so prevalent that travellers often had to stop and brush them away every two minutes. Margaret Brewster noted how in Cannes, unlike in Britain, mosquitoes dominated conversation. Writing to her Scottish friends back home she remarked, 'In your tranquil unbitten Scotch home you can have no idea of the social weight of mosquitoes.'[74] Perhaps British people's lack of experience with swarms of insects made them susceptible to bizarre reactions when faced with the pests on the Continent. On her trip through Germany and Switzerland, Eliza Salvin commented on how the fly population was biting and bleeding the horses. The flies were so numerous and actively biting that she admitted, 'I dreamt of flies with bloody bodies all night long. They came flying about me with long feelers and the more I brushed them away the more they came.'[75]

During the first half of the nineteenth century, quarantining rituals to prevent the spread of cholera were particularly noisome to travellers. Those entering ports or approaching borders from plague areas were confined for from three to 30 days aboard ships or in specially built *lazarettos*. Any physical contact between the detainees and people outside was strictly forbidden. When John Marsh arrived by boat in Copenhagen, he was immediately isolated for five days in a building separated from the outside world by two wooden fences 7 feet high and 8–10 feet apart.[76] Some mid-century *lazarettos* adopted fumigation of travellers and luggage as an extra precautionary measure. Inmates spent at least ten minutes breathing lime and camphor fumes from inside a sealed, whitewashed room. No wonder one traveller referred to quarantining as 'that abomination of travelling'. Alexander Dunlop was particularly critical of the practice. As he passed the Straits of Gibraltar, he wrote enthusiastically of the mountains, white cottages and vineyards in view. Only the threat of six days in a Maltese *lazaretto* kept him from insisting on a stopover. The prospect of such confinement had him fulminating:

> What damned nonsense the quarantine laws are! Can scarcely understand a government in a sane state of mind authorising such utterly ridiculous and useless a farce – No plague or cholera was ever stopped by them – and then the provoking detention to travellers – and the loss of time to those who trade or traffic with quarantine ports is incalculable besides being vexatious and frivolous.[77]

Less routine discomforts and delays resulted from the presence or absence of recent inventions. Travelling stoves known as 'Etnas' were popular with British tourists determined to have their tea. Filled with lava, Etnas were harmless unless leaky, as one train passenger discovered when a stream of lava flowing along the carriage floor set fire to her portmanteau. A different sort of inconvenience sometimes occurred because of the absence of typewriters. For example, Italian sentries detained a man carrying a British Foreign Office passport because the handwritten date on the document was not legible. Observing his predicament, a Toynbee Traveller wrote that the detainee 'thanks to a badly written date on his passport was taught to pray for the speedy introduction of the typewriter into our Foreign Office.'[78] As late as the 1980s, his prayer had not been answered.

Some annoyances of travelling were so severe as to be more properly termed 'hazards'. These mostly involved accidents to do with horses, carriages and trains. Alp scaling frequently required travelling on paths inhospitable to wheeled vehicles. Climbers either walked or hired mules and horses for such expeditions. Salvin and companions chose the latter, and put themselves in the hands of an experienced guide before ascending a Swiss mountain. All was well until one horse decided to lie down in the road with cousin Emmie atop. The guide apologized profusely, saying that his animal only wanted to roll. Eliza was livid and lashed out in her journal,

> He laughed...and said...it only wanted to roll poor thing! Only! If the rider chanced to be underneath during that pleasing little diversion, it would be an – only? With a precipice on one side and no protection between us and it, such an occurrence was exciting.[79]

Excitement could be had on a diligence as well. Despite their weight, diligences did occasionally overturn due to drivers being tipsy or going too fast down hills. Smaller carriages could also be dangerous, as friends of the Combes found out when theirs tumbled over a precipice not far from Baden-Baden. As Combe explained it, the carriage drag did not fit the wheel and thus slipped off on a downhill stretch. The harness then snapped, sending the carriage forward on the horses and eventually over a six-foot precipice. As it rolled it disintegrated, with the result that the occupants sustained severe cuts and bruises.[80]

Trains were no safer, with crashes generating plentiful copy for newspapers and travel journals over the course of the nineteenth century. One traveller riding a Scotland-bound train in 1856 was delayed for several hours because of what he termed a 'fearful' wreck. Five minutes before his train arrived at a North English station, a passenger train had slammed into a cargo train carelessly left standing in the station. The wreck blocked the tracks and left five people dead. When his train finally rolled forward again, he described the scene of the tragedy saying, 'A fearful sight presented itself. Engines doubled up; Carriages completely slivered to pieces; the Rails torn up; and covered with blood; whilst goods of various descriptions, including a quantity of fish, lay scattered in every direction.'[81] A year later from the Hotel Windsor in Paris, Father Antony Hutchison wrote home about the accident he had just experienced on a train from Boulogne. He and other passengers noticed their carriage hurtling at a tremendous pace just before a succession of bangs and shocks. By the time they stopped,

> The engine had got off the rails...it had then run in a slanting direction across the line still dragging the train, at last it had crossed the down line knocking the rails all to pieces and in the end had gone clean away into a field where having made a deep trench for itself it

had tipped over on one side the tender had followed and turned over on the other side, breaking both its axles, then came a luggage van which was greatly smashed and battered... next were the three passenger carriages all off the line.[82]

These travellers were lucky; no one in the train suffered the least injury. But had the train jumped the track on the left side instead of the right, Hutchison noted it would have been a much more serious incident, as they would have plunged down a 10-foot embankment.

Hutchison did not say why the Boulogne train derailed. The most common cause of train crashes at the time Hutchison crossed the Continent was collision, commonly caused by single waggons or trucks being left standing on the tracks.[83] Next in frequency were crashes arising from engines or carriages jumping the rails, like the one Hutchison described. They might be caused by some obstruction such as blocks of wood or bars of iron being left on the rails. Engines were also derailed by cattle that had forced their way through inadequate fencing and wandered onto the tracks. Broken axles or wheels as well as defects in the rails themselves caused some trains to leave the track. A final cause of railway accidents was human neglect of the points and switches, or mechanisms enabling trains to pass from one line of rails to another.

The railway in all its facets, including its potential for destruction, embodied the new industrial age.[84] Unprecedented speeds of 35–40 miles per hour symbolized the accelerated rate of change and sense of progress accompanying industrialization. Railway time which eventually eliminated whimsicality from clocks reflected the precision and standardization inherent in machine production. When boarding either a first-, second- or third-class carriage, passengers were reminded of the class system which emerged more clearly with the rise of factories and urban sprawl. Finally, the 'fearful' wrecks described in travel journals revealed the potentially destructive power of technology. Whether one considers transport systems, the workplace or domestic space, the possibility of violence and havoc increased dramatically as machinery was adopted and improved. Train crashes were typically so sudden, uncontrollable and catastrophic that they transformed assumptions about illness. Prior to the last quarter of the nineteenth century, medical thinking attributed shock from accidents to physical injury of the spine. 'Railway spine' was a recognized medical condition for which one could receive legal compensation. By the late 1880s, however, 'traumatic neurosis' – a psychological rather than physical condition – had become the accepted explanation for post-accident shock. The disorientation and violence resulting from train wrecks were unprecedented and so severe, said medical experts, that purely psychic trauma often occurred.

This is perhaps a rather gruesome place to conclude a discussion of travel and tourism in the Victorian period, but also a fitting one. For in addition to the industrialization process, railways embodied many characteristics of the nineteenth-century commercialized world of travel – democratization, standardization, predictability and loss of autonomy. As more people left home to encounter new peoples and places, their collective identities moved more sharply into focus. The following chapters explore how travelling worked to reinforce, reveal and sometimes challenge national identities in particular. We begin with a discussion of landscape, often the first thing travellers encountered when experiencing other countries, and perhaps the most enduring aspect of their own.

2
Landscape and Climate

In Kazuo Ishiguro's Booker prize-winning novel *The Remains of the Day*, the English landscape and English butler are intimately linked. Darlington Hall's butler, Stevens, explains the connection as he relaxes in a Salisbury guesthouse after a day's drive through the West Country. The expedition took him near the Berkshire border where he climbed a steep but beckoning footpath for a hill-top view of the surrounding countryside. From that elevated position where a light breeze caressed his face, Stevens felt that the English landscape was 'the most deeply satisfying in the world'. It possessed, he thought, a quality found in no other national landscape – the quality of greatness. By 'great' Stevens did not mean dramatic or spectacular. Quite the contrary. The beauty of the English landscape was great, in Stevens's view, because of its 'calmness' and 'sense of restraint'. At this point, Stevens's thoughts shifted from the rolling countryside to the reserved English butler.

According to Stevens, England is the only country which can boast of having true butlers as opposed to manservants. He comments on the Celts and Continental Europeans, noting how they lack the emotional restraint so essential for maintaining the professional exterior characteristic of a true, dignified butler. On the other hand, the best English butlers are, like the English landscape, 'great' and 'true' because of their unique capacity for restraint. As Stevens put it, 'It is with such men as it is with the English landscape seen at its best as I did this morning: when one encounters them, one simply *knows* one is in the presence of greatness.'[1]

These guesthouse musings reveal certain key themes discussed in this chapter on Victorian attitudes towards landscape. First, they suggest that people imagine a nation to have a unique landscape. In other words, landscape is an integral part of national identity, and in this case the identity is English as opposed to Celtic or British. Victorian travellers also typically identified with a localized English, Scottish or Welsh landscape as opposed to a more overarching British or Celtic one, although in some contexts and when thinking of certain qualities they did imagine a British landscape. Second, a nation is characterized as much by the physical position its people choose to adopt when viewing and appreciating landscape as it is by the landscape itself. Stevens's preference for looking down rather than out across or up at landscape has been typical of people from all parts of Britain. Third, there is a close relationship, or mutual influence, between a nation's landscape and its people, such that they come to exhibit similar qualities, at least in people's minds. David Lowenthal argues that this relationship has been closer in England than anywhere else in Europe.[2] According to Lowenthal, in no country but England has landscape so clearly embodied national virtues and a national way of life. Victorian travel journals suggest that this very close relationship between landscape and people was thought to exist in Scotland as well. Finally, as Stevens suggests, the English landscape and people have tended to exhibit restraint and moderateness and to be averse to the dramatic, majestic and extreme. These characteristics became more sharply focused in English people's minds as they travelled around Scotland, Wales and the Continent, commenting on the very 'un-English' landscapes they encountered. The Scots and Welsh, on the other hand, were more at home in majestic settings.

Before discussing these and other issues, we must clarify what is meant by landscape.[3] For Stevens, landscape refers to countryside characteristics, a narrow but frequently used sense of the term. The usage adopted here is a broader one encompassing the *perceived* attributes of any surrounding outdoor environment, whether it be countryside, city, town, village or garden. Emphasis is on how and what people saw or imagined when they described a particular outdoor environment rather than on what was actually there. Landscape is thus treated as a component of culture. What people saw or noticed, what they ignored, and the meaning they invested when they cast an eye over and described an outdoor scene are assumed to provide important insights into their identity and values. Thus Daniel Defoe (1660–1731), who ignored ruins and rushed through mountain terrain pronouncing it a 'horrid' sight, represented a cultural milieu very different from the later Romantic era when the rage among travellers was to explore every mountain and ruin with sketchbook in hand. This chapter investigates what Victorian travellers had in sight and mind when they described landscape as British, English, Scottish or Welsh. It gives equal attention to those landscape characteristics they found unfamiliar or unappealing because not like those of their native land.

Travel journals reveal just how interdependent landscape and national identity were to the Victorians. They clearly reflect the view that national landscapes are distinct and that people's pride in and loyalty to a nation are firmly rooted in its landscape. On his expedition to the Black Forest, Charles Wood noted how the boundary between Holland and Germany and that between England and Scotland were clearly marked by changes in landscape. These natural boundaries separated the nations in both their geographic and human sense, according to Wood. In crossing from Holland into Germany he remarked, 'The German hills and undulations plainly declared that we were in a new country and amongst another race.'[4] Landscape declarations along the Scotland–England border were not so clear to James Murray, compiler of the initial *Oxford English Dictionary*.[5] When as a young boy he first saw the small stream that ran in a deep ditch marking the border between Scotland and England, he was told to straddle the ditch. Carefully placing one foot in each country, he thought of his map of Britain with some puzzlement. The map displayed Scotland and England in contrasting colours, forming a very distinct boundary between the two territories. But as he straddled the actual boundary, no difference appeared between the barren views north and south of the ditch. What is important is not that Murray failed to see any dramatic change in landscape at the border point, but rather that he took it for granted that such a change existed. Largely because of map representations, people tended to assume and imagine that borders between countries marked different landscapes as well as peoples.

Wood and other travellers recognized the existence of a sense of mutual belonging between a nation's people and its landscape that could generate intense feelings of pride and loyalty. Caroline Corner wrote of such pride while touring the Rhineland where she was a foreigner very conscious of not belonging and of thus having no claim to the landscape. To her, the Rhine was the most beautiful river on earth. While revelling in its beauty, she realized her inability ever to feel pride in the river, for she was not German and thus the Rhine would never be hers. As testimony for this bond between nationality, landscape and pride, Corner quoted Longfellow who said of the same river, 'Oh, the pride of the German heart in this noble river....By heavens! if I were a German, I would be proud of it, too.'[6] The words reflect the widespread assumption among Victorians that a national group feels, at the core of its being, a pride in its nation's landscape features.

In addition to pride, travellers linked loyal and affectionate feelings for a nation to landscape. On his first journey to England, Hugh Miller judged its landscape to be different from and much inferior to his own Scottish one. He grew weary of the many artificial, human-made elements in the English landscape, particularly the hedged enclosures. They had him longing for the 'bold natural features' characterizing Scotland's countryside, and the yearning prompted him to comment on the significance of such features:

> One likes to know the place of one's birth by other than artificial marks, – by some hoary mountain...by some wild range of precipitous coast...by some lonely glen...Who could fight for a country without features...[7]

His remark suggests that the ultimate expression of loyalty in the modern world – a willingness to fight and die for one's country – was bound up, at least in part, with landscape. It also implies that, because of landscape, the Scots had more reason to be militant as a people than did the English. Another Scotsman, G.A. Ramsay, pronounced on his people's love of his country's natural features when he addressed the Scottish Mountaineering Club saying, 'The love of scenery and of hills is implanted in the heart of every Scot as part of his very birthright; our mountains have been the moulders of our national character.'[8] Landscape features inspired affection for England as well. While touring Portugal, Margaret Law stumbled on a seemingly English patch of scenery. With its sheep-dotted hills, cultivated fields, fresh wind and crossable stream, the scene reminded her of home, or in her affectionate phrase, 'dear old England'.[9]

Ramsay's address is a very direct expression of the connection between landscape and national identity, exemplifying the intimate link between landscape and people that Lowenthal associated with the English more than with any other European people. It also suggests, as do Wood's and Miller's remarks about scenery, that Victorians stressed distinctions between England and Scotland when thinking of landscape. Most travel journals do make these distinctions, and the bulk of this chapter thus focuses on the perceived attributes of an English, a Scottish and a Welsh landscape – not of a shared British one. But there is some evidence in the journals of a Britain-wide sharing of attitudes towards the outdoor environment which should not be ignored. These attitudes concern climate and atmosphere (factors influencing how people perceive and relate to landscape), the preferred position from which to view landscape and the human scale of the natural environment.

When travelling on the Continent, people from Britain were struck by how different the European climate was from that of Britain as a whole. Some travellers even resorted to the infrequently used term 'British' when writing of the climate at home. Jemima Morrell, for example, always used 'England' and 'English' to refer to her native land, except when speaking of 'British mildness' to characterize its weather. Other travellers categorized climate as being either 'southern' or 'northern', identifying European weather as 'southern' and that across the Channel as 'northern'. By a northern, or British, climate, travellers meant grey skies, veiled rays and plenty of damp, chilly days. It was, in their view, an ungenial climate lacking in sensuousness and grace. Although many travellers left Britain so they could relax under sunnier Continental skies, they nevertheless took pride in and boasted of their own less inviting climate. As they saw it, the weather in Britain, unlike that in Europe, was mellow and mild, never subjecting one to extreme heat or cold. Summer sun, for example, was easier to enjoy in England than in France where it was too severe to be tolerable for most of the day. John MacGregor was well situated to draw such a comparison, travelling as he did by canoe. He estimated that 'in a week of common summer weather we see more of the sun in England than in France, for we seldom have so much of it at once as to compel us to close our eyes against its fierce rays.' He and other travellers from Britain favoured the twilight in their native land as well. It was a lengthy, 'delicious season of musing and long shadows' as opposed to the short spell of light after sunset typical of the sunny south.[10]

Travellers recognized that their relatively damp but mellow climate had implications for social and cultural life. Though not extremely harsh, the British climate with its long winters was nevertheless one from which people often needed to seek refuge indoors. This helps explain, according to travel journals, why home life and comfort were so much more highly valued on the British side of the Channel than in the South. Continental Europeans' life of alfresco concerts, evening strolls and café conversation was as unknown in Britain as was cosy domestic life in Europe. Travelling through Italy, J.R. Green commented disapprovingly on the absence of 'hearth and home' noting, 'An Italian doctor or an Italian lawyer knows nothing of the cosy evenings of the North, of the bright fire, the brighter chat round it, or the quiet book till sleep comes....We have so much winter that we have faced it...and beaten it.'[11] A poor person from Britain might not have been so inclined to declare winter 'beaten'. The battle to survive in Britain was much more costly and exhausting than it was in Continental countries, especially in the very warm southerly ones such as Italy, Spain or Portugal. A year before her death, William Wordsworth's daughter, Dorothy Quillinan, toured Portugal hoping to improve her health and incidentally English perceptions of the Portuguese. She observed that the sort of starving poverty found in England did not exist in Portugal. In explaining the difference, she pointed out, 'One grand advantage that the poor of Portugal have over ours is their glorious climate. They require little fuel and little clothing.'[12] Quillinan was obviously as interested in preserving an uncritical attitude towards the English as in elevating perceptions of the Portuguese. That is, instead of attributing the 'starving poverty' in England to such human-generated factors as laissez-faire economics and unthrottled industrial forces, she linked it to climate for which her countryfolk could not be held responsible.

Turning from the social to the aesthetic realm, climate and atmospheric conditions had a significant effect on use of and tolerance for colour, especially in architectural design and painting. Soon after arriving on the Continent, travellers often expressed surprise at the colourful building exteriors. Anna Howitt, for example, wrote home from Munich where she settled to study art, 'I had no conception, till I came here, of the wonderful beauty of *colour* in architecture.' Similarly, Jane Sanderson noted on her travels, 'Colour seems everything in Italy, never a house without bright blue, green, orange, or some varied hues, but all in good taste and seeming to harmonize with the brightness of the landscape.'[13] In Portugal, though the houses were painted crimson, pink, green or yellow, each with a painted balcony full of every coloured flower, Margaret Law did not find the effect gaudy. These travellers and others from the 'North' realized that bold colours did not clash with the bright, sunny Continental landscape the way they did with Britain's duller skies and 'murky' atmosphere.

Travellers from all parts of Britain returning home from the Continent spoke disapprovingly of the black haze, dingy brick and streets, and houses all grimy and bleak found in British cities. Coal was the culprit, though frequent fog, mists and drizzle intensified the dinginess. The smoke and grime were not only unpleasant to the eye, but also detrimental to physical well-being. The Welshman Sir Lewis Morris had almost forgotten how bad London air made him feel until he had been back in the capital for several hours. Proceeding to London from Dover where he had just arrived from the Continent, he noted how 'wholesome' and 'lovely' the countryside looked compared to

Continental scenery. Then he approached London Bridge complaining, 'We got once more into murky atmosphere squalid streets villainy and wretchedness, after lively Brussels and the dapper cleanly Dutch towns. I had not breathed smoke and filth for 9 hours before I felt as seedy and bilious and uncomfortable as I did before I left for the continent.'[14] The 'murky' atmosphere enveloping Britain as a whole simply did not benefit human health or show off colour and buildings to advantage the way the more transparent atmosphere on the Continent did. A panoramic view in France or Italy presented the most distant objects with a distinctness and a boldness of colour hardly ever seen in Britain. While in Paris, the Scotsman John Dunlop remarked on how enchanting it was to see buildings devoid of grime through a clean atmosphere. But although he was enchanted with the clean and clear appearance, it did not make him feel at home. He admitted, 'There will always be to one accustomed to the dark look of English houses, a feeling somewhat akin to discomfort in the outward appearance of the whitewashed French buildings.'[15]

Buildings in Britain tended to present greyish or terracotta exteriors with more colourful decoration inside. Continental cathedrals often did just the reverse, as a group of Toynbee Travellers discovered when they visited the Duomo in Florence. One traveller explained his initial disappointment with the church's interior:

> The contrast between the brilliant exterior with its dazzling mosaic of white and brown marble slabs and the bare dull walls inside is very striking and strongly impresses itself upon those who are used to a reversal of this arrangement in obedience to climate.[16]

In Genoa, Nona Bellairs's tour of churches had her eyes growing weary of strongly coloured exterior pillars, steps and floors, and she sighed saying, 'One of our grey old minsters with their painted windows would be a relief.'[17] Even the form of religiosity sanctioned by cathedrals was thought to be influenced by climate, as MacGregor argued after attending a saint's day ceremony in France. Although the procession seemed strange to him, he conceded that 'deep devotion, silent in its depth, is for the north and not for this radiant sun'.[18] The French, he admitted, required a public religion of bold colours, actions and sounds.

In addition to perceptions about climate and atmosphere, natives of Britain shared attitudes about how best to view an outdoor scene, whether in the city or countryside. They preferred looking down, and thus trekked up to high ground, especially when travelling through hilly, mountainous terrain. Murray's earliest guidebook encouraged this bird's-eye stance, advising, 'The quickest mode of acquiring a good idea of any place is to take the earliest opportunity of ascending some tower or eminence, from which there is a commanding view.'[19] M.F. Tupper did just that in Augsburg where he 'went up to the top of a church tower to look round panoramically: it is always the most compendious method of making oneself master of the position, and learning a city at a glance.'[20] Travellers sought and favoured similar heights when gazing at countryside scenes. In their journals, they sometimes compared the viewing opportunities provided by roads, always praising those running closest to mountain tops. The Albthal and Wehrathal valleys in the Black Forest enabled Charles Wood to draw such a comparison. In the former, the road was far up the mountain side, allowing for a continuously downward gaze. Travelling its path was exhilarating for Wood, who declared, 'You seem to be above it all, to command all; a sense of wings, of soaring, takes possession of you.' The Wehrathal road, by contrast, ran on a level with the valley stream, offering a much inferior prospect in Wood's estimation. From its ground-level position, Wood argued, 'There is no looking into great depths, which always gives a far stronger sense of the sublime and the splendid than looking upwards from the depth itself.'[21] Eliza Salvin confessed to a similar prejudice when she encouraged other travellers to ascend the Bernese Alps where 'one feels so free'. In her opinion, 'Looking up at them from the vallies [did] not fill one with the same awe and wonder.'[22] Lakes, too, required a downward gaze, as Thomas Letts made clear during his tour of Scotland and the Lake District. He first glimpsed Loch Lomond while travelling a road running along the foot of the surrounding mountains. The experience was a disappointment not only due to bad weather, but also because 'so low a road is rarely competent to convey a just sense of Lake scenery'.[23]

Like these English travellers, Scottish women and men sought peak views with a passion. Alison Cunningham did not wish to reach the top of just any Alp. She admitted, 'I've a strong desire to get to the highest peak of the Alps.'[24] Perhaps in her nursing capacity, she instilled in the young R.L. Stevenson the same love of summit reaching. On his donkey trip through France, he sought out the Pic de Finiels peak which towered 5,600 feet over the Languedoc countryside. From its height he could see the Mediterranean, and the experience prompted him to say with an imperial air, 'Like stout Cortez when, with eagle eyes, he stared on the Pacific, I took possession, in my own name, of a new quarter of the world.'[25] Although Cunningham's and Stevenson's comments suggest a desire among Scots for downward glances at scenery, some English travellers believed the desire to be more of an English than a Scottish or Welsh one. C.L. Smith thought the Scots preferred an outward to a downward view. He came to this conclusion while looking out over Loch Tay at views considered by the Scots to be 'the finest in Scotland'. For Smith, the vistas were disappointing, and he decided that a fine view in Scotland meant 'nothing more than that you can see a very long way, beauty being considered identical with extension, just as among the Hottentots'.[26] Smith is drawing a clear distinction here between the Scots and the English, by linking the former to what was regarded by many at the time as an 'uncivilized' African tribe. On his walking tour of Wales, Borrow noted a marked difference in attitude towards hill-top prospects between himself and the Welshman who accompanied him. As they passed a hill summit, Borrow remarked about how much they would have enjoyed 'a glorious prospect down' if it had not been so dark and drizzly. He then qualified his remarks: 'I should say that I should have enjoyed a glorious prospect, for John Jones, like a true mountaineer, cared not a brass farthing for prospects.'[27]

Whether felt by English or Scottish travellers, the attractions of summit perches may have had something to do with the British landscape itself. According to travellers from Britain, the country's landscape differed from that of the Continent in its being wholly human in scale. That is, no plot of land was so high or inaccessible that it could not be reached in a day's journey. Even the tallest mountains such as Ben Nevis (highest in Britain at 4,406 ft; compare to Switzerland's Mt. Blanc at 15,600 ft), Snowdon (highest in Wales at 3,560 ft), and Cader Idris could be ascended by both men and women in a day. Snowdon, for example, took the average tourist three hours to climb, and nearly all travellers to North Wales made the ascent. Of the Highlands a Scottish traveller noted, 'There is very little difficulty experienced in ascending any of the finer Scottish hills.'[28] Though not considered one of the 'finer hills', Ben Nevis's summit could be reached in 3 1/2 to 4 hours, with the descent taking less time. Even the lakes in Britain were small enough to be seen comprehensively as lakes, rather than as boundless inland seas. In short, the British were accustomed to hill-top views and to an accessible, obstacle-free landscape when it came to rambling and gazing. This assumption of accessibility helps explain why Elizabeth Sewell looked with disfavour upon much of the German landscape – a landscape Murray's guides depicted as having a 'character of wildness and loneliness'. As Sewell passed through German countryside she complained, 'There have been very few lanes amongst the fields, and I have always had an uncomfortable feeling in looking at them, as if I could not get from one part to another without walking amongst corn or jumping over ditches.'[29] This seemingly unwelcoming landscape contrasted with Britain's which offered many inviting footpaths to the rambler. Similarly, the small scale of Britain's natural sites, including rivers, may account for Christina Struthers's negative first impression of the Rhine. When first setting eyes on the river, she exclaimed, '[We] learned for ourselves how ugly to a Scotch eye is the glacier water – one's first idea is that the river is in *spate*! all the more that there is such an enormous volume of water rolling between these banks.' She went on to say that travellers enthusiastic about Rhine scenery had to be those 'who only know Germany, Holland & the like'.[30] Even insects on the Continent seemed larger than those in Britain. On her trip through Switzerland, grasshoppers as big as frogs and huge butterflies caused Mary Dundas to conclude, 'Everything here is on a large scale – excepting poor little humanity – we are quite dwarfed by... the general vastness of our surroundings.'[31]

It is interesting to note the emotions inspired by summit views, given that natives of Britain were so enamoured of and accustomed to them. Gazing down from Snowdon, T.W. Fisher admitted, 'I felt lord over an immense tract, I drank in the view slowly... then had some brandy & water', a favourite mountain top refreshment.[32] Fisher's remark together with travellers previously discussed comments suggest that these views generated feelings of commanding, possessing, being a master, soaring, and being free – the very feelings associated with an over-confident, imperial mentality. Perhaps the British landscape played a part in motivating its people to claim possession of distant lands and to rule over and command other peoples, while at the same time declaring that they themselves were free and never would be slaves. The British were admittedly not the only imperialists, but they were the most 'successful' ones, if one measures success by extent and duration of empire.

The manageable scale of Britain's landscape generated the perception among travellers that it was more humanized than other landscapes. Like Lowenthal, they recognized that a close relationship – almost a fusion – between humans and nature set Britain apart from other countries. T.N. Talfourd articulated the intimacy best when he was vacationing in Switzerland. He praised Swiss scenery for being grand and bountiful, but noted its lack of individual character and inability to incorporate human feelings and thoughts. The British landscape, he argued, was superior in these respects. In his words, the advantage of the Swiss scenes will be found in their richer affluence of accompaniment; that of British, in that individuality of character which partly belongs to their own features, and partly consists in their aptitude for blending with the feelings and thoughts of him who loves them.[33]

He went on to explain how centuries of human struggles, loves, joys and sorrows lay preserved in the British countryside. Even the tops of hills and mountains in Britain, unlike those of the unreachable Alps, bore witness to human history with their many ruins of towers, castles and earthen forts. Similar thoughts occurred to Elizabeth Carne just after she returned to Pau from a four-day expedition in the Pyrenees. She compared the grand mountains of the Pyrenees chain and the tamer, more modest hills, or *coteaux*, surrounding Pau where she was enjoying three months' rest. Like Talfourd, she preferred the hills which were reminiscent of home and more easily integrated into her daily life and 'common humanity'. They had soothed, cheered and refreshed her in a way that the Pyrenees never could, given their tendency to dwarf human cares and trials. Thus her remarks upon returning to Pau, 'Welcome back the tamer coteaux; welcome their chequered clouds and sunshine; welcome my common, busy, happy, human life.'[34]

These attitudes towards climate, preferred viewing position and countryside scale reflect a Britain-wide context for thinking about and relating to landscape. But most perceptions of landscape were framed within a less inclusive English, Scottish or Welsh context. That is, the three groups defined themselves and their landscapes in opposition to each other (the opposing of England to Scotland and Wales is most apparent) as much as to the Continent. In so doing, they used different languages to imagine and describe their landscapes. The Scots, for example, resorted to such terms as rugged, wild, bold, barren, grand, savage, lonely and mountainous when writing about their native landscape, while the English imagined their land as soft, gentle, cheerful, neat, flat and fertile. Their languages and perceptions say something about how the different national groups valued and conceptualized grandeur and majesty, liberty, order, ruralness, hierarchy and productivity.

English travellers made comments about buildings and landscape indicative of an aversion to the grand and majestic, or at least of a sense that the two qualities were very un-English. Continental cathedrals tended to elicit hostility towards grand-scale architecture. E.A. Freeman felt very much at home in Nevers Cathedral because its proportions seemed more English than French. That is, at Nevers, he was 'not overwhelmed with the soaring majesty of some of the greater French minsters'.[35] He went on to praise the English landscape for its many modest parish churches as compared to those in France, where grand minsters were revived and preserved at the expense of many parish churches after the revolutionary suppression of religious institutions.

English hostility to majesty is even more apparent when looking at reactions to countryside landscape, particularly to mountains. Travellers admitted that the Continent offered grand mountain chains like the Alps and Pyrenees which fascinated and astonished, especially at first sight. But after an initial feeling of awe in the presence of such grandeur, they quickly became uncomfortable and longed to take refuge in their own more modest English hills and mountains. Journal writers from England repeatedly spoke of feeling oppressed, imprisoned or hemmed in by the Continent's majestic mountain scenery. Like Freeman who was displeased by the magnificent proportion of French cathedrals, Mary Eyre was distressed by the Pyrenees, which seemed to tower over her like a cathedral fashioned by God. She expressed her desperation:

> On each side rose the rocky walls upon which the blue sky seemed to rest; while before me, still loftier mountains appeared to hem me in. The whole scene was inexpressibly awful and solemn; it seemed a temple to the Divinity built by his own hands...I never before so completely realized the majesty of God. I could hardly breathe, I was oppressed even to tears, and I felt thankful I was alone.[36]

T.N. Talfourd experienced similar sentiments in Switzerland where he felt like a dwarf subjected to the 'frowning tyranny' and 'excess of grandeur' of the Alps. He described how 'the spirits sink among great mountain tops almost as if beneath a weight of care; and some shivering sense of oppression comes over us.'[37] Other English travellers wrote of how the overwhelming sense of insignificance elicited by grand mountains made gazing at them almost too painful to bear.

Sky-scraping mountains like the Alps and the Pyrenees clearly violated English people's sense of proportion and scale. In their view, pleasing mountains were ones with easily accessible summits. Towering peaks seemed impassable barriers and thus produced, in many English travellers, a feeling of confinement, especially when viewed from a valley. As Martha Lamont pointed out, 'Mountains must either be ascended, and the country looked at from them, or they must be seen from a distance, when every effect of light produces a change in them; otherwise, they are oppressive.'[38] Charles Wood agreed on the importance of distance.

The watering-places in the Kniebis-Baths district, he argued, were shut in by mountains of 'too close proximity, that after a while inevitably becomes oppressive'.[39] Even parts of the less towering Welsh and Scottish mounatins sometimes seemed stifling to the English whose native mountains were modest by comparison. At Beddgellert in North Wales Samuel Linder became greatly distressed by the hills that, in his view, 'enclose us on every side...and appear to intercept ventilation. It is rather like a prison.'[40] This prison-like sensation occurred much more often, however, in the more majestic Continental mountains.

In addition to their hemmed-in feeling, Alp-high mountains' capacity for producing danger and adventure was unattractive to some English travellers, particularly to women. The mountains challenged the quiet, relatively risk-free life so highly cherished by English men and women. This preference for the safe and undramatic moved more sharply into focus for Elizabeth Sewell as she eavesdropped on conversations in Swiss mountain villages. The talk was mostly of avalanches, glaciers, torrents and precipices, all illustrated by the many pictures of adventurous expeditions decorating inn walls. She was struck by how different these exchanges were from typical ones back home, which tended to focus on friends, family, schools or interesting villages and towns. In Switzerland, she realized, 'It seems quite as natural for persons to be leading a scrambling life, full of risk, as it is in England for them to be sitting down every day to the same quiet occupations, and taking walks over smooth fields and along broad highways.'[41] The English and even the British landscape was much less conducive than Switzerland's to nervy, dangerous outings. Even when climbing Britain's highest mountains, the risk was very low. According to Murray's handbook for North Wales, a guide was not needed for ascending Snowdon in good weather. In the handbook's estimation, 'There is nothing about the excursion calling for any but moderate exertion, care, and nerve.' Similarly, the guide for Scotland noted how the Highland mountains offered a 'spice of excitement' but 'rarely any danger'. The greatest risk for travellers arose 'not so much from inaccessible scrambles, as the mistaking their way, and being overtaken by mist'.[42]

Sewell may have underestimated the English desire for adventure. Although life in England itself may have been relatively risk-free, it was also in England that the first Alpine Club in Europe was founded in 1857. Between that date and 1890, 823 men, mostly of professional, middle-class status, joined the club dedicated to scrambling up every major peak in the Alps.[43] Many English women joined Alpine excursions as well, trekking over rocks and glaciers with the men. No national group in Europe displayed such a passion for peak climbing as the English. Somewhat defensively, the president of the Scottish Mountaineering Club explained why the English were the first to form an Alpine mountaineering club. Ramsay speculated:

> Perhaps their own dull flats drove them in sheer desperation to seek for heights elsewhere; perhaps the very paucity of their climbers drove them for self-defence into combination: whereas in Scotland, every man has his hill or mountain at his door, every man is potentially a mountaineer; and a mountaineering club, in its simple sense, must thus have included nothing less than the entire nation.[44]

Scholars' explanations of the English-British fondness for mountaineering range more broadly to include the expansion of railway networks, widespread romantic sentiment, a need to express masculinity and a desire to assert the conquering drive of a determined imperial power.[45]

Romantic sentiment is the motivation for mountain viewing and climbing most evident in English travellers' journals. It can clearly be seen in the ambivalent attitude towards mountains, whether Continental or British, expressed in many journals. Travellers from England, even those with a penchant for climbing, considered majestic mountains un-English, and many felt uncomfortable and out of place in their presence. In addition to grand, awesome, oppressive, awful and frowning, terms such as frightful, tortuous, perilous, painful, gloomy, savage and stern filled the mountain sections of travellers' journals. The discourse suggests that Continental mountain chains were repellent to English people's undramatic sensibilities and very different from the English landscape always characterized by the native population as smiling, cheerful, soothing, and so forth. But interspersed among this negative mountain discourse are such terms as fine, enchanting, romantic and venerable, suggesting an irresistible attraction among many to the peaks, precipices and gorges, no matter how frightful or frowning. Simon Schama has termed this romantic attraction to the dramatic and the horrible as 'agreeable terror', a characteristic central to picturesque taste, according to Andrews.[46] The picturesque tourist sought landscape that roused the emotions rather than scenes that prompted reason to survey.

An excellent example of this ambivalence about majestic mountains appears in a lovingly produced journal by an Alp climber who identifies himself simply as 'An Englishman'. The gilt-edged pages covered with detailed sketches and type-like handwriting are carefully bound in a lockable volume entitled 'Among the Alps'. In describing his adventures with friends and guides, the author resorted to all the above-mentioned mountain discourse, especially when recounting their experiences at the 'tortuous' Guill Pass and Gorge. At one point, they had to cross the face of a perpendicular cliff by a narrow pathway with 'overhanging cliff above' and 'a yawning gulf below'. Keeping his eyes firmly fixed on his footsteps, the author emerged safely with the others, all looking at each other 'with a gravity of visage that spoke [their] mutual sentiments'. They shared a 'richly earned' bottle of wine and light repast before tackling the 'dreadful trade in prospect' of descending a cliff face by rope ladder in order to reach a much celebrated cavern. To give a final 'screw' to his courage, the author lit one of his cherished cigars, and then planted his foot on the first of many rungs. It was not until he reached the rock shelf over 20 feet below and exchanged congratulations with the others that he realized his cigar had fallen from his mouth – an assurance that, in his words, 'my attention had been otherwise directed, and my nerves somewhat flurried'. As they stood in the bowels of the mountain gazing at the 'forlorn void' and 'dreadful sublimity' presented by the cavern, the author noted, 'The occurrence of a thunder-storm...would have greatly deepened the romance of the situation.' Lacking any such thunderous clouds, they laid claim to the cavern with some carvings, before returning to the ladder. The upward climb was 'terrific' because 'the wind had become gusty and the ropes seemed to sway between life and death.'[47] Once at the top, they laughed triumphantly and indulged in a second, more aggressive assault on the refreshment basket. A more classic depiction of 'agreeable terror' would be hard to find, though the English did not have to cross the Channel to indulge in such 'romantic' adventures.

Scotland in particular drew hordes of English tourists in search of a respite from the calming, orderly nature of their familiar landscape. The distinctions in fact and perception between lands could be a source of attraction for tourists, in that a primary purpose of the touristic act was to partake of experiences and places different from those of home. Novels, poems, paintings and tourist literature had taught the English that, in contrast to their country, Scotland was a romantic land of dramatic, sublime scenery and age-old tales guaranteed to spice the imagination.[48] Travel journals depicted Scotland in this very fashion. At the end of a Scottish tour, one traveller wrote of imposing heathy mountains and moors, lovely lakes, thundering falls, rugged river beds and sublime rocks, not forgetting 'all the fabled patriotic tales, and all the cherished associations blended oft with these – Scotland!'[49] Travellers bound for Scotland hoped and expected to have their passions excited temporarily by this combination of literary associations and overpowering scenery. Most were not disappointed. Edmund Gosse found his passions heightened by West Coast scenery. As he steamed out of the Sound of Mull on a sunny day with jagged hills in view, he recorded, 'An exultation such as I have seldom felt, filled me and I found my cheeks flushed, and my heart beating fast.'[50] A English lady touring the Highlands with a female friend and two men wrote of the 'strange fancies' they often experienced, such as when one of the gentlemen sat at a large round table imagining himself as King Arthur. She attributed the fancies, in part, to the 'rarefied state of the atmosphere' that induced a drunken-like state.[51] She also regarded Glen and mountain scenery as mind-altering and appealing to the imagination. After a day's sightseeing in the Highlands, she napped for an hour enjoying the scenery 'again in dreams'. One of the gentlemen read through an old newspaper, but with an eye transformed by their new surroundings. As she explained his perception of the paper, 'In a fresh place [it] seem'd like fresh information or else from the time that had elaps'd since reading it before it had really become so to him.' Their next stretch of mountain-bound scenery offered such a variety of 'wild romantic picturesque or sublime views' that she thought it a place an artist's 'loftiest imagination would be pleas'd to revel amidst or delineate with the magic touches of his pencil'. Her comments suggest that Scotland's air and scenes transported the mind from the rational world to one more dreamlike, imaginary and magical.

An experience this foursome with their nine-year-old guide had at a waterfall near Callander illustrates clearly Scotland's capacity to inspire a fanciful state of mind. From the brink of a precipice on which they perched with a bottle of wine and some biscuits, the author described the scene. Water cascaded over 'Craggy Rock in splendid foamings', forming a pool of still black water below known locally as 'the Devil's pal'. She thought the designation appropriate, as the pool was 'inky black' and contrasted markedly with the snow-white foamings above giving a 'most imposing effect'. The whole scene was 'truly romantic' and 'picturesque', especially given the small wooden bridge crossing the Cataract and the unexpected wanderer. As they sat absorbing the 'solitary grandeur' of the place, a small girl in a scarlet cloak appeared out of nowhere and stood on the bridge looking over the fall. The colourful figure offered 'a very suitable and pleasing effect – It was just what an artist would have introduced had he been sketching the view.' In this romantic setting they listened to the 'roaring torrent' below, letting their imaginations and fancies run wild.

They began to talk of loved ones and home and, 'in imagination (quickened amid such scenery)', started to converse with them as if they were there and part of the scene. They felt in their hearts 'the feelings of the poet' as they talked and admired the view. Suddenly, a gentleman in the group was seized by an 'extraordinary desire' to perform a christening. He proposed to rename the nearby Bracklin Bridge 'Craven Bridge' after the chapel near their home. Though astonished by the proposal, the others agreed to comply, because they 'were at all times ready to gratify each others' peculiarities or *fancies*'. He then 'dash'd' the near empty wine bottle against the side of a rock before hurling it into the torrent below. As it disappeared beneath the foam, he pronounced the following words, 'Bracklin Bridge, I will that henceforth you be call'd Craven Bridge!' The respondents yelled, 'Amen! Amen.' They then sat 'wrapp'd in wonder' at their surroundings so remote from human touches and with an appearance of 'savage wildness and gloom that could not be surpass'd'. Some time passed before they began to retrace their steps over the apparently 'unbeaten' track of mountain over which they had come. The author found herself so overpowered by the recent excitement that she could hardly walk.

This incident exemplifies, in several ways, English people's relationship with Scotland and with mountainous landscape in general. Scotland was, first of all, different enough from England to be a desirable tourist destination for the English. Specifically, the romantic, sublime scenery contrasted with England's soothing, gentle, tamed and highly humanized landscape. English tourists went to Scotland to be temporarily piqued and unsoothed, believing the sublime scenes with their literary associations to be fuel for the imagination and passions. But though they sought the flights of fancy engendered by Scotland's magnificent, relatively remote settings, they were also disturbed by their overpowering quality, much the same as they were by the Alps or the Pyrenees. On the precipice near Bracklin Bridge, one gazer attempted to alleviate such discomfort by satisfying his very English urge to tame the landscape. That is, he enacted the conquering, humanizing ritual of bestowing on the site a name linked with home.

Although English travellers communed with Scotland's wildest landscape, they maintained distance, at least perceptually, from the local inhabitants. Scholars have written about the Anglo-Saxon view of Celts in the nineteenth century.[52] While Anglo-Saxons thought of themselves as rational and able to experience irrationality only with some external stimulus such as sublime scenery, they believed Celts to be naturally passionate and irrational. The Celts could thus, in their view, still believe in the ghosts and legends haunting Scotland's landscape in a way that the more sceptical English could only pretend to do. One such sceptical Englishman found the flowers, foliage and fauna around Loch Katrine enchanting. In fact, the scene was so romantic, he admitted, 'One almost became a convert to the belief of the natives of the district, that the incidents related in Scott's charming dramatic poem, really occurred.'[53] His use of 'almost' clearly separates him from Celtic credulity. The foursome at Bracklin Bridge perceived themselves, even in their most dramatic and passionate state, to be so different from the locals as to be shocking. In the process of tossing a bottle and renaming the bridge, they became aware that gazers' eyes were turned on them. Two local children in search of their companion (the guide) 'stood staring with astonishment' at the display of passion on the precipice.

Scottish travellers distanced themselves from the English as well by composing eulogies on mountains and mountain scenery. Although Ramsay's narrowly focused, patriotic speculation about English people's urges to club together for mountain climbing may not adequately explain their love of Alp scaling, it does hint at differences between the English and the Scots when it comes to attitudes towards mountains. The Scots were more at home with mountains and did not express the same feelings of oppression as the English did when confronted with steep slopes and towering summits. This difference can no doubt be attributed to the more mountainous Scottish landscape alluded to by Ramsay. Even the so-called 'Scottish Lowlands' were more mountainous than any stretch of landscape in England. In fact, Murray's *Handbook for Travellers in Scotland* (1883) suggested that the South of Scotland was miscalled the 'Lowlands', since it is 'for the most part a mass of mountains or round-backed hills'. Scots often spoke fondly of the grandeur conveyed by Scotland's most mountainous areas. Even the highly acclaimed Rhine scenery seemed deficient compared to Scotland's mountain scenery. According to the Scotsman William Chambers, the prettiest part of a Rhine cruise included the middle stretch from Cologne up to Mayence (Mainz). But beautiful as this river scenery was, he admitted, 'Nowhere...in the whole hundred miles from Cologne upwards, does the scenery possess those qualities of sublimity and grandeur which we find in such savage regions as Glencoe – the generally limited height of the mountain steeps necessarily precluding any character of that kind.'[54] One Scotsman spoke proudly of 'our noble Scottish hills' and suggested that the grandest and most impressive mountain scenery in Great Britain was not Ben Nevis, but the more modest Cuillins in Skye, the highest of them only about 2,600 ft. For this mountain enthusiast, shape and covering rather than height rendered mountains magnificent. Although the Cuillins were not towering, they rose 'stern and sharp from the sea...shaped on the extremist alpine model, but with wild and wondrous variety – scowling dark and naked from base to peak.'[55]

Mountains, whether wild, bleak or grand, were not frightful or alienating to the Scots. In fact, they were perceived to embody the Scottish landscape and national character. Nothing expresses this perception better than an article on the 'Access to Mountains Bill' published in *The Scotsman* (1888). That bill was designed to prevent the closing off of Scottish mountains to ramblers in the interest of sport, particularly deer hunting. In defence of the bill the article claimed:

> Man is, no doubt, a climbing animal...Scotsmen have this climbing quality developed to its highest point. The Scotsman, if he is not exactly born with his foot upon his native heath, at least takes to the heather as naturally as a duck to water. The mountain and the flood, the brown heath and shaggy wood, have no terrors for him. They are often his only inheritance, and he never can be induced to abandon his rights of succession. Even when the Scotsman goes to London, which is the most denationalising of all places, you find him settling upon Hampstead Heath, or some other of the scarcely perceptible eminences.[56]

The words imply that nothing, not even England's grandest city, could suppress the most salient of Scottish national characteristics – love of, or at-homeness in, the mountains. Scotland's heath, hills and mountains were treasured birthrights, setting the Scots apart as a people, especially from the English.

Given this national trait, it is not surprising that Continental mountains did not disorient and distress Scottish travellers as much as they did English ones. When travelling through Continental mountain chains, Scottish men and women tended to praise the sky-piercing, rugged, irregular peaks for their beauty rather than to criticize them for their confining or chaotic nature. The Dundee merchant and traveller William Edward Baxter thought that the mountains between Innsbruck and Landek had no equals for romantic beauty. He remarked on their varied shapes saying, 'At one time they present to view lofty symmetrical cones, at another sharply outlined pinnacles, and occasionally peaks of the most fantastic forms...few of them having massive rounded summits, like those in our native land. The effect of the scenery is thus much enhanced.'[57] Standing on a plateau with Mont Blanc in view, Christina Struthers from Aberdeen was also enchanted by the scenery, as her positive description suggests, 'The whole glorious range lay in its majesty Mont Blanc with its soft rounded top surrounded by these marvellous Aiguilles which seem to shoot a thousand spires up to heaven. I felt a thrill of deep solemnity, and thanked God that I saw that great sight.'[58] George Combe was also 'thrilled' by the silence, solitude and grandeur of the mountains 'steep as perpendicular walls' near Berchtesgaden. He even regarded a ravine road sandwiched between high mountains as 'beautiful' rather than confining. His English wife was not so enamoured of majestic mountain scenery as he. At their lodgings located between Salzburg and Innsbruck, she stayed room-bound attending to her journal in order to avoid gazing on 'la belle nature – which is however here *too* awful and grand not to be rather oppressive to the spirits'.[59]

As in the case with Scotland, travellers imagined Wales as a mountainous country, and, like the Scots, the Welsh displayed a deep attachment to mountains. Although a Welsh national community distinct from England was not apparent when looking at the Established Church, the Union Jack or the administrative apparatus, there were marked differences regarding landscape. This was especially true of North Wales whose craggy, often barren mountainous scenery resembled the Scottish Highlands more than any terrain in England. The rounder hills cultivated to the very top characteristic of the South seemed English in proportion and lushness, and one English traveller said of the southwest area around Pembroke and Carmarthen, 'The country throughout would be thought pretty in England.' But travellers from all parts of Britain perceived Wales to be a wild, rugged, mountainous country very different from England, and even from Scotland. No matter how stunning Scottish hills appeared, the Welsh patriot Henry Richard felt compelled to give Wales the edge in the contest for beautiful scenery. Gazing at the Ochil hills in Scotland, he found the atmosphere 'magical' and the landscape so impressive as to embody 'a kind of spiritual beauty'. But when comparing the hills to his native landscape he noted, 'They lack the rich colouring which some of our Welsh hills display from their abundance of heather.'[60] Travellers from England were not always so positively disposed towards Welsh mountains. Characterizing Wales as a mountainous country, Samuel Linder complained of the landscape's effect on the inhabitants. The castle at Llangollen with its gate manned by six children seeking fees prompted his complaint. Linder explained the youthful garrison with conviction, 'It is one of the characteristics of mountainous countries, that the inhabitants are fond of building castles, and levying blackmail on all travellers. The descendants of the Welsh retain all their ancestors fondness for this habit.'[61] A Welsh woman or man might have pointed out to Linder that the most impressive and famous castles in Wales (in all of medieval Europe, for that matter) were built by the English king, Edward I (1272–1307) in order to subjugate the Welsh once and for all. The issue here, however, is not whether the Welsh possessed castle-building urges or not. What is important in the context of this chapter on landscape and identity is the prevailing perceptions expressed by Linder that Wales was a mountainous country and that there was an interdependent relationship between the landscape and its people.

Welsh journal writers never expressed a fondness for castles, but they did rhapsodize on the subject of mountains and mountain scenery. In 1859, W.T. Griffith left his home in North Wales for the first time bound for medical studies in London. During his time as a student, he composed a three-volume journal focused mostly on his spiritual thoughts and condition. But the journals also contain accounts of his trips back home where he visited meaningful places and scenes, mostly in the mountains. He took daily strolls in the mountains in the early mornings and evenings, commenting on the joy of being 'among delicious solitudes, where *the thin air fans my panting frame*, inspiring me...with purer thoughts, nobler aspirations, and sublimer reflection'.[62] Similarly, Henry Richard found mountains comforting and uplifting. While travelling on the Continent, he bestowed this eulogy on the majestic scenery:

> There is something unspeakably soothing and elevating to my mind in mountain scenery. They seem to repose in such calm and imperturbable dignity the hoary watchers of innumerable ages that have flown in all their vicissitude and turbulence at their feet, while they remain unchanged and immovable, looking down with a sort of grave pity on the shifting varieties of human life. One generation cometh and another goeth, but the earth (and especially its everlasting mountains) abideth for ever.[63]

His comments are very different from those of most English travellers who were oppressed, pained or awed by mountains but not typically soothed. It is also interesting that, for Richard, mountains were a source of permanence and stability; they were not, as many English gazers argued, the products of nature in its most chaotic and convulsive state. In Richard's view, humans were the changing, capricious force, lending less meaning and longevity to a landscape than the mountains. The implication is that a mountainous country such as Wales instils in people a more deeply rooted, permanent attachment to landscape than a country without mountains.

In addition to a sense of scale and proportion, travellers' comments about mountains and other landscape features have implications for their notion of liberty. As we have seen, majestic mountains clearly offended the English sense of liberty. They were seen as barriers, and English people associated freedom with a landscape like their own, devoid of such obstructions to views. Other aspects of the English landscape were invested with the quality of liberty as well, including the tidal sea enveloping its shores. When travelling through countryside, the poet J.A. Symonds loved to imagine how a painter might depict the land, light and sky. In his travel writing, he used words effectively to create pictures of the places he visited. His favourite destination was Italy, and during a stay in the fashionable spa town of Viareggio, he lingered near the edge of a wooden pier to indulge in the sense of freedom inspired by the evening sea breeze. 'There is,' he noted, 'a feeling of "immensity, liberty, action" here, which is not common in Italy. It reminds us of England; and to-night the Mediterranean had the rough force of a tidal sea.' Perhaps the expanse of sea surrounding Britain helped to create the feeling of immensity and liberty, despite the landscape's small scale. Symonds certainly associated liberty with a view of the sea as opposed to one of an expanse of land. In comparing the two, he asserted, 'There are suggestions... of immensity, of liberty, of action, presented by the boundless horizons and the changeful changeless tracts of ocean which no plain possesses.'[64]

English travellers infused even trees and livestock behaviour with significance concerning liberty. Linking trees and liberty was not new in the Victorian period.[65] The Anglo-Saxons regarded the forest as the seat of English liberty. According to English mythology, a forest tree deflected an arrow killing the Norman heir, William Rufus, whose father, William the Conqueror, had violated the traditional woodland rights of grazing and gleaning. The English continued to remember and mythologize forest freedoms that existed before the Normans transformed the forests into exclusive hunting grounds where only the king had rights. During the eighteenth-century struggle against France, the heart of oak was depicted as the mainstay of English liberty. This hardest and stoutest of woods was valued both as a symbol of the nation and as the key construction material for the primary defender of English freedom – the Navy. For the Victorians, it was the arrangement of trees in the countryside rather than the qualities of a particular tree which had implications for liberty and authority. French trees, for example, seemed regimented and authoritarian, standing as they often did in soldier-like ranks. One traveller declared them to be 'under an Imperial necessity to form into line'.[66] In contrast, English trees appeared to be scattered naturally and randomly about the landscape, and thus to embody the sort of liberated spirit so highly valued by the English. Cattle in England were thought to symbolize freedom as well. Unlike on the Continent where they lived a confining stable life, English cattle grazed relatively freely over the countryside much like the human inhabitants.

Attitudes towards landscape reveal that the English notion of liberty did not imply unbounded freedom or anarchy. What characterized the English and their landscape was a capacity for embodying liberty and order *simultaneously*. Perhaps this combination is what Stevens had in mind when he used the term 'restraint' to sum up the English landscape and the English butler. According to travellers from England, their landscape manifested order and restraint by means of its neatness and cheerfulness, its natural irregularity and moderation, and its variety.

Comparisons made between Continental and English landscape reveal that the latter typically was perceived as neat and trim. Travel journals are full of these two terms applied to buildings and outdoor scenes reminiscent of England. Matilda Edwards thought Anjou had 'an English aspect' about it because of its 'neat little cottages, with flower-garden, and newly constructed villas of middle-class owners...there is order and tidiness, and a look of prosperity everywhere.'[67] Other travellers noted how 'neat compact construction' of buildings and 'neatly-gabled wood framed villages' gave an English look to certain parts of France and Germany.[68] Trimmed lawns and hedges also were perceived as English, and travel journals contain numerous outbursts against the straggly, run-wild look of both sorts of greenery on the Continent. During her stay in Munich, Anna Howitt visited a well-known German artist's studio set in what, to her English eyes, was a very unattractive field. Not wanting to appear the carping type, she distanced herself from any negative stance by putting her critical remarks into the mouth of a generic Englishman. She thus wrote, '"Very untidy all this!" remarks your Englishman, recalling his trim lawn and shrubbery at home: "a boy is wanted here to pull up these rank weeds, and a roller to roll that gravel and grass!"' Similarly, Eleanor Price pointed out while visiting a château park in France, 'Round about an English chateau these grass slopes and banks would be kept in a very different kind of order: but we have no trim lawns here.'[69]

Rugged, wild-looking landscape clearly was at odds with the English sense of order. The Pyrenees, for example, were in one traveller's estimation so 'rugged and massive, as to convey the idea of their having been the waves of a chaotic world, suddenly arrested in their foam and fury, and fixed for ever.'[70] Another traveller thought that the lofty, jagged peaks around Lucerne appeared unsettled and belligerent, standing up 'as if prepared for war'.[71] Journals typically speak critically of wild, rugged terrain, noting how markedly it differs from anything in England. In contrast to such rugged, chaotic landscapes, the English countryside seemed comfortable and soothing. Travellers from England used such adjectives as soft, smooth, gentle, peaceable, cheerful and smiling to describe their native hills, views and trees. Thus unlike the threatening summits surrounding Lucerne, English hills appeared 'soft, and smooth, and peaceable-looking'.[72] Wandering around Versailles, T.N. Talfourd captured the friendly, unintimidating quality of English landscape while admiring a vista, 'The prospect of a richly wooded plain, with low hills in the distance, wore that home-like aspect which makes the common-places of nature so welcome, and I felt how consoling such a gentle English-like view must be to sojourners in a strange land.'[73] Perhaps what all these adjectives imply is a perception of the English landscape as being more domesticated than landscapes on the Continent.

English travellers expressed a similar perception when travelling around Britain, imagining their landscape as markedly different from that of Wales and Scotland with respect to order, neatness and 'civilized' touches. In their view, Wales and Scotland were 'wild', 'rugged', 'barren' and 'desolate' compared to England. Guidebooks conditioned travellers to think in this manner. Murray's guide for North Wales, for example, summarized the area's most grand, wild and distinct scenes, leaving out the pretty vale of Clwyd 'because its swelling hills more nearly resemble soft English scenes'.[74] One young traveller, who was born in South Wales but lived most of her life in London, noted how English-like southwest Wales appeared, admitting, 'I should hardly have thought myself in Wales today, if it had not been for the old women on horseback with their black hats and red petticoats.'[75] She could not believe she was in Wales because, in her mind, Wales was more wild, rugged and mountainous than any land in England. English travellers in North Wales and the Scottish Highlands often spoke about how unaccustomed they were to the barren, desolate prospects presented by the landscape. The scenes clearly violated their sense of order and seemed the product of turbulent natural forces unknown in England. Cader Idris and other mountains, for example, displayed 'disordered confusion' with their jagged, scattered rocks. According to one traveller, Cader Idris 'seemed the consequence of some dreadful convulsive effect of nature.... The result of which was a scene of savage wildness, and awful sublimity.' Other travellers spoke of the 'primeval barrenness and disorder' of Welsh mountains and gorges, regarding them as the 'effect of some primeval earthquake.'[76] Many were 'fearful' of the scenery, something that was never true in England. Even the intrepid traveller George Borrow, whose three-volume travel journal was entitled *Wild Wales*, felt uncomfortable wandering through the wilder parts of the countryside. A deep lake made him think of crocodiles and beavers and other things 'monstrous and horrible'.

Given this fearful, desolate feeling, it is no wonder that English travellers in Wales or Scotland frequently heaved a sigh of relief when they encountered a patch of scenery reminiscent of England or crossed the border back into their native land. Thus Clement Ingleby was greatly relieved to leave behind the wild, barren mountains of Glencroe to enter Glen Ant. The latter glen was surrounded by mountains completely covered with a variety of trees so that not a barren rock could be seen. Furthermore, thousands of trees shrouded the river, lending a safe, sheltered feel to the landscape. Ingleby spoke of the change of scene as a transition from 'the sublime to the picturesque' noting, '[It] is very pleasing and one almost feels rejoiced at entering a range of scenery so much more congenial to English feelings, than scenes more rugged wild and barren.'[77] Signs of human habitation in even the bleakest landscape were also appealing to the English, and thus they felt more comfortable in Wales than in Scotland. Regarding a scattering of houses in the mountains, one traveller declared, 'Wales is in this respect far superior to Scotland, I have seen nothing here at all similar to the moors and deer forests of Scotland, but every district however bleak or bare appears to be comparatively well populated.'[78] Other travellers noted how 'cheerful' a scattering of residences made even the most secluded scene.

No landscape was, however, as cheerful, beautiful and orderly to English travellers as their native one. Arriving back in England after a trip through Ireland and Wales, Charles Lucey admired the scenery and felt pleased to be greeting a 'familiar friend'. He exclaimed, 'I saw more neatness and order in the farms and villages and more appearance of comfort... than I had met with in Wales or Ireland during the whole period of my journey.'[79] Another traveller crossing the border from Wales into England at Oswestry noted:

> the more flat and Englishified became the scenery, it had none of the sublimity of North Wales, none of the barren desolation of that district, but the fertile fields, growing beneath a plentiful harvest, and the green hills covered with rich, and beautiful pasture, had a very beautiful and picturesque appearance, and we felt at home, among such rustic and familiar scenery.[80]

Orderly, neat, fertile, productive and beautiful were terms often ascribed to the English landscape, but rarely to Scottish or Welsh scenery. The different landscape languages clearly suggest that English travellers identified with an English as opposed to a British landscape when they travelled around Britain.

Although tame and orderly were terms associated with England's landscape, the type of order valued was not one of geometric precision. Such highly controlled precision was an extreme, unnatural form of order distasteful to the English. We have already noted the English dislike of regimented rows of trees. They also denounced a close clipping or pollarding of branches which rendered them uniform and sacrificed their natural shapes. A good example of this hostility to extreme order and control can be seen in English attitudes to Holland's landscape. The earliest Murray guide to the Continent depicted Holland as a country 'hardly endurable' to live in. It went on to justify this unflattering depiction in terms of natural landscape. In Holland, the guide argued, the laws of nature were reversed. For example, the sea was higher than the land, making ship hulls rise above chimneys. Humans were thus forced to exert an extreme control over nature in order to survive. Rivers ran in canals, pollarded trees stood in ranks, and the wind was a slave to the many mills. To sum up the obsession with control in Holland the guide noted, 'Even the cows' tails, in other countries proverbial for growing downwards... here grow upwards: for, with the view of promoting the cleanliness of the animal while in the stall, the tail is tied up to a ring in the roof of the stable.'[81]

To this highly disciplined type of order, the English preferred a more moderate one embodying neatness as well as a natural irregularity. Moderation was key, and travellers from England often bestowed praise on their climate and landscape for changing only in moderate and gradual ways. Rarely would a person in England leave home shivering and return later the same day broiled. Nor would a traveller in England experience sudden, dramatic shifts from urban to rural landscape or from flat fields to hills as in many other countries. Sudden changes in landscape and volatility in climate were thought to produce fiery, passionate people prone to acts of violence and ferocious dispositions. Murray's guide to France reinforced this view with its negative description of Provence. The author criticized the region for its Mistral-induced sudden shifts in weather from scorching heat to piercing cold. Given the severity of the weather, it was no wonder that the people were 'rude if not brutal in manner, coarse in aspect, and harsh in speech'.[82]

This English preference for moderation as opposed to extremes in landscape can be seen when looking at descriptions of bridges. The English have been characterized by some scholars as a people with a love for rural and commercial life and an aversion to industrial and engineering activity.[83] Thus it is interesting to note that the landscape sites receiving the most detailed attention in travellers' journals are bridges – not the picturesque foot bridges spanning streams and small rivers, but rather the huge engineering feats such as the Forth Railway Bridge or the Tubular and Suspension Bridges connecting Wales and Anglesey. Even a journal entitled 'Picturesque Trip in Summer' engaged in a more rapturous discussion of these two bridges than of any other landscape feature. Five pages of text and two of illustrations detail the characteristics and cost of the Tubular Bridge being built at the time (1850) a mile from the Suspension Bridge (opened 1826). One of the things this author noted about the latter bridge was its pleasing quality of being enormous in size and weight and at the same time very light and elegant to the eye. Another traveller captured the bridge's appeal this way, 'The wonderful combination of majestic solidity and grandeur with the extreme of elegant lightness is remarkable in the highest degree.'[84] This paradoxical combination of opposites balanced and thus tempered the bridge's extreme qualities, appealing to the English love of moderation. Thus in travellers' estimation, dramatic products of the industrial world such as steel or suspension bridges reinforced rather than spoiled key characteristics of the traditional English rural landscape. Travellers' reflections on bridges suggest that the English resorted to nature and traditional values in order to come to terms with their aggressively commercial, increasingly industrialized world. In so doing, they were not simply looking as reactionaries back to a 'golden age', but rather were trying to use the past and the natural world as vehicles for accommodating changes in the present. In other words, the English displayed an ambivalence about – not an outright rejection of – things modern and industrial.[85]

Extreme uniformity or sameness was also displeasing to the English sense of order and aesthetics in landscape. Their journals frequently confessed to great impatience with monotonous scenery, especially that created by straight roads. And when such roads were lined with poplars so straight as to seem 'picked out of some great box of Nuremberg toys', they were too wearisome to endure.[86] Journal outbursts also targeted scenes presenting only a single type of tree, reserving the most vehement criticism for evergreens. Frederick William Faber found many defects in Greek scenery such as the absence of valleys, water and woodland areas. But he was most annoyed by the sameness of the evergreens. As he put it, 'There is no grouping or blending of divers greens, no masses of foliage, no tall stems or antler-like branches. Besides, there is an invariable dulness in the green of evergreens.'[87] Elizabeth Sewell had a similar reaction to the large fir forests covering Swiss mountain sides. Although she could appreciate their grandness and solemnity, she would have been 'sorry to exchange our variety of trees, – oaks and beeches, elms and birches, etc., for them'.[88] Long expanses of uniform terrain, whether flat field or rugged mountain, disappointed English eyes as well. For the Reverend Trench, his ride through Scottish mountain scenery would have been unbearably dreary had it not been for the variety in the sky above. The soporific slopes suddenly riveted his attention because of 'a quick succession of bright blue sky, of thick dark clouds flying fast over the heights around, and of warm flowing sunshine. These colours and changes of the sky...quite obviated any thing like dreariness or monotony in our course.'[89] He also admitted to appreciating certain picturesque mountain faces with their varied mixture of rocks and winding hollows displaying a pleasing blend of grey, green, brown and purple hues.

Clearly, variety was an important component of what the English considered a well-ordered, attractive landscape. They regarded their national landscape as superior to others because of its varied features. Although small in area, England presented scenery ranging from flat fens and gently undulating downs to hills and modest mountain precipices. Moreover, one did not have to cover hundreds of miles in order to encounter a change of scene as was sometimes the case on the Continent. Murray's guidebook to France estimated that a traveller in England could count on a change in natural features almost every 10 miles. Along with this variety of natural features, winding roads and lush green hedgerows worked to dispel monotony from the English countryside. The latter created irregular divisions and subdivisions in the landscape, ensuring that one would never be faced with a continuous, uniform expanse of land. Most travellers from England bemoaned the lack of hedgerows as they passed great extents of open country or large fenceless fields on the Continent. On his first trip to Germany, William Howitt noted with some exasperation, 'Here you look in vain for anything like the green fields and hedge-rows of England.... It [rural Germany] is all one fenceless and ploughed field.'[90] Elizabeth Carne found the same lack of boundaries and borders in France. She recognized a degree of mutual influence between the French and the English in regions close by the Channel. In Kent, the locals copied French-style turreted houses, while around Boulogne the English hedgerow struggled to take root. Unfortunately for English eyes, it did not get far, as it was 'soon obliged to yield to the unbounded liberty of French lands'.[91] Here again we find the notion that 'unbounded liberty' is un-English. Perceptions of landscape reveal that the English valued a combination of liberty and order that might be termed 'restraint'. In their view, such typically English landscape characteristics as scattered trees, a tidal sea, roaming cattle and easily accessible mountains symbolized liberty; hedgerows, soft, undulating hills, neatly grown lawns and varied, naturally irregular scenery represented order. Both qualities of liberty and order merged in England's landscape and people to create a natural presentation that was, in fact, very deliberately constructed.

What seemed natural and orderly to the English appeared unattractive and artificial to the Scots. The two people's reactions to landscape were as distinct as the landscapes themselves. James Smith's and Hugh Miller's comments on the English countryside are very revealing in this respect. Ironically, they sound much like English people's grumblings about country views on the Continent. During his ride from Lille to Brussels, Smith observed the landscape, drawing comparisons with the English scenery he had seen:

> We found the country all along remarkably flat and intersected by the monotonous hedge rows which so fill England. Like England too the country was broken up into a multitude and diversity of small fields. In fact the best mode of characterising both Belgium and England is to describe them as flat countries cut up into slips, patches, and corners. It is but very rarely that one'e eye could rest on what we might call a continuous field. Even within the enclosures by the hedges, no continuous crop was seen, but the various crops scattered in patches.... This to our eyes was a decided defect in the system of agriculture.[92]

Similarly, as Miller cast his eyes over English scenery, it was not prospects composed of diverse natural features that stood out in his mind, but rather the many unvarying expanses of flat, fertile fields. They appeared like blank tablets on which humans could express themselves in whatever fashion they pleased. And, in Miller's view, the human touch intruded everywhere into the English landscape, lending a sense of artificiality which he found oppressive. In particular, he grew weary of what seemed like an infinity of hedgerows criss-crossing the land 'in undistinguishable sameness, like a net, on the face of the landscape'. He longed for 'the wild free moors and bold natural features of [his] own poor country'.[93] Miller thus shared with the English a hostility to unvarying landscape, but he differed when it came to acceptable sources of diversity. To Miller, manmade hedgerows were as monotonous and stifling to a free spirit as were the endless stretch of level fields. It was 'bold natural features' and 'wild' landscape without a trace of human hands that provided him with a feeling of freedom and a pleasing sense of diversity.

Miller and other travellers, both Scottish and English, recognized marked distinctions between the landscapes north and south of the Tweed, and they used differing vocabularies when describing them. Eyeing the terrain around York, Miller noted how the vast expanse of fertile acres offered a striking contrast to prospects at home. Even in Scotland's most agriculturally productive areas, Miller commented, 'There is no extensive prospect...that does not include its wide ranges of waste, and its steep mountain sides, never furrowed by the plough.'[94] Other travellers likened Continental areas 'bare of cultivation' to Scotland, especially to its moors. Thus the traveller Henry Blackburn associated 'half-cultivated' Brittany with Scotland as strongly as he linked fertile Normandy to England. Such associations could only occur as a result of Blackburn and others turning a blind eye to England's moors, which they did when they imagined typical English landscape. Similarly, a *vetturino* ride south from Siena brought Scotland to Dickens's mind. Not far from the city, lush, cultivated hills turn into severe, treeless ones whose eroded white gulleys have the rugged look of Alp-high peaks. Evidence of water abounds, but little of fertility. As Dickens entered this area of Tuscany, he wrote of 'a region gradually becoming bleaker and wilder, until it became as bare and desolate as any Scottish moors'.[95] Instead of soft, trim and gentle, the Scottish landscape seemed wild, bleak, grand, savage, sour and unfriendly to Scottish and English eyes. But unlike the English, the Scots were comforted and felt liberated by the wild, desolate Scottish landscape that bore less evidence of human influence and taming. In other words, they placed great emphasis on the quality of liberty in landscape, and very little on that of order.

As we have seen, when the Scots imagined links between their landscape and national identity they thought of mountains. Thus the previously quoted view, 'Our mountains have been the moulders of our national character'. For the English, on the other hand, ruralness most clearly embodied the connection between their landscape and national character, or way of life. In their view, England's countryside reflected the essence of ruralness more than any other landscape in Britain or on the Continent. It might even be said that when travellers thought of England, they imagined rural scenes and life, despite the urban sprawl characterizing more and more of England in the nineteenth century. When on the Continent, Frederick Faber experienced homesickness more than most travellers. He would suddenly become dreamy-eyed, with images of England eclipsing the foreign scenes before him. Once on a balcony in the Bosphorus, he fell into such a state, reciting a Wordsworth stanza to satisfy his longing for home:

> The cock that crows, the smoke that curls, that sound of bells; those boys who in yon meadow ground In white-sleeved shirts are playing; and the roar of the waves breaking on the chalky shore – All – all so English.[96]

The 'all' composed of farm animal sound, hearth smoke, parish church and village cricket captures the rural domesticity perceived to be central to English people's lifestyle.

English travellers did cherish the rural or country life above any other, and complained of its absence when travelling. In southern Italy, James Cobbett expressed an intense dislike for the local way of life. He bemoaned the lack of farmhouses and cottages, as well as the preference for cramming into filthy towns and villages instead of living among the fields. In defence of his disapproving remarks, he stated, 'Not to dislike this is more than can be expected of the least prejudiced Englishman.'[97] George Borrow expressed a prejudice in favour of the rural during his tour of Wales. Heading south from Llangollen, he crossed a bridge from which he obtained a westward view of something he admitted to liking more than the wild grandeur typical of Wales. In the distance about 100 yards away was a watermill and a herd of pigs cooling themselves in the river. After describing the scene, he summed it up as one 'of quiet rural life'. Murray's first guide to the Continent reflected the same affection for country living. In explaining why watering places as opposed to country houses were such popular rendez-vous in Germany for socializing, the guide pointed out, 'The pleasures of a country life are as yet almost unknown in Germany; those mingled pleasures of enjoyment of scenery and rural beauties, domestic tranquillity and fire-side comforts, which so many of our own poets have enthusiastically described, and which every Englishman relishes.'[98]

Travellers from England did not deny that other peoples had a concept of rural life and values, but they did believe that their concept was distinct. As J. Cobbett said while touring the area around Florence, 'Our common idea of the *rural* in England is, indeed, very different from any thing to be seen here.' Similarly, W. Howitt noted on his trip through rural Germany, 'What we call country life in England is here unknown.'[99] What did Cobbett, Howitt and other English travellers have in mind when they used the terms 'rural' and 'country'? Scanning the German countryside, Howitt summed up the English notion of ruralness more comprehensively than most of his countrymen:

> Here you look in vain for anything like the green fields and hedgerows of England, with their scattered trees, groups of beautiful cattle or flocks grazing in peace, and sweet cottages, farm-houses, and beautiful mansions of the gentry. It is all one fenceless and ploughed field... the population is not scattered along as in England, over hill and dale, in groups and single residences of various grades and degrees of interest... The people are collected into villages of the most prosaic kind, and no gentry reside amongst them.[100]

Of the components of English ruralness mentioned here, the one singled out most frequently in travel journals is the presence of parks and country houses. Seen in the distance from the top of nearly every hill of woodland in England, they were thought to enliven the landscape and to provide centres of civilization. Noting the lack of progressiveness and refinement in the Pyrenees region of France, Mary Eyre attributed it to the absence of country squires and clergymen. Gentlemen's country houses were also symbolic of two highly cherished English values: hierarchical ordering of social relations and a fluidity between town and country life. We have already noted Cobbett's aversion to southern Italians' tendency to forsake the countryside in favour of urban life. English travellers regarded the relative absence of gentry residences in the Continental countryside as indicative of an antagonism between town and country they found foreign and alienating. It also signified, according to one proud traveller, a lingering lawlessness and insecurity unknown in England. In explaining why English town architecture fell short of French standards, E.A. Freeman very patriotically transformed a seemingly inferior quality into a superior one. English towns had fewer fine houses than French ones, he argued,

> because it was possible earlier in England than in France for a man who had not a castle of his own to be safe without seeking the shelter of a fortified town. France has nothing to set against the series of houses in the open country, or in mere undefended market-towns, manor houses, parsonages, houses of every kind, which England can show.[101]

English rural life centring on country houses thus symbolized an age-old heritage of liberty and lawfulness that Continental Europeans could not claim.

Nigel Everett has referred to this image of hierarchical, harmonious relations in the countryside, where the grandest country house was seen as an integral part of the local rural community and town, as the 'Tory' view of landscape.[102] It contrasts markedly, according to Everett, with the coexisting Whig view that de-emphasized hierarchy and social connections in favour of the isolated, self-interested individual appropriating nature for personal use and display. For those embracing the Tory view, all parts of a rural community seemed connected and orderly at the same time that they were free and unrestrained. Perhaps the Tory view is found more frequently in travellers' journals because it is more consistent with that combination of liberty and order so highly valued by the English and central to their image of England's natural landscape.

Howitt's comments on Germany reveal other essential elements of English ruralness. We noted previously the qualities of scattered distribution and hedgerow field boundaries when discussing the air of liberty and natural order about the English countryside. Equally characteristic was the deep-green colouring of fields, hedgerows and foliage. According to Cobbett and others, this verdure rendered the English rural landscape softer to the eye than any on the Continent. The scattering of deciduous trees in England enhanced the sensation of softness, as their leaves seemed far more delicate than the evergreen needles so plentiful across the Channel. In addition to softness and delicacy, a 'sweetness' emanated from the cottages which were as pervasive as grander country houses in English rural settings. Travellers regarded the cottage as a peculiarly English thing. Other countries certainly had what might be called modest farmhouses, huts or cabins, but they did not 'convey those ideas of prettiness, neatness, and comfort, which are, in the minds of English people, almost inseparable from the word *cottage*'.[103] Country cottages provided the element of cheerful domesticity that was at the heart of English ruralness, and that will be discussed further in chapter 4.

The English clearly displayed a feeling of superiority regarding their countryside landscape. It seemed to embody, in their minds, a cluster of positive, highly cherished qualities – to represent all that was finest about England and the English. The sentiments were often very different, however, when it came to cityscapes. Edward Wilberforce expressed the difference directly when he noted, 'Entering on foreign travel, the first thing that strikes you as a pleasant contrast to England, is the gaiety and brightness of Continental towns. Returning to England, the first thing that strikes you is the beauty of the country.'[104] Gaiety and brightness are two of a stream of positive terms adopted by English travellers to describe Continental towns and cities. Others include agreeable, quaint, warm, dazzling, pure, pretty, clean and cheerful. Such terms came to mind as travellers admired gabled buildings, whitewashed walls, airy streets, enticing shops and sun-drenched, red-tiled roofs. These attractions contrasted so markedly with things at home, that a return to England's city settings sometimes generated shock, even horror.

As Nona Bellairs travelled by train into London after a delightful stay in Paris, she gazed 'in speechless horror at its smoke and blackness'. She went on to compare the two cities, noting how Paris's many virtues only served to highlight just how 'big and dull and heavy' London was, with even its people lumbering along as if weighed down by business cares.[105] Commercial bustle did seem to characterize London as opposed to Continental cities, as one long-time Londoner noted. He had just returned after touring the Continent and was struck by how small and confined the houses appeared with their slate – not tiled – roofs. But what was most stiking was the 'apparent confusion and *utter* business' that suddenly seemed 'most astonishing and dumbfoundering – nothing is done *slowly* in London – people drive, walk, think *and live* more quickly here than any where else and Time is the greatest object the Cockney seems to think of.'[106] Interestingly, this business bustle is not associated with the English generally, but is confined to the working-class Eastenders of London. The restricted association reflects the prevailing view that, though business might thrive in and even characterize an English city and a particular social group, it did not embody what was perceived by travellers to be Englishness any more than did city life itself.

Although on the whole they reacted negatively to their cities, English travellers did find some things about them worth praising. They tended to be qualities providing a sense of liberty and natural irregularity. Thus England's relatively wide city streets and buildings of only modest height contrasted favourably with many Continental cities whose narrower streets lined with taller buildings appeared dark and suffocating. The absence of patios was another virtue of England's cities. These walled inner courtyards were characteristic of southern European towns, as Dorothy Quillinan discovered while touring Portugal. Feeling as hemmed in by a Seville patio as other travellers felt by a circle of Alps, Quillinan exploded, 'To be shut up within four walls, be they of the purest and whitest marble, soon becomes oppressive to the spirits; and I fairly longed to knock down some of those Moorish pillars, that I might get at the view beyond.'[107] Even when Belem's palace gardens provided her with a view, she was disappointed. For the focal point was an obviously unnatural, busy public road separating the gardens from a river beyond. In England, she noted, the garden would have run right down to the water's edge in order to preserve a natural look and to insulate the garden grounds from city cares and bustle. Quillinan quickly explained that 'English feeling prompted this remark'. Unlike the English who cherished gardens as a refuge from urban and public life, the Portuguese, according to Quillinan, valued them as a stage for public display. Thus no garden in Portugal was complete without a well-travelled road or street within easy view.

City walls and fortifications were equally offensive to the English spirit of liberty, and travellers from England boasted of their freer, less fortified cities. Without walls, English cities could expand at will where taste and fortune led them, giving that appearance of natural irregularity so highly valued by the English. With respect to this value, even dingy, dull London with its skyscraping spires had the edge over Paris, at least when viewed from above. On his last day in the French capital, T.N. Talfourd climbed the Place Vendôme column for a bird's-eye view of the city. Despite the clouds, he drew comparisons between gazing down at Paris and at London and concluded,

> London, so regarded, infinitely surpasses Paris.... Thus surveyed, Paris loses the impression which its piled, huddled, crowded, buildings produce... and the sense of magnificence conveyed by the long

piles of the Louvre and the Tuileries, and looks like a mass of square-built houses in the midst of a flat country, without the irregular grace of those frequent spires 'whose silent fingers point to heaven'.[108]

Such grace was absent from Paris gardens as well. Earlier in his visit Talfourd had commented on the 'perverse regularity' of the Tuileries garden layout. To the English eye, Continental gardens seemed either too regular and formal to be pleasing, or too untidy to be inviting. That appealing look of neat and natural irregularity with winding walks, smooth turf and tidy flowerbeds was not to be found.

Although the English boasted of and identified with certain aspects of their towns and cities, they did not regard them as an embodiment of their core values the way they did the countryside. But they did identify both their urban and rural landscapes with a quality they much applauded – productivity. Thus travellers praised England's deep-green fields and foliage not only for their soft appearance, but also for their fertility. One reason for the English aversion to wild, untamed countryside landscape was that it was uncultivated and, therefore, unproductive. Even Murray reflected the importance attached to wealth and productivity in England. Travellers clutching Murray's guide to France crossed the Channel predisposed to think of Normandy as almost an extension of England. In fact, the guide described Normandy with its verdure, winding dales, hedgerows, thatched cottages and chalk cliffs as the best part of France because most like England in appearance. Murray associated Normandy's landscape and people with productivity. That the Normans conquered England long ago was a pleasant memory, according to the travel authority, because of England's resulting prosperity. Thus the handbook argued that along with the familiar landscape, the English traveller in Normandy 'may also take pleasure in remembering that this was the cradle whence came the wise and hardy bands of conquerors from whose possession of England that country dates her rising prosperity and greatness.'[109] Interestingly, the Normans were denigrated rather than praised when the subject was English liberty, a quality whose roots were seen to lie in England's Anglo-Saxon rather than Norman heritage.

Along with their countryside landscape, English travellers thought their cities presented an air of productivity. In comparing Paris and London, Nona Bellairs was struck by the absence of any business look in the French capital. It seemed carefree, gay and festive, as if incapable of generating a brow-furrowing worry. London, on the other hand, was 'big and dull', weighed down by 'the ceaseless roll of its lumbering waggons of merchandize – the care-worn contracted brows of its labouring thousands.'[110] Even its priests, she noted, hurried along, blending in with the general business bustle. Drawing a similar comparison between cities, T.N. Talfourd focused on their rivers. The Seine he described as a 'lucid avenue' providing a 'glorious division of the city'. But unlike the Thames, he argued, it 'lacks the world of masts, indicating enormous wealth, and carrying the mind to a thousand remote shores, which tower into the murky sky below London bridge'.[111] Other English travellers on the Continent had to remind themselves that they were not in one of their native towns or cities when they saw quays crammed with commercial traffic or engine chimneys, smoke and other symbols of manufacturing wealth. To Saunderson Walker the most attractive part of Marseilles was the harbour where the thronged quays presented 'a bustle of commerce that much resembles the home of a "nation of shopkeepers" – as we were termed'.[112]

Clearly, perceptions of landscape and climate say something about a nation's values with respect to a variety of things besides the natural environment, including a sense of aesthetics and proportion, preferred manner of displaying religiosity, concepts of liberty, order, hierarchy and productivity, and so forth. This chapter has argued that treks around Europe tended to highlight a British identity in travellers' minds regarding landscape and climate. That is, people from all three main regions of Britain became more aware of the sensitivities they shared when it came to a sense of pleasing proportion, tolerance for colour, preferred stance from which to view landscape and a need to humanize the natural environment. Travel within Britain, on the other hand, was more likely to enhance distinct English, Scottish and Welsh sensitivities to landscape, particularly regarding notions of liberty, order, ruralness and productivity. Geographic context was thus significant in determining how Victorians imagined themselves and their landscapes. It was perhaps an even more significant determinant of national imagining in the area of religion, as we will see in the following chapter.

3
Religion

The fifth of November, commonly referred to today as 'Firework' or 'Bonfire Night', is the closest thing the English have to a national day.[1] Since Parliament's passing of the Anniversary Days Observance Act in 1859, the celebration has been a secular one with no official links to any church or religious group. This was certainly not how the festivity began in the early seventeenth century when it was known as 'Gunpowder Treason Day'. The name commemorates an unsuccessful attempt on 5 November 1605 by Guy Fawkes and other Catholic conspirators to blow up the King and Parliament with 36 barrels of gunpowder. Parliament legislated the plot's failure into the national memory in 1606 by passing an Act to make 5 November a day of public thanksgiving for God's favouring of the English and their Protestantism. The thanksgiving day was officially part of the Church of England calendar. Until well into the nineteenth century, Protestant patriotism and anti-Catholic sentiments were at the heart of this national day of celebration. Its endurance in the nineteenth century reveals the tenacious link between Protestantism and national identity in England and in Britain.

This alliance between Protestantism and an English collective identity had been forged by the end of the sixteenth century. Mary Tudor (Queen of England and Wales from 1553 to 1558) inadvertently contributed to the alliance by marrying King Philip of Spain (Europe's most powerful Catholic ruler), reuniting the English Church with Rome and burning Protestant believers at Smithfield.[2] These acts greatly intensified a fear held by people in England across the social spectrum – that of foreign influence, in this case Spanish and papal. Taken together, Mary's actions worked to link Catholicism in people's minds with this dreaded influence of outside powers. Protestantism, by contrast, became associated with English patriotism and independence, an association fully cemented under Mary's successor, Elizabeth I (1558–1603), who returned the English Church to the Protestant fold, where it has remained ever since. Her accession day, 17 November, became the first in a series of Protestant triumphs to be incorporated into the national calendar and celebrated throughout the land.[3] Others included England's defeat of the Spanish Armada in 1588, the previously mentioned subverting of the Gunpowder Plot to blow up Parliament and the failure of King James's son, the Prince of Wales' attempt to negotiate a marriage with the Catholic Spanish Infanta in 1623. English people saw these events as indisputable evidence that God sided with their Protestant kingdom, and they celebrated them exuberantly for having saved England from the evils and thraldom of Catholicism.

England was 'saved' again in 1688, this time from the threat of a Catholic king and heir. In June 1688, James II (1685–88) and his second wife, Mary of Modena, who were both overt Catholics by the 1680s, gave birth to a son. Ignoring his subjects' Protestant sympathies, James announced that the Pope had consented to be the child's godfather, making it clear that the boy was to be raised a Catholic. According to the laws of hereditary succession, a son took precedence over daughters, and this meant that this Catholic prince rather than his elder Protestant half-sisters, Mary and Anne, would inherit the throne. Ten days after his birth, leaders in England made overtures to Mary's husband, the Dutch leader, William of Orange, inviting him to protect his wife's right to the Crown. Even Tory leaders, for whom the doctrine of legitimate succession was a cherished principle, supported altering the succession in this case to save England from the Catholic Stuarts. William accepted the challenge, arriving in England with an army that forced James to flee to France with his wife and son. Parliament bestowed the Crown jointly on William and Mary, with the succession to go to their children if they had any (which they did not) and then Mary's younger sister, Anne, and her children. Anne's 18 pregnancies did not result in a child who lived beyond infancy, and thus in 1701 Parliament passed an Act of Settlement investing the Crown in the nearest Protestant branch of the Stuart family – Sophia, Electress of Hanover, and her son George (who reigned as George I from 1714 to 1727). Once again, Tories forsook the creed of legitimacy to perpetuate Protestantism on the throne.

Colin Haydon's recent study argues for a consistent and continuous anti-Catholic belief in England from the seventeenth until well into the eighteenth century. In fact, Haydon claims that for most of the period from 1714 to 1780 anti-Catholicism 'could be seen as the chief ideological commitment of the nation'.[4] Events in Britain and on the Continent, including the Jacobite Rebellions in 1715 of James II's son and in 1745 of his grandson, together with the frequent persecution of Protestants by Continental rulers, kept anti-Catholic sentiment alive. The law also encouraged a view of Catholics as outcasts. For most of the eighteenth century, a harsh penal code deprived Catholics in Britain of political and property rights, as well as the right to worship.[5] Moreover, a barrage of propaganda fuelled intense hostility towards Catholics, or 'Papists' as they were derisively termed. Taken together, almanacs, prints, sermons, broadsheets, rhymes, clubs, pamphlets and Pope-burning pageants painted, in the popular mind, an indelible impression of Papists as evil. The English populace feared and mocked them as agents of despotic power, believers in superstitious, false Christianity and persecutors of heretics.

Recognizing the virulent nature of anti-Catholicism in Britain as a whole, Linda Colley focused on its role in the formation of a Protestant identity.[6] According to Colley, a shared Protestantism was one of the key factors that allowed a British national identity to emerge after the Act uniting Scotland with England and Wales in 1707. That Act of Union recognized the Anglican Church of England as the Established Church in England and Wales, and the Presbyterian Kirk as the Established Church in Scotland. After 1707 the British saw themselves, says Colley, as a chosen people blessed for their Protestantism and superior in every way to Continental Europeans, especially to the Catholic French with whom they were at war for much of the eighteenth century. The recurrent wars with France helped to fuel anti-Catholicism in Britain and to fix Protestantism at the centre of a fledgling sense of Britishness.

After the second Jacobite Rebellion in 1745, political threats from Catholic Stuart pretenders declined, and the Pope officially recognized George III as legitimate King of Britain in 1766. War with Catholic France finally came to an end in 1815. From that year until the beginning of the First World War, Britain was not involved in a major military conflict with any Catholic European power. Furthermore, certain pieces of legislation reveal the emergence of a more relaxed attitude towards Catholics. In the late eighteenth century laws restricting Catholics' property rights were repealed, and in 1829 Catholic Emancipation became law, giving full political rights to Catholics for the first time.[7] The Roman Catholic Church hierarchy of archbishops, bishops and priests became lawful again in England and Wales in 1850 and in Scotland in 1878, and, as mentioned earlier, in 1859 Parliament removed from the books legislation enacted in 1606 declaring 5 November a day of public thanksgiving. Did a sense of Britishness revolving around Protestantism prevail in the Victorian period despite the absence of war against Catholic Europe and the rise of more tolerant policies towards Catholics in Britain? Travellers' journals confirm the centrality of religion to national identity throughout Victoria's reign. But they also suggest that the religious dimension of identity was too complex to be explained adequately by a Protestant versus Catholic model. Not surprisingly, Protestant travellers from different parts of Britain emphasized a shared Protestantism when they were travelling in Catholic areas of Europe. But in Protestant European countries or when touring around Britain itself, they tended to stress the divisions and tensions within Protestantism and to identify with their particular brand of English, Welsh or Scottish Protestantism. Their journals thus reveal that Protestantism was as much a divisive as a unifying force among people from Victorian Britain and that context is crucially important to any discussion of religious and national identity.[8]

Before discussing travellers' religious identities, we need to be clear about the religious geography of Britain that was the main context in which the identities developed.[9] Although the majority of Britons may have shared an allegiance to Protestantism in the Victorian period, no British, or Britain-wide, Church of any denomination existed. Britain contained a cluster of confessional groups with radically different concentrations depending on location, giving distinct religious identities to England, Scotland and Wales, as well as to cities and regions within these larger entities. The main confessional groups were Anglicans, Presbyterians, Methodists, Baptists, Congregationalists, Quakers, Unitarians and Catholics.

In England, the Anglican Church (Church of England) was the dominant, or established, Church, linked directly to the state through both the monarch, who was its head, and certain bishops, who sat in the House of Lords. Parliament regularly legislated for the Church and, until the 1860s, all people in England had to pay Church rates for the upkeep of parish churches. Although it was the Established Church with the most widespread national coverage – 14,077 places of worship at mid-century – leaders were surprised to learn from the religious census of 1851 that nearly half of the 11 million people (out of a total population of roughly 18 million in England and Wales) attending church on Census Sunday were not members of the Church of England. Nonconformist sects, particularly Methodism, grew at a faster rate than the Church of England in the early nineteenth century, and were strongest in Cornwall and the northern industrial areas (the smaller Baptist and Congregationalist sects were strongest in the South). During the second half of the nineteenth century, Catholics were the fastest growing of the major denominations in England, due largely to the influx of Irish after the 1840s famine. By 1901, the 570 places of Catholic worship recorded in the 1851 census had swelled to 1,536, with the Catholic community in England estimated at around 1.5 million, 80 per cent of it Irish.

In Scotland, the vast majority of the population was Presbyterian, but there were three main Presbyterian Churches by the mid-nineteenth century. The Established Kirk was, like the Church of England, subject to parliamentary control and had the most attendances of any single church on Census Sunday in 1851. Its total attendances (566,409), however, fell far short of those of the other two Presbyterian Churches combined (892,114), making it clear that it was no longer the Scottish National Church. The Free Church broke away from the Established Kirk in 1843 (see discussion below), experiencing a remarkable growth immediately thereafter. By 1851 it had nearly as many churches and attendances as the Kirk, making it a rival National Church despite its severing of all connections with the state. This new Free Church attracted commercial and industrial families as well as people in the Highlands and Islands where the Kirk had historically been weakest. The other Presbyterian Church in Scotland was the United Presbyterian which had been collecting secessionist groups since the eighteenth century.

Compared to the Anglican Church, all three Scottish Presbyterian Churches were austere and bleak, with their chanting and prohibiting of instrumental music. For those in Scotland drawn to more High Church ritual, there existed the Episcopalian Church which used the English Book of Common Prayer but was not under Church of England jurisdiction. The smallest of the six major religious groups in Scotland (43,904 attendances in 1851), it was most popular with the gentry. In that the Episcopal Church provided a forum for High Church sounds and display, it helps explain the weakness of Catholicism in Scotland. Support of the Catholic Church was largely confined to Irish immigrants in the Clyde Valley.

Church attendances in general were better in Scotland than in England, but they were strongest of all in Wales. The established Anglican Church (the same as in England, often termed the 'Church in Wales') did not, however, reap the benefits of Welsh religiosity. Less than 20 per cent of those attending church participated in Anglican services. The Anglican Church in Wales, lacking money and manpower, was ill-equipped to stem the tide of nonconformity (Protestant sects not conforming to the Established Church). Anglican parish clergy in Wales were the worst paid in the whole Church, and many bishops appointed to Welsh sees ignored their responsibilities, regarding their appointments as merely stepping-stones to something more attractive in England. Although Welsh-language Bibles had existed since the sixteenth century when England and Wales were united, most nineteenth-century Anglican clergy in Wales could not speak Welsh, despite the fact that the language was still widely used by the native population. The Church in Wales did not appoint a Welsh-speaking bishop until 1870. In contrast, most nonconformist preachers in Wales did speak Welsh, with the result that chapels became linked with Welsh nationalist feelings in the nineteenth century. The growth of nonconformity was dramatic even by mid-century when the Sunday census recorded 675,877 nonconformist chapel attendances compared with 155,066 Anglican. Despite the weakness of the Church in Wales, it was not finally disestablished until 1920. In addition to being disestablished, the Church was disendowed, with the money then divided between the University of Wales, the National Library and county councils.

Having established some 'facts' regarding religious geography in Britain during the Victorian period, we can now turn to travellers' religious identities. In other words, we can turn to the world of perception and imagination. That world is much harder to understand and document than such things as church growth, membership and attendance. In the realm of perception, specific church or chapel (term often used for nonconformist churches) identities sometimes seemed insignificant and at other times appeared to embody the defining characteristics of peoples and places.

As we have noted, most travellers bound for the Continent armed themselves with one or more guidebooks before venturing across the Channel. These guides provided not only lists of *what* to see, but also preconceptions about *how* to see, even when it came to religious life. The earliest Murray guidebook to the Continent (1836), for example, reinforced the long-held notion of a natural antipathy and inseparable gulf between Protestantism and Catholicism. It even maintained that a union of Catholics and Protestants in a single nation-state was unthinkable. In its opening section on Belgium the travel authority asserted, 'The Belgians differ from the Dutch in two essential points, which are quite sufficient to make them a distinct nation, incapable of any permanent union: they are French in inclination, and Roman Catholic in religion.'[10]

This centuries-old tendency to see the Christian world as polarized between the monolithic forces of Protestantism and Catholicism survived long after the publication of Murray's first guide. Along with guidebook assumptions and maps, nineteenth-century travellers carried with them a mental map of Europe divided into Catholic and Protestant areas, each with its sacred shrines or pilgrimage sites. They regarded Rome as the primary Catholic site and such places as Geneva and Worms as shrines for Protestant believers, regardless of their sect or nationality. An English Alp climber said of Geneva, 'By a great Protestant nation like England it must ever be remembered and loved for its promptitude in embracing, an untiring zeal in establishing and consolidating, the doctrines of the Reformation.' The Welshman Henry Richard, who was minister of a Congregational chapel in London from 1835 to 1850, expressed a similar reverence for Worms. During a trip to the town, he made a point of standing on the very spot where occurred, in his view, 'one of the greatest and sublimest scenes in the history of the world'. It was the site where, in 1521, a Diet convened at which Luther refused to recant his Protestant beliefs. The building had been razed, but an elm tree a mile and a half away under which Luther supposedly rested on his way to Worms was still standing. Richard hiked to the tree and broke off two small twigs 'to bear with [him] as a memento of a spot so fraught with thrilling interest'. Upon returning to the town, he wrote a letter dated Worms to his mother and enclosed a leaf from 'Luther's tree' because he knew it 'would intensely interest her mind'.[11] Whether or not Richard correctly identified the Diet site or Luther ever sat under the elm christened 'Luther's tree' is unimportant. What is significant is that Richard and others elevated these sites to the status of Protestant shrines. The shrines suggest that, in certain contexts, Protestants from all parts of Britain imagined themselves to be linked together in a common community.

The view of the Christian world as a contest between distinct Protestant and Catholic camps was especially apparent among Protestant people from Britain when they travelled through Catholic areas of Europe. They repeatedly identified with and extolled the virtues of Protestantism, while noting the many evils of Catholicism. In order to understand the implications of this perceived duality for their collective identity, it is essential to explore what travellers had in mind when they used the terms 'Protestantism' and 'Catholicism'. In other words, it is important to explore what qualities travellers were identifying with when they imagined themselves as Protestant, and were divorcing themselves from when they denounced Catholicism. For in addition to being religious labels, the terms were code words for a whole range of cultural attributes, some very secular in nature.

In its narrowest and least frequently used sense, Protestantism referred to certain religious beliefs and practices characteristic of Britain as a whole. Clergymen travellers tended to stress Protestantism's doctrinal aspects, particularly its opposition to Catholic belief in transubstantiation, purgatory, confession and the power of the Virgin Mary. They also drew attention to the Protestant emphasis on the authority of the Bible and individual conscience rather than that of church officials, so highly valued by Catholics. Protestant travellers who were not part of the clergy often depicted Protestantism as a simple and serious religion devoid of spectacle and decoration pandering to the emotions. Prompted by his tours of Catholic churches in Munich, the Oxford graduate M.F. Tupper argued:

> We Protestants take the truer view of religion 'in Spirit and in truth,' and are apter to hide our feelings on the matter than to display them: but Papists may seem somewhat to be commended too in adding the cedar and gold, the willing offerings of Art and jewellery.... However... in most instances all such decoration helps only to degrade – because to amuse – the once spiritual worshipper, and has a tendency to defeat the holy purposes of Religion.[12]

The canoe enthusiast John MacGregor also talked of the sombre, reflective side of Protestant religiosity and attributed it to climate. The French, he argued, lived in the open air and thus required a very public, gregarious religion full of colour and music. This insight occurred to him at a Catholic procession in Nancy when he noted, 'Deep devotion, silent in its depth, is for the north and not for this radiant sun.'[13] The Protestant preference for quiet worship was compatible with Bible reading, an activity highly valued by all Protestants. Unlike Catholics, they stressed the importance of the masses having access to God's word as expressed in Scripture. Many travellers from Britain bemoaned the lack of Bibles on the Continent, and some of the more evangelically-inclined smuggled Scripture stashes through customs for dispensing at strategic moments, that is, when officials were not around to notice.

More often than not, travellers used 'Protestantism' in reference to secular qualities. In their minds, the term clearly encompassed a cluster of characteristics whose connection to theology and religious ritual seems tenuous at best. For example, they associated Protestantism with education and a diffusion of culture and enlightenment among men and women. When commenting on Protestant communities in France, the prolific travel writer Matilda Betham-Edwards noted how the women read widely and were thus *au courant* with the political and literary world. Brittany presented, to her eyes, a marked contrast. In that area where most young women were educated by nuns, Edwards observed disapprovingly, 'You never see or hear of a book.' She did not attribute this difference to the Protestant emphasis on reading the Bible for one's self, but rather on a 'spirit of inquiry' which she and many other travellers regarded as integral to Protestantism and foreign to Catholicism. Because of this spirit of inquiry and emphasis on education, travel writers argued that Protestantism engendered high levels of tolerance and enlightenment not found in Catholic communities. Of Montbeliard, one of the most Protestant *départements* in France, Edwards said, 'We find a toleration here absolutely unknown in most parts of France, and a generally diffused enlightenment equally wanting where Catholicism dominates.'[14]

In addition to rational inquiry, enlightenment and open-mindedness, travellers had domestic morality and cleanliness in mind when they used the term 'Protestantism'. Their journals are full of comments about how beneficial Protestant priests and pastors were to home life in their communities. In explaining the benefits they noted that, because Protestant clergymen married, they were better able to set standards of domestic virtue and to offer relevant advice on domestic matters than Catholic clergy, who had to suffer enforced isolation from the domestic life and affections. A virtuous home was also a clean one, and travellers argued that Protestant churches and clergy were more apt than Catholic ones to encourage good hygiene in their followers. As they saw it, the Catholic Church taught that the body was sinful and not to be exposed for washing. This view prompted Edwards to remark with disdain, 'Nuns must of necessity be as dirty as human beings can well be, seeing in what abhorrence they regard the notion of stripping naked to perform daily ablutions...the priests appear as dirty as they are.'[15]

The final secular dimension of Protestantism as revealed by travellers' journals included order, enterprising spirit and prosperity, the three usually seen as connected. These qualities suddenly manifested themselves to and elicited praise from travellers as they passed from Catholic into Protestant areas, particularly in Switzerland and France. Jemima Morrell from Yorkshire was one of a group of 64 tourists who accompanied Cook on his first excursion tour to Switzerland in 1863. The first half of her journal talks mostly of ignorant peasants and dirty, unaccommodating chalets. But after negotiating a steep descent to Frutigen, a marked change of scene occurs. As Morrell explained it, 'The chalets along the road were of greater pretensions than any we had seen, the gardens tidier, and some enterprise displayed in a new hotel with tastefully planned grounds, but was not all this easily accounted for? We were in a Protestant Canton.' Similarly, on coming into Zurich, M.F. Tupper noted, 'In Protestant, and therefore eminently prosperous, Zurich Popery is a quiet unrampant animal.'[16] Other travellers noted the more cheerful cottages, larger farmhouses, cleaner pastures, better fences and more plentiful fountains to be found in Protestant as opposed to Catholic cantons. Judging from Reverend Trench's discussion of an area in southern France, nearly all travellers commented on these sorts of contrasts between cantons in Switzerland. Regarding the district between Pau and Puyoo Trench observed:

> The whole district... offered, in unbroken succession, that attractive scene which good country-houses, neat cottages, cherished gardens, and highly cultivated fields must always compose.... And when I mention that this day we were in a very Protestant country [for France], and that we naturally compared the appearance of this people and districts with many other departments, entirely Popish,... the observations almost universally formed by travellers as to the respective mien of different cantons in Switzerland, according to the prevalent religion, naturally recurred to my mind, and received here a testimony corroborative of their truth.[17]

Victorian travellers clearly projected onto the Europe they experienced the traditional image of the Christian world as one divided into two antagonistic religious groups. That is, they perceived the Continent as a collection of distinct, antithetical communities defined either by Protestantism, which they identified with and praised (though not always completely, as we will see), or by Catholicism, which they usually denounced. The imagined oppositional relationship between the two religions is apparent in Edwards's account of a holiday in France when she states matter-of-factly, 'Protestantism means cleanliness, education, and domestic morality, and Catholicism the reverse.'[18]

The perceived reverse, or opposing, characteristics of Catholicism received attention from guidebooks to the Continent and from nearly every Continental tourist from Britain. Such guides adopted a protective stance towards readers, advising them to exercise a wariness with respect to the religion. In his *Cautions to Continental Travellers* (1818), the Anglican vicar J.W. Cunningham unleashed pages of objections to Popery and

Papists, especially to their subversion of the Gospel, their veneration of the Virgin Mary and their elevation of priestly power. That power was especially insidious, thought Cunningham, in the confession box where crafty priests could manipulate the consciences and monies of their parishioners. Later Victorian guidebooks ignored religious beliefs and practices when offering warnings, and focused instead on travellers' conduct in Catholic Churches. Murray's *Handbook for Travellers in France* (1843) admonished:

> Englishmen and Protestants, admitted into Roman Catholic churches, at times are often inconsiderate in talking aloud, laughing, and stamping with their feet while the service is going on.... Our countrymen have a reputation for pugnacity in France: let them therefore be especially cautious not to make use of their fists, however great the provocation, otherwise they will rue it.[19]

One has only to read Protestant travellers' journals to understand the source of this inconsiderateness. Such journals reveal a general lack of respect for Catholicism and its services, particularly for the smells, setting and rituals in the churches.

To Protestants, Catholic forms of devotion seemed very strange – more like commercial transactions, theatrical performances and operatic evenings than religious experiences. In describing Catholics and their religious practices as well as when representing themselves, Protestant travellers adopted a discourse that recent scholars have termed 'colonial'.[20] For example, depictions of Catholics include such words as 'dark', 'dirty', 'ignorant' and 'strange' which cast Catholic 'others' in a subordinate position relative to Protestant gazers. According to postcolonial theorists, this discourse reveals the 'Euroimperialist mind' (Britons are lumped together with Europeans by these scholars) with its orientation to 'othering' and subordinating. It is true that travellers from Britain and Europe used this discourse when writing about places and peoples their home countries were subjecting to imperialist acts of conquest. But their use of it when representing each other as well should cause us to question how appropriate such terms as 'colonial' and 'imperialist' are for the discourse. They certainly are appropriate when English travellers depicted Gaelic-speaking Irish or Welsh clergy as coarse, dirty and disgusting, which they sometimes did.[21] The English subjected Ireland and Wales to 'imperial expansionism', to use Mary Pratt's term. But are the terms appropriate when the same travellers used the discourse to represent Catholic priests in Notre Dame or St.

Peter's? There is a problematic tendency among postcolonial theorists to see every act committed and word uttered by a Briton or European as 'colonial' or 'imperialist', regardless of context. By investing everything European with an imperialist meaning, these theorists render imperialism itself a meaningless concept. I prefer to think of this discourse as an 'othering' one which in some contexts is motivated by imperialist mindsets and intentions, and in others is not.

This 'othering' discourse is reminiscent of the anti-Catholic rhetoric which had been aggressively dispensed in Britain since the sixteenth century. We can thus assume that travel through Catholic Europe worked mostly to reinforce, rather than to alter, preconceived ideas about Catholicism. There is, however, one important difference between the anti-Catholicism felt by Victorian travellers and that expressed in Britain prior to the nineteenth century. The element of fear, whether of Catholic powers or of persecution of Protestants by Catholics, which was so much a part of earlier anti-Catholicism, is absent in Victorian travel journals. Instead of being seen as a bloodcurdling threat, these travel journals suggest that Catholicism had come to be regarded simply as strange and repulsive. Its unattractive aspects were still viewed as detrimental, but only to Catholics themselves. Perhaps this view explains why pity rather than hostility greeted Father Dalgairns on his return from France to Guernsey in 1847. He had just become a Catholic priest and wrote to J.H. Newman of his reception in Guernsey, 'Most of the people here have received me more in sorrow than in anger, though some have been rude. Some have been very kind and you cannot tell how painful it is to be amongst kind Protestants.'[22]

The clergy embodied the strange, unacceptable nature of Catholicism in Protestant travellers' eyes. In both their behaviour and appearance, Catholic priests seemed far too irreverent and uncouth to inspire a spiritual frame of mind. One visitor to Pisa's Duomo spoke disapprovingly of the 'strange intonations and mumblings' emanating from priests in the choir, and William Gladstone objected to Catholic priests' Turveydrop-like rhythms in church. After attending Mass in Calais he informed his wife, 'When I saw the amazing accumulation of gestures, and evolutions almost dancing master like of their priests in celebrating service it never fails to prompt a puritanical reaction in my mind.'[23] The Quaker John Marsh was equally displeased by Calais. For him the city was 'a dark, low place, containing many monks, priests and soldiers' who greatly contributed to its darkness.[24] In addition to darkness, one gets the impression from travellers' journals that 'intolerable smells' were a constant accompaniment of Roman Catholicism.

According to Nona Bellairs and many others, priests were largely responsible for the dirtiness and odours travellers associated with Catholic churches and towns. At a church in Nice she remarked with some deprecation, 'The dress of the priest was dirty and common, the cathedral was also very dirty, and the spitting most offensive. Even while adoring the Host, a priest would turn round and spit.' She also thought Catholic clergy exhibited a preference for religious festivals as opposed to cleanliness and tidiness. In Italy she observed preparations for the festival of the Immaculate Conception. A group of monks were hanging dozens of tin hearts on a canopy protecting a picture of the Virgin Mary. The scene prompted her to complain, 'They were knocking and hammering away, while their cemetery was a wilderness of untidiness and dirt.'[25] Such filth and aversion to respectability were only to be expected, argued many travellers, from a priesthood deprived of wifely influence and domestic niceties. Nuns, too, were criticized for their celibate, cloistered lives, making them unable to perform domestic 'kindnesses'.

Travellers associated deprivation itself with Catholicism. They saw the Church hierarchy as a tyrannical one which kept the Scriptures and learning from the masses, thus encouraging superstition, ignorance and poverty. Its members seemed to value splendid churches, squadrons of priests and sumptuous ritual, but not education in morality and industriousness. In his journal devoted mainly to Continental schools, the Scotsman William Chambers described the Catholic city of Cologne, with its filthy streets, stagnating pools and uneducated populace, as 'disgraceful'. He attributed this to 'the political and ecclesiastical thraldom' dominating the city.[26] The English Quaker Samuel J. Capper had a similar impression as he wandered through France during the Franco-Prussian War commenting on the low moral tone of its inhabitants. This moral tone prevailed, according to Capper, 'because religion in the form of Roman Catholicism has, for centuries, been the strongest bulwark of ignorance and superstition, and tyranny, and the most powerful foe to human rights, liberty and progress.'[27] A Toynbee Traveller visiting Florence emphasized how visiting a Catholic country enabled an Englishman to appreciate the value of his native land, particularly its freedom from superstition. He spoke of the Catholic rituals he witnessed as 'mummeries', and felt pity for Duomo worshippers as he stated, 'Surely it can need only the light of truth to rise amongst them to free them from the galling yoke of the priestly superstition.'[28] The yoke rendered a country like Italy 'low in the scale of civilization and national respectability', as one traveller put it.[29]

Travel journals repeatedly allude to alleged priestly powers that border on the magical and numb the rational mind. For example, when a Catholic believer explained to Robert Louis Stevenson's nurse that fonts contain ordinary water made holy by a priest, she thought to herself, 'Deluded mortals'. Stevenson was equally unable to take Catholic belief and devotion seriously. On his canoe trip through France, an old woman engaged in her devotions caught his eye. He observed her movements in church, noting how she went from altar to altar dedicating an equal number of beads and length of time to each shrine. The ritual was bewildering and dispiriting to him. Instead of accepting it as evidence of sincere faith or belief, he could make sense of the offerings only as a rational commercial transaction. In describing the woman's devotions Stevenson said condescendingly,

> Like a prudent capitalist with a somewhat cynical view of the commercial prospect, she desired to place her supplications in a great variety of heavenly securities. She would risk nothing on the credit of any single intercessor.... I could only think of it as a dull, transparent jugglery, based upon unconscious unbelief.[30]

Stevenson's words say more about his disdain for the irrational realm of faith and religious ritual than they do about the woman's spirituality. Another Scotsman felt certain that if Catholicism were explained in the abstract to *rational* believers in the faith (and he did think there were such persons in the Catholic Church), they would treat the religion with ridicule and contempt.

Travellers from Britain saw themselves as embodying rationality and criticized Catholicism for its irrationality, particularly for its theatrical nature designed for emotional appeal. Henry Clark Barlow offered a vivid description of the emotional dimension of Catholicism:

> Indeed Catholicism as we see it on the continent appears a *system of emotions*... hence the visible appeals to the sights, the pictures, the crosses, the ceremonies – the pomp and the splendour – the appeal to the ear, the music and singing... the kissing of crosses and attempts to raise inward feelings of love, in short all the means resorted to appear to have for their object the cultivation of religious feelings.[31]

The ceremonies, music and sights in Catholic Churches were very strange and sometimes upsetting to Protestant travellers. While studying medicine in London, the Welshman W.T. Griffith attended a

Catholic chapel on Christmas Eve. The priests made 'unearthly yelling sounds' and their service was so 'gross and addressed to the senses; so superstitious and absurd that [he] shuddered by witnessing them... It was painful to see the delusion of the people, several of them were intoxicated... counting their beads and crossing themselves in the most ridiculous and absurd manner.' Griffith was so distressed when he returned to his room, that he prayed that the 'terrible system of priestcraft' would soon be abandoned.[32]

Other journals speak of Catholic worship music as being more appropriate for the opera house or a quadrille gathering than for a sacred setting. Wordsworth's daughter, Dorothy Quillinan, said of the church music for a service honouring St. Cecilia that it 'too frequently recalled passages that we had heard at the opera House'.[33] Catholic church settings appeared to belong to the operatic or theatre world as well. At St. Peter's in Rome, Charles Dickens attended a High Mass that seemed staged for high drama. As he described the 'droll and tawdry' scene, 'A large space behind the altar, was fitted up with boxes, shaped like those at the Italian Opera in England, but in their decoration much more gaudy. In the centre of the kind of theatre thus railed off, was a canopied dais with the Pope's chair upon it.'[34] For Protestants, this sort of ostentatious setting combined with stirring music could inspire intense sensuality, but only the most superficial religiosity. Furthermore, the sensuousness seemed to signal weakness and effeminacy. The Revd. Hugh Price Hughes, a Methodist minister who was born in Wales but lived his adult life in England, went so far as to attribute France's defeat in the Franco-Prussian War to the sensual nature of Catholicism. Standing on a high point overlooking Marseilles in 1900, the preacher commented on his visit to the nearby Church of the Virgin:

> As I read the votive tablets, and smelt the sensuous incense, and felt the sentiment that filled the very atmosphere of the much embellished and painted shrine, I understood once more why France was defeated by Germany, and realised... why Mohammedanism, in its austere and iconoclastic youth, triumphed over the decadent, sensuous, effeminate Christianity of the Levant.[35]

His words suggest that during the increasingly militaristic turn-of-the-century era, even religion was infused with martial meaning. That is, in addition to education, rational inquiry, domestic virtue, cleanliness and order, Protestantism (Prussia was primarily Protestant) came to be associated with manliness and military superiority.

One aspect of Catholic Church settings and ceremonies which was especially shocking and horrifying to Protestant travellers was imagery in the form of paintings, statues, dolls and shrines. Journals describe church walls covered with nightmarish depictions of the anguish of the flesh. No matter which direction one turned, scenes full of pained expressions, gaping wounds, spurting blood and tormented souls seemed to meet the eye. Dickens found St. Stefano Rotondo particularly grotesque. Scanning its walls he recoiled in horror exclaiming:

> Such a panorama of horror and butchery no man could imagine in his sleep, though he were to eat a whole pig, raw, for supper. Grey-bearded men being boiled, fried, grilled, crimped, singed, eaten by wild beasts, worried by dogs, buried alive, torn asunder by horses, chopped up small with hatchets: women having their breasts torn with iron pincers, their tongues cut out, their ears screwed off... these are among the mildest subjects.[36]

The miracle play at Ober-Ammergau indulged, according to one spectator, Anna Mary Howitt, in a similar display of ghastliness. During the play's second part she noted, 'There was no sparing of agony, and blood, and horror.' As she and her companion turned away from the spectacle 'sick with horror', she was surprised to see an audience of absorbed faces. Travellers from Britain were often surprised at how a Catholic audience responded with reverence to imagery they found repulsive or silly. On the festival day for St. Paul in Malta, for example, Reverend Hughes was stunned by the crowd's behaviour at the traditional procession. As several men carrying a huge wooden statue of St. Paul walked by, the crowd offered a roaring, almost frenzied, reception to the image as if it were St. Paul himself.[37] The Scotswoman Alice Cunningham was equally surprised to see a group of Catholic men treating a doll as the actual Saviour who could heal the sick. The behaviour seemed so childish as she made clear, 'We were quite shocked to see it, and shocked at men believing in such gross superstition... It might have delighted children, but how grown-up men can so far deceive themselves with such childish things, is all a mystery to me.'[38] This reverence among Catholics for wood, paint, dolls and gore seemed pagan-like and indicative of a low level of intelligence and culture. For Protestants, the sacred and divine could properly be represented by light and space, but never by tangible images or material objects. The latter were considered to be merely 'forgeries of divinity'.

James Smith thought that two cakes he purchased in Switzerland summed up the profane nature of Catholic imagery. The cakes had been made in moulds so that each displayed a sharp and well-defined impression. On one was a Madonna and Child, while the other pictured a gentleman with a rose behind his back and a woman holding a broom. The latter one was entitled 'The Amorous Old Gentleman'. From this purchase, he was 'impressed with this principle as running through the whole system of Popery – namely the Levelling of the loftiest concerns of the soul and the Glory of God himself, with the meanest and most trifling things of earth.'[39] It seemed to him a mockery of the spiritual to represent Mary as an everyday piece of food and to juxtapose the Virgin with a vulgar, amorous couple.

Protestant travellers wielded a certain derogatory discourse when summing up this material dimension of Catholicism. Their journals are full of words such as trash, tinsel, tawdry, tasteless and trumpery to describe the many objects 'littering' the churches and countryside in Catholic territories. On entering the cathedral in Vienne, Julia Pardoe admired its 48 lofty columns of rare marble. But the pleasing architectural effect was marred, in her estimation, 'by the excessive taste for tawdry ornament... a taste that has clothed these finely proportioned pillars in crimson velvet for two-thirds of their height; while the numerous altars are laden with gold-leaf, foil, and discoloured lace.' Whether the objects were crimson velvet and discoloured lace, artificial flowers, gaudily dressed wax dolls, gilded ornaments, wayside shrines or framed pictures of the Virgin, they signified, for Protestants, the lack of taste, solemnity and refinement characterizing Catholicism. Such Catholic trappings were thought especially disgusting and offensive when cluttering roadsides and bridges amidst beautiful countryside. Travelling through Catholic Germany and Switzerland, William Howitt regarded the combination of roadside religion and majestic scenery as a union of the ridiculous and sublime which was jarring to the eye and insulting to the Almighty. Approaching a mountainous area he fulminated, 'In the very face of the Alps... before the handiworks of God's greatness and the beauty of his poetic revelations of himself in mountain and overarching heaven, they have dared to set up their most impudent forgeries of divinity.'[40] He was particularly incensed that the 'forgeries' used 'ghastliness and bloodiness' as a decorative theme. Smith described and illustrated his journal with two types of roadside shrines in Catholic Switzerland. One was a pole with a board at the top equipped with a little covering to keep off rain. The board typically presented a coloured lithograph. The other consisted of a stone-built chamber neatly plastered and whitewashed inside and containing such stucco statuary as the nude body of Christ dangling over Mary's lap. He summed up the shrines as offering 'beastly engravings and nude and unseemly stucco figures'.

The above descriptions of Catholicism and Protestantism suggest an almost militant allegiance to the latter among travellers from all parts of Britain. In that sense, they support Colley's argument for a shared religious identity in Britain. But these descriptions tell only part of a much more complex story that both reveals the non-monolithic nature of Protestantism and Catholicism and challenges the notion of a religiously-based Britishness. Many of the above travellers' comments were prompted by direct confrontations with Continental Catholicism. Such confrontations tended to mask temporarily the many divisions between Protestants. The Continent was not, however, all Catholic. When attending services in Continental Protestant churches and, especially, when travelling around Britain, travellers expressed the divisiveness inherent in Protestantism *and* the national distinctions between people of Britain.[41] Furthermore, not all Continental travellers from Britain were Protestant. Some were Catholic and felt themselves to be both Catholic and English, suggesting that national identity did not always rest on, but could sometimes transcend, religious affiliation.

Journals of trips through Protestant parts of Europe reveal that travellers often identified with the way Protestantism manifested itself in England, Scotland or Wales – hardly ever Britain – rather than with Protestantism as a whole. To Henry Mayhew, for example, Protestantism in Germany was as foreign and subversive of liberty as was Catholicism. This realization struck him when he became aware that baptism in the established Protestant Church was required by German law. He thought of the English provision of Public Registrar's Offices for those outside the Anglican Church and pronounced on the German system, 'This is a form of religious tyranny that, thank Heaven! advanced notions upon such matters have long ago, in England, blown to the winds.'[42] Other English travellers felt that their home-grown variety of Protestantism was warm and friendly compared to Protestantism on the Continent. According to E.V. Lucas, Dutch Protestant churches clearly revealed the difference. In the interest of sterile, chilly religiosity, the Dutch had, he argued, whitewashed away all the external grace and charm in their churches. Comparing England and Holland with respect to religion Lucas maintained, 'In the simplest English village church one receives some impression of the friendliness of religion; but in Holland...religion seems to be a cold if not a repellent thing.'[43] The earliest Murray guide to the Continent (1836) dispensed a similar view. Travellers read that Dutch churches were barren and of little interest compared to Catholic churches in Belgium, and that ministers wore the puritanical garb of Charles I's time. According to Emma Ward, French Protestant churches were equally devoid of warmth and welcoming touches. The 'bare, cold, drab-coloured conventicle at Caen' prompted longings for home and journal entries such as, 'Oh! these sad Sundays! There is no day in France so hard for the English exiles.' She was most relieved to arrive in Paris where English money had financed a 'sunny, bright, perfectly well-appointed' Protestant sanctuary.[44] Guidebooks informed travellers regarding the location throughout Europe of English and Scottish churches so they could, like Ward, seek refuge amidst a familiar form of religiosity.

The traveller Margaret Brewster also found her thoughts wandering back home, in her case to Scotland, when she experienced Continental Protestantism. After worshipping with Christian Brethren in Paris she confessed, 'I always return from my ecclesiastical aberrations with a warmer gratitude for the Church of our own land – of our Scottish hills and our old martyrs.' One has the feeling from her words that she saw the Scottish Church as being as permanent and natural a part of Scotland as the landscape. As she travelled South in France, she felt even more out of place worshipping in Nîmes, the headquarters of French Protestantism. The city was home to 15,000 Protestants who had two large churches and a chapel to choose from on Sundays. The services Brewster chose to join distressed her greatly, for they seemed to give offence to the serious spirit of her Protestantism and to smack of 'religion walking in silver slippers'. As she explained, 'It was painful to see in churches...so many inattentive countenances, and to hear, before and after the service, as much irreverant whispering and chattering as we find among Roman Catholic worshippers.'[45] For the writer Dinah Craik, who went to the Continent for the first time in 1870, Protestant services in France were, in some ways, distinctly French. In fact, her evaluation of hymns suggests that Protestant services in general had national characteristics. Commenting on French Protestant hymns she noted, 'They were neither English nor Scotch psalm-tunes, nor German chorales; and, of course, they were utterly removed from anything in the Roman Catholic service.'[46] Craik's comments were based on a familiarity with both English and Scottish churches. Although born and raised in England, she married a Scot who introduced her to churches in his native land.

Differences in the musical traditions of Protestant churches occurred to John Dunlop as well during his Sunday visits to a French Protestant church. In comparing the services to those in his native Scotland, he was particularly struck by the beautiful music. He noted how the hymns were all set to written music, dispensed to worshippers in a book. Taking issue with those who considered Scotland a 'musical nation', he went on to discuss the 'disagreeable' and 'miserable' psalm-singing in Scottish churches. As he saw it, the only Scottish music worth hearing was of a very old date. The musical talents of more recent generations of Scots had been corrupted, he maintained, 'by the wretched system of psalmody practised for 200 years in the Scotch Kirk. Instrumental music being banished from sacred buildings as profane, a system of Psalm-singing at once the most disagreeable and miserable has been used in public worship.' While in France, he also noted differences between the English church there and his kirk back home. He filled a page in his journal talking of the mild and gentle manner of preaching, noting that, though devoid of anything 'piquante', the service was very proper and exemplary. The sermon, however, he found somewhat surprising, because 'deficient in that doctrinal and political theology which is so much prized in Scotland.'[47]

Welsh religiosity offered additional variations with respect to the sounds heard in Protestant churches. Although the Anglican Church of England was technically the Established church in Wales, only a minority of Welsh – mostly the Anglicised gentry – attended its services. Wales was a bastion of Protestant nonconformity in the nineteenth century, with the majority of the population attending dissenting chapels. As MP for Methyr Tydfil, Henry Richard was a firm upholder of Welsh and nonconformist rights, and a strong opponent of state interference in religious matters. During his trips to the Continent to attend Protestant Bible Society meetings, his encounters with Catholic and Protestant religiosity had him comparing what he experienced there with chapel practices in Wales. Interestingly, the nature of Welsh preaching seemed to him more Catholic in some ways than Protestant. This recognition occurred to him near the railway station in Cologne where he witnessed a very flamboyant Catholic procession. As he listened to a priest chanting part of the service, he noted how the sound reminded him 'as it has done frequently before of the tone in Welsh preaching. There is precisely the same measured and musical recitative, and it seemed... that the tone was in fact derived by traditional remembrance from the chants of the Catholic worship.' Given the alleged bonds between Protestants, it is intriguing that Richard felt at home with Catholic chanting, but somewhat disoriented when attending a Lutheran church in Paris that displayed a table supporting a small figure of Jesus on the cross 'very much as you see in Catholic Churches'.[48]

Continental travellers' tendency to link Scotland with communities outside Britain when thinking of religion provides additional evidence challenging a Britain-wide religious identity. For example, the Scottish traveller William E. Baxter pondered the issue of church–state relations as he wandered around central and southern Europe. State churches such as the Protestant one in Prussia seemed, in his estimation, to stifle freedom of sentiment. He was highly critical of their policy of forcing adherence and payment of fees, and argued in favour of separation of church and state. Prompted by such musings, he praised religious attitudes in his native land and asserted, 'We speak of Scotland in the same category as New England, because the great majority of her people support dissent... Anti-State Church Associations have the best of the argument.'[49] For very different reasons, Mrs Craik drew parallels between French Protestant churches and Presbyterian churches in Scotland. While attending a Protestant church in France, she noticed that the altar and pulpit familiar to her English eyes were replaced by 'the same sort of rostrum which one sees in Scotch Presbyterian churches'. Similarly, the pastor in his ordinary dress looked 'not unlike a Scotch Free Church minister' and the congregation was '*sitting* to sing, as they do in Scotland'.[50] Such comments certainly make one wonder just how strong the sense of community was among Protestants in Britain.

When touring Britain, travellers were even more aware of the divergent and divisive strands of Protestant religiosity. The heightened awareness left no doubt in their minds that, at least in a religious sense, Scotland, England and Wales were three distinct nations. On a superficial level, they recognized that the appearance of churches varied in the three main parts of Britain. Passing from Scotland into his native England, it was the churches that made Reverend Francis Trench aware of having crossed a border between different peoples and environments. On re-entering England he remarked:

> We stopped at a pleasant inn, about a mile on the English side of the border. The character of the old village church told us, in a moment, where we were. I had seen nothing of a similar appearance throughout all Scotland.[51]

George Borrow was more specific about the distinguishing mark of Welsh churches. Admiring a church near Llangollen, he noted that, instead of the sky-piercing spire typical of English landscapes, it had a 'little erection on its roof, so usual to Welsh churches, for holding a bell'.[52]

More significant were the differences noticed concerning religious attitudes and beliefs. Minutes after crossing into Scotland at Gretna Green, Trench encountered religious opinions foreign to his English ears. Of the first church he saw he asked a local man whether it drew a Sunday congregation. The man responded that it did not because the priest was a 'patronage man', and he then proceeded to lecture Trench on the evils of patronage – the practice of allowing ministers to be chosen by owners of land on which churches stood rather than by congregations. This practice was prohibited in the Church of Scotland by the 1707 Act of Union, but restored by the English-dominated British Parliament in 1712. Many Scots viewed this as betrayal carried out in the interest of landowners, the most anglicized group in Scotland. The Scotsman near Gretna Green spoke with a passion and conviction that Trench found surprising, for patronage was 'a subject totally disregarded in England'.[53]

Other religious issues of vital importance to the Scots seemed equally strange to the Anglican reverend, especially the split in the Presbyterian Church of Scotland resulting in the formation of the Free, or Secession, Church in 1843. The 1707 Act of Union which created the political entity of Great Britain with a single Parliament based in Westminster recognized the Presbyterian Church as dominant in Scotland. Throughout the eighteenth century, various small groups broke away from the Presbyterian Church of Scotland, or the Kirk, to form new sects. The 1843 split was a major one between moderate Presbyterians (supporters of the Kirk) and more radical Evangelicals fired by both missionary zeal and hostility to subordination of church to state (Parliament). In that year more than 40 per cent of the Kirk's ministers gave up their salaries and left to form a new Church, the Free Church of Scotland, over which the British Parliament in Westminster had no control and in which there was to be no patronage. Trench spent several chapters discussing this split because he recognized that the sentiments underlying it would be very difficult for English people, whether Anglicans or Dissenters, to understand. To highlight the gulf between England and Scotland on the matter, he quoted a Continental Protestant clergyman:

> The matter is one purely Scotch, and as the Scotch Church occupies a peculiar position in the Protestant world, the whole affair must be treated on its own ground. All abstract theories, all transference of English views and theories applied to it can only mislead.[54]

Trench also felt 'a stranger' to the idea of church autonomy – a principle held dear by many Scots, and even defended to the death by some. In the rest of Britain, Trench argued, people did not find it problematic to acknowledge Christ as the spiritual head of the Church, while at the same time deferring to a secular head of the Church such as the monarch. As believers in church autonomy, on the other hand, many Scots regarded Christ as the only head of the Church. In their view, the Church was thus independent of any secular power. When pointing out how peculiarly Scotch this view was Trench wrote, 'I am well aware that it is very difficult for people...if not Scotch, nor bred up in that country, to realize...the strength and depth, with which these convictions are embraced in the national spirit and religious heart of this land.'[55] His words suggest that religious belief was thought to be a meaningful indicator of national spirit, in this case of Scottish national spirit.

Other English people travelling in Scotland found religious services to exude Scottishness. In general, Scottish religious services seemed to be performed with a propriety and solemnity not found in England. Clement Ingleby remarked after attending the cathedral in Glasgow, 'The Scotch attend to their external duties in Religion with much greater regularity and propriety than the English.'[56] The one aspect of Scottish services that appeared 'undevout' was behaviour during singing. Scottish congregations remained seated when they sung the praise of God, unlike English ones. C.L. Smith attended services in the Episcopal Church of Scotland and was surprised to find that he did not feel at home, given that this church was more like the Church of England than any other in Scotland. Expressing how out of place the Scotsman conducting the service made him feel, Smith complained:

> He was a fair reader, and gave a good explanatory sermon on the uses of the Mosaic Law; but it was *all* explanatory, with no practical address. There was one curious innovation, adopted probably out of deference to the Scottish Presbyterian notion; he himself gave out the Psalm, and read the first two lines of it. He also wore white gloves.[57]

Thus even the Episcopal Church which used the English Prayer Book had a distinctly Scottish feel about it, raising further doubts about the strength of a common British religiosity.

Journals by Scottish travellers in England offer a similar challenge to the notion that people from Britain felt united by a shared Protestantism. When mustering evidence for the gulf between England and

Scotland regarding religious matters, Trench quoted a Continental clergyman. But had he been writing a year later, he could have resorted to the words of Hugh Miller – a Scottish nationalist and fervent Presbyterian – who declared:

> The errors committed by the Government of the country in legislating for Scotland in matters of religion, as if it were not a separate nation, possessed of a distinct and strongly-marked character of its own, but a mere province of England, have led invariably to disaster and suffering.[58]

This statement came at the end of a journal full of comments on the profound religious differences between Scotland and England. For Miller, these differences determined the two peoples' distinct social and intellectual character. Regarding social character, Miller observed that community life in England was much less intimate and sociable than in Scotland. As he put it, 'Nothing struck my Scotch eyes in the rural districts as more unwonted and peculiar than the state of separatism which neighbours of a class that in Scotland would be on the most intimate terms, maintain with respect to each other.'[59] He related this English separatism to the independent, insulated Churches characteristic of England. Scotland, by contrast, was more a country of a National Church which, in Miller's view, helped explain the more sociable, integrated communities.

Scottish and English travellers alike noted how religious issues were much more hotly debated by all social groups in Scotland than they were in England. Once, while discussing doctrinal matters, Miller encountered an English commercial gentleman who thought the Scotch 'a strange people' for getting so exercised about religion and inquired of Miller, 'What good does all your theology do you?' Miller was quick to respond, 'It has awakened [Scottish people's] intellects, and taught them how to think. The development of the popular mind in Scotland is a result of its theology.' Miller believed that Scotland, much more than England, was characterized by a diffuse intellect, and he attributed the difference to religion. The dominant Anglican form of religion in England, he argued, revolved around liturgy and ceremony, which, though capable of inspiring sincere devotion, 'have no tendency to exercise the thinking faculties'. In Scotland, on the other hand, religion focused more on the sermon and adhered to the doctrine of Calvinism which, according to Miller, was 'the best possible of all schoolmasters for teaching a religious people to think'. The English Church leaned more towards Arminianism (based on the idea of free will rather than Calvinistic predestination), 'a greatly less awakening system of doctrine than the Calvinism of Scotland,' in Miller's view. Miller believed that Calvinism made people feel bound by destiny, and that the feeling engendered a sort of scrutinizing mentality not likely to be inspired by the Arminian feeling of freedom.[60]

Perhaps the solemnity of religiosity in Scotland helps explain why Frances MacKenzie was so surprised when she attended her first Anglican service. It was in Durham Cathedral, and she and her family were 'shocked with the profaneness' of what they saw. The hurried way the prayers were gobbled and chanted seemed 'marvellously similar to Romish ceremonies'.[61] The speed of prayer presentation might have been related to the sparse attendance, there being only two ladies in the congregation on that Tuesday evening.

Like the Scots, the Welsh were perceived as being more serious than the English about religious matters. Travellers from England commented on how even small Welsh villages contained numerous chapels well attended by interested rather than yawning worshippers. Most Welsh men and women strongly supported dissenting sects, and were hostile towards the state relgious establishment, or English Church in Wales. According to one English traveller, the Welsh dissented 'from not only the doctrines, but the *theory* of our Established Church'. By theory, he meant the principle or idea of a dominant Church which was accepted, he argued, in England, Scotland and most of Ireland (as long as it was the Catholic Church that was dominant), but not in Wales.[62]

Such perceptions of divisions within Protestantism became more widespread in the nineteenth century when increasing numbers of people travelled. They should make us cautious about adopting the Protestant versus Catholic model to explain religious identity in Victorian Britain. Given the tradition of regarding Catholics as the evil 'other', one might assume that travellers perceived the Catholicism they experienced on the Continent as monolithic, and thus as more in line with the model. This was not, however, always the case. As a result of their travels, people came to recognize that, like Protestantism, Catholicism was not a uniform thing, but rather a diverse phenomenon with regional and national characteristics. According to their journals, it was primarily the material, aesthetic characteristics of Catholicism that varied. Milan Cathedral tended to highlight the distinctions between Catholic aesthetics in northern and southern Italy. Descriptions of the cathedral leave little doubt that travellers from Britain favoured and felt more at home with the *relatively* austere Northern variety. Lt. Col. Legge, for example, noted of Milan's grandest church, 'There was scarcely any tawdry... within, and but a few statues in bad taste, so that it is far better than the more southern Italian churches.' Similarly, the Quaker traveller Catherine Braithwaite stood admiring the cathedral, expressing with some relief, 'After so many churches with paintings, and frescoes and statues in, it was quite a pleasure to see the simple but grand Gothic style of the interior; the fine columns with their carved capitals.'[63] For Andrew and Agnes Donaldson (née Twining), Catholic churches and religiosity in France heightened awareness of the religious culture Italians shared. After being in Italy for approximately four months, the couple with their children made their way home stopping for a time in Paris. The contrast with Italy was marked, as they made clear in their remarks about Nôtre Dame, 'We felt the interior cold and were impressed with the want of reality after the real religious fervour of the the [sic] Italians and the constantly used churches of Italy.'[64]

Moving further north, Catholicism in England stood out as distinct in the minds of those who had travelled to the Continent. Although the majority of people in England were Protestant, the number of Catholics increased throughout the nineteenth century, especially during the 1840s with the influx of Irish to mostly urban areas. In that decade, the Catholic population of London rose from 100,000 to 150,000, so that London housed almost as many Catholics as Rome, whose total population in 1850 was only 175,000.[65] Heading north from London in 1846, Revd. Trench stopped at a recently opened Romish chapel not far from Derby. The decor compared favourably with what he had seen during his recent trek through France and Spain as his description of the chapel's appearance reveals, 'The inside of the latter edifice was very simple, in comparison with foreign churches, neither did I notice figures of the crowned Virgin or other reprehensible ornaments and decorations, similar to those in which Popery delights abroad.'[66] He went on to express his fear that priests and Jesuits steeped in Continental Catholicism would undoubtedly introduce such 'reprehensible ornaments' into England in the near future. His fear suggests that 'Popish decoration', instead of being a natural part of English Catholicism, had to be imposed from the outside. Frederick Faber was in an even better position to draw comparisons between Continental and English Catholicism, for he eventually experienced both as a Catholic. Shortly before renouncing his Anglican faith in favour of Catholicism, he travelled to the Continent determined to worship there as if he were already a Catholic. By the time he reached Cologne, the rowdiness and imagery in the churches combined to make him feel homesick and out of place. As he put it:

I determined... to conform to the Catholic Ritual here... But it all will not do. The careless irreverence, the noise, the going in and out, the spitting of the priests on the Alter steps, the distressing and may I use the word: indecent representations of our B. Lord – I cannot get over them... I cannot lean on a foreign church even while moving and living in it. There is no quietness, no being able to hide oneself in its penitent services.[67]

Even after he converted to Catholicism in 1845, Faber continued to find Continental religiosity unfulfilling. In Florence he wrote home to Brother Strickson, 'There is something in English Catholicism which I like far, far better than anything I see abroad.'[68] Although he did not specify what it was he liked, we can safely assume, given the previous quote, that he found English Catholicism to be less gaudy visually and more sombre in tone. Despite his eventual founding of the Italianate Bromptom Oratory, Faber was committed to perpetuating an English form of Catholicism. His clearly stated religious goal was to 'harmonize the ancient and modern spirituality of the Church... and to put it before English Catholics in an English shape, translated into native thought and feeling, as well as language.'[69] Faber's religious preference and goal are important to note here because they indicate that nations put their stamp even on Catholicism, the Christian denomination with the most overt claims to universality.

These comments showing the plurality of Protestantisms and Catholicisms suggest that the Protestant versus Catholic model of religious identity, by assuming that the two religions were monoliths, masks as much as it reveals. It also obscures the reality during the Victorian period by implying a purely antagonistic relationship between the two religions. In fact, Protestant travellers did not always see Catholicism as something to criticize and oppose. Most of them were critical and did regard Catholicism as strange – as the 'Other'. But even some critics were surprised to find themselves drawn to certain facets of Catholicism and to feel slightly less satisfied with Protestantism after sojourning on the Continent. Their experiences suggest that, at least for some travellers, exposure to the Continent worked to alter – not merely to reinforce – negative preconceptions about Catholicism. Perhaps this shift in attitude helps explain why rabid Catholic-baiting in sermons was not so readily accepted as it had been in earlier times. Agnes Twining, for example, found a service conducted in Germany by a Society for the Propagation of the Gospel Chaplain to be very alienating. In her view, it was 'dreary' and 'the sermon was merely a raid against Roman Catholics'.[70]

Some travellers found that their negative reactions to Catholicism mingled with a new-found appreciation for its beautiful settings and sounds. As noted above, Miss Howitt was horrified by the gruesome display at a miracle play in Ober-Ammergau. She spoke condescendingly of Catholics' 'child-like faith' and of the beggars around her as the 'disgusting fungi of Catholicism'. But of a Corpus Christi procession in Munich she remarked, 'It was very beautiful. My soul seemed calmed and exalted.' At High Mass later in the day she declared, 'I had no conception how sublimely beautiful is this chapel... the crowd of worshipping people, the strains of music, the incense, all produced an overpowering effect.'[71] Alexander Dunlop was overpowered as well, in his case by a visit to the Sistine Chapel where he heard the famous 'Miserere'. As he stood wedged between 'a fat Bishop and a Dominican Friar', he thought at first how 'stupid and tiresome' was all the chanting. His thoughts flashed back to an earlier ceremony at St. Peter's where the spectacle had him heaving a sigh of relief at the thought that Protestants had 'heads as well as hearts and passions'. But then the 'Miserere' began, and he recorded:

> It is magnificent – splendid – overpowering – indeed to me the impression of a mixture of awe and delight was such as I had never before felt anywhere... my feelings were such as to prompt me to say to myself – 'I wish this could last forever.'... I felt as if I had never heard anything that deserved the name of *Sacred* music before.[72]

Dunlop had realized that he was not immune to Catholicism's appeal to the senses and feelings. Charles Churchill was also surprised to find himself drawn to the ceremonial side of Catholicism. Attending High Mass in Cologne, he commented on how grand the service was and how much more beautiful his own familiar Protestant church services would be 'with the same externals and accompaniments'.[73]

Thomas Macaulay was another traveller who found himself drawn to the aesthetic aspect of Catholicism.[74] When he first arrived in Italy in 1836, he was critical of Catholicism, using the standard collection of derogatory terms found in so many British travellers' journals. As time passed, however, this negative vocabulary gradually disappeared from his writing, and Macaulay became more and more enamoured of the beautiful churches and the ritual of the Mass. He went so far as to praise the Italians for their lively, festive form of worship, noting how it contrasted so markedly with the more sombre religious expression in England. Upon returning to England, Macaulay unleashed a barrage of attacks on the English Protestant form of religiosity, with its endless chanting, poor sermons, inattentive congregations and loud talking. His attacks make clear the degree to which travellers could be transformed by their journeys and thus motivated to change their native societies as well.

Many travellers expressed contempt for the 'trash and trumpery' trappings of Catholicism. Yet when visiting Catholic churches, some confessed to being very impressed with the art inspired by the faith. While standing in St. Peter's, for example, the Scotsman J.B. Greenshields was struck for the first time by the thought that the Catholic Church had 'done more towards the promotion of the fine arts than all the world has done'.[75] Lancashire-born Martha Lamont came to the same conclusion as she toured Belgian churches offering Reubens paintings and Mozart Masses. She could not help but admit how much better Catholicism was than Protestantism at inspiring and preserving the arts. And, as a romance devotee, she was drawn to the Catholic religion with its talk of Gothic churches and of taking the veil. Attending service at the church in St. Etienne she rhapsodized:

> Altogether the scene was so beautiful, the music so touching, the odour of the incense so agreeable, it was all so unlike what we see at home, and so much like what we only read of, that I began to sigh... I am so much fascinated by this gothic church, and its *gothic* ceremonies, that I intend, very soon, to visit Notre Dame, which should be doubly interesting to me after reading Victor Hugo's romance.[76]

Another English woman, Margaret Law, was attracted to several aspects of the Catholic Church. Although it had a rigid hierarchy of officials, she felt there was an absence of ranking within Catholic congregations, unlike in many Protestant churches. According to her, in the Catholic Church 'there is no distinction of persons; an elegantly dressed female will enter, and kneel beside the poorest beggar.' She was pleased by this egalitarian spirit, thinking it appropriate for the house of God. Law was also attracted, unlike most English travellers, to the many roadside crosses in Catholic countries, thinking it a pity that Protestants cast aside this 'fitting emblem of the religion we profess' (presumably she meant Christianity). She thought the cross 'under God's free Heavens' should be no less revered than a church building, something Protestants regarded as sacred. As was true for other Protestant travellers, her tolerance for Catholicism had its limits, even when it came to investing roadside crosses with sacred meaning. She had been admiring one of these crosses while resting on a stone under a majestic elm tree. Minutes after she left her seat, one of the larger branches snapped in the wind, falling directly on the stone with a crashing sound that startled her. She realized that, had she not left the shaded spot exactly when she did, she would have been severely injured, perhaps even killed. The thought made her declare, 'Here was a miracle for the superstitious.' She then went on to distance herself from 'superstitious', presumably Catholic, behaviour by saying, 'Instead of hanging an additional garland on the cross I contented myself with an inward thanksgiving for my escape which was truly providential.'[77] In other words, she was not willing to engage in a ritual that could be construed as her giving thanks to the cross, rather than to God, for her fate. Such unwillingness reflects Protestants' distaste for the idolotry they associated with Catholicism.

Even more than the beauty and art, travellers applauded the piety and earnest religiosity they witnessed in Catholic churches. For some, this earnestness prompted the disturbing realization of just how lukewarm devotional energy was back home. Four years before he converted to Catholicism, Frederick Faber attended a Catholic service in Austria which left him painfully aware of the anaemic religiosity in his own church. As the Mass began with rising incense and rousing song, Faber thought of how his own country's faith ran 'in thin and scattered rivulets', and he looked with 'envious surprise' at the 'pure, hearty, earnest faith' surrounding him.[78] Such comments coming from a near convert to Catholicism are not surprising, but life-long Protestants said similar things. Henry Clark Barlow, for example, did not wish to worship amidst altars, images, crosses and Madonnas, yet in their defence he argued, 'The cultivation of pious sentiments and religious impressions, dispositions and habitudes of resignation and love are worth all the means that Romanism has invented for the purpose.'[79] One such means in Ostend was an altar supporting a huge wooden doll representing the Virgin Mary. Frances Trollope was in Ostend for the festive celebration of Fête-Dieu and denounced the doll decoration as being 'childishly grotesque'. That is, she did so until an adoring believer made her see the image in a more positive light. As Trollope sat watching a woman display reverence towards the doll, she admitted:

> I was touched by the unmistakeable devotion of a poor old woman, who kneeled on the pavement before it... perhaps, there is something sublime in the state of mind, which allows not the senses to dwell on the object before them, but, occupied alone by the holiness of the symbol, is raised by it to such thoughts of heaven, as chase all

feelings but those of devotion. That this is often the case with sincere Roman Catholics I have no doubt.[80]

Even a caustic travel writer like Trollope lost all inclination to criticize the gaudily dressed doll once she witnessed the feeling and devotion it inspired.

Two Scottish travellers thought their native Presbyterian Churches could learn a thing or two from Catholicism. John Dunlop had no doubt that the Catholic faith was founded on a 'grand delusion', but he appreciated its churches being always open for prayer and meditation. The practice encouraged, in his view, pious habits, and he wondered, 'Could the Free Church not take this subject into consideration?'[81] Similarly, the fervour of Vesper chanting by a Varenna congregation made Combe more critical of Scottish religiosity. He thought about how much more effective such daily devotions were at nurturing a pious population 'than the sole Sunday exercises of Scotland.' With its long and lofty settings and rousing ceremonies, Catholicism suddenly seemed attractive. In thinking of Protestant Presbyterians back home, Combe admitted that they 'have lost the emotional power and substitute only a cold, barren, self-esteeming dogmatism in its place'. Though his praise for and temporary attraction to Catholicism were genuine, they were not unqualified. Combe clearly regarded Italians as having suffered greatly because of their religious devotion. According to Combe, the power of Catholic religious sentiments in Italy appeared 'wonderful', until one looked at the productivity of the land and people. He declared:

> If the wealth, the talent, and the labour that are entombed in Churches and their ornaments in Italy, had all been applied to improving the physical condition of the land, and the moral and intellectual condition of the people...how different might have been the results!...Let the good take courage. The day is on the wing...when the same powers will be better directed, and we hope will bring forth richer fruits.[82]

Thus although Combe could understand Catholicism's appeal and even feel the appeal himself when observing Catholic ceremonies, he did view the religious devotion it inspired as too all-consuming and too Church-oriented. For Combe, religiosity was truly admirable only if it did not detract from economic productivity. One has the feeling that, in the end, he preferred a church that expected only Sunday attentions from its members, leaving them free to enlarge their minds – and bank accounts – during the rest of the week. This discussion of religion and national identity has focused mostly on Protestant travellers from England and Scotland, noting how their collective identities were bound up with various forms of Protestantism. What sort of national identity did Catholic travellers from England feel? Did they feel themselves to be un-British, or un-English because of their Catholicism – to be a marked 'Other'? Journals by Catholic travellers indicate that a Catholic identity did not necessarily preclude an English identity. Perhaps the gradual eroding of anti-Catholic sentiment coupled with the perception of a distinctly English form of Catholicism made it possible for someone to feel both English and Catholic in the Victorian period. This was certainly the case with Father Faber. On his trips to the Continent several years before his conversion, Faber frequently felt homesick for England. At such moments, he would enter a dreamy sort of state during which images of England eclipsed the Continental scenes in front of him. His England included green valleys and rural settings, parish churches, domestic hearths, village cricket and white cliffs. After he became a Catholic, visits to the Continent still had him longing for England. When in Paris he admitted to his Catholic friends at home, 'I scarcely think of anything but you and England all day long. I can find no services any where like those at St. Chad's' (the Catholic church in Birmingham). Similarly, while in Florence he wrote to one of his Brothers, 'I am a prisoner caged up; I pine to be in England, to work for England, to be with you all again.'[83] The work Faber alluded to was the conversion of England to Catholicism. He certainly identified England as Protestant, and thus often spoke of 'poor England' and 'poor faithless England'. But rather than making him feel an outsider, England's Protestantism gave meaning to his life and provided him with a cause – that of converting his homeland to the Catholic faith. Thus if anything, Faber's Catholicism intensified his passion for and identification with England. It may also have been true that English Catholics such as Faber proclaimed their Englishness all the more strongly in order to distinguish themselves from the Irish Catholics flooding into England in the 1840s and from such Catholic converts as Cardinal H.E. Manning who became more Roman than the Romans.

Mary Heimann's recent study reinforces the idea that Catholicism in England was distinct from that on the Continent, particularly with respect to devotional practices.[84] Heimann argued that the more earnest religiosity characteristic of Catholicism after 1840 was a reinvigorated recusant (Old Catholic) one – not a Roman one. Instead of Roman devotions being adopted in England after 1850, Heimann showed that old recusant devotional traditions were revived and altered to suit the times. She concluded that developments in English Catholicism during the Victorian period were similar to those in other English religious groups – an increased earnestness and intensity, desire for simplicity and concern about growing secularization and alienation of the industrial poor from organized religion.

In this chapter on the religious dimension of national identity I have emphasized several things. First, certain aspects of culture such as aesthetic sense and devotional behaviour sometimes cut across religious lines. Thus English Catholics and Protestants could and did see eye to eye regarding church aesthetics. A second and similar point is that religiosity could transcend national boundaries in certain contexts, such as when Protestants of differing nationalities confronted Catholicism and felt united in their similar reactions. Third, a national or even regional culture put its stamp on a particular religion such that an English or a Scottish Protestant was sometimes aware of how his or her religion differed from other Protestantisms, including each other's. Taken together, these three observations suggest a final and most important point: context is key to understanding how religion contributes to people's collective identity. These four themes are perhaps highlighted most clearly by Victorian travellers' comments on the Sabbath.

More than Catholicism, the Sabbath as observed on the Continent engendered a feeling of shared identity among travellers from Britain. Whether Quaker, Evangelical Protestant, high Anglican, Presbyterian, Catholic or areligious, travellers from England, Scotland and Wales felt out of place and of one mind when touring the Continent on Sundays. And they did so regardless of whether they were in Catholic or Protestant areas. Murray's first guide to the Continent offered a warning about Sabbaths across the Channel. When discussing gardens and houses of public recreation on the outskirts of many German towns, the guidebook admonished,

> It is true the time when these places are most frequented, and when the music and dancing are kept up with the greatest spirit, is the Sunday afternoon, which may... shock the feelings of an English or Scotchman, accustomed to the rigorous Sabbath-keeping of his own country.[85]

Although such guidebook warnings may have softened the 'shock', travellers were still surprised and disappointed at the absence on the

Continent of church-going bells and respectable processions of family groups bound for Sunday worship. Instead, they found bustling markets, open shops, routine weekly labour and an energetic pursuit of pleasure on Sundays. Even in a 'citadel of Protestantism' like Geneva and in Nîmes, a centre of French Protestantism, very unsabbatical sights and sounds prevailed. Jemima Morrell spent her first Sunday on the Continent in Geneva where she noted, 'Here we first learned the characteristics of a Continental Sabbath, which was painful enough to English eyes.'[86] Frederick Fryer, a Quaker, happened to be in Nîmes for the opening of the Montpelier–Nîmes Railway which generated 'grand entertainments, in spite of its being the Sabbath. In the arena there was a sort of bullfight...a shameful exhibition for a partly Protestant town like this in the 19th century.'[87] While staying in Berlin, the Welshman Henry Richard compared Sabbath Sundays in Germany to those in England. He thought it curious that 'in no other country, not even in Protestant Germany or Switzerland, has there ever prevailed such rigid notions about the observance of the Sabbath as in England.'[88] He attributed the English Sunday not to the Reformation, but to Puritanism in particular. The Catholic sympathizer Frederick Faber displayed a slightly more liberal attitude to the Sabbath. He had no objections to music and open gardens on Sunday. But even he found Sunday in the very Protestant town of Dresden too much to bear. He remarked, 'Dresdeners seem to regard coffee and music and leafy walks as far too tame a way of spending their Sunday afternoons...there was every species of gambling, smoking, drinking, singing.'[89]

The traveller Margaret Fountaine was someone we might expect to have been oblivious to Sunday frivolity on the Continent, for she led a very unconventional life. A country clergyman's daughter born near Norwich in 1862, she had a very formal upbringing. But in her late teens, she flouted convention by falling in love with *and* aggressively pursuing an Irish alcoholic. When that pursuit finally failed, she decided to spend her modest private income on world travel in order to study butterflies, among other things. For the rest of her life she romped through distant countryside chasing winged creatures and 'wild, gipsy-looking' men. A Syrian man married with children was her devoted travelling companion for 28 years. In short, it would be hard to chronicle a more unconventional life for a Victorian Englishwoman. Yet this rugged individualist was very conventional when it came to the Sabbath. On a Sunday in Naples she refused to join in a game of cards. In Nôtre Dame Cathedral on Sunday she likened the organ sound to 'the warning voice of Heaven speaking to this gay abandoned city that hath no Sabbath, for see, within sight of the very walls of this holy edifice the Bird Market is filled with buyers and sellers, regardless of God's day.'[90]

As travellers from Britain perceived it, Sabbath obervances on the Continent clearly cut across religious and national lines. Similarly, these observances elicited uniformly negative reactions among travellers from Britain regardless of their religious persuasion or native region within Britain. They thus fostered a feeling of unity among all Britons. But in certain contexts, particularly when Britons travelled around their native island or encountered each other on the Continent, differences between English and Scottish Sabbath behaviours seemed paramount. Murray's handbooks predisposed travellers to think of differences between England and Scotland with respect to the Sabbath. Offering travel 'hints' to an assumed English audience, the Murray's *Handbook for Travellers in Scotland* (1883) admonished, 'One is to remember that the Scotch Sabbath is excessively rigorous.' Journals suggest that travellers took the advice to heart. When staying in Glasgow, for example, one English traveller looked with some disdain on the sombre Scottish Sunday. He was particularly distressed to find the window blinds drawn in most houses. As he walked from his hotel to the cathedral he lashed out, 'Is it not reasonable to suppose that GOD would have forbidden the glorious Sun to shine on the Sabbath, if he had intended it to be the day of gloom which these Pharisees would make it.'[91] He then went on to describe the gloom and monotony pervading the city and the 'sanctimonious fear' on people's faces, as if a reprimand from the Almighty were imminent. Revd. Trench also experienced his first Scottish Sabbath in Glasgow and was struck by how it differed from Sundays in London. As he stood savouring the quiet and repose of a Sunday afternoon, he declared,

> I looked up the long line formed by the Trongate and Argyle Street, just at the time when the chief stir might have been expected, and I could not see one single vehicle abroad. What a contast with a similar view, at the same time of day, down Oxford Street or Piccadilly, the corresponding thoroughfares of London.[92]

The English Sunday also stood out as more liberal in the Scotsman William Chambers's mind as he witnessed a Dutch Sabbath. He noted that although the Sabbath was observed in Holland with slightly more strictness than in other areas of the Continent, it was nevertheless much less sombre and strict than in Scotland. The Dutch Sabbath was more like the English, according to Chambers. As he explained it, in Holland 'both stage-coaches and treckschuits plied on Sundays, and... the people recreated themselves out of doors as in England.'[93]

A Swiss rather than Dutch Sabbath caused Chambers's countryman James Smith to make distinctions between the Scots and the English when it came to Sunday attitudes and behaviours. On a Sunday in Basle, Smith and his Scottish friends refreshed themselves at a *table d'hôte* serving six courses to between 80 and 100 people. He reflected on all the requisite cooking and cleaning labour and concluded that no one employed by the *table d'hôte* had sufficient time to enjoy and observe the Sabbath. Although the conclusion disturbed him, he noted that the other diners were unconcerned because they were 'mostly English, and probably not accustomed as we to estimate the amount of Sabbath labour'.[94] His food became more palatable as he fantasized about the day when Sabbaths on the Continent would be honoured and all the huge inns and hotels would thus close. Once he left Switzerland, such fantasies seemed less likely to come true. For the profane nature of a Swiss Sabbath disappeared from his thoughts and concerns when he went to Paris and witnessed real 'evils' on Sunday.

This chapter takes issue with scholars such as John Wolffe who argue that, in the area of religion, a British cultural identity was more strongly felt in Victorian Britain than the local nationalisms of Scottishness, Welshness and Englishness. I have argued that religion was an integral part of the larger culture, with religious identity including a cluster of very secular values. These values suggest that travellers were conscious of a British religious identity when they were in Catholic areas of Europe, but of more local religious and national identities when they were travelling in Protestant Europe or in Britain itself. The chapter also questions the view that Protestantism and Catholicism were monolithic ideologies, by showing how nations put their distinct stamp on these belief systems as much as they put their stamp on particular nations. What emerges once again is the key role that geographic context played in the process of national imagining among Victorian Britons.

4
Customs, Comfort and Class

I was 30 before I left the United States for the first time. A dissertation requirement and a grant sent me to London where the British Library became home for over a year. On the morning after touching down at Gatwick Airport, I realized the significance of breakfast for national identity. With tray in hand, I stood beside another jet-lagged American who seemed as suspicious as I was of the fare spread before us in Crosby Hall's famous Tudor dining room. The sight of baked beans, porridge and boiled eggs in egg cups made us feel more American than ever and less hungry than usual at breakfast time. Toast would be safest, we thought, until a most peculiar rack appeared containing six equidistant pieces standing soldier-like, and too cold to butter. Months later after I had crossed the Channel, I realized that our taste buds were not the only ones particularly patriotic first thing in the morning. When trying to book accommodations at tourist information offices, I was sometimes asked whether I preferred to stay at a place catering for Americans, English or some other national group. When I inquired what distinguished one place from another, I was told mainly breakfast, because tourists typically were least willing to deviate from their familiar eating habits during the morning meal.

Eating and drinking rituals are part of those taken-for-granted daily habits that contribute to making people identify themselves and appear to others as a distinct national group. This was true in the Victorian period as well. Other such habits included manners, preferred recreational activities, methods of relaxing or making oneself comfortable, and rituals of social ranking. They put an identifying stamp on a people or place, as Henry Blackburn discovered when staying in the Pyrenean town of Bagnères de Bigorre. The town was popular with English residents abroad, and Blackburn explained what, besides the English language, gave the town such a homelike, English atmosphere. It was the familiar 'click of croquet', taste of pale ale, subdued behaviour in the streets and other 'signs of our nationality everywhere' that made the technically French town seem English, according to Blackburn.[1] The daily habits of other national groups were just as effective at proclaiming their collective identities, making British travellers on the Continent aware they had left Britain's shores. Their journals reveal that a myriad of details including *table d'hôte* tastes, body language, styles of dress and carpetless hotel rooms let them know very quickly that they had arrived at Boulogne, Dieppe or some other Continental town.

This chapter on customs, comfort and class explores the minutiae of daily life that Victorian travellers identified as English, Scottish, Welsh or British. Travel journals suggest that the daily customs most significant for these national identities were those concerning food and drink, manners and recreation. In some cases the customs reflect a British identity, in others separate Scottish, Welsh and English ones. The vast majority of journals by English travellers also reveal the centrality of the concept of comfort for Englishness, a concept discussed here in the context of the British emphasis on home life and recreations. Finally, the chapter examines the obsession with and methods of social ranking that made people from all parts of Britain feel markedly distinct from Continental Europeans. These seemingly surface matters of behaviour were just as important for creating and maintaining a sense of national identity as the more deliberately orchestrated state-sponsored rituals performed at royal festivities, schools, churches and law courts. The best-selling author Samuel Smiles was one Victorian among many who recognized the all-encompassing influence of manners, for example. Comparing their influence to that of laws, he thought the former more all pervasive. In his words, 'Morals and manners... are of greater importance than laws, which are but one of their manifestations. The law touches us here and there, but manners are about us everywhere, pervading society like the air we breathe.'[2]

Travellers' reactions to Continental food and drink clearly reveal the existence of a British dimension to the palate during the Victorian period. More than any other single eatable item, meat marked the British as distinct from Continental Europeans according to travellers from England and Scotland.[3] Journal criticisms of lean and flabby *table d'hôte* meat and the ever-present culinary disguises to make it palatable prompted praises for the quality and quantity of meat back home. It was so superior, said many travellers, that it needed no smothering sauce or spice. On the British side of the Channel, simple, unadorned meat was preferred and thought to be tasty, fortifying and plentiful. During her stay in France, Martha Lamont noted that the adult population did not look healthy. Echoing the sentiments expressed in Hogarth's earlier prints contrasting portly, beef-fed Englishmen with scrawny, effeminate Frenchmen who dined on frogs and soup, Lamont explained that too many 'eggs, and frogs, and vegetables' and the absence of 'English roast beef' caused 'the grown persons [to] have a very dried-up look'.[4] In Germany, the Mayhew family inspired astonished looks because of their daily consumption of meat and other animal products. As Mayhew told it, 'When we first came to the town, it was a positive nine days' marvel among the citizens, as to the quantity of animal food consumed by our family... and yet our fare was simple plain English living without even meat at breakfast or supper.'[5] The Mayhews dined on beef or mutton once a day, whereas the Germans typically partook of meat two or three times a week, filling up daily on potatoes, vegetables, soups and dumplings. Another English traveller drew a distinction between the typical cut of meat served in England and that offered in Germany. In his view, German dinners appeared 'rather strange to our English taste'. He attributed the 'strangeness' to there being 'no joints of meat', the Germans preferring to avoid the carver by indulging in boiled beef, chops or cutlets.[6]

In a study of the meat trade in Britain from the mid-nineteenth century until the First World War, Richard Perren argued that, except for bread, 'meat was the most important food of the British people'.[7] He thus corroborated travellers' comments regarding the significance of meat. But Perren's study also reveals the irony of 'English roast beef' as a symbol for the prosperity and superior quality of things English or British. This symbol figured prominently in Hogarth's eighteenth-century prints as well as in nineteenth-century travellers' journals, though less so as the century wore on. It was part of the language of national identity, particularly among the English. Yet during the Victorian period people in England ate increasing amounts of meat from Ireland, Wales and Scotland. Furthermore, free trade budgets and refrigerated containers dramatically increased the amount of meat Britain imported first from Europe and then from North America and the Empire. In the 1860s, 10 per cent of the meat consumed in Britain was imported; by 1914 the figure had risen to 40 per cent. When chilled meat began arriving in Britain from North America in the early 1870s, there was such a craze for the product that shops would sell their entire supply in several hours. Perren tells of a shop in Liverpool where such a rush of customers appeared the morning American meat went on sale that a policeman had to be summoned to maintain order. Britain also imported North American livestock, most of which was slaughtered in port towns. Such port-killed meat was closer in quality to the supposedly cherished home-fed variety. In comparing the quality of port-killed US meat to British meat, Perren suggested it was Scottish rather than English beef that was the best Britain had to offer, at least by the last quarter of the nineteenth century. He noted, 'Of course, the port-killed US meat was never good enough to compete with the best home-fed Scottish beef, but it did compare favourably with a sizeable proportion of the English beef that was sold.'[8] Thus not only was English beef no longer the finest in Britain by the late Victorian period; much of the beef eaten in England and other parts of Britain was European, American and Australian – not English. It is true that *roast* beef was a peculiarly English thing, in that the English preferred their meat roasted, which meant buying the most expensive cuts of meat. The Scots, on the other hand, typically boiled or stewed meat, and thus could get by with cheaper cuts. The growth of a Britain-wide meat market made possible by steam ships and railways made these sorts of dietary differences more apparent.

Milk and butter were the two other animal products considered indispensable by both the English and the Scots. Travellers complained repeatedly about having to consume tea without milk, and bread without butter, on the Continent. Being aware of the Continental preference for coffee, they packed plenty of tea before leaving home, never dreaming that milk to accompany it would be difficult to come by. One traveller in Trieste became so desperate that she stirred the yolk of an egg into her tea when no milk was to be had. For determined travellers in Reggio who wished for milk at breakfast time, Edward Lear advised sitting 'in the middle of the road with a jug at early dawn, for unless you seize the critical moment of the goats passing through the town, you may wish in vain.'[9] He had no advice for obtaining butter which, to the astonishment of travellers from Britain, the Italians knew nothing about and never used.

With respect to beverages, the English even more than the Scots identified passionately with tea. For English travellers, the want of tea and kettles was the privation hardest to endure when living abroad. Equally difficult was actually drinking the tea occasionally found across the Channel. While travelling in Brittany, the Welshman J.H. Lewis struggled to sip the tea made with salt water presented hospitably for his pleasure. He admitted, 'I drank it every drop for politeness sake but fear I must have made some wry faces.'[10] Scottish travellers seemed to abandon their tea-drinking rituals with more ease. In Brussels, James Smith and his friends indulged for the first time in *café au lait*. Pleasantly surprised by the taste, he confessed, 'We found it so agreeable that without regret we bade adieu to Tea. I did not see Tea till I came to Geneva, and there I got Tea so trashy that I was glad to abandon all wish for it till I got across the Channel.'[11] No English traveller ever admitted to abandoning tea willingly or gladly.

Most travellers from Britain as a whole attached more importance than did Smith to their tea-drinking habits. For them, the significance of tea went beyond merely its familiar, much-loved aroma and flavour. In the Scotsman G. Combe's view, tea-drinking was a great enhancer of sociability. He noted how the absence of tea-drinking on the Continent made entering societies there difficult for British travellers. When explaining why he and his wife made no progress at getting into German society, for example, he remarked, 'The Germans... drink no tea... They cannot ask us to dinner, nor to tea... nor can we ask them to tea.'[12] English travellers were more apt to emphasize the importance of tea for domesticity. Along with the hearth, tea and the tea-kettle symbolized the warm, nurturing domestic life so highly valued by the English. Thus faced with an absence of kettles in France, Matilda B. Edwards daydreamed of cosy English firesides and remarked, 'What a homely poetry is awakened in every English heart at the hissing of the tea-kettle.'[13] Linder experienced the same 'homely' feeling at a Welsh inn when the proprietor served tea after dinner. He associated the beverage with a cosy, curtain-drawn environment shielding the sipper from the outside world. In his words, 'It is indeed a comfort when the evening is cold and wet to draw the curtain, light the candles, and leisurely indulge in a good cup of that refreshing beverage which cheers but not inebriates.'[14] Tea and kettles were so adored by the English as to be thought of as much-loved family members. Frederick Faber, for example, declared a familial affection for the drink after hearing an Italian doctor speak of it positively. The doctor explained that the English in Italy were more immune than coffee-drinking Italians from ague because they retained their 'national habit of scalding themselves internally with tea'. Faber confessed in a letter, 'I could have hugged him; hearing the praises of tea is like listening to a eulogy on one's parents or brothers.'[15]

Although considered less homely and generally wholesome, beer was the other drink favoured by the British. This liking was not new in the Victorian period. Eighteenth-century prints depicted a hearty John Bull fortified by generous quantities of roast beef and beer. Unlike tea-sipping, beer-drinking was not thought of as a peculiarly British national habit. A taste for beer transcended national boundaries much like Protestantism. In fact, the writer and traveller Henry Barlow posited a direct link between beer and Protestantism as he stood in a gallery admiring Luther's stoneware drinking mug. It occurred to him that the Protestant English, Dutch and Germans were all known for their beer-drinking, and he explained the phenomenon by suggesting that *'Luther set the example'*.[16]

Aversions to culinary practices are just as revealing of national habits and values as preferences for specific food and drink items. Journals by Scottish and English travellers rarely have anything good to say about the sauces bathing many Continental dishes. They were associated with deviousness designed to hide substandard fare. One travel writer advised against tasting mysterious sauces and singled out the 'dark glutinous' ones as particularly dangerous. He told of his experience at a celebrated French hotel when a waiter encouraged him to order a special *plat très excellent*. The plate arrived full of a dark suspicious-looking sauce that seemed to cover 'a pair of brown kid gloves'. Much to his horror, the gloves turned out to be pig's ears.[17] This startled visitor and many other travellers from England and Scotland proclaimed proudly the virtues of their natural, sauce-free style of cooking. In Britain unlike on the Continent, travellers argued, the meat was of such high quality and cooked with such care that it was served simply so as to maximize its natural flavour. Only Welsh travellers expressed criticism of meat served in Britain, suggesting either that they did not identify so strongly with this particular dietary item or sought to distance themselves from the English. Welshmen such as Sir Lewis Morris and Sir J.H. Lewis may have been less inclined than Scotsmen to identify with things English because, as we have seen, Wales retained less real institutional independence from England. Morris was born and educated in Carmarthen and eventually became vice-president of the University College of Wales in Aberystwyth. Two years after he was called to the Bar (in 1863), Morris toured Belgium, Holland and the Rhineland area. As he was about to partake of his first dinner aboard a Rhine steamer he exclaimed, 'For a steamboat and recollecting that a dinner on board in England would be simply an abomination consisting of a raw beefsteak... or leg of mutton and capers and strong cheese the spread was really astonishing.' A fellow Welshman was equally unimpressed with meat quality and preparation in England. Comparing the meat offered in English and French hotels he concluded, 'What a difference in food there is between English and French Hotels! The meat has a flavour that one cannot find in the best English hotels.'[18]

The *au naturel* method of cooking meat that most English and some Scottish travellers applauded and identified with had significance in their minds for more than simply the quality of ingredients. It symbolized the honest, sincere nature of Britain's people as well. Travellers often contrasted the 'truthfulness of disposition', 'honesty of purpose' and 'openness of intercouse' characterizing their native people with the hypocrisy of Continental Europeans. In Margaret Law's view, the lack of mutual trust among the Portuguese explained their unpatriotic nature. For her, truth, or sincerity, and patriotism were intimately linked. The Portuguese could not love their country or have faith in their countryfolk because, as she saw it, 'No one [in Portugal] trusts another, and therefore no one thinks it necessary to keep his word.'[19] Miss Taylor and other travellers had a very different impression of the Scots. After visiting several Scottish cottages she noted, 'There is certainly something peculiarly striking in the manners and conversation of the Scotch. They evince much sincerity and honesty.'[20] Mrs Ellis thought the English especially displayed a high regard for truth in social and domestic life and that this quality formed 'the only true basis of national and individual greatness.'[21] Gerald Newman was the first scholar to note the centrality of sincerity for English national identity. He argued that by the Victorian period, people believed sincerity to be *the* English national trait. By sincerity, English artists and writers meant innocence, honesty, originality, frankness and moral independence as opposed to the artful, deceptive, conventional, imitative qualities thought to characterize Continental Europeans, particularly the French. Travel journals, especially those by English travellers, express this sincere ideal most clearly when meat is the topic of discussion. But they also suggest that sincerity was a quality perceived to be characteristic not only of the English, but also of the Scots.

In addition to avoiding sauces, British plain-style cooking and eating involved keeping varied flavours separate and shunning pungent tastes, especially onion and garlic. Being somewhat compartmentalized, British taste buds recoiled from mingling such things as sweets and sours, several vegetables in one dish, or different types of drink. German cooking offended M.F. Tupper with its typical medleys of sweets and sours. He complained of the roast fowls and stewed prunes, ducks and preserved apricots, and beef and cherries typically served at the *tables d'hôte*. As if these combinations were not violation enough of his sense of culinary order, he then had to endure 'vegetables served together, peas, minced cabbages, and potatoes, etc.'. The whole experience led him to declare sarcastically, 'I should never wonder to see onions stewed in sugar, candied oysters, and strawberries *à l'huile.*'[22] Even without sugar, onions were not a favourite flavouring device among the British. They regarded it as no compliment to say of a dish that it tasted of onions. Hence Martha Lamont's astonishment at discovering that the French prepared and seemed to relish a soup cooked of onions alone. Garlic was the target of even greater condemnation in travel journals. Whether as a flavour in food or an odour on the breath, it was considered an affront to British sensibilities. Perhaps the largely indoor life of people in Britain rendered them less tolerant of pungent foods and spices than people on the Continent who lived more in the open air.

Most travellers from Britain thought their natural, unspiced cooking was superior to what they found on the Continent. The English in particular also took great pride in the quantities of food eaten in their native land. Hearty English meals symbolized the prosperity of England and contrasted, in travellers' minds, with the infinitesimal portions and dainty eating found on the Continent. That disparager of dark sauces warned travellers about to leave England that they would be exchanging 'the substantial, salutary, and ample diet of "good old English fare" for the "airy nothings" of cookery that sets off bad meat with high-sounding names'.[23] Charles Wood's eating experiences in Holland reinforced this view. Even when he encountered food and drink items associated with the English, they were served in a stinting way that seemed very foreign to him. In Hoorn, for example, tea was a staple beverage as it was in England. The tea-sets, however, were so different as to shock Wood and his family. Instead of the 'substantial vessels' they were accustomed to in England, the tea cups in Hoorn were handleless and no larger than eggshells. The teapot was correspondingly tiny such that, in Wood's words, 'The whole equipage would have served to furnish a large doll's house.' A cheese sandwich he ordered in Rotterdam seemed similarly dainty and lacking in substance. Instead of 'cutting their cheese in thick, sensible, English-like squares', the Dutch decorated the roll with 'transparent slices' of cheese.[24]

The Scots also identified themselves with heartiness and prosperity, but tended to do so by referring to human and animal body sizes rather than to the size of food and drink portions at table. This type of measuring mentality appears most clearly in two journals by young Scottish travellers experiencing the Continent for the first time. As with other first-time foreign travellers, they took nothing for granted and thus recorded a wealth of detail about their impressions. One of the travellers was a young woman invited by her sister and brother-in-law to join them in Copenhagen. She had not been on the Continent long when she expressed regret that Continental men were 'so small' compared to 'our tall, vigorous Scotsmen'.[25] John Dunlop had similar thoughts as he made his way from Boulogne to Paris where he was to study medicine. He observed the countryside and people carefully, noting how the latter seemed pleasantly cheerful, contented and civil. But despite the apparent contentment, Dunlop was struck more strongly by the 'uncomfortable emptiness' characterizing everything he saw. As he explained it:

> The men were thin, and thinly clothed; the cows lean and miserably small, the horses small, and ill-cared for and even the pigs seem to participate in this universal dearth of 'substantiality' to use an odd phrase... pigs they certainly were, but our common saying 'as fat as pigs' would not by any means apply to them, for they were miserably lean and the idea of eating them was far from pleasant.[26]

The depiction is reminiscent of Hogarth's prints representing everything English as substantial and all things French as enervated and emaciated, suggesting that this national imagery and language of 'substantiality' were as popular in Scotland as in England.

Journals of tours to the Continent are full of comments regarding food and drink that reveal a mostly British dimension when it came to travellers' taste buds. When travelling around Britain, on the other hand, journal writers were less inclined to offer remarks about food, perhaps because their sense of taste was less often startled or offended. An exception occurs in journals by English travellers who ventured north of the Tweed. They complained about the bread found in all parts of Scotland. Typically purchased rather than baked at home, it seemed to the English to be both too heavy and too sour. One traveller's taste buds became especially exasperated in the Highlands where he expressed the wish that 'English cooks' would teach their culinary skills to the local population. A kale pot perceived to be bubbling with broth, mince, haggis and vegetables prompted the wish. In his view, the pot contents 'with Southern stomachs are just the things to make a rout, [e]specially when aided, by their atrocious bread, [m]ore sour than very nice; – heavier than lead.'[27] His comments reflect English people's aversion to and suspicion of Scotch broth. Murray's guide to Scotland warned its mostly English readers somewhat sympathetically that, when touring north of the Tweed, they would have to 'put up with Scotch broth'. In consuming such broth, one of the things they would be putting up with was cuts of meat viewed as 'inferior' to those for roasting so popular in England. Along with heaviness, salt and acid had something to do with English dislike of Scottish bread, and vice versa. The average salt in bread doughs in England was 3.5–5 lb per sack of 280 lb. of flour, while in Scotland the average was often as high as 8 lb.[28] The Scots also used longer fermentation periods when preparing bread, increasing its acidic flavour. These differences explain why the English found Scottish bread salty and sour, and the Scots detected hardly any taste at all in English bread.

Along with customs surrounding food and drink, those concerning manners sharpened travellers' sense of national identity. The term 'manners' is interpreted broadly here to include general demeanour, body language and stylized behaviours sanctioned by society. Touring the Continent highlighted in travellers' minds a certain English quality. That quality was an arrogant bearing reflected most obviously by English tourists' refusal both to defer to and to try to understand other people's customs. Instead, they typically turned up their noses at foreign dishes and habits, seldom made any effort to speak a foreign language and congregated almost exclusively with other English folk while travelling in foreign lands. Gissing deemed them 'Fools! Fools!' for doing so, suggesting that not all English people considered this form of arrogance a virtue. It is true that Gissing was more likely to display a condescending attitude towards his own countryfolk, than towards foreigners. But other English journal writers wrote about their native people's aloofness and arrogance as well. Nona Bellairs described the English as snail-like, travelling through foreign lands as if with a house on their back to provide shelter from anything strange and unfamiliar. Given the English passion for reading and travelling, Eleanor Price found it amazing that, at the end of the nineteenth century, the English were still so blinded by their own prejudices as to be incapable of understanding others. As she put it,

> It is almost as rare now as fifty years ago to meet with an English person who understands the French, or is even fair enough to confess that he does not understand them. And we are much more arrogant in our remarks than they in theirs. They laugh at us; we snarl at them.[29]

Nearly 50 years earlier the first Murray guide to France warned its English readers of their bad reputation on the Continent. They were thought to be arrogant and disinclined to show respect for customs and beliefs different from their own. In Catholic churches, for example, they displayed a lack of consideration by talking aloud and stamping their feet during services.

This perceived arrogance may have had something to do with the very reserved behaviour that nearly all travellers from Britain identified with. In their journals, they used the term 'reserved', but also 'stiff', 'cold', 'sullen' and 'shy' to describe the generally emotionless demeanour that set them off collectively from Continental Europeans. A variety of experiences underscored this British tendency to maintain distance and to keep feelings private. Soon after arriving at Calais, Lady Campbell-Bannerman and her husband ignored friendly gestures from the French and chose to keep to themselves. As they rode the train to Amiens, a French couple tried to engage them in converstion, but to no avail. Lady Campbell-Bannerman confessed, 'We stupidly and English like did not meet them halfway so very little conversation passed betweeen us.'[30] Conversation was scarce at *tables d'hôte* as well when the diners were mostly British. When they were mainly French or German, however, travel journals noted repeatedly, and with some disdain, how the table conversation never ceased. Martha Lamont actually lost her appetite during her first dinner at a Parisian boarding house because of the energetic conversation and annoying animation. 'What distorting of faces, shrugging of shoulders, tossing of arms, slapping of hands! What jumping up and sitting down!', she recorded in her journal. To settle her stomach, she 'remembered the perfect silence of an English boarding-school dinner' and proceeded to pick at her food.[31] She would have felt equally out of place at a Continental railway station where the theatrical, demonstrative behaviours were surprising to British travellers. Standing at the station in Sens, the Yorkshire woman Jemima Morrell admitted,

> You might travel the length of Great Britain and yet never see the semi-theatrical yet joyous meeting and greeting between Monsieur and Madame, on the latter leaving the station, as they kissed each cheek repeatedly then kissed again, the same repeated with compound interest on *le petit enfant*![32]

In short, there was a warmth and exuberance about social exchanges on the Continent that nearly all travellers recognized as very un-British.

George Combe thought that an inability among the Scots and English to sympathize with others' vivid feelings was responsible for the reserved British manner.[33] He expressed this view while watching the public behaviour of two German newlyweds. They were always placed together at parties, according to Combe, where she '[hung] on his arm and [smiled] in his face with the most undisguised satisfaction'. Much to the Scotsman's surprise, the couple's friends did not regard this overt expression as indelicate or wrong, but rather sympathized with the young bride's emotions. Thinking of similar couples in Edinburgh, Combe indicated how unlikely it would be for them to engage in such public displays of affection. 'If they did,' he declared, 'their manners would be censured.' Combe went on to justify this aversion to public display by citing Chesterfield who advised never to manifest any emotion in company unless all present could sympathize with the sentiment. According to Combe, people in England (presumably used here for England and Scotland), unlike those in Germany, typically would 'not sympathize with the emotions of a young couple vividly in love' and thus such couples restrained their feelings when in public. Combe did admit to envying the ease with which Germans entered into sympathy with the feelings of others, especially in this case when the sentiments were so 'natural, virtuous, and happy'.

Travellers from Scotland and England did not identify any more strongly with the familiarity of manner between servants and employers and that between parents and children on the Continent. Mrs Ellis declared the former to be 'rather startling to our English reserve'.[34] Instead of keeping their distance as was usual in Britain, explained Ellis, servants in France felt free to come often into your room to chat or to impart the news. Equally free relations existed between parents and children, much to British travellers' surprise. During her stay in France, the playful antics between a father and his sons caused Mrs Craik to remark,

> In England, and especially in Scotland, however deep and tender the love, there is always a certain distance kept up. Now these lads played tricks with their father that would have made a British parent's hair stand on end with horror, fondling over him the while with a kind of rough caressing that was queer, certainly, to us undemonstrative islanders.[35]

Violations of the British sense of distance could not only startle and surprise travellers, but make them feel extremely uncomfortable as well. German body language during serious conversation caused Mary Shelley to squirm and to long desperately to run away. It seemed to her that the Germans could argue only if they rested a hand on their listener's shoulder and drew their face close to the other's. This sort of posturing was far too intimate for the British, whose sense of personal space required more distance between persons.

House names also reveal the British desire to keep feelings private, at least when compared with names in Holland. In naming their country houses, Dutch merchants tended to opt for emotionally charged phrases such as 'Beyond Expectation', 'Our Contentment', 'Pleasure and Rest', 'My Desire Satisfied' or 'Joy and Peace'. Travellers sometimes made fun of these names which seemed too suggestive of the occupants inside. In Britain, by contrast, typical house names like 'Chatsworth', 'Belle-vue', 'Cedars', 'Towers' or 'Wave Crest' were impersonal and lacking in any expression of sentiment.[36] In Germany, the toy shops rather than the houses brought British reticence to mind. While looking over the toys in a Frankfurt shop, Miss Edwards noted how comical they were. She and her travelling companion could not help laughing no matter which direction they turned, something they would never have been inspired to do by the toys back home. The experience sent her away wondering, 'How is it that the Germans manage to throw so much fun into their toys? Our English dolls, dolls' houses, and ships, are as stiff as possible, and cannot possibly be laughed at. Here everything cracks a joke with you.'[37] Her musings suggest that children in Britain were groomed from an early age in the 'stiffness' of manner that would be expected of them in adult life.

Some travellers not only recognized reserved, stiff manners as a British national trait, they criticized them as well, especially after an extended stay across the Channel where social relations were so much warmer and more congenial. Following her Alpine tour, Sophia Holworthy concluded, 'The kindly interchange of combined familiarity and respect between masters and servants, which you see abroad, is far pleasanter and more human, than the silent coldness we maintain.'[38] Relations between social equals in Britain seemed similarly formal and frigid and thus unattractive to Hugh Jerningham. He confessed, 'How striking, how little attractive is that innate reserve and sullenness so peculiar to Englishmen, in which we... entrench ourselves against every possibility of extending our acquaintance with our fellow-creatures, by any other than the formally accredited medium of personal presentation.'[39] His first meeting with a group of Frenchmen at a fête rendered his countrymen's reserve all the more unattractive. As a total stranger, he was immediately put at ease by a genuine warmth and kindness that he admitted would never be bestowed on one of them visiting England. Explaining the difference, he maintained that the English were much too shy to put a stranger at ease by being truly easy and congenial themselves.

Perhaps this shyness helps explain why the British attached such importance to formal behavioural rituals, or what Lord Chesterfield termed the 'graces'. These graces inspired confidence about how to behave in specific situations and thus obviated the need to rely on feelings and spontaneity as a guide to behaviour. We can sense the degree of importance placed on these rituals by looking at Margaret Fountaine's reactions to Italian behaviour. Fountaine felt so out of place in her native England, that she left it for good at an early age to pursue a wandering life. When she was not chasing butterflies, she was attempting to lure attractive men. Few Victorian women from Britain flouted convention so completely as she did. But despite all the overt iconoclasm and attempts to shed her national identity, Fountaine carried with her the British high regard for formal behavioural rules. During a romp through Italy, she received a postcard from the father of an Italian friend. The man's son had been hiking in the mountains with Fountaine and was experiencing snow blindness. After reading the postcard Fountaine exclaimed, 'As to Papa Bruno, I hardly knew what to think of him, signing himself with affectionate salutations on a postcard, and *no* acquaintance!'[40] If Fountaine maintained respect for such etiquette, how much more strongly must her more conventional countryfolk have deferred to them. Conduct and etiquette books detailing proper behaviour certainly flooded the British market in the late eighteenth and nineteenth centuries.

It might seem that this reverence for formal behavioural rules contradicted the sincere ideal so central to British identity. How could people be truly sincere if their behaviour conformed to convention instead of to their own internal feelings? Writers of conduct and etiquette books did not recognize this contradiction because they identified sincerity as the underlying principle of their behavioural code.[41] That is, they grounded their behavioural rules in unchanging moral principles and social ethics rather than in the fickle dictates of fashion based on a select group of people's momentary whims. Conduct and etiquette arbiters regarded fashionable mores as inherently deceptive and insincere because conducive to imitativeness and a reverence for public approbation rather than innerdirectedness. Their morally charged behavioural conventions were thus an attack on the other-directedness of fashion and a plea for moral independence – a central component of the sincere ideal. In this case, it is the meaning people invested in behavioural rules rather than the rules themselves that confirms the centrality of sincerity as a British ideal.

British travellers' preoccupation with formality and their lack of ease in social settings made them feel less truly well mannered than

Europeans. They recognized that a roughness of exterior and an absence of grace and gentleness characterized their countryfolk. Robert Louis Stevenson used the terms 'abrupt' and 'uncouth' to describe his native Midlothian manners. According to Charles Wood, English people were just as lacking when it came to a gentle courtesy of manner. Only those men and women wealthy enough to have spent considerable time outside England had the advantage, in Wood's view, of having 'their national traits and reserve and a certain uncongeniality of manner softened down by frequent intercourse with other nations, and the enlargening influences of travel.'[42] The British lack of gentleness was most apparent in their treatment of those they perceived as beneath them in the social scale. George Borrow thought his countrymen's greatest foible was their tendency to be 'extremely insolent to those whom they considered below them'. Other travellers contrasted the gentle and affectionate attitude towards the aged and the poor in France with the cold, stern treatment in Britain symbolized by the workhouse.

Some travellers believed that the lack of warmth and respect shown to the lower orders in Britain explained, in part, why this group displayed little affinity for politeness as compared to their Continental counterparts. According to James Cobbett, labourers in Europe were too decent in their demeanour to deserve the terms such as ' "swinish multitude" ' and ' "basest populace" ' applied to the same group in Britain. It seemed to most travellers that ill-mannered, vulgar behaviour by the 'people' or 'working classes' was a national trait in Britain. While attending a celebration for the patron saint of Bagnères de Bigorre, Mary Eyre asked, 'Why is it that the English working classes are so much more clumsy and vulgar than French people of the same rank?'[43] The Scotswoman Janet Robertson thought the labourers of Edinburgh were 'without principle' and 'without feeling' and that their coarseness and public 'ferocity' were attributable to high levels of intoxication. Drunkenness was apparently no excuse for bad manners in France. In fact, Miss Carne commented that too many drinks tended to produce in French country people 'exaggerated demonstrations of politeness' much preferable to 'the coarse oath and rough blow' typically encountered back home.[44]

There were travellers who found fault with Continental manners and thought those in their native land much superior. But the faults tended to involve bodily habits and matters of refinement rather than exchanges between human beings. For example, an advice book on travel warned readers about foreigners' knife and fork rituals. Singled out for discussion was the all-too-common table habit of employing a fork tine to remove troublesome scraps of food or fibres from the teeth.

Spitting on the ground at the *table d'hôte* was just as common in Europe and even more unacceptable to the British. Landlords sometimes begged patrons to refrain from spitting when there were 'English' at the table. Fanny Kemble's disgust in France was not confined to *table d'hôte* meals. No matter what the occasion, she noted disapprovingly, a Frenchman 'hawks and spits close to your cheek, blows his nose like a trumpet in your ear, and yawns and coughs under your nose.'[45] Some travellers explained this casualness about bodily functions as resulting from the warmer Continental climate. In their view, sunshine encouraged a love of ease conducive to 'a thousand little slovenlinesses most revolting to an English eye'. Unkempt hair and half-covered feet were two such vulgarities inducing a smug sense of refinement in travellers from Britain. Thus we might say that travellers identified behaviours combining refinement and reserve as typically British.

In some cases journal remarks about manners have implications for recreational activities, the third category of customs reinforcing a sense of national identity among travellers. It is clear from discussions on the rowdiness and bad manners of the British populace that drinking to excess was indulged in often enough to be considered a national pastime. Drunkenness was so common in Britain as to be designated 'the great sin of our great cities' and 'that great curse of our population' by two travellers.[46] Journals suggest that Europeans consumed large quantities of drink, but did so quietly and without giving offence. Their civility sharpened travellers' awareness of the vulgar British way of drinking as if the goal were to get loud and rowdy. On the streets and at fairs in Britain drunkenness and blackguardism were common and very visible. Public festivities in Italy were thus a surprise to George Gissing who declared, 'Ever since I came to Italy I have not seen one drunken man, not one.'[47]

Many travellers found it refreshing to see so many Europeans able to amuse themselves in public without getting tipsy. Perhaps the British drank to excess because they were not as adept at amusing themselves naturally while in a sober state. Travel journals certainly suggest a deficiency in this area, as if amusement and pleasure aroused twinges of guilt in the British. After attending a carnival in Italy, J.R. Green commented on the joyousness characterizing the revellers. Their naturally fun-loving spirit contrasted markedly in his mind with the typical crowd at an English fair whose fun and amusement had to be artificially created, not only by alcohol, but also by such 'complicated apparatus' as clowns, moveable theatres, vans with fat women and two-headed calves. Summing up the difference between English and Italian festivals, Green remarked, 'An English peasant goes to be amused, and the clown finds it wonderfully hard work to amuse him. The peasant of Italy goes to Carnival to amuse himself.... He is full of joyousness and fun ... is himself the fun of the fair. His neighbour does precisely the same.'[48] Travelling in Portugal, Margaret Law concluded that the rigorous work schedule in England accounted for people's inability to amuse themselves. Unlike the Portuguese, the English worked too much, in her view, and were thus too weary to relax and enjoy their leisure time. Admittedly, the southern Europeans were renowned for their pleasure-loving cultures, but even the Germans seemed more amenable to relaxing and having fun than the English. Watching evening strolls in the gardens of Germany, Charles Wood thought them more lighthearted than any entertainments in England. People walked, sat on benches, talked and listened to music in such an easy, carefree manner, that Wood noted, 'The English do not understand amusing themselves after this manner; they are more heavy even than the Germans, at any rate in their recreations.'[49]

Although Scottish and English travellers both identified rowdy recreational drinking by the masses as national traits, they drew a distinction between their two countries when it came to mind-enhancing leisure activities among the lower orders. On his travels through Scotland, particularly its major cities, Revd. Trench was struck by the vast number of libraries, bookshops and publishers as compared to England. They touched the lives of all classes in Scotland, as the well-stocked bookshelves of even the poorer cottages revealed. Trench noted how the humblest domestic libraries and the common people's conversation reflected an intellectual calibre higher than that among the same group in England. Thinking of sermons, he realized that they, too, were much more argumentative and intellectually sophisticated in Scotland. Miss Taylor was also impressed with the enthusiasm for reading among all classes in Scotland. In her words,

> The Scotch are well educated and fond of reading. I have seen the carmen pull out a book and read while waiting for their company and others reading as they walk along. There is a steadiness in the countenances and manner of the middle order of men... an address and phraseology superior to the same class of our people – amongst all classes, even the poorest, there is a readiness to communicate information, or answer questions.[50]

The mental acuity of Scotland's masses stood out as a distinguishing national characteristic in Hugh Miller's mind as he encountered the

English populace during his first trip south of the Tweed. Of the common people in England he said,

> I have no hesitation in affirming, that their minds lie much more profoundly asleep than those of the common people of Scotland. We have no class north of the Tweed that corresponds with the class of ruddy, round-faced, vacant English, so abundant in the rural districts, and whose very physiognomy... indicates intellect yet unawakened. The reflective habits of the Scottish people have set their stamp on the national countenance. What strikes the Scotch traveller in this unawakened class of the English, is their want of curiosity.[51]

Frances Mackenzie felt a similar pride in the awakened minds of the Scottish masses as she travelled through Belgium admiring the Meuse scenery. Comparing her poorer countryfolk to the local inhabitants along the Meuse, she exclaimed, 'How many little things in these lands remind one of the gratitude too often alas! forgotten, which one *ought* to feel for the privilege of being born in a land where a more moral and intellectual training enlarges and refines the minds of the lower classes.'[52]

In mentioning education, Taylor identified a key difference between Scotland and England.[53] Scotland placed more emphasis on education, particularly of the poor and the lower middle classes. Scottish Reformation leaders outlined a national system of schools to include a school at every church, a schoolmaster in every village and a college in each notable town. Although the plan was not implemented at the time, it did lead to a significant expansion of education in the seventeenth century, with an emphasis on providing a school in every parish. In 1696 the Scottish Parliament passed an Act for the Settling of Schools, stating that Scottish landowners were to build a school in their parish if one did not already exist. A rate on landed property was to provide the funds, and Kirk presbyteries were to inspect the schools, whose main function was to teach literacy skills to all. In addition, parish schoolmasters were expected to teach Latin to those boys wishing to attend university. At the opening of the nineteenth century, Scotland's four universities were cheaper and had a more open admissions policy than Oxford or Cambridge.

The 1696 Act remained the basis of Scottish education legislation until 1872. It helped sustain the belief that Scottish education was uniquely democratic, despite the fact that the Act did not apply to cities where educational provision became increasingly inadequate as the urban population swelled in the nineteenth century. Nevertheless, by the mid-nineteenth century when literacy was first measured by the signature test, Scotland had a literacy rate of 89 per cent for men and 77 per cent for women, compared to 70 per cent and 59 per cent for England and Wales.[54] With the passing of the Education (Scotland) Act in 1872, education became compulsory for all Scottish children between the ages of 5 and 13. Parliament was slower to compel parents to send their children to school in England and Wales. The 1870 Education Act was an enabling Act; it did not make schooling compulsory. Not until 1880 did it become compulsory in England and Wales, at that time for all children until the age of 10. In 1893 the school leaving age was raised to 11, to 12 in 1899, and to 14 in 1918. At secondary level, one Scottish child in 200 received some education by the late nineteenth century. This figure may not seem impressive until compared with that for England where it was 1 in 1,300.[55] Thus although Scottish and English writers may have exaggerated the democratic nature of Scottish education, the above figures suggest that Scottish schools were more successful than their English counterparts at providing a basic education for all social classes.

The type of education offered in Scottish and English schools differed as well. Scottish education was much more authoritarian and based on learning by rote, with very little attention given to moulding character. Unlike the English, who tended to value education as a means for developing character and conferring social status, the Scots valued it as practical training for a vocation or occupation. Scottish schools, influenced no doubt by this preference for the practical and a strict Calvinist religiosity, thus discouraged an interest and education in the arts. The Scotsman William Baxter's vehement criticism of the Young Englanders reflects the high value placed in Scotland on reflective and useful activities as opposed to the arts.[56] He took the group to task for its belief that social stability could best be achieved by encouraging amusements and fine arts among the masses rather than 'useful' arts. By 'useful' he meant those arts cultivated in reading rooms, literary clubs and machine shops for which Scotland was particularly known. He warned 'Old England' that books, ships and machine shops were infinitely more beneficial to a nation's well-being than frivolous amusements or fine arts like painting and sculpting. Throughout the nineteenth century and into the twentieth, the Scots accorded higher status than did the English to technical, practical studies.

Travellers rarely noted any distinctly Welsh form of recreation. When they did, singing was the activity mentioned. Travellers sometimes remarked on how the Welsh seemed to enjoy singing during religious services. One journal commented on the pride a local guide took in Welsh minstrelsy. He thought it superior to any other, and was happy to demonstrate by singing a native tune half in Welsh, half in English. Poetry and music had long been the focus of popular and elite culture in Wales. Eisteddfodau, or competitions for Welsh poets and musicians, have a long history. Heated disputes between Welsh bards were recorded as early as the sixth century, with the first formal competition, or eisteddfod, occurring at Cardigan in 1176. Such formal competitions took place until the sixteenth century, when the Anglicization of the Welsh gentry led to a decline in the prestige of Welsh language and culture. Although unofficial bardic contests continued in pubs and alehouses, it was not until 1789 that a formal eisteddfod was organized once again. Inspired by the nationalism and ideals of the French Revolution, patriotic societies of London Welshmen put together this first modern bardic competition at Corwen in Denbighshire. Regional eisteddfodau have been popular since the late eighteenth century, with over 500 eisteddfodau occurring in the nineteenth century, including an annual National Eisteddfod for the whole of Wales. In 1863, the president of the National Eisteddfod commented on the recreational passions and pleasures of various national and regional groups, including the Welsh. He imagined the English to display a passion for horseracing, the French a passion for dancing and the Highlanders a passion for reels, sword dancing and pitching the caber. Proclaiming his respect for these various passions, he asked that other people respect the Welsh 'national passion for the Eisteddfod'. In explaining this passion he declared, 'We Welsh are an impulsive, impassioned people, proud of our country and all that belongs to it. From the very earliest traditions... it will be found that we have been fondly attached to poetry and music.'[57]

Murray's *Handbook for Travellers in South Wales* characterized the Welsh in just the same way as did this Welsh patriot.[58] That is, it depicted the Welsh as 'a kindly, generous, and impulsive race' with a love for music and 'a lively imagination and poetic temperament'. Furthermore, the Welsh had a strong sense of themselves as a nation, with the Eisteddfodau serving to preserve 'the germ of nationality which is such a distinguishing feature in Welsh character'. But accompanying these guidebook remarks were highly critical and condescending comments about the Welsh, which help explain, perhaps, the Welshman's plea for respect of Welsh national passions. This Murray guide to Wales was clearly written for an English audience and from a well-to-do,

English/Anglican point of view. It talked of the 'rude miners' of southern Wales as having recently been 'softened' by the effects of agricultural activities. This 'softening' should be a great source of relief, the guide suggested, to all those 'who remember the lawlessness and ignorance which characterized Chartism'. Commenting on Welsh religiosity, the handbook characterized nonconformity as something to be 'coped with', and it 'feared' that the Church had not made much progress in this regard. This was one reason the Welsh were not to be trusted. In Wales, according to the guide, 'There is often to be met with a sad want of truth and straightforwardness, and a love of prevarication... lack of truthfulness is a fault lamentably prevalent.' Such a view indicates that sincerity was not thought to characterize the Welsh as it was the English and the Scots. The guide thus predisposed its mostly English readers to think of themselves and their recreations as very distinct from the Welsh.

Instead of intellectual and musical leisure pursuits, the English were known for physical recreation in the form of formal exercise or sport. Because of their sporting inclinations, some travellers thought the English looked healthier than peoples elsewhere. Miss Edwards, for example, pointed out how robust and enterprising English girls were compared to the French. She attributed their vigour to regular walking out of doors for health and recreation, something French girls never did. In France, according to Edwards, women might walk to pay visits or to attend Mass, but never simply to exercise the body, for recreational exercise was 'masculine, unwomanly, and eccentric to a feminine French mind'.[59] Law found similar attitudes prevalent among Portuguese girls. They were surprised to hear about the gardening and recreational walking activities of English girls, as gardening and walking for any other reason than to pay visits were unknown to Portuguese women. Law speculated that Portuguese propriety was responsible for the preference for sedentary habits. According to her understanding, it was not considered proper in Portugal for an unmarried lady to be seen without her *duenna* (governess), a view Law described as 'a kind of slavery preventing free exercise'.[60]

But most travel journals suggest that exercise and organized games were not typically indulged in by European males either. Only in England were athletic activities so popular as to be considered an 'obsession'. Of golf, football and cricket, the Englishman I.A.R. Wylie said, 'These are the matters of importance. They fill pages of our newspapers, whose German contemporaries give their space to drama, and art, and literature.'[61] Maggie Browne pointed out that, although German youths played 'ball' and 'touch', they knew nothing of cricket, football or other organized games and 'would do well to learn a few good English outdoor games'.[62] Learning games was an integral part of education in England, at least for boys. To the English, playgrounds were as necessary for developing young men's physiques and team spirit as classrooms were for broadening their minds. In fact, schools often gave priority to playgrounds, with contemporaries pointing out how dingy classrooms contrasted strongly with superbly kept cricket grounds. This passion for playgrounds was uppermost in E.V. Lucas's mind as he wandered through Holland, particularly its meadows. Imagining how the landscape would change if the English ever conquered the country, he wrote, first of all, of how meadows full of cattle would quickly be transformed into athletic grounds. Though a deliberate exaggeration, the image captures the importance attached in England to a strenuous, athletic outdoor life as if nature were meant to be merely a 'background for sport'.[63]

Climate in England may have contributed to this emphasis on organized outdoor exercise. The few short periods of the year when warm, dry days could be counted on no doubt encouraged people to make the most of them by engaging in strenuous, well-planned activities. To live and relax outdoors in the way Continental Europeans did as if the open air were an extension of domestic space was very foreign to people from all parts of Britain. Scottish and English travellers often commented on the differences in attitude towards public, outdoor life on the two sides of the Channel. An English brother and sister staying in the Aveyron area of France summed up the contrast best. Though the locals were enamoured of the outdoor life, they argued, it was 'not the active, boating, tennis-playing, cricketing, and generally athletic existence to which we English are addicted'. It was, instead, a 'sit-outside-under-the-shade-with-one's-work-or-cup-of-coffee kind of life' to which they were attracted. One might use the less cumbersome phrase 'outdoor domesticity' to describe the life. Whatever the phrase, it was a style of life the British did not understand or find attractive. Seeing people relax oudoors in public by sipping, sitting, conversing, knitting, reading or doing any other activity frequently performed indoors made the British uncomfortable. They felt as if they were 'intruding [themselves] into other people's private affairs'.[64] In their view, such activities should occur in a private garden if engaged in out of doors. The many more restaurants on the Continent suggest that private dining was preferred in Britain as well. Even celebrating a national triumph in public was something the British did only haltingly. Just after hearing good news from the Crimea, Eliza Salvin attended a celebratory street procession in Paris where, much to her surprise, soldiers fraternized with the crowd. When someone suggested to her that surely there would be similar revelling in London, she followed up her positive response with the qualification, 'It takes English people a much longer time to get ready to rejoice publicly, however.'[65]

Except when exercising or playing sports which of necessity occurred outdoors, people in Britain tended to spend their leisure time in the privacy of their gardens and especially of their homes. Whereas in Europe people socialized after work in cafés or while strolling the streets, in Britain they were much more likely to gather around private firesides. Thomas Smith stated the centrality of home life for Englishness when he wrote,

> No other nation has accepted the home as the foundation of national life to the same degree as England; no other nation esteems the influences of home higher than the English; in no other land is it so easy to found a home, and nowhere else does the law protect the home as in England, which deserves the title – the Home of Homes.[66]

Other travel journals concur with Smith's view and are often critical of the passion for public places so prevalent on the Continent. Mrs Ellis found it remarkable that no word existed in the French language synonymous with the English word 'home' which had such a hold over the hearts of her nation. Disapproving of those who forsook the hearth for public haunts, she declared, 'Certainly there must be some national or constitutional defect in the habits of a people, who seek their amusement and their interest any where rather than at home.'[67] According to Talfourd and Mayhew, the defect was a moral one. Both travellers argued that the unhappy children's faces and lack of discipline they witnessed on the Continent stemmed from an absence of home life and the moral guidance it alone could provide. This moral guidance which, 'to the pride of every Englishman, is found alone in his own country', was more important to the English than all the learning and scholastic lessons of the classroom.[68]

The Scotsman James Smith thought the idea of and reverence for home as private domestic space were common throughout Britain. In his view, 'Home. Home. It is the Briton's nest – and he builds his fireside wherever he dwells – In the land of strangers his thoughts always wander Home.'[69] The terms 'nest' and 'fireside' suggest the sort of cosy domesticity that English travellers in particular associated with home. But the last line hints at a different concept of home – one more often found in journals by Scottish and Welsh travellers. The line juxtaposes a 'land of strangers' with 'Home', the latter term implying homeland in this case rather than domestic space. Smith clearly expressed this notion of home as native place when spotting bluebells on the Continent. Recognizing the flower as the same variety commonly found in Scotland, he picked a sample and pressed it into his journal where it still remains to illustrate the text. In describing the specimen he said, 'I was delighted to see it and greeted it at every step as a memento of Home.' When returning home to Wales, W.T. Griffith expressed a similar view of home as a native place full of familiar flora, fauna, sites and memories. In his words:

> At Home! Home! my native place, where in childhood I learned life's first lessons, where I gathered buttercups and daisies, and sat beneath the shady limetrees, making floral coronets.... How these recollections cling to us wherever we go! How sweet and welcome is that which greets our visit to our native place! The very birds and flowers seem to have loving messages, and old scenes and old spots smile at our approach.[70]

English travellers were more likely to associate 'England' rather than 'Home' with certain sites, scenes and flowers, reserving the latter term for their fireside environment.

Interestingly, the cherishing of home coexisted among the English and the Scots with a passion for travelling and a willingness to emigrate to far-flung parts of the globe. One might say that the domestic circle in the two countries functioned as a coherent unit for welcoming in the outside world of friends, but also as a base from which to venture out into the larger world. Many travellers commented on how much more attached Continental Europeans were than the British to their native lands and thus less likely to travel and, especially, to emigrate. In France, for example, emigration was 'a thing to be dreaded – a very last resource'.[71] In this sense, one could argue that Europeans clung tenaciously to their homelands but not to their home space created by walls, a roof and a hearth. Perhaps they did so because they considered home to be the streets, cafés, public gardens, and so forth of their native land rather than the roof under which they typically slept. Similarly, the English and Scottish willingness to be uprooted from their homeland may have had something to do with their concept of home as a particular physical space, or 'nest', one creates and the life generated within it. Such a space could easily be built anywhere in the world, as Smith suggested.

The emphasis placed on home was linked to another value at the heart of Englishness in particular – comfort. Most journals by travellers from England spoke about 'English comforts' as qualities distinct from anything on the Continent or in other parts of Britain. Murray guides warned English travellers bound for other lands that they were the only people who understood the word 'comfort' and would thus need to be equipped with a generous supply of good temper and forbearance. The majority of comforts identified by journal writers as English and as lacking in other countries were domestic ones. Three of those most commonly mentioned were carpets, fires and plenty of hot water for bathing. Contributing to the warmth and snugness of an English home, the first two contrasted with the cold, bare but polished floors and dreary-looking ineffective stoves typical of homes across the Channel. Hotel and inn accommodations outside England caused continual complaints about the inadequate water supply. After numerous outbursts about insufficient water for washing during her trip through America, Fanny Kemble then found the situation equally bad in France. Of her ablutionary opportunities she fulminated:

> [I] find myself now in one of the best hotels in Paris, with a thing like a small cream-jug for a water vessel in my bedroom, and a basin as big as a little pudding-bowl: moreover, when I asked for warm water this morning for my toilet, they produced a little copper pot, with an allowance such as the youngest gentleman, shaving the faintest hopes of a beard, might have found insufficient for his purposes – in short, I believe England is the only place in the world where people are not disgustingly dirty.[72]

Other items categorized as 'English comforts' were curtains, blankets, airy rooms, spring-cushioned sofas, soap in hotel rooms and drains.

Underground pipes were so categorized because of their importance for cleanliness, a key component of English comfort. Whether imagining streets or people, the English thought of theirs as considerably cleaner than everyone else's. *Trottoirs* (pavement for walking) and adequate drains accounted for the cleanliness of English streets, according to travellers. So closely did English travellers associate clean streets with their native land that they assumed any modern drainage on the Continent had been installed to please their countryfolk. The compiler of the Toynbee Travellers' Florence logbook, for example, said of the Italian city, '[It] is so over run with our fellow Countrymen and the drainage has been so far advanced to suit their fastidious requirements that but for the narrow streets, quaint old bridges and the bright blue sky, one might often have felt oneself in an English holiday resort.' The author went on to point out how a visit to Florence by Queen Victoria caused a frenzy of cleaning in the city, and thus she/he called for annual tours of Continental towns by the royal family 'as a philanthropic mission in order to induce foreign governments to disinfect their towns'.[73] This very sporadic cleaning for occasions contrasted markedly in travellers' estimation with daily cleaning in England of houses and other buildings. Journals note how English notions of cleanliness and comfort were reflected in the regular scrubbing of doorsteps and floors. Disgusted with the generations of dirt amidst an abundance of water in the Pyrenean area of France, Mary Eyre recorded, 'It is not the custom to wash the floor of the rooms, or the passages, or the shop floors, or the counters, or tables, or anything that is commonly washed *every day* in England.'[74] Even the floors and stairs of poor labourers in England, travellers emphasized, presented a spotless cleanliness compared to their counterparts' in Europe, or in Scotland for that matter.

The patriotic Toynbee traveller may have exaggerated English countryfolk's influence on Continental street design and cleanliness. It is true that many nineteenth-century urban improvements were pioneered in London.[75] Gas lighting of streets, for example, made its first appearance in London (1812), helping to reduce crime in the city. Other capital cities followed London's example, with Vienna's streets becoming gas-lit by mid-century. London also led the way in sewage removal. In 1844, a public body took control of the city's drainage system. Within 30 years London could boast a more comprehensive drainage system for sewage removal than any other European city. At the time, there were public tours of Paris sewers but not of London's because the former drained surface water but not sewage, which was still removed in carts. Yet by 1888 when the Toynbee travellers went to Florence, Paris not London was the model city – the city of the future – to which others looked when redesigning their cities. This fact was clear to the Parisian Victor Tissot when he visited Vienna in the early 1880s. Looking around the city he concluded smugly, 'Whatever people say, and whatever they do, the influence of Paris reigns supreme.'[76] This influence can be attributed in large part to Baron Georges E. Haussmann and Emperor Napoleon III. Between 1850 and 1872, Haussmann implemented Napoleon III's plans for redesigning France's capital city. The plans included wide, tree-lined boulevards, public parks, sewers for drainage, aqueducts for bringing clean water and improved public transport from the city centre to its outskirts. Made possible by a combination of government money and private capital, these improvements in Paris were copied in the late nineteenth century by other governments and city planners, especially in Vienna. In fact, Paris's influence on Continental urban planning was so great that one scholar coined the verb 'Haussmannize' to sum up what was done to transform cities in Europe during the last quarter of the nineteenth century.

Although the English associated themselves with cleanliness, they did not perceive this quality to be characteristic of people from other parts of Britain. Thus Beatrix Potter described the Scotch as 'a filthy people'. Not only were the rural cottages in Scotland thought to be caked with grime and unpleasantly odorous, but the urban residences as well. Unlike the English, the Scots tended to live in apartments as did most Continental Europeans. This meant that a single building contained several residences, one on each floor, all with a shared staircase. To the English, this style of city living was not conducive to wholesome domestic life or to comfort and cleanliness. The likelihood of carousing neighbours and the existence of three or four kitchens with their clash of steams and smells would threaten, in their view, occupants' moral fibre, not to mention their nasal passages. In explaining how various peoples coped with this inferior living arrangement Miss Carne declared derisively, 'The French live much out-of-doors, the Scotch have no noses.'[77]

In Britain notions of comfort and cleanliness were sometimes vehicles for marking distinctions between classes and ethnic groups even within the main national groups. As he crossed from England into Scotland, Thomas Letts declared, '[T]hey seemed to understand as little as did our Coachman the essentials to make an Englishman even moderately comfortable.'[78] Here the essentials of comfort were imagined to mark Englishmen as distinct not only from the Scots, but also from English servants, both groups being lumped together on the basis of their being ignorant of such essentials. In other cases, Welsh, Scottish and English travellers identified 'Gaels' as the 'Other' when it came to cleanliness and comfort. On his tour of Scotland, the Welsh patriot Henry Richard visited the Ramsays, a wealthy Scottish family living at Kidalton House not far from Glasgow. During an evening stroll around the property, Ramsay gave his visitor a tour of some cottages he had built for his workers. Richard admired the cottages, pronouncing them to be 'very good', despite their surroundings and interiors which seemed 'dirty and untidy'. After noting how Mrs Ramsay complained of not being able to get the occupants to adopt 'clean and orderly habits', Richard went on to explain, 'Most of the inhabitants are Gaels and most of them talk Gaelic.'[79] English travellers to Scotland also associated Gaelic residences with an absence of comfort and cleanliness. After partaking of the lunchtime hospitality of a Gaelic family in the Highlands, an English lady then cast her 'enquiring' eye around the 'dwelling', as if it were on display for her consumption. She found the inside 'barren of interest' because there were 'no curtains... nor anything of ornament or comfort to be seen'. Furthermore, 'dirt and disorder' marked the whole interior which was regularly filled with black smoke due to the lack of a chimney pot. This 'picture' of filthy, unadorned living was 'sometimes completed by a pig or a few fowls strutting into the apartment with an air of consequence as great as that of the *owner* of the cottage as they do in Wales only perhaps a little less fearlessly.'[80] Here Gaelic Highlanders, the Welsh and pompous-looking animals are included in a single disorderly picture from which the English lady very definitely excluded herself.

We have already noted that the cleanliness English people associated with themselves did not extend to England's atmosphere or to the outside of her buildings. In fact, travellers were amazed by the clean, whitewashed building exteriors on the Continent. Perhaps their soot-begrimed building façades inspired more assiduous scrubbing of steps and inside floors. But touring Holland made English travellers recognize certain limitations to their obsession with cleanliness, even regarding domestic interiors. Just as the Dutch were too extremely precise in their controlling of nature for English tastes, they also were too extreme when it came to scrubbing. Every Saturday, they waged a brushing, mopping, scrubbing and scraping war against spiders, spots and grime. In certain rooms, particularly the sitting or drawing room, this cleaning frenzy was followed by a furniture-covering ritual before the door was closed and all left to await next week's burst of brushing. In detailing this Saturday cleaning habit, Murray's guide said somewhat sarcastically, 'The contents of the apartment are worn out, not by use, but by repeated cleanings.'[81] To the English, this Dutch habit was an abuse of domestic furniture which was meant to be used everyday for providing comfort rather than preserved in a pristine state like a museum piece.

In addition to cleanliness, usefulness was part of the English concept of comfort. Whereas English buildings and material objects made travellers think of comfort and utility, Continental ones brought terms such as magnificent, ornamental, tasteful, handsome and beautiful to mind. Elizabeth Carne explained the difference by contrasting 'order' which she associated with England and 'good taste' which she thought prevailed in France. As she understood the terms, order was 'the good taste which belongs to comfort and utility, and good taste the order which belongs to enjoyment and beauty'.[82] Many specific objects and settings including houses, doors, windows, hotel rooms, fountains and libraries reflected, in travellers' minds, the two contrasting value systems. All the marble, lacquer, polish, ormolu and other finery in German houses, for example, seemed chilling to M.F. Tupper and thus very impractical in winter. He admired their beauty, however, concluding, 'Comfort is not the word for continental houses, but magnificence.'[83] Gazing at the front door and windows of an Italian villa inhabited by an English family, Nona Bellairs said it was immediately obvious they had been Anglicized. That is, the doors were designed to admit people but to shut out the cold, and the windows to let air in when open but keep it out when shut. In other words, they functioned properly and thus 'spoke of comfort and usefulness'. Judging by travel journals and guides, most Continental inn and hotel rooms had not been Anglicized. Landlords apparently spent more money on frivolous finery than on practical matters of eating and sleeping. Murray's guide to Holland and Belgium complained of insufficient food at *tables d'hôte* and the flimsiness of partition walls with their 'communicating' doors between bedrooms. Reflecting the English emphasis on comfort and utility, the guide remonstrated, 'Landlords would do well to remember that the traveller cares more for a substantial dinner and a quiet night's rest, than for paint, gilding, and chandeliers.'[84] This same contrast between ornament and utility struck Mary Shelley as she contemplated how the French and the English used water. After wandering around Paris, she decided that fountains symbolized the French and pipes the English. In other words, the French used water ornamentally and thus lacked enough for utility, while the English did just the reverse. Noting how much more cheerful and gay Paris was than London she admitted, 'The *coup d'oeil* of a fountain is more pleasing than the consciousness of a pipe underground.'[85]

Edward Wilberforce explained how libraries embodied similar sorts of national values. During the nineteenth century, national cultures became institutionalized with the emergence of such things as Dictionaries of National Biography, state-financed schools, National Theatres, National Museums and Galleries, and National Libraries. In particular, Wilberforce compared the values embodied by the British Library with those of the main library in Munich. With its domed, well-ventilated room, comfortable chairs, and individual desks complete with book rest and blotting pad, Wilberforce suggested the British Library promoted comfort for readers in every possible way. He did not say the same of the Munich library reading room. The outside was gorgeous with marble steps reminiscent of a palace built for luxury and show. But the inside was, according to Wilberforce, 'low and dark, vaulted like a crypt, with heavy pillars; the fittings consist in two long bare tables, at which everyone reads, without a desk to support books, or any convenience for transcribing.'[86] Thus like houses, fountains, water pipes and hotel rooms, libraries highlighted perceived cultural differences between the English who valued comfort and practicality and the Continental Europeans who cheerfully sacrificed both values for splendour and ornament.

Welsh and Scottish travellers were more apt to criticize things English when it came to comfort. In other words, they thought in terms of English discomforts, and were less likely than the English to identify with the notion of comfort. English travellers rarely had anything positive to say about Continental beds. They complained about the lack of bedsteads with posts and especially about the absence of insulating curtains. The Welshman Lewis Morris had a different view. After a night in a Belgian inn, he spoke of the bed as being 'exquisitely comfortable as only non English beds can be'.[87] As mentioned above, English travellers fulminated against Continental windows for their inability to prevent drafts. For the Scotsman James Smith, on the other hand, it was English windows that seemed inimical to comfort. During a stay in Brussels, he was struck by the 'multiplicity and size of the windows'. The wealth of glass and light caused him to reflect on the relatively windowless buildings across the Channel, and then to denounce the taxes on glass and window light first passed by Parliament in 1695. He recorded, 'It is impossible to reflect on the latter of these taxes without being indignant at the authority which imposed it – there is no question that it operated to reduce our domestic architecture so far as health and comfort are concerned to the same sort of cramped existence as a Chinese lady's foot.'[88] Those taxes were in place from 1695 until 1851, causing people to fill in existing windows and to be very sparing when creating new ones. Touring Britain today, one can still spot eighteenth-century houses with fake windows, designed obviously for the appearance of symmetry rather than the admission of light. Given this practice, it is ironic that Victorian travellers from England were so inclined to find fault with Continental windows for being ineffective.

Taken together, travellers' comments on comfort and manners suggest an interesting paradox. Continental environments, both domestic and public, were perceived to be lacking in warmth and comfort. But the people themselves seemed remarkably warm, comfortable and free-and-easy in their manner. To put the contrast another way, Europeans appeared very willing to sacrifice ease for elegance in furnishings, but refused to renounce any liberties when it came to talking, laughing, frolicking, and so forth. Miss Edwards recognized the contrast clearly when she said of French attitudes, 'The privilege of making as much noise as one pleases is much more valued than that of spacious dining-rooms, easy-chairs, and comfortable sleeping accommodation.'[89] Travellers depicted the English as just the opposite. That is, physical environments in England were warm and comfortable, but the people were cold and ill at ease. Perhaps the English resorted to generating warmth and comfort with external material objects because they felt inadequate at creating them from within by means of their bearing and manner. Thus we might conclude that people on both sides of the Channel valued warmth and comfort, but expressed the qualities in very different ways.

Along with eating and drinking habits, manners, forms of recreation and notions of comfort, rituals of social ranking reinforced people's sense of national identity. Scots and English travellers noted how much more aristocratic and overtly hierarchical society was in Britain than on the Continent. Whereas journal writers sometimes commented on the high regard for democracy and equality in Europe, especially in France, they never used these two terms when imagining Britain. Instead, they described the British as 'aristocratic insulars', 'aristocratical throughout', nestled privately in 'aristocratic secludedness' and stable because devoted to the 'aristocratical principle'. Most travellers spoke positively of aristocratic influence and attributed the squalor they saw in Europe to its absence. Thus Breton country life was, in Matilda Edwards's estimation, very different from anything to be found in England. Villages had an air of squalor and neglect, with dung-heaps near dwellings and bare-footed, dishevelled-looking residents. Alluding to the absence of gentlemen's houses and married clergy, she reasoned, 'Where, indeed, should emulation and improvement come from?'[90] Similarly, Mary Eyre spoke disparagingly of the homes and people in the South of France, noting how every peasant in the area owned his own land. She argued that the tumble-down look would disappear and 'these people would have far more real comfort if the land belonged to intelligent, kind landlords, able to cultivate it properly, and who would take care that the cottages on their estates were well built... fit abodes for human beings.'[91] William Howitt expressed an equally paternalistic view on seeing the rural masses in Germany, most of whom were landowners. At the same time that he recognized how much more free and independent these peasant proprietors were than the typical landless agricultural labourers back home, he maintained that the beneficial influence of wealth, taste and intelligence was missing, unlike in England.

This respect for aristocracy coexisted in Britain with a very visible and seemingly rigid social hierarchy. The high value placed by the British on hierarchy and on maintaining class distinctions is clearly revealed by travellers' surprise at and negative reactions to the mingling of ranks they commonly encountered in Continental countries whether in railway stations, schools, recreational areas or private homes. For example, waiting for trains on the Continent annoyed British travellers because there appeared to be no separation in station waiting-rooms between passengers of different classes. Furthermore, the time spent in a waiting-room could be lengthy, as passengers were prohibited from stepping on to the platform and boarding carriages until just before departure time. In British railway stations, on the other hand, travellers noted approvingly that mixing of classes was minimal because ticket holders could abandon the waiting room for the platform and board their first, second or third class carriage at their leisure. Schools in England also reinforced hierarchy to a greater extent than French schools, in Miss Edwards's view. Pointing out how the English had different schools for professionals, farmers, shopkeepers and the 'people', she added, 'You no more expect to find a rich man's child attending the latter than a chimney-sweeps son at the Grammar School.'[92] Not so in France, where the École Communale dispensed the same education to children regardless of their parents' occupation or bank account.

We have already discussed how a more democratic spirit infused the Scottish education system. It is also true that Scottish travellers were slightly more apt than English ones to criticize behaving and judging others, according to rank. During a tour of Germany, George Combe took the English staying there to task because of their preference for mixing only with locals of the highest rank. He noted how they snubbed middle-class Germans in favour of the highest circles on whom they attempted to force their acquaintance by leaving cards without a prior introduction. Although in their own country these English were 'far below the highest rank', Combe explained that 'their national pride prompts them here to consider themselves as fit associates only for Princesses, Barons, and Counts.' For Combe, this assumption of airs was 'mean and presumptuous', and he refused to behave in such a manner. Leaving no cards with Germans, he and his wife cultivated acquaintances only after meeting them, if they were agreeable *and* 'without any regard to rank'.[93] Furthermore, they purposely sent apologies when invited to a ball at which the Duke of Saxe Weimar and other nobles were to be present, so they could distance themselves from all the English bent on attending simply so they could say they had met the Duke.

Travel journals suggest that hierarchical relations between social groups were most aggressively maintained in Britain at places of amusement and within private homes between employers and servants. Whether at horse races, public gardens, concerts or other entertainment venues open to all, the British arranged prices to ensure a segregation of classes. Europeans were less likely to do so, often charging, except at the opera, only one low price for all. This European pricing practice resulted in a greater mixing of classes which, to Edwards, showed 'how fundamentally democratic is the [French] national character'.[94] Similarly, the Scotsman William Chambers noted with some amazement how the Duke of Nassau, sovereign of a state, mingled with *table d'hôte* guests on Sundays at a popular watering place in Germany. Such encounters, he commented, 'excite no surprise in continental society, in which... there is a familiarity between high and low... that could not for a moment be sanctioned in Britain.'[95] As mentioned above, familiarity characterized relations between employers and servants on the Continent as well, much to British travellers' surprise. The customary demureness and silence of British servants when in the presence of their employers did not exist in Continental households. Instead, servants in Europe regularly exchanged words, smiles, and so forth with their 'masters' as if they were part of the family. Some travellers admitted that carriages travelling European streets with a woman servant in the rumble immediately elicited a 'There go English!' exclamation from the locals.[96] As Martha Lamont explained it, a Continental lady did not consider it in any way degrading to sit beside her maidservant and converse inside a carriage, and thus only rumbles belonging to the British functioned as rank markers.

Rituals of social ranking are sometimes very subtle and thus difficult to interpret, especially if one is observing them in a foreign country. There is no doubt that British travellers perceived their society to be more obsessed than Europe with hierarchy and keeping the classes separate. But in some cases they may have been keying on the absence in Europe of their own familiar ranking rituals and thus been blind to the different ones operating all around them. In European train station waiting-rooms, for example, prosperous middle-class British travellers may have found themselves rubbing shoulders with the garlic-scented masses because they were unaware of the local habit among more well-to-do passengers of arriving by taxi only minutes before departure.[97] Unlike in Britain, it was true in Europe that passengers were prohibited from stepping on to the platform until just before departure time. Thus to avoid mingling with the masses in waiting rooms, first- and second-class passengers sent their servants ahead to buy tickets and negotiate luggage, so all they had to do was make a last-minute appearance for boarding.

A more nuanced view of British attitudes emerges if one combines the above clear-cut depiction of British society as rigidly hierarchical with other less direct comments in travel journals. When travellers talked of population distribution in whole countries as opposed to that at particular public places, they emphasized the greater degree of mixing of social groups in Britain than anywhere in Europe. That is, a population of all classes, richest to poorest, lived throughout the whole of Britain. Unlike in France or Germany, it was impossible to travel for miles through the rural parts of Britain and see only peasant establishments. Houses of gentlefolk and middle-class families dotted the countryside as well, integrating all classes into the local communities. The many mechanisms employed by the British for maintaining lines between classes in public places should be considered in the context of their highly integrated residential communities. They may have been more likely to perceive a need for such mechanisms than were Europeans whose home-based communities were so much more segregated by class.

Travel journals also suggest that hierarchical social relations coexisted in Britain with greater degrees of social ambition. Many travellers sensed that, compared to their own countryfolk, Continental people were without ambition beyond their social stations. The feeling prompted them to remark on how different things were at home where people 'seldom look upon their present position as permanent'.[98] In British society, travellers repeatedly noted, one class continually trod on the heels of another with its members spending beyond their means in an effort to inflate their social worth. When explaining the ease with which Germans of all classes mingled at watering places, Murray's *Handbook* painted a portrait of Germans that clearly set them apart from the social-climbing British. In Germany, the *Handbook* argued, 'not only the privileges of nobility, but of all grades are so clearly understood, and kept distinct, that all parties, however intimate they may seem to be in public, know the exact boundaries of their position in society, and act accordingly.'[99] The portrait suggests that, at least in Germany, rank was so highly internalized and taken for granted that overt methods of segregating social groups were unnecessary. It does not indicate, however, that Germans were more oblivious to hierarchy than the British, but rather that they maintained it in different ways.

What these comments suggest is that travellers imagined Britain's social hierarchy to be, paradoxically, both more fluid and more rigid than that on the Continent. One traveller's journal reveals clearly how this combination of fluidity and rigidity operated, at least at the perceptual level. The traveller is the anonymous woman from England who recorded the 'romantic' adventure at Bracken Bridge.[100] At one point during her tour of Scotland, she saw Lord Glenlyon and a friend walking his dogs in her vicinity. She carefully scanned his physiognomy and gait, and decided that he was handsome and very gentlemanly. Although she did not speak with him, she admitted that, had there been fewer in her party, she would have 'enter'd into conversation with him'. She then went on to justify such familiarity between two people of very different rank. As she saw things, 'My vanity perhaps led me to feel myself on a level with him on the only grounds that ought to equalize matters namely Education and Respectability – And I flatter'd myself that I should have been recognized by a gentleman as a Lady and therefore as his equal.' In other words, when imagining herself in relation to a perceived superior, hierarchy collapsed in her mind, and equality prevailed.

Her perception was very different when she was in the presence of people she regarded as her 'inferiors'. During the same tour, she conversed with a poor Highland family. Given Highlanders 'perfectly uncultivated minds', she was frequently surprised by their 'natural good understanding'. The particular family she met appeared 'more civilized' than most. She described the man as wearing the Highland costume of sandals and kilt, and as doffing his 'bonnet' when she entered his dwelling. His wife – later described as a 'kind hearted hospitable creature' – rose when the traveller appeared, brushed down a chair, and placed it for her to be seated. The same was done for her friend. The couple's four daughters sat by a window that was so small 'it admitted only enough light to make darkness visible'. They sat working despite the darkness, but 'left off work now and then to gaze at each other then at us as tho'' they had never seen a human being above their own standing in the world.' In this case, the hierarchy did not collapse in her mind. She saw herself as superior to these Highlanders, and automatically assumed that they perceived her and her friend as above them in the world. With the Lord, she was able to imagine herself his equal, and assumed he would perceive her as such. There were no grounds for such perceptual fluidity or equality in this case when she was the one with superior rank. Thus notions of social hierarchy were fluid or rigid depending on context.

Context emerges here once again as key to understanding how the rituals of everyday life contributed to a sense of national belonging in Victorian Britain. When travelling on the Continent, men and women were most apt to feel a shared sense of Britishness regarding food and drink, reserve and refinement at least among the middle and upper classes, rowdy drinking among the masses, cosy domesticity and hierarchical social relations. Even in these areas, differences between national groups were apparent. The Scots, for example, seemed less obsessed with hierarchy than the English. Both the Scots and the Welsh, though they identified with cosy domesticity, embraced another concept of home as well – one implying native place rather than fireside and family. Travel around Britain revealed other qualities highlighting distinctions between the English, Scots and Welsh. The Scots identified themselves and were identified by others as having a diffuse intellect due to their religion and superior education system. The English thought that they were the only people in the world who embraced comfort and cleanliness, while both the Scots and Welsh divorced themselves from what the English considered comfort. They spoke of English 'discomforts'. Travel within Britain also revealed how exclusive imaginings of the nation could be, with travellers restricting their images to certain classes or ethnic groups, particularly when it came to refinement and cleanliness. There was an arrogance about this kind of imagining that evaporated when the experience of travel confronted people with challenges to their taken-for-granted national identities, as the next chapter on liberty, language and history suggests.

5
Liberty, Language and History

A Victorian Certificate of Nationality clearly reveals the centrality of the monarch to Britons' concept of the nation and state. In certifying British nationality, such a document confirms that a particular individual is 'a Subject of Her Britannic Majesty' – not a citizen of the British nation or the United Kingdom. David Cannadine has argued that the monarch was, in the last quarter of the nineteenth century, celebrated as symbol of the nation in a more grandiose manner than ever before.[1] In fact, he suggests it was during this period that the British became experts at, rather than bunglers of, royal stagings and pageantry. Given that many other European monarchies had disappeared by the early twentieth century, the British were able, as they are still, to convince themselves and others that elaborately staged royal rituals are part of a long-standing and unique British tradition – one existing since time immemorial. By so doing, says Cannadine, the British invest not only their monarchy, but also their nation with historical continuity, when, in fact, both have been recently invented or constructed.

Since the publication in 1983 of Anderson's *Imagined Communities* and Hobsbawm's and Ranger's *The Invention of Tradition*, it has been fashionable to speak of cultural traditions and nations as inventions constructed at a particular moment in time, rather than as age-old phenomena existing since time immemorial. Like Cannadine, scholars have emphasized the relative newness of nations and traditions, attempting to locate the historical moment when they emerged. Colley, for example, argued that the British nation was invented, or first imagined, during the eighteenth century when a shared Protestantism together with almost continual war with Catholic France united the peoples of Britain such that they defined themselves collectively as Britons, rather than as English, Scots and Welsh. Similarly, the supposedly ancient Scottish national traditions of kilts and clan tartans were, according to Hugh Trevor-Roper, inventions of the eighteenth century. He points out ironically that an English Quaker industrialist originated the kilt in the middle of the century. The garment was then popularized by the Highland Regiments, romanticism and Sir Walter Scott.[2]

By focusing on the mental processes of imagination and invention, these arguments have made us aware of the creative, protean nature of national identity and tradition. Instead of depicting people as passive recipients of natural, age-old collective identities, we are now more likely to talk of them as active participants in the creation and re-creation of their national identities and traditions. So far so good. Carried too far, however, these arguments can blind us to the continuities shaping national identity. In the course of waging war against a Catholic enemy in the eighteenth century, Britons may have become self-conscious as never before of a shared loyalty to Britain – perhaps even of a shared Britishness. But one of the central ingredients of that Britishness was liberty, a quality the English in particular had imagined themselves to possess for centuries. In fact, from at least as far back as the sixteenth century until well into the twentieth, the English and then the British identified themselves more often with liberty than with any other single characteristic. Does this fact negate the notion of ever-changing, artificially constructed national identities? Not exactly.

Although the English have continued for much of their history to identify their nation with liberty, the specific things invested with meaning for liberty have changed over time. In the later sixteenth century English people stressed the religious dimension of English liberty, regarding their Protestantism as its greatest safeguard and sign. Protestantism symbolized English independence and freedom from control by a foreign power such as the Pope or a Catholic Continental ruler. Satirical prints suggest that the notion of liberty had broadened in scope by the eighteenth century to include not only religious but political and economic elements as well. British liberty was still linked to Protestantism, particularly to the belief that all worshippers should have direct access to God's word. But it was also associated with Parliament and constitutional monarchy. Prints produced before the French Revolution contrasted the liberty of Britain's Protestant religion and constitutional monarchy with the despotism of France's Catholic Church and absolute monarchy.[3] These two French institutions appeared in prints as plunderers of the people. During and after the Revolution prints linked British liberty to the prosperity of the nation by opposing its inherent wealth and order to the poverty and anarchy characteristic of French liberty. John Bull's robustness and diet of roast beef and beer became a device among satirists for symbolizing the prosperous, orderly nature of British liberty.[4]

What these examples and this chapter suggest is that national identity formation is not simply a matter of inventing and artificially constructing something new. National identity often rests on age-old outlooks and traditions which are continually invested with new meanings depending on circumstances. Thus liberty continued throughout the Victorian period to be a central component of British people's collective identity. We have already noted how Victorian travellers invested the British landscape with the quality of liberty. The landscape attributes perceived to embody liberty, however, did not continue unchanged from the Hanoverian into the Victorian period. Our discussion of trees made this point clear. Instead of people imagining British liberty to reside in the heart of oak as they had done in the eighteenth century, nineteenth-century travellers perceived it to be most clearly represented by the scattered distribution of Britain's trees, whether oak, ash, or any other type. Similarly, this chapter will show how people from Britain continued to identify themselves with a form of government conducive to liberty. But the aspects of government most often associated with liberty shifted from a constitutional form of monarchy to a non-intrusive state devoid, at least in contrast to Continental states, of meddlesome officials and rules. The chapter will also reveal how encounters with other countries as well as experiences within Britain particularly regarding language made travellers more acutely aware of how liberty was stifled in Britain. Travel journals thus suggest that people from Britain identified themselves with liberty in some areas, and with tyranny or oppression in others.

Before discussing the significance of government for perceptions of liberty among people from Britain, a few additional points need to be made regarding landscape and religion. We have already seen how travellers imagined their landscape and Protestantism to embody the highly cherished quality of liberty in certain specific ways. In the case of landscape, they perceived not only scattered trees but also free-ranging cattle, accessible countryside and mountains, and the surrounding water as clear evidence of the liberty characterizing Britain's landscape and people. Travel on the Continent certainly worked to intensify this perception, particularly when it came to the matter of accessibility. The freedom of movement afforded by Britain's landscape moved more sharply into focus as travellers found their map-designed travel plans foiled by Continental mountain chains. Elizabeth Sewell, for example, felt the need to justify to British readers, who might be looking at a map, her route from Switzerland to Innsbruck, capital of the Tyrol. Although Switzerland and the Tyrol region were contiguous, she pointed out that her touring party had to proceed in very round-about fashion from Switzerland to Italy and then into the Tyrol. Explaining this indirect route she noted,

> Though Switzerland and the Tyrol lie side by side, there are great mountains rising up to separate them like the walls of a house, and if you wish to go from one to the other, you cannot break down the wall, but must as it were go out of the door into the street, and then enter at the other door. This is just what we intend to do.

Sewell felt compelled to offer this explanation because she knew her countrymen and women who had not been to Europe would assume they could 'look at a map and fancy you can travel from one country to another as you can from London to York.'[5] As Sewell suggests, the British were accustomed in their own country to being able to plot travel plans from a map without having to worry about encountering unscaleable walls or barriers along the way. Without the experience of foreign travel, they would very likely have taken this freedom of movement for granted and thus not regarded it as a peculiarly British characteristic.

We have seen how J.A. Symonds associated freedom with the tidal seas surrounding Britain. Rough waters in the Mediterranean brought the association to mind. Elizabeth Carne had similar thoughts crossing the Channel on her return home from a stay on the Continent. Her excitement about disembarking in England once again inspired patriotic sentiments, so much so that her pride in the country seemed to swell with each wave bringing her closer to Folkstone. Even the ship's roll had a friendly, home-like feel, as she made clear, 'The wild wind and the great waves belonged to England in their strength and freedom... I welcomed them as they seemed to welcome me.'[6] The implication here is that England shared the qualities of strength and freedom with the wind and waves, legitimizing her possession of these two natural phenomena. It did not occur to Carne that France might have an equally valid claim to the 'liberated' stirrings in the Channel, because she did not imagine France to embody liberty.

In addition to choppy water, Carne and others associated the hedges so characteristic of England's landscape with liberty. Journal writers frequently bemoaned the absence of hedge divisions in Continental fields, and were thus pleasantly surprised on the few occasions when they did appear. Not far from Pau, for example, Carne felt very much at home as she walked through very English-like lanes, admiring the fields criss-crossed by hedges. The country looked 'more like England than France', and the recognition caused her to reflect on the significance of hedges. She recalled hearing the view that English hedges were products of a former age when small proprietors free from the demands and pressures of aristocratic landlords occupied much of the land. It therefore seemed appropriate, in her view, that hedges mark this particular part of southern France where '"the ancient constitution was singularly favourable to liberty"' and the soil divided among a population of labouring proprietors.[7] Thus for Carne, hedges symbolized economic independence and freedom from aristocratic influence, liberties she recognized as being more prevalent in England during times past than in her own era.

As noted earlier, travellers from Britain had many qualities in mind, including liberty, when they used the term Protestantism. The liberating dimension of Protestantism was most apparent when travellers confronted Catholicism directly. Observing Catholic rituals, for example, made Protestants from Britain more aware of how free they were from superstitious behaviours and beliefs. Visits to convents had them celebrating the physical freedom afforded by Protestantism. Thomas Cook's first foreign tour took Lucilla Lincolne and other eager travellers up the Rhine in 1855. Along the way, Miss Lincolne toured a convent for the first time and felt profoundly sorry for the 'inmates'. Upon leaving she declared, 'I [felt] thankful once more to breathe the free, pure air, and thankful, oh most thankful! that my religion was not one which would confine its votaries by bolts and bars.' Travellers thought Protestantism was as liberating to the mind as to the body. It was so in their view for two main reasons. First, by promoting literacy and encouraging all worshippers to read the Bible for themselves, Protestantism rendered people less dependent on the authority of priests and more able to interpret God's word for themselves. Second, the variety of churches within Protestantism seemed conducive to a freer rein for intellects and consciences than the single, unified Catholic Church. In commenting on the many places of Protestant worship in Cannes, the Scotswoman Margaret Brewster took issue with the Catholic view that they signified a lack of Christian union and were, therefore, a disadvantage. She argued that a diversity of churches 'might be made a powerful argument in favour of the Christian love and charity resulting from liberty of conscience.... Surely many of the errors of the Church in all ages have been caused by struggles after what never can be attained in this world – unity, or uniformity of mind.'[8]

Victorian travellers from Britain most often associated liberty with England's – rather than Britain's – political principles and governmental system. They regarded England's political system as the only one in the world characterized by that peculiar combination of freedom and restraint that travellers saw in the English landscape as well. Mrs Trollope identified this quality most clearly when she said, 'The Constitution of ENGLAND... is the only one which appears to be formed in reasonable, honest, and holy conformity to the freedom of man as a human being, and to the necessary restraint inevitable upon his becoming one of a civilized, social compact.'[9] Travellers from Britain identified with and took great pride in their 'responsible constitutional government', and assumed people everywhere would desire the same form of government once they were educated about its principles and practices. In fact, English people in particular were encouraged to export their political principles to all corners of the globe.

The Foreign Office articulated this imperialist mission clearly in its 1850 memorandum proposing to reduce the charge for British passports. As noted earlier, before fees were reduced in 1851 British passports were expensive, at £2 7s 6d. Given that foreign ministers in London issued passports to British subjects free of charge, Britons travelling to the Continent rarely bothered to purchase a Foreign Office British passport. In 1850, however, the Austrian government started requiring British travellers to show a British passport in order to enter northern Italy. For the Foreign Office, the Austrians had transformed the issue of passport fees from a purely revenue issue into a political one. In its memorandum on fees, the Foreign Office stated that cheap British passports encouraging travellers to cross the Channel were now in the 'vital interest of England'. As the memorandum explained:

> It is for the interest of England that the political principles of Englishmen should be known and appreciated by the People of every Country on the face of the Globe; and it is useful to an Englishman that he should have every opportunity of seeing and hearing *all* that is to be seen and heard on the Continent, and of comparing and contrasting the Governments of other Countries with the Government and Institutions of his own... rather than allow Austria or any other Despotick State an excuse for repelling Englishmen from their frontiers, because they may not have chosen to provide themselves with our costly Passport, it would be better for us to abandon the revenue view

of the question altogether; and at once issue our Passports to all respectable applicants at an amount of fee which would be just sufficient to cover the Cost of the Stamp and the expense of the Passport Office – say 7s 6d each.[10]

The proposed fee was adopted in 1851. Considerable confidence underlay this memorandum in that there is not even a hint of fear that a comparison of governments would cast England in a disadvantageous light. The memorandum conveys a certain arrogance and condescension as well. English political principles – especially liberty – are perceived as being more valuable than any others, and it is assumed that people the world over should embrace and appreciate these principles. It clearly did not occur to the memorandum's author that such an assumption could be perceived as an offensive violation of liberty – the liberty to appreciate one's own non-English political principles.

Mary Shelley conveyed the same pride and confidence in England's governmental institutions and assumed that the English had already been active in exporting the love of freedom underlying them. Thinking globally, she stated, 'The aspiration for free institutions all over the world has its source in England.' She argued that even the seed of the American colonists' struggle for political freedoms against the British government 'was all sown by us'.[11] These comments were prompted by her travels in Italy where she noted that the fight against oppression among Italians was kept alive by the 'swarms of English' touring the country. Similarly, travellers' remarks about visits to Waterloo make it clear that they believed Britain preserved 'the World's liberties' or 'the Liberties of Europe' (the two were equated) on that Belgian field in 1815. They were unwilling to accord other peoples a share in the victory, least of all the Belgians. James Smith, who wrote passionately and at great length about his tour of Waterloo, was very critical of the Belgians as he gazed on and then ascended the Belgian mound. Standing about 300 feet high on the highest ridge of the field, this cone of earth supported an over-sized lion – monument to Belgian bravery during Waterloo. Smith described the site as 'a huge deformity' costing the Belgian government four years of labour and a sum it refused to reveal. What disturbed Smith more than the monument's appearance was his conviction that its very existence was wholly unwarranted. The campaign records, as he understood them, confirmed that 'in all the battles the Belgians fled in terror'. He concluded that the only consolation to be gained from the monument was that 'neither the ugly hill nor the big Lion will run away'.[12]

In the political and governmental realm, travellers from England, Scotland and Wales frequently identified the absence of an intrusive State as the primary source of liberty in Britain. The minimalist role of central government in Britain became more apparent to travellers once they had crossed the Channel where the State seemed a 'golden idol... before which the nations of the Continent fall down and worship'.[13] Being greeted on the Continent by an 'espionage' system of passport checks and customs searches made people from Britain realize how free they were to travel around their islands without the State keeping tabs on their behaviours and whereabouts. Travel guides and journals are full of comments about how the British feel their cherished liberties infringed on particularly by the passport system in Continental states which appeared to employ an army of officials to invade people's privacy and monitor their every movement. Murray's guides warned travellers about all the unfamiliar annoyances they would encounter on the Continent from intrusive state regulations and officials, especially from those connected with travel documents. The guide to France, for example, instructed readers on the importance and vexations of the passport, noting,

> The gens-d'armes are authorized to call for it not only in frontier and fortified towns, but in remote villages: they may stop you on the highway, or waylay you as you descend from the diligence, may force themselves into the salle à manger, or enter your bed-room, to demand a sight of this precious document. It is needless to expatiate on this restraint so inconsistent with the freedom which an Englishman enjoys at home... it is the custom of the country, and the stranger must conform, or has no business to set his foot in it.[14]

Retreating slightly from its critical tone, the guide went on to say that the police and officials performed their checks with civility, and that they were prohibited from entering a private home to check passports unless they possessed a warrant. What is significant for this discussion of liberty is that the state ritual of monitoring travellers is characterized unquestionably here as a violation of the freedoms held dear by Englishmen.

Although Murray's guide used the term 'Englishman' presumably in deference to its intended English audience, journals of tours to the Continent reveal that travellers from all parts of Britain associated liberty with their low-profile state. Arriving at Calais, Julia Pardoe regarded the throngs of custom-house officers with their lanterns and demands as well as the soldiers stationed in the passage way to insure single-file queues as very foreign and offensive to her liberties. In describing the scene, she characterized it as 'so perfectly un-English, that I involuntarily sought for my passport, and drew my breath hard, with the sensation of having bartered somewhat of my accustomed liberty for a foreign thrall.'[15] Similarly, negotiating the passport and custom-house examinations in Belgium made Robert Burn conscious of how foreign travel cost him certain freedoms. He pondered how he was 'no longer a free agent – no longer at liberty to roam... as in brave old England, but tracked from place to place.'[16] The Scotsman A.G. Dunlop regarded the police monitoring of travellers and passports in Europe as not only disagreeable and absurd, but also 'most repugnant to the feelings of a British subject'.[17] One proud British subject was not sure how to evaluate all the uniformed officers stationed at passport and customs offices. He admitted, 'In all the stations we saw gens d'armes. To a British subject accustomed simply to Porters, at the most in railway uniform, the presence of military armed with swords, bayonettes and muskets was whether more ridiculous or more oppressive, I know not how [to] decide.'[18]

After showing his passport numerous times, T.N. Talfourd concluded that such documents were inconsistent with the principles of a civilized country. He fulminated, 'Surely the system of passports is wholly unworthy of civilised, peaceful Europe in the nineteenth century!'[19] Travel entrepreneur Thomas Cook agreed, as his comments to Lord Lyons on the stringent passport/*visé* requirements imposed by the French government during the Franco-Prussian War reveal. In the summer of 1871 he told Lyons, 'The very fact of a passport and *visa* being required awakens fear in the more timid class of travellers.... The passport is also regarded by a large class of... travellers as utterly incompatible with the freedom of commercial and social intercourse which characterizes the present age.'[20] Even the British Foreign Office objected to certain infringements of liberty inflicted by the Continental passport system. In many European countries passports included what were known as '*signalement*'. They were personal details about the bearer such as hair colour, stature, age, eye colour, nose, complexion, mouth, chin, and so forth. Many Continental countries, especially Belgium and Austria, tried to persuade the British Foreign Office to add *signalement* to its passports, but to no avail. Itemizing these sorts of personal characteristics seemed to British government officials unnecessarily vexatious and offensive to travellers. Sir H. Seymour, the British Minister in Belgium, dispatched a memorandum protesting at the

Belgian government's insistence on *signalement*, and the delays caused British travellers because of their not having them listed on their passports. Seymour was instructed to express 'the hope of H.M.'s government, that a government founded like that of Belgium on principles of liberality, would not have recourse to a system of "signalement" on Passports, which was wholly ineffectual... and offensive to travellers to whom it was applied.'[21] These instructions together with British travellers' objections to Continental passport rituals have interesting implications for the relationship between passports and national identity. A passport technically provided others, particularly foreign officials, with certification of the bearer's nationality. But a passport also had the unintended consequence of heightening the bearer's awareness of his or her own national identity and values. In the case of British travellers, the experience of carrying a passport around the Continent made them more conscious of the liberty afforded by their relatively inconspicuous state.

Travellers encountered state officials most directly during passport and customs checks. But such officials seemed to be ever-present on the Continent, regulating and supervising life to a degree unknown in Britain. Travellers associated this officialdom with authoritarianism and militarism, and its relative absence in their native land as evidence of the liberty embodied by the British. Upon leaving the walled town of Nimeguen with its military officers and soldiers stationed to supervise every arrival and departure, the Scotsman William Chambers declared, 'Whatever may be the degree of personal liberty existing in Holland, it is still far below that which prevails in his [the Englishman's] own free country. Escaping from these insignia of a military system, we were glad to take our place in the steamer.'[22] Edward Wilberforce thought the top-heavy, meddlesome state in Germany was just as suffocating and stifling to liberty. Surprised by the mass of orders and instructions issued by the Government, Wilberforce asserted, 'Surely it is not necessary for Government to poke its nose into all private concerns, to have magistrates, and police, and common councils, and commercial councils... to control the affairs of the citizens, and to protect what is in no need of protection.'[23] More than any other official, the gendarme symbolized to British travellers all this deference to authority. With their cocked hats, blue coats, silver lace and well-trained horses, they seemed to display an unattractively imperious air. Margaret Brewster spoke proudly of her prejudice against and E.H. Barker of his lack of respect for these agents of the state. Recounting his meeting with a gendarme while studying buildings in an Alpine village, Barker stated, 'We advanced upon him with that absence of awe in the presence of cocked hats and gaudy uniforms which is one of the consequences of being born in a country that has little respect for such emblems of authority.'[24] Even British children thought the gendarme a foreign figure of fun. Agnes Twining Donaldson noted how amused her children were at the strange appearance of people and things in Boulogne. Her daughter asked whether the gendarmes were 'real men' or 'tend men'. By the latter she assumed the youngster meant figures at Madame Tussaud's.

The vast majority of travellers confessed in their journals a prejudice against gendarmes. But not all did. To Eliza Salvin, for example, gendarmes were aids to ease and efficiency. That much vaunted liberty from them in Britain was, in her view, freedom only to be disorderly and inconvenienced. This realization occurred to her after a night-time crossing from Boulogne to Folkstone where, in the absence of officials for guidance, she struggled to find her way to the station. Conflicting directions sent her first one way and then another until finally she blurted out, 'We thought it the better plan to have a gens d'armes [sic] at one's elbow to send one in the right direction, rather than be left to one's fate in the dark, to be sent first to one place then another and all equally wrong.'[25] Thus for Salvin, the heightened awareness of national identity and values – in this case of English liberties – afforded by foreign travel elicited a critical rather than a patriotic response.

Salvin's view, however, was very much the exception amongst an outpouring of diatribes against Continental officialdom. Some of the most vehement criticisms of government meddling appeared in journals by Welsh and Scottish travellers, a reflection, perhaps, of frustrations generated at home in Wales and Scotland by an English dominated Parliament and central government. While travelling in Germany, Henry Richard visited a school in Frankfurt. The school was run by a committee of parents, but subject nevertheless to government surveillance when it came to subjects taught, textbooks, and so forth. After touring the school, Richard recorded, 'Nothing can be worse in its effect on the entire character of Continental countries than this perpetual and officious intermeddling of the Government in all the affairs of life, and the consequent dependence of the people upon political measures as the means of social and national regeneration.' Richard's prejudice against political measures as a vehicle for achieving national regeneration stemmed no doubt, in part, from the recognition that his native Wales had been overwhelmed politically by England for centuries. For the Welsh, national regeneration was something most effectively achieved in the cultural realm, by means of language preservation and music.

From a Scottish perspective, John Dunlop expressed a similar hostility to dependence on the state.[26] The French government prompted his outburst. In particular, such things as uniformed schoolchildren, licensed schoolmasters and regulated cab fares led him to conclude that the Government in France controlled everything, much to the detriment of the French people. Though it was the French and not the British who adopted a formal Declaration of the Rights of Man, Dunlop nevertheless maintained that they had 'little idea of what the rights of man are in reality'. In his view, eternal Government interference crushed any 'spirit of individual enterprise which is the soul of a country' and 'something every man should have'. Dunlop admitted that French men were well educated in an intellectual sense, but were lacking in 'that kind of education which makes a nation'. By the latter, he meant training in organizing for the purpose of achieving things for themselves. In other words, he thought the French a mere 'mob', incapable of governing themselves because they were so accustomed to the state doing everything for them. Such observations led him to declare, 'Liberty is a word only known in England and in the United States of America.' Since he clearly considered himself to be privy to this knowledge of liberty, one assumes he was using 'England' here to include all of Britain.

If we reduce our focus from the over-arching state to the smaller realms of local communities, domestic environments and isolated individuals, liberty emerges as an identifying characteristic of Britons as well. Travellers from Britain perceived their native local communities to be much more free of State, or central, government, interference than those on the Continent. The signs of British local liberties were many. For E.A. Freeman, church architecture provided confirmation of such liberties. When travelling on the Continent Freeman was most interested in visiting the castles and churches of off-the-beaten-track smaller cities because he brought to them few preconceptions. In commenting on church architecture in France, he noted how much more standardized it was than England's, as if it had been dictated by a central authority. In France, he wrote, 'Neither local nor personal taste had such free play as they had in England. It would be hard to find the same kind of difference in the same number of great French Gothic churches, as those which distinguish the early Gothic of Wells from the early Gothic of Ely.'[27] It was the filthy water in Marseilles that had Fanny Kemble singing the praises of England's local freedoms. She argued that proposals for cleaning the water were ineffective because of the centralized nature of the French political system. That is, solutions for all local problems were discussed and devised in Paris which, she believed, was too far from their source. Her stay in Marseilles rendered her more aware than ever of the benefits of England's freedom from such centralization. She wrote in her journal, 'How much coming abroad makes us love England!'[28]

Only after living on the Continent did Elizabeth Carne recognize the importance of laws for liberty at the local and national levels in England. Perhaps it would be more accurate to say the absence of laws, for she strongly criticized the numerous laws imposed by local and national government in Continental countries to regulate every aspect of behaviour. It seemed to her that the reading aloud of new town regulations by green-coated officials who beat drums as they called them out was a daily occurrence in French towns. She maintained that instead of such government regulation by law, the English preferred regulation by freely competing social groups and interests. In her words:

> It needs a residence abroad to make one comprehend the full extent of English freedom. Our local, like our national laws, are framed on the principle that it is better to check social evils by the friction of social interests, than by direct interference. For example, we restrain overcharges in trade, not by perpetually making laws against cheating, but by throwing open all trades, trusting the interest of the shopkeeper to keep him from selling his goods at a higher price than is comparable with a fair profit.[29]

Like Carne, William Chambers perceived English towns to be freer than most of those on the Continent. Frankfurt, however, was more like an English town according to Chambers, and it is revealing to note the qualities that made it seem English. As Chambers explained, 'Frankfort was the most English-looking town we had seen on the continent.... The reason for this is, that Frankfort is a free town ... and, by the good sense of its government, has been stripped of its walls and fortifications, leaving the town to expand where taste or opulence may direct.'[30] In this case, government was viewed as a promoter of liberty because of its efforts to eliminate militaristic structures and symbols from Frankfurt in the interest of growth and development, particularly commercial, as Chambers made clear.

Scottish and English travellers linked the domestic realm in England with liberty as well. Once again, the absence of state interference is noted, as is house design. Regarding the former, William Baxter (a Scot) commented on the liberty English parents enjoyed to influence and control their children as compared to parents in Prussia who had to turn their children over at the age of seven to the state for schooling. He added that the Prussian State also imposed conscription in the army once males reached the age of 20. Interestingly, Baxter seemed to value liberty more than education as the following remark suggests, 'Unfettered liberty of speech, mind, industry, and action, has exalted the English masses, illiterate though they be, immeasurably above these educated vassals of the Prussian government.' He was particularly proud that Britain (his term) would '[n]ever... be thus converted into a vast hospital, its parents treated as incapable of managing their own concerns, and its children forcibly removed from parental control and influence! These Prussians originate more evils than most men are aware of, by thus making the state stand *in loco parentis.*'[31]

Other travellers contrasted the liberty afforded by English house design with the barracks-like quality of Continental apartments. English houses typically included all floors of a building, allowing for the sort of privacy and freedom from other occupants' kitchen smells, noises, and so forth. T.F.A. Smith looked with disapproval on living arrangements in German cities where a building typically had different families on each floor, with the landlord often occupying the ground floor apartment. Instead of liberty, this arrangement encouraged, according to Smith, energetic enforcement of house rules regulating everything from times for piano playing to methods of flower watering. In his words, it did not provide '[t]he privacy and seclusion which an Englishman values so highly.... The landlord is the house policeman, so that even the German better-class homes are not free from barrack-yard discipline. Your comings and goings are duly observed, those of visitors likewise.'[32] In southern Europe it was the walled courtyards, or patios, which had Dorothy Quillinan longing for the freedoms provided by an English home, particularly the freedom to partake of a view.

Limiting our focus to the single individual, travellers thought of England as offering the most liberty in this area as well. In fact, the English considered themselves willing to sacrifice certain conveniences in order to preserve their individual rights, especially to property. E.V. Lucas noticed how few light railways England had in comparison to Holland which was covered with them. Explaining the difference, Lucas declared, '[W]e can never have such conveniences, England being a free country in which individual rights come first.'[33] He went on to point out that Holland existed for the state instead of the individual and thus showed little concern for ruining private property by criss-crossing it with tram and rail lines. Touring Italy, Mrs Trollope was struck more by the individual's right to freedom of thought and speech in England rather than by his or her right to property. After talking with a Tuscan, she remarked on the little cause he had for political grievances. This did not imply, however, that he had the same rights as English people in her estimation. She qualified her comment by noting, 'I do not mean to say that every Tuscan subject can claim and hold fast, as his indefeasible right, the English privilege of thinking and of avowing his thoughts.'[34] For Trollope, this particular 'English privilege' was the most important one a society or civilization could adopt and embrace.

Although Continental touring highlighted liberty as a national trait in British travellers' minds, it did so only with respect to certain aspects of British life. The British landscape devoid as it was of barriers to roaming, and the Protestant religion with its emphasis on access to God's word for all, seemed to embody liberty. An even more frequently mentioned symbol of liberty was the British political and legal systems, regarded by travellers as conducive to freedom because of their restraint in employing officials and laws to regulate people's lives. In other areas, however, trips to the Continent and around Britain itself worked to make travellers more aware of ways liberty was stifled in Britain. We must be careful here because, by definition, travel involves escaping from the routines and pressures of daily life, and thus often underscores in travellers' minds, at least for the duration of a journey, the confining nature of home. For example, on the second day of John MacGregor's canoe trip around Europe he remarked, 'There began a strange feeling of *freedom* and *novelty* which lasted to the end of the tour.' In this sense, a traveller from anywhere in the world would feel the routines of home inhibiting to liberty when compared to the 'novelty' afforded by the act of travelling. Such a feeling, though helpful for understanding the nature of travel, is obviously not a meaningful indicator of national identity. Thus my focus is not on travellers' daily home routines, but rather on those liberty-suppressing qualities that journal writers associated with their national group, conventions, and institutions. These qualities suggest that, though travellers from Britain identified their landscape, churches and government with liberty, they associated their moral and social conventions with nothing short of tyranny. In some cases such as policies regarding language, even the government was seen as hostile to liberty. Travel journals also indicate that women were more apt than men to experience, as a result of travelling, an enhanced recognition of barriers to liberty in Britain.

When touring the Continent, women travellers became more conscious of the despotism of social hierarchy in their native land, while men commented more on the inhibiting strictures regarding personal appearance. Detailing the restrictions on liberty in various countries, Martha Lamont exclaimed, 'Look at England, where the despotism of castes, a social despotism exists, of even a worse sort than that of a tyrannical monarch.'[35] Other travellers were so painfully aware of this social despotism that they were unable to enjoy themselves in social settings on the Continent. In Munich, Anna Howitt attended a militia ball where she felt most uncomfortable. Unlike in England, there was a mingling of social classes, with aristocrats dancing freely with 'plebeian partners'. She and her friends were so disconcerted, worrying about whether they were aristocratic or plebeian enough, that they refrained from dancing the whole evening. Miss Carne encountered similar sorts of 'democratic' entertainments in Pau, where the *préfets* hosted balls open to all classes. According to convention, women had to dance with whomever asked them, or else not at all, and there were no introductions. Such social mixing in public without introductions was shocking to Carne and other English visitors to Pau, but they nevertheless attended the balls, which they would not have felt so free to do at home.

Male travellers spoke of a different tyranny from which they felt relief when they were no longer in Britain – the tyranny of trappings related to appearance. We have already noted John MacGregor's delight at feeling free to forsake hat and braces once he arrived on the Continent. He also mentioned abondoning his razor, a freedom welcomed by other British men as well. The prevalence of beards and moustaches in Germany made M.F. Tupper bemoan the more bare-faced look expected in Britain. He concluded that facial hair gave 'a very manly look to the people'. Feeling somewhat oppressed as an Englishman, he confessed, 'I wish that we English had more real freedom in the matter of shaving: free as we boast ourselves, that iron rod – a pretty sharp one – the razor rules us still.'[36] Tupper did not have long to wait for his longed-for freedom. The 1850s when he wrote was a transitional decade regarding attitudes towards beards. Although an 1854 *Westminster Review* article noted that 'In England...public opinion...is perhaps harder on the beard than it is anywhere else', a popular etiquette book published five years later expressed approval of beards.[37] By 1870, beards no longer needed defending in Britain, having become thoroughly respectable.

Touring the Continent, men and women became more aware than ever of the pressures of pretentious living in England in particular.

Travellers noted how much cheaper the cost of living was in Europe because, unlike in England, people did not place high value on maintaining an ostentatious lifestyle. They had fewer servants, lived more within their means, and did not let limited means inhibit them from mixing as equals in their local society. Many journals expressed relief at the freedom from extravagance afforded by travel or residence outside of Britain. According to Edward Wilberforce who lived for a time in Munich, the 'social tyranny' in England was so great, 'that many Englishmen take shelter in foreign residence'.[38] By 'social tyranny' he meant the pressures of public opinion, or Mrs Grundy, of extravagant living beyond one's means, and of servants lecturing one about the manner of living in the richest houses where they have been accustomed to being employed. Even Mary Shelley who regarded England as the source of liberty in a political and legal sense, thought of England as oppressive socially. In particular, the practice of judging others and oneself according to material possessions, income and connections led to an obsession with luxury that seemed stifling, especially when contrasted with the apparent nonchalance about such things on the Continent.

There were other ways in which British travellers imagined themselves slaves to social and moral conventions. Compared to the Continent, they thought Britain allowed little scope for individuality, particularly among the middle and upper classes as well as among women. Such thoughts occurred to I.A.R. Wylie who went to live in Germany during the opening years of the twentieth century – a time when hostility to Germany was rampant in the British press. He wrote at length about German schools, comparing them to public schools at home. As Wylie saw it, German classrooms were conducive to independence and individuality among students because schoolmasters did not attempt to mould character by means of moral influence. Although German boys were schooled to possess the same sense of discipline, Wylie argued that their opinions, character and attitudes towards life were left free to develop along independent paths. Not so in Britain where public schools were like 'China manufactories', shaping character above all else and thus turning out students 'all bearing the same hallmark'. Wylie believed it nearly impossible for a boy to come out of a public school with an independent personality. In his view, 'The Englishman fancies he is brought up as an independent manly character because he is allowed a certain amount of physical freedom.... But morally and mentally he is gagged and bound hand and foot.'[39]

As repressive as this deference to unoriginality and convention was for men, it was even more so for women, in Wylie's estimation. Wylie noted over and over again how dominated the English were by conventions regarding morals and taste, so much so that they were frightened by anyone who flouted the rules in order to follow their fancies, and tended to label such independent spirits as 'mad'. He went on to say, 'If the offender happens to be a woman there is no limit to our horror and disgust.'[40] Other travel journals confirm this lack of tolerance for singularity in women. A tourist site in Llangollen often generated journal outbursts against its women occupants. The site was known as Plas Newydd, home for over 50 years to Lady Eleanor Butler and Sarah Ponsonby. Fleeing the demands of late eighteenth-century fashionable society, these two women of aristocratic background retired on £280 a year to the lush Dee Valley where they lived a relatively quiet, but not reclusive, life. During the Regency period, their home became a favourite stopping-off point for literary and fashionable travellers, including the Duke of Wellington, Sir Walter Scott and William Wordsworth.

Plas Newydd, with its Gothic decor, remains a popular tourist site today. The most recent *Rough Guide to Wales* bills its Regency occupants as 'the country's most celebrated lesbians'. This is not how Victorian travellers thought of the ladies. Many were perplexed and somewhat disturbed by their singular behaviour. One writer who published letters from Llangollen in a Sheffield newspaper depicted the ladies as a mystery. Had the nearby abbey of Valle Crucis still been active, the writer suggested it would have been perfectly acceptable for such ladies of noble birth to forsake 'the boudoir for the serge gown of the convent'. But Butler and Ponsonby were 'neither religious devotees nor misanthropic recluses'. The only other possibility, and the most likely one, to this puzzled writer's way of thinking was that one or both of them had been 'disappointed in love'.[41] His account reflects the prevailing view in the Victorian period that the nunnery, misanthrope, and rejection just about exhausted the possible reasons for a woman remaining unmarried – a view that gave women very little liberty to choose the unmarried state.

Another visitor to Llangollen was less charitable towards the ladies. R.W. Long found their house 'rude' and 'strange' in its decor, and their habits 'equally singular'. The habits he mentioned were their literary and philosophical tastes and their masculine appearance. Based on engravings he had seen in Wales and Chester, he described them as having 'very masculine features, hair...brushed but rough and not very long and wearing a kind of loose riding habit fashioned above like a loose coat'.[42] Little tolerance was shown towards such unfeminine-looking women. The Welshman Henry Richard encountered a similar woman at a hotel in Switzerland. Although at first intriguing to his eye, in the end he found her behaviours 'absurd'. She clearly violated all the social conventions about eating and promenading. At the *table d'hôte*, for example, she talked in a 'loud masculine voice', put her elbows on the table and bit her bread. After dinner, she walked up and down the balcony 'with a stick in her hand, and a large hat set on one side of her head, smoking cigarettes and talking in a loud man-like voice with absurd...gesticulations'.[43] About the same time Richard was in Switzerland (1880), Charles Wood toured Holland noting how fashionable it was for women to be strong-minded and masculine. He clearly did not approve of the fashion. In a station waiting-room, he noticed a tall woman rushing about with her hands and mouth full. Wood described the woman as 'big' and 'ungainly' who, when running, 'reminded you of a frolicsome cow'. Somewhat disgusted, he asked, 'Why are there such women? Why were they not all made to tread softly and go gently, and be everything that is feminine?'[44]

For Margaret Fountaine, travel abroad made her realize how completely stifled she had been all her life by English conventions. Only outside England did she feel free to realize and discover her 'true' self – the born naturalist that had been repressed by her traditional upbringing. Had she been a man, she would likely have come to Europe as an educated naturalist, seeking and recording information according to a well thought-out plan. As it was, she first experienced the delight of chasing and securing butterfly specimens in Switzerland, noting, 'I was a born naturalist, though all these years for want of anything to excite it, it had lain dormant within me.' After her first trip to Europe, she returned to England thinking she 'had learnt to enjoy life in a new way. The great void was being filled.'[45] One of the things she learned about was her own power, especially that of attracting and rejecting men. For the rest of her life, spent almost entirely abroad, she enjoyed teasing and flirting with men to an extent she would not have felt free to do at home. In most cases, she would lure them and then walk away proudly without another thought, revelling not only in her power, but also in the feeling that she was continually getting back at Septimus – the Irish alcoholic who jilted her. As she explained it, 'I love to be a woman, and feel that power which a man can never possess, the power, however, that is only the power to reject.' Her experiences abroad were so liberating and transforming that she was unable to return to England for any length of time, even in her dreams. Once when staying at Lake Como, she dreamed of returning to her Norwich home. Lying on the grass of her local tennis ground, she felt in her dream 'dissatisfied and impatient'. At the point of no longer being able to stand the sensation of suffocating, she sprang up and found herself in Italy. When she did return to England, she felt completely alienated and out of place. In her words, 'I had no taste for the home that was no home to me... I almost felt a stranger in my own country; I looked upon my own countrymen as foreigners.'[46] In this woman's case, English national identity and her personal identity were so at odds that she had to renounce the former in order to realize the latter.

Although Fountaine experienced a more negative reaction to her English upbringing than most, the sense of freedom and independence afforded by the act of travelling abroad – in some cases alone and unprotected – heightened awareness in other women's minds as well of ways their lives at home were restrained and unfree. When Eliza Anne Salvin went to Germany with her mother and sister, she described the group as 'Three unprotected females without a servant and very independent we feel.'[47] Servants, governesses and male authority figures were all shackles women felt relieved to be free of once they left Britain. Sophia Holworthy was aware of her lack of liberty long before she left England. In the preface to her journal, she revealed, 'As a child I had gipsy dreams, that when I was grown up, and had escaped from governesses and masters, I should wander forth all day.'[48] She accomplished her 'gipsy' dream in the 1880s when she embarked on an 18-month tour of Switzerland, France and Italy. Travelling alone and mostly on foot, she revelled in her freedom from nagging governesses as well as male guides, noting how Badaekers made her independent of the latter. (This feeling of independence was slightly illusory, in that a male author composed the guidelines and advice in her Badaekers.)

Mary Eyre from Yorkshire travelled in a similarly solitary and independent manner, mostly in the South of France. Interested in observing and recording French life rather than in socializing with other English tourists and fashionable locals, she travelled relatively unencumbered, taking only a small waterproof stuff bag. The bag contained one spare dress, a light shawl, two changes of various kinds of underclothing, two pairs of shoes, pens, pencils, paper, the 'inevitable' Murray, and a prayer-book. For Eyre, travelling was a means of coping with and liberating herself from the unproductive, useless lifestyle for which English gentlewomen like herself were reared. A lack of training and education were the restraints at home uppermost in her mind, and she thus went abroad and composed a journal to 'show other poor gentlewomen brought up like myself to no occupation, that they may do better than stay lamenting over their past prosperity in gloom and isolation and discomfort at home.'⁴⁹ Comfort here implies psychological and emotional peace of mind rather than such things as fires, carpets and draught-proof windows. Eyre suggests that, in this sense, England was very much a source of *dis*comfort, especially for well-to-do women.

Julia Pardoe, also Yorkshire-born, was slightly less openly enthusiastic about the liberated feeling she experienced in the South of France. She, too, travelled alone, noting how the adventure made her more aware than ever of how dependent English women were, and how difficult it was for them to break the cycle of dependence. At home, women's dependent state rendered their energies, inclinations and powers stagnant and torpid, according to Pardoe. From the cradle, Pardoe argued, '[Women] are walled round within the charmed circle of domestic guardianship – they are habituated to obedience and self-distrust.'⁵⁰ One reason Pardoe ventured abroad was to illustrate to herself and others how self-reliant and independent women could be, if circumstances demanded it. And yet, she also maintained that a woman paid a psychological price for acting independently, such that underneath the self-reliant exterior there was likely to be a 'shrinking sensitivity' and an 'alienated heart'. She seemed to have paid this price.

In her journal composed of letters to a friend, she noted repeatedly how emotionally wrenching the separation from home was for her. As she got further and further from her hearth, she recorded, 'My heart is heavy; and my spirit sad. I cannot forget, even amid all my enthusiasm, that every hour is widening the distance between me and my home.'⁵¹ She admitted, despite her hankering for the independence afforded by travel, that she and other women 'love the tendence, the counsels, and the cares of those who are dear to [them]'. They did so, in her view, not only because convention encouraged them to be dependent, but also because women were more *naturally* helpless than men. As she saw it, 'To women the task of partial self-reliance is necessarily tenfold more different and painful; they are, both naturally and socially, more dependent than men.'⁵² Had she not been addressing her remarks to a friend living with the Pardoe family, she might have written less of homesickness and natural dependence and more of her independent adventure. Certainly, she must have felt a sufficient level of frustration with her home life to cross the Channel in the first place. Her ambiguous manner of coping with independence is evident, on the one hand, by her bold pronouncement in the journal's opening pages that she owed her friends and family no explanation for what motivated her to travel, and on the other by the apologetic, lachrymose tone she adopted when writing about her separation from the attentions and support of loved ones. What is not ambiguous is that she felt repressed by the dependent state she was expected to exist in at home.

For the Scotswoman Janet Robertson, it was the law in Britain that seemed oppressive to women, a recognition that occurred to her in Paris where she sought refuge in a pension for women during the turmoil of 1848. To her way of thinking, France contrasted favourably with Britain rather than adversely as was usually the case with British travellers. The difference may have had to do with Scotland's close links with France historically. At any rate, as the barricades emerged and the streets filled with malcontents, Robertson pondered whether it was worse to be enmeshed in the intricacies of British law or the sort of 'civil war' raging outside. She decided that British law was worse, especially for women, because it victimized them. Civil wars, she argued, threw the distressed together, whereas law fostered selfishness and suspicion. In her words:

> Yes! most certainly, I would prefer again living through the horrors of the French Revolution of 1848, to encountering the heart-sickening and tortuous details of the law in tranquil Britain; where it has always appeared to me that the heavier purse gains the day, and where helpless and unsuspicious woman is generally the victim!

Robertson did not appear helpless as she travelled through Italy and France, but she was correct about British women being disadvantaged in the eyes of the law for much of the nineteenth century. It was particularly true that married women in England and Wales were subjugated legally. At mid-century when Robertson wrote, married women had no property rights in law, no right to divorce except by an extremely costly private Act of Parliament, and were oppressed by a double standard of morality, which made adultery committed by a woman a worse legal offence than that committed by a man. (Under Scottish law, women were more easily able to divorce on grounds of adultery or desertion.) It was even true that women legally had no nationality in their own right. That is, a British-born woman who married a foreigner legally assumed his nationality and was no longer entitled to a British passport, given only to British-born subjects, Ionians or those who had become naturalized.[53] If such a woman divorced or became a widow, she could obtain a British passport only by becoming naturalized, as was true for anyone – with the exception of Ionians – not born in Britain. Passport regulations thus reflected the general principle enshrined in British law that a married woman had no identity or status independent of her husband.

A number of travel journals drew distinctions between the liberties afforded married and single women, whether in England or Europe. Most travellers concluded that married English women had fewer liberties than those on the Continent, and single women more. The perception was that Continental women, once married, were freer to say and do what they pleased than their English counterparts. Hugh Jerningham concluded while visiting Normandy, 'In France marriage is the establishment of woman's freedom; in England, that of woman's dependence.'[54] According to Betham-Edwards, who travelled extensively in France, the freedom for French women at marriage was that of being treated as an adult rather than as a child. She pointed out that, in France, as long as an unmarried woman's mother lived, she was treated as a child, no matter how old she was. This was not the case in England. When an English girl left school, for example, Edwards explained how she was given her own allowance for dress and personal expenses. She recorded, 'I well remember the astonishment of a French lady at seeing an English girl of twenty-five write out a cheque in her own name. Such a thing, she informed me, she had never heard of.'[55]

In general, English women travellers, especially unmarried ones, clearly felt more liberated than the spinsters they observed on the Continent when it came to issues of parental control and occupational opportunities. The lack of independence among Italian girls was particularly noticeable to Miss Lucas, when she compared them to girls from Britain. Observing 'Scotch and English girls' in Rome, she noted how they went about the city in 'an independent sort of way' which provided a 'good example to Italian girls'. It appeared to her that Italian young women were beginning to 'complain bitterly of the restraint they [were] kept in'.[56] Mary Shelley thought the Scots women were even more independent than the English. In Milan where she was about to board a *vetturino* carriage bound for Geneva, she discovered that three other ladies had booked the carriage as well. Shelley sent her maid to cast an eye over them, and the woman came back to inform her that they were three Irish ladies, judging from accent. Somewhat perplexed, Shelley wondered what could have prompted Irish ladies to travel 'unprotected' or 'unattended'. The mystery was solved when she met the women whose rich 'Doric accent' told her in an instant they were Scots. As she explained it, 'The enigma vanishes on the discovery of their native land; for there is something in Scotch-women more independent than in English and Irish.'

In the realm of occupational opportunities, Edwards talked of how many more single, professional women there were in England, and how much freer they were than the same group in France. Discussing the French lady doctor, occulist, dentist or advocate, Edwards admitted she had more freedoms than a young French woman in fashionable society, at least with respect to what books she read, theatre she attended and guests she received. But even compared to professional women in France, Edwards maintained, 'The freedom from restraint enjoyed by English and American spinsterhood would look subversive, anarchical, Nihilistic in French eyes.'[57] We might conclude that the experience of foreign travel made British women more conscious of their lack of liberty at home, but that comparisons between themselves and European women – especially single ones – made them feel somewhat liberated, particularly when it came to occupational opportunities in the professions.

One thing stifling to mental and physical freedoms for women especially, whether married or single, was the British perception of gender spheres. Britons had rather clear-cut notions regarding appropriate activities for men and women, regardless of individual inclinations. For example, the political, diplomatic and military spheres were imagined to be closed to women. Travel, especially to the Continent, highlighted in people's minds these sorts of barriers. Thus Henry Richard found an Electoral Club meeting in Paris a surprising experience. One of the surprises was that speakers read their speeches, a practice that would have generated roars of laughter, according to Richard, at any election meeting in England.[58] But the other surprise was the large number of women not only present, but deeply interested in the proceedings as well. To Richard's and other British travellers' way of thinking, women were not supposed to be involved or interested in politics.

Nona Bellairs clearly felt this restriction as she drew comparisons in her journal between policies towards slaves in the United States and England. Although a vehement opponent of slavery, she nevertheless criticized English policy for setting slaves free in a penniless state to make their way in the world. She wound up her discussion on the subject by saying somewhat deferentially, 'This is a subject beyond a woman's pen, and should be met by the arguments of men, rather than by the fictitious creations of a lady's brain, or by drawing-room petitions.'[59] This view no doubt worked to discourage many women from participating in politics, even if the participation took place in the feminine space of the drawing room. Yet despite Bellairs' deference to gender sphere imagining, she nevertheless spent a page and a half of her journal arguing about this supposedly male concern. Her words confirm the existence in people's minds of gender spheres, but her actions suggest that sphere boundaries were able to be stretched and even violated, something scholars have increasingly recognized in recent years.

Martha Lamont wrestled in a similar way with her supposedly unfeminine interest in battlefields. On a trip to Brussels, she passed several such fields. Finding herself drawn emotionally to the sites, she felt it necessary to justify her reaction by arguing, 'As a woman, I have no right to love battle-fields, nor do I love them; but it would be impossible for me to pass over any field of battle without my feelings being stirred to their profoundest depths, as it were in sympathy with the long-past struggles of the now peaceful fighters.'[60] Her unfeminine interest was acceptable, in her mind, only because it was rooted in the very feminine realms of emotion and sympathy. In the second half of the nineteenth century, increasing numbers of women attempted to expand their interests and scope for action by claiming that the traditionally male public sphere would benefit from an injection of such qualities as sympathy and morality considered natural in women. Like Lamont, they ironically used gender sphere ideology to undermine barriers between the female and male domains.

Those barriers affected the working world, such that appropriate work activity was determined by gender. Thus it was perfectly natural, according to John Forbes, to see women tending the cemeteries in Innsbruck. He noted how all the planting and watering was done by women, as well as most of the devout kneeling in churches. This division of labour was appropriate because, in his words, 'Woman's holier and tenderer heart constitutes her the natural interpreter and minister in all offices where the affections are chiefly concerned.'[61] Other types of work engaged in by Continental women were surprising to British travellers. Frederick Fryer was struck 'rather forcibly' by seeing so many women managing shops on the Continent, something rarely seen across the Channel. Meat stalls and railways also afforded women employment opportunities not found in Britain. In Bruges, Elizabeth Sewell found it 'very strange' that 'women often kept the meat stalls, just as butchers do in England'.[62] During her first trip to France, the surprising sight of women railway officials – even 'signalwomen' – prompted Mrs D. Craik to praise French women for their willingness to work. She felt they were less ashamed of working than women back home. Perhaps the signalwomen were so startling because of women's assumed ignorance regarding machinery. When Mary Dundas first crossed the Channel, she spent considerable time at the window of an engine room. Impressed by the scene, she admitted, 'Machinery always fascinates me though I know nothing about it.' She went on to explain how engines made one feel small and great simultaneously. As she saw it, they rendered one 'small in comparison with the power of the machinery and great in that one's brother men have discovered and invented the powers, and the means of using them.'[63] She clearly located machinery in the male sphere, imagining that women could take pride in its powers, but only one step removed by taking pride in the men creating the machines.

The work activity on the Continent that most clearly violated British travellers' notion of gender spheres was field labour by women. Travellers from England and Scotland noted over and over again how shocked they were to find Continental women engaging in burdensome, outdoor labour along side men, whether the work be breaking stones, ploughing, spreading manure, or lugging heavy loads on their backs. This was men's work, in most travellers' view, and the women performing it displayed to their eyes the coarse, weatherbeaten look of men. One traveller said of such female labourers, 'If it were not for their petticoats, I should not know them from men.'[64] The Scotsman James Smith thought this practice of employing women like men led to other 'abusive' behaviour in the Continental countryside. He was particularly concerned about the cows that were commonly seen drawing heavy carts all over Switzerland. Of these carts he said, 'To a Scotch eye and feeling they are very disgusting – and grating to one's thought of what is due to a cow's comfort. But when the women are wrought like men, no wonder that cows are called on for horse's labour.'[65] Regarding the unceasing out-of-door labour typical of Continental women, William Howitt maintained that English working-class women would complain if married and blush if single were they to be seen 'sweltering in these labours, more like ponies and patient asses than according to our notions of women and their work.'[66] Interestingly, at the very time Howitt's words were published (1842), committees presented illustrations to Parliament showing English women in the mines on their hands and knees hauling coal carts strapped to their bodies as if they were draught animals. Parliament responded with the Mines Act of 1842 barring women and children from the mines, despite the protests of many women miners who felt the Act denied them a relatively lucrative form of employment.

One reason Howitt and others objected to women working all day in the fields was that such fatiguing activity violated their image of ideal womanhood. In England in particular, women were admired for their delicate form and physical limitations, neither of which was maintained by back-breaking physical work. The sturdy women of Tuscany prompted James Cobbett to reflect on his more 'elegant' and 'delicate' countrywomen. To his way of thinking, 'The little hand, with taper fingers, and knuckles hardly to be seen; the small round wrist, from which the arm imperceptibly swells in soft continuation to the elbow; this kind of charm, which is found... in England, does not belong to the women of Tuscany.'[67] Men especially found this delicate look charming because it made women appear to be dependent on male physical strength and guidance. M.F. Tupper had no doubt that women's physical limitations forced them to rely on men, even when they were travelling independently. While mountain climbing in Switzerland he exclaimed, 'I can scarcely believe that ladies sometimes cross the glacier; but our guide said so; and no doubt they do, somehow or other, by means of his iron help.'[68] Even independent women travellers deferred, in part, to the delicacy expected of them. Mrs Trollope, for example, had second thoughts about a very difficult and fatiguing walk she took to a wild, secluded village. Although she 'gloried in the enterprise, when it was achieved', she admitted that she very likely would have urged her companions to go without her had she known how physically demanding the excursion was. In fact, she concluded her account of the expedition by saying, 'I do not recommend the expedition to my travelling readers; particularly if they be ladies, for it is a most fatiguing one.'[69] Martha Lamont clearly paid little heed to such advice. As she was ascending Montanvert to see the Mer de Glace, she explained the long debate she had had with herself that morning about whether she should climb the mountain at all. Her mother had written many times to remind her not to go up any 'fatiguing mountains'. Despite her mother's instructions, she could not bring herself to 'give up the pleasure, or the pain' of making the ascent. She ended her self-defence by inquiring of the reader (her mother being one of them), 'Do you not think I was good to debate the matter at all? I think so.'[70] Trollope and Lamont both acknowledged the delicacy expected of themselves and others as women, but their deference did not stop them from violating the expectations. Their experiences thus reveal how travel worked to make people conscious of and at the same time more able to challenge ideals imposed on them at home.

Another reason travellers disapproved of women working in the fields is that such outdoor labourers had insufficient time to keep their homes neat and tidy and to tend to their family's needs. Mary Eyre discussed at some length the disadvantages of women doing physical work in the fields. Throughout the Pyrenean part of France where she travelled, the ploughs were small and light, and women typically followed the ploughman breaking clods, or spreading manure by hand among the furrows. Of such work Eyre remarked with some disgust, 'It is impossible to estimate *the demoralization* to which women's working with men, whether in English collieries or Pyrenean slopes, occasions.'[71] (At least she acknowledged that some English working-class women did engage in back-breaking work with men.) Part of the 'demoralization' occurred because homes were neglected and dirty. Eyre recounted her attempt to convince a French peasant that it was unhealthy and uneconomical for his wife to do field work. She told him of the typical Yorkshire labourer who, because his wife stayed at home, returned each night to a well-cooked supper and a clean and tidy cottage. Speaking then of the man's own wife, Eyre noted how field work prevented her from doing such things as mending his clothes, making his children's and keeping a well-ordered home. She finished by saying, 'I think you would find you saved more if the women stayed at home and attended to their own proper work.'[72]

By 'proper work', Eyre clearly had in mind scrubbing the floors, among other things. At one place where she stayed in the south of France, Eyre requested that the floor be scrubbed. Her hosts promised to comply, though floor cleaning was not routine work in France as it was in England. When she next returned to the establishment, she found the husband on his knees scrubbing, with the wife, according to Eyre, 'standing by, admiring his work and doing nothing. What a model husband! Fancy an Englishman scouring a floor while his wife stands idly by.'[73] Men in England did not clean floors because the English considered this type of work to be women's. In France, on the other hand, floor scouring was neither men's nor women's work, nor was the domestic realm clearly designated as women's domain. Servant couples in France, for example, frequently worked together in the same house, doing similar sorts of domestic work.

Eyre's comments reflect the prevailing view in Victorian Britain that the domestic realm was feminine, and the outdoor, public realm masculine. Whether working-class or well-to-do, women belonged in the home when working or relaxing, according to this view. Typical labour for working-class women was thought to be tending to their family and doing the physical work of housekeeping, that of well-to-do women meeting their family's needs and supervising the physical housekeeping labours carried out by servants. Travellers' journals suggest that the domestic realm, though highly valued by men as a place to retreat, was not one in which they could function naturally. In fact, they felt unable to generate the cheerful comfort of domesticity without the aid of women. In Paris, Henry Richard and his male companions were at a loss regarding what to do with their evenings. As he explained it, 'After toiling long with body and mind... we feel the need of some relaxation and a little cheerful domestic society.... But we have none here, and so we linger out our evening reading or walking as best we may.'[74] They had no domestic society because there were no women present with which to share the evenings. Similarly, Agnes Twining thought women were much more adept than men at functioning in the domestic realm. When she, her sister, her father and his male companion were travelling in Switzerland, Twining pitied the two men whenever it rained. She did so because she imagined they had nothing to do, suitable male activities being such things as mountain climbing or glacier trekking in her mind. The women, on the other hand, had plenty to do on the wet, house-bound days, given their love of sketching, sewing, reading and playing music.

Travel journals by British women reflect their strong tie to the domestic sphere. Unlike men, women travellers referred frequently to home and family in their journals, and some travel journals by women were composed of letters they wrote home to family members while travelling. Women often expressed a longing for home and doubts about the virtues of travelling, something men almost never did. In these ways, women travellers sought to maintain emotional ties with home, no matter how many miles away from the hearth they ventured. They clearly did not feel as free as men to indulge themselves in the joys of travelling. Independent travellers Lamont and Pardoe both began their journals by admitting how sad they were to be leaving home. Lamont felt the need to justify her tour abroad and to downplay the excitement of travel. In her words, 'We cannot help wishing to see those places which are famous in history... yet after all, travelling is... a finer thing in imagination than in reality.'[75] Even when she revelled in being alone at some stunningly beautiful spot, she always added a qualification addressed to her mother such as, 'The wish to have you near me robs me of half my enjoyment.' What is important here is not whether her qualifications were true or not, but rather the fact that she, like other women, felt the need to appear as if she put home and family before her own interests and pleasure.

Male and female travellers actually fell into gender-defined activities, especially on organized tours. One can see such patterns by looking at the Toynbee Travellers Club which sponsored a number of group tours in the late nineteenth and early twentieth centuries. A club pamphlet lists names and addresses of members as well as the various expeditions taken and logbooks kept. Of the 41 expeditions, *all* were led by men, with the exception of one to Brittany in 1910, which had one male and two female leaders. Thus men clearly assumed or were granted leadership roles. But when it came to compiling illustrated logbooks, women had a more active role. Of the 15 logbooks listed, eleven had at least one woman among the compilers, and six were compiled by a woman working alone. One is reminded of meetings in the late twentieth-century workplace where men often run the proceedings while women record the minutes.

This discussion has shown that travellers from Britain identified themselves with the quality or principle of liberty. This identification did not apply, however, to all facets of life. Travellers typically regarded 'British liberty' as residing in Protestantism, an accessible, island landscape and a political system characterized by constitutional monarchy and a non-obtrusive state. But Continental travel also helped to highlight how being British meant feeling inhibited and adhering to certain limitations on liberty, particularly when it came to social and moral behaviours. Women travellers were more apt than men to comment on such limitations. Aside from this difference between the genders, travel journals suggest that people from different parts of Britain imagined themselves to share certain kinds of liberty and certain inhibitions. If we shift the focus to journals of tours around Britain, comments about the bond of liberty in areas other than landscape become scarce. The emphasis is more on things that make the peoples of Britain feel separated from one another. We have already looked at some things – religion, attitudes to mountains and other landscape details, food, and so forth. Two others that have implications for liberty are language and history.

When travelling on the Continent, people from Britain were lumped together by the locals as 'English'. This was largely because they all spoke the English language, and Europeans were better able to identify this similarity rather than any differences in dialect or accent that would have marked them as Scottish or Welsh as opposed to English. Scottish travellers often identified themselves as 'English' when on the Continent in deference to local people's perceptions, as we will see more clearly in chapter 6. And travellers from England felt close linguistic links to the Scots when they were amidst French, German and Italian speakers. Thus at a Continental *table d'hôte*, the Englishman John Marsh noted with some relief, 'I sat next a Scotchman and it was quite a pleasure to have one with whom I could converse.'[76] Martha Lamont, an Englishwoman from Lancashire whose middle name 'MacDonald' suggests Scottish roots, was surprised to find her enthusiasm for Robert Burns's Scottish language poems heightened by her exposure to German, French and Italian books during a stay in Geneva. Lamont explained how she found a book of Burns's poems in her host's library, the 'Scotch' of which was unintelligible to him. Of her excitement upon reading Burns she said, '[A]t home I should not have relished him so. Perhaps something of my delight, indeed, arose from the foreign place I was in.'[77] These experiences suggest that foreign travel tended to highlight the linguistic similarities and bonds between Britons. Travel around Britain, however, often did just the opposite.

During the Victorian period it was only in England that the people spoke a single language. Such linguistic homogeneity, even in England, was a relatively recent phenomenon. A traveller to Cornwall could still have heard Cornish – part of the same Cymric Celtic language group as Welsh – as late as the mid-eighteenth century. At about the time Cornish died out, a movement got underway to standardize written English by means of dictionaries. The battle between the forces of standardization and localization continued on into the Victorian era, affecting spoken as well as written English. It was during Victoria's reign that the notion of 'the Queen's English' or Received Pronunciation (RP), first emerged.[78] This London/southeast England accent had become the hallmark of the educated elite by the late nineteenth century. Upper- and middle-class children from all over Britain were forced by public schoolmasters and peer pressure to shed their regional accents in favour of RP. No longer was anyone aspiring to a political or professional career at liberty, as had been Sir Robert Peel, to retain a provincial English, Scottish or Welsh accent. In fact, Scots and Welshmen who were prominent in public life had felt the need to shed their more obvious differences in vocabulary and accent as early as the eighteenth century. Thus we might say that linguistic liberty, especially among the elite, declined during the Victorian period.

Linguistic diversity however did survive among other groups, being most pronounced in those regions furthest from London. Murray's *Handbook for Travellers in Cornwall* (1879) warned its readers that they 'may be frequently puzzled by provincial expressions' in Cornwall. The Cornish language was no longer spoken, but the guide explained that there remained a dialect, or vocabulary, that was unfamiliar to people from other parts of England. For example, the use of the term 'townplace' for an open space in front of a farmhouse was so unfamiliar and un-English that the guide suggested it would be 'as Hebrew' to one uninitiated in the local dialect. In other regions of England, it was the accent that stood out as distinct. At mid-century, Miss S. Taylor travelled north from her home in Birmingham, a region known for its distinct accent. (According to today's hierarchy of accents in Britain, it is still one of the least valued.) While walking round Durham, very un-English sounds confronted her ears. She recorded, 'The people speak a peculiar dialect with a very broad accent. When two or three were in conversation, it sounded like an unknown tongue.' Similarly, returning home to London in 1890 from his first trip to Scotland, W.A. Stephenson noted, 'The Newcastle folks are very *broad* talkers, I think worse than the Scotch.'[79]

While English travellers found their countryfolk who spoke with unfamiliar English accents and dialects disorienting and sometimes aversive, they did not find it impossible to communicate with them. Nor did such linguistic differences make them feel as if they were among a foreign people or 'race'. Though specific words and sounds might seem as un-English 'as Hebrew', the term most likely to be used for an unfamiliar dialect or accent was 'provincial' rather than 'foreign'. This was not the case in Wales where in 1840 roughly two-thirds of the population spoke Welsh, over half of them speaking no English. By 1891 the percentage of the population able to speak Welsh had dropped to just over half, but in absolute numbers there were more Welsh speakers in 1901 than there had been a century earlier.[80] The majority lived in the north and west where the English were less inclined to settle. The only area of official or public life where Welsh was prominent during the nineteenth century was in the churches and chapels. In other areas of officialdom, English had gradually been replacing Welsh since the sixteenth century when the latter language was prohibited as an official form of communication. This meant that the Welsh gentry became English-speaking long before the masses.

The Anglo-Saxons who began invading Britain in the fifth century referred to the native Celtic Britons they pushed west as *wealas*, meaning foreigners, from which comes the word 'Welsh'. It is clear from Victorian travellers' journals that Welsh speakers were still thought of by the English as foreigners rather than as fellow countrymen. While touring North Wales in the late nineteenth century, George Gissing encountered many conversations in Welsh. He wrote to his German friend,

> it is a strange thing to hear this (to me) unintelligible tongue in my native island.... Strange to think that these people have a better

right in England than I have, and that my language is a modern, newfangled thing, compared with theirs.'[81]

Gissing not only was conscious of the marked differences between his language and Welsh, but also imagined the people speaking the language as being different collectively from himself and his people. Hence his use of 'these people' to distinguish them from his own people. Another English traveller in Wales admitted that he would not have found it odd to hear Welsh on the Continent, but to encounter a totally unintelligible language in Britain was very strange to him. He compared Welsh to all the other languages he had heard, and confessed that it 'cut them all out for oddness'.[82] Others thought the Welsh language sounded so rough and bizarre that it required a unique sort of throat to speak it – one designed like a nutmeg-grater.

In addition to being demanding on the throat, the English poked fun at Welsh for being dislocating to the jaw. Travellers often referred to Welsh jaw-dislocating names. A postcard entrepreneur in Llandudro capitalized on this tendency, producing a two-foot long card entitled 'The Great Jaw-Breaker, or An Englishman's Cure for Lock-Jaw'. Stretching the length of the card in large red caps is the 58–letter name of a parish on the Anglesea side of the Menai Bridge: LLANFAIRPWLL-GWYNGYLLGOGERYCHWYRNDROBWLL-LLANDISILIOGOGOGOCH. Although this was the official name, for posting's sake the shorter version of Llanfair, P.G. was used. The literal translation of the whole name is 'The Church of Saint Mary in a hollow of white hazel near to the rapid whirlpool and to St. Disilio Church near to a Red Cave'.[83]

The English went beyond ridicule to denouncing the Welsh language. In the 1840s three English barristers led a commission to inquire into the state of Welsh education. The lengthy Blue Book report denounced Welsh standards of education in every respect, arguing that ignorance and immorality characterized the people. These qualities were mainly attributable, in the commission's view, to the Welsh language. Echoing the commissioners' condescending remarks, Combe noted while travelling through North Wales in the early 1850s, 'The Welsh language is a great obstruction to the improvement of the people.'[84] Outraged by the report's findings, prominent Welshmen energetically defended their country, pointing out the incompetence of and unfair methods used by the commissioners. Furthermore, this official slight upon their country intensified a feeling of national consciousness, elevating the Welsh language to a position of prominence as a symbol of the nation. We might say that the Welsh language signified the nationalism of the

Welsh, and the intolerance of the English-dominated State in which they lived. Travel journals suggest that many Welsh people, including those who had been Anglicized, clung to the Welsh language as an important component of a national identity distinguishing them from the English in particular. George Borrow discovered this on the many occasions when he spoke Welsh to non-English speakers in Wales. Instead of appreciating his knowledge of their language, Welsh speakers were hostile towards Borrow, often falling silent when they realized he understood what they were saying. One woman said to him in exasperation, 'After all, what right have the English to come here speaking Welsh, which belongs to the Welsh alone, who in fact are the only people that understand it.' After travelling for a week in North Wales, Charles New commented, 'It [Welsh] is not like the old Saxon, but has kept quite apart – "a perfect tongue, refusing to mix with any other." The Welsh cling to it very tenaciously.'[85] The development of the English language suggests that the exclusion and hostility went both ways. English has always been a borrowing language, having absorbed a substantial vocabulary from Latin, Danish, French, and many other languages the world over. Yet there is almost no trace of the Celtic languages in English. Old English contained only about a dozen Celtic words.[86]

The Welsh felt closer linguistic bonds with the Celtic Bretons across the Channel than they did with any group within their native island. The traditional Breton-French onion sellers who bicycled through Wales had no difficulty communicating with their Welsh-speaking patrons. Similarly, in 1900 while travelling in Brittany, Welsh politician and patriot Sir J.H. Lewis felt close linguistic links between his people and the Bretons. Riding in an omnibus with several local folk, he noted, 'I opened fire, as usual, by telling them we came from Wales and spoke a language very like Breton, then repeated a number of words common to both languages. This seems to be the shortest cut to these people's hearts.... They become friendly and communicative once this bond of sympathy is established', a bond that Englishmen like Borrow speaking Welsh in Wales did not experience.[87] Language clearly remained an important vehicle among the Welsh for preserving distinctions between themselves and other peoples from Britain during the nineteenth century.

Language was less a source of national identity for the Scots than for the Welsh. This may be attributable to the Scots having other sources of distinct identity the Welsh did not have, such as an established Kirk and unique systems of law and education. Certainly the Scots did not consider the Celtic language of Gaelic as Scotland's national language. By the time Victoria ascended the throne, Gaelic could be heard only in the Highlands, and by the end of the nineteenth century was spoken by only some 5 per cent of the population. Scottish Lowlanders were as apt as the English to view Highland Gaelic as a foreign tongue, despite their having adopted other aspects of Highland culture, notably the kilt and clan tartans, as symbols of the Scottish nation.

The Scots tongue in its pure form did not survive among even 5 per cent of the population.[88] As different from English as Dutch is from German, Scots had been in steady retreat as a written and spoken language since the early seventeenth century when King James and the Scottish court relocated to London and all official documents were produced in English. From this time on, Scottish aristocrats sent their children to English tutors and schools. But even those Scots who were not well-to-do felt pressure to learn English. They did so because James insisted that all churches in Scotland use the newly authorized English-language version of the Bible in their services. (No Scots translation of this version of the New Testament was published until 1983.) Throughout the seventeenth and eighteenth centuries, Anglicization went on in kirk, school and home until the Scots tongue survived only in the verse and song of writers like Robert Burns. By the Victorian period, the majority of people in Scotland spoke English flavoured with certain words and word-order patterns from Scots and a broad Scottish accent – what one early nineteenth-century traveller referred to as a 'curious patois'. Interestingly, this traveller and others noted that the most standard English in Scotland was spoken in the Highlands during the first half of the nineteenth century. This was because many Highlanders had only recently been taught English, and had learned the language grammatically in school as one would learn a foreign language.

Language clearly was a force for both unity and diversity among people from Britain. It contributed to unity in that the Celtic languages lost out to a common English language spoken by the vast majority of Britons. Furthermore, the establishment of received pronunciation, stifling as it was to linguistic liberty, forged a linguistically uniform British elite. Travellers from Britain were most aware of their linguistic links when they were on the Continent among non-English speakers. Within Britain and outside the elite, however, the diversity characterizing spoken language in particular was most striking. Half the Welsh and a tiny minority of Highlanders still spoke Celtic languages at the end of the nineteenth century. But even among English speakers, unique vocabularies, word-order patterns and accents lent distinct linguistic identities to the various regions of Britain. And, although RP unified members of the elite, it simultaneously separated that group from others along class rather than regional or national lines.

Although travel journals are replete with comments about such things as churches, landscape features and people's habits, there is very little discussion of historical sites and memorabilia. What discussion does exist, however, is very revealing of British travellers' attitudes towards the past. Scholars as well as many national communities have noted the importance of a shared past for national identity. Nations are constantly reinforcing the shared feeling by means of celebrations, commemorative monuments and rituals, songs, myths, and so forth. A classic example in Britain is the fifth of November celebrations commemorating the failed Gunpowder Plot of 1605, a celebration David Cressy noted was an early example of 'legislated memory'. But even when Britons join together to celebrate or commemorate 5 November or another aspect of the past they share, the meaning attached to the celebration by various individuals and groups can be very different, as Cressy so persuasively shows. In other words the past, like language, can be a force that both unifies and separates.

A Continental historical site receiving considerable attention in British travellers' journals was the Waterloo battlefield in Belgium. This was a truly *British* national shrine – that is, one that people from various parts of Britain visited, were proud of and invested similar meaning in. They even commemorated the battle at home when naming crackers, rail stations and bridges. Being momentarily sensitive to a French perspective, R.L. Stevenson wrote, 'I wonder...what they call *Waterloo* crackers in *France*; perhaps *Austerlitz* crackers... Do you remember the *Frenchman* who, travelling by way of *Southampton*, was put down in *Waterloo* Station, and had to drive across *Waterloo* Bridge? He had a mind to go home again, it seems.'[89] Given Colley's thesis about the role of war against France in forging British pride and national identity during the eighteenth and early nineteenth centuries, it is not surprising that the Waterloo site had a Britain-wide significance and emotional appeal. Travellers who wrote of it talked of how moved they were to see the field, the monuments, and to think of the nearly 45,000 men – 15,000 of them British or troops of the allies – who died there in June 1815. They had no doubt about what the British soldiers at Waterloo fought and died for; the 'Freedom of Europe', the 'World's Liberties' and the 'Freedom of Nations' were phrases typically used to sum up what the campaign stood for. Thus when commemorating the Battle of Waterloo, the British were imagining themselves as the world's great preservers of liberty, though the image was somewhat exaggerated. British troops composed a third of the total Allied force, with Dutch, Belgians and Hanoverians constituting most of the rest.

By the time Victorian travellers made the trek to Waterloo field, the area had become not only an important historical site, but also a tacky tourist one. Journals are full of outbursts directed at begging children, grasping guides and dishonest relic vendors, innkeepers and coach drivers. The deception and aggressive commercialism cast a pall for British travellers over this most symbolic of places. They complained, for example, of entrepreneurs capitalizing on the Marquis of Anglesey's (Henry William Paget, commander of Allied cavalry) amputated leg, which had been buried in a nearby garden complete with a monument to the lost limb. For a hefty price, one could purchase a piece of leather supposedly cut from the boot removed from the Marquis's leg before amputation. One traveller pointed out that if the pieces of boot sold were joined together in one, there would be sufficient leather to make boots for an army. Other equally rapacious vendors offered such relics from the fight as brass eagles, buttons and lead ornaments. Journals explained that these tourist treasures were actually made in Birmingham and then sent to Waterloo for burial until they were appropriately dusted, rusted and ready for sale. British travellers thus regarded the Waterloo field as symbol both of liberty from European despotism and of enslavement to rampant commercialism.

Given that travel journals often denounce the market atmosphere at Waterloo, one wonders who bought all the manufactured relics. James Smith was most certainly not among those enticed and 'befooled'. His journal reveals most graphically the seriousness with which British travellers approached Waterloo. From Dumbarton just northwest of Glasgow, Smith was touring the Continent for the first time in 1855. He kept a meticulous journal revealing his obsession with accuracy and authenticity. In describing a bluebell, for example, he was not content with mere words. He pressed one on the page beside his text so the reader could see the flower. If he made a mistake in writing, he pasted pieces of paper in the journal with corrected words or phrases. Smith documented his journal with tickets, bills, brochures and so forth, and even these he felt compelled to correct to avoid giving the slightest misconception. A bill from his *pension* in Rigi presented an illustration of the inn whose deception Smith had to make clear. Thus at the bottom of the bill he added, 'Note. The picture gives a tolerable view of the Inn – but the surrounding scenery is grotesquely unlike.'

Smith was not a man to be satisfied with false relics. On this former battlefield, which was now peaceful pasture, Smith waged his own personal war against the cut-throat commercialism all around him. He made a point of recording, 'I bought no relics.' For him, the Waterloo battlefield was a sacred place from which he was determined to take home 'real relics'. He thought of his garden back home, and then proceeded to stuff his pocket, first with a seed from an ear of wheat growing close by the monument to Sir Alexander Gordon (Wellington's personal aide-de-camp). Slightly west of this hallowed ground, he clutched a clod of soil which, once wrapped in paper, filled his pocket as well. Finally, Smith stepped to the part of the field on which 'the decisive combat with the Imperials took end' to find some brilliant red poppies with flowers that had gone to seed. He carefully picked some, nestling them side by side with his 'gathered clod'. Feeling deeply satisfied and somewhat triumphant, Smith declared, '[I]n some choice spot of my garden I shall have poppies from the field of Waterloo growing in soil over which the feet of our guards passed in death less courage to decide the destiny of the World's liberties. These are real relics from the field of Waterloo. Poppies descended through forty generations.'[90]

The Battle of Waterloo was an historical event whose memory was shared and celebrated by people from different parts of Britain. In that sense it was part of a British past and heritage relived by means of pilgrimages to the field. Smith made clear that the coach carrying him around Waterloo was crammed with 'English and Scotch'. The site supports Colley's view that it was military pursuits more than any other that bound the peoples of Britain together, or forged them into a nation. But for most of history the peoples of Britain fought against rather than with each other, and recorded and remembered separate rather than shared pasts. The sense of separate pasts lingered on into the Victorian period and was particularly prominent in travellers' minds when they toured Britain itself.

If we consider travellers' attitudes to historical sites and statues in Scotland, for example, the lack of a common memory among the Scots and English seems paramount. When Scots toured their own country, they were, unlike the English in Scotland, as interested in visiting historical sites as in viewing scenery. In fact, they often wrote in more detail about places like Holyrood Palace and Edinburgh Castle than about Highland scenes. Places and memorabilia to do with Scottish monarchs received the most attention. In writing about Edinburgh Castle, one traveller made a special note of seeing the room where

James VI was born, as well as the Scottish regalia. Scottish visitors to Holyrood Palace wrote at great length in their journals about 'Queen Mary's' apartments – one even drew a floor plan of the rooms in a journal, adding detailed descriptions of the items in each room. While touring the Palace one traveller wrote, 'Here we visited in due order all the apartments that are shown, and of course we were most especially charmed with the remains of the Chapel and with the rooms associated with Queen Mary's history.' It is interesting that Scottish travellers often used the title 'Queen Mary' whereas English travellers almost always referred to the Scottish monarch as 'Mary Queen of Scots' – a phrase that clearly distances the Queen from themselves. Even the Scottish landscape brought memories of native monarchs to Scottish travellers' minds. While travelling not far from Edinburgh, a traveller recorded, 'I suppose we must have passed under the precipice from which Alexander the III had his unhappy fall.'[91] The record referred to the King's death in 1286 when he rode over a cliff in a rainstorm while trying to return home.

The Scottish countryside often brought literary scenes and lines – particularly those of Sur Walter Scott – to English travellers' minds, but almost never historical events. Journals by English tourists reveal not only an ignorance of but also an indifference and even an hostility to Scotland's past. Some writers confessed to being unable to recall the Scottish monarchs and to finding their history boring. Edmund Gosse made no attempt to hide his condescending attitude towards Scottish historical sites and monarchs. It was all he could do to stay awake at Holyrood Palace, a place he admitted was the least interesting to him in all of Scotland. Stories surrounding the Palace that were fascinating to Scottish travellers had Gosse rolling his eyes. As he described his visit,

> We saw all through the rooms redolent of that unpleasant personage, Mary Queen of Scots; we viewed with weary eyes beds that had been slept in by veritable sovereigns, and tapestries that had decked the rooms of several monarchs celebrated for their inanity or their vices. Also, with an air of great mystery, our sceptical vision was allowed to rest on the black stain of Rizzio's blood. I doubt whether a microscope would discover much blood there. Then came the portrait gallery, with all the Scotch Kings since Fergus I, whose blessed memory dates back to some 300 B.C.![92]

Neither Scotland's historical sites nor the Scottish countryside had any historical meaning for Gosse. They were things to mock, but nothing with which he could identify himself or England. Similarly, another English traveller confessed, 'I cannot love the Scotish nation, they're too assuming, proud, much given to self laudation.'[93] He then went on to criticize the many monuments to Scottish patriots, heroes and statesmen displayed all over Scotland, as if the Scots were offensively arrogant for commemorating a past this traveller did not share.

We have seen in this chapter, as in the others, the coexistence of unity and diversity in the national imagining process. The quality of liberty, which travellers from all parts of Britain identified with most strongly when they were on the Continent, seemed most apparent in the context of their thinking about landscape, religion and the state. Regarding the latter, it was their relatively non-intrusive state that stood out in travellers' minds as the source of British liberty. On the other hand, travel to the Continent also highlighted for travellers ways in which life in Britain stifled liberty. All travellers, but especially women, became more self-conscious of the social and moral tyranny they had to endure at home. Travel inside Britain also made people aware of limits to liberty, but in a way that underscored distinct Welsh, English and Scots identities, especially when it came to language and history. This fluidity with respect to identity is clearest when looking at the discourse/terminology of national imagining.

6
The Discourse of National Identity among Victorian Travellers

In so far as travellers from Britain were encouraged to carry a Foreign Office passport, it is surprising that any confusion about their national identity should have existed. All such documents stated very clearly that the bearers were 'British subjects'. Yet ambiguity greeted British travellers upon their setting foot on the closest foreign shore. Whether in Calais or any other part of Europe, British subjects were, despite their passports, universally thought of and referred to as 'English'. As noted above, this use of 'English' was no doubt a result of Europeans Identifying the English – rather than British – language spoken by travellers from Britain. They often referred to American travellers as 'English' for the same reason.

When touring the Continent, travellers from Britain typically deferred to this tendency to lump all people from the British Isles together as 'English'. Robert Louis Stevenson, for example, wrote at length about his Scottishness when in America, but nearly always identified himself as an 'Englishman' if talking with Europeans. His nurse, Alison Cunningham, explained this flexibility regarding national identity terminology. When Stevenson was a boy, Cunningham accompanied the family to the Continent and kept a journal. During these trips she frequently felt homesick for 'bonnie Scotland' and scanned the papers to glean news of her native land. Her journal is full of statements such as, 'Scotland is my home, and I yearn to be there.' Yet when talking with the locals, she usually spoke of herself as 'English'. As she explained it:

> At the table d'hote yesterday a man...asked me if I were English. I said Yes. When I was asked that at first, I used to say 'Scotch,' and they told me it was all the same, but I told this fellow I was from England, so after a little he said, 'Are you not Scotch?' I said, 'Of

course, I am'... I said I was proud of Scotland, and proud to say I was a native of it.[1]

The conversation helps explain why many travellers from Scotland referred to themselves as 'English' in the European context even though, like Cunningham, they thought of themselves and each other as 'Scotch'.

Encounters with Europeans do not by themselves explain Victorian travellers' imprecise usage of national identity terminology. What this study has shown is that British travellers' many ways of imagining national identity were anything but consistent and precise. Instead, ambiguity and contradiction were at the heart of the national imagining process, despite the official documents such as passports where certainty and uniformity regarding national identity reigned. How could it have been otherwise in a state that was technically known as the United Kingdom of Great Britain and Ireland, but commonly referred to as Great Britain, Britain, the three Kingdoms (England, Scotland and Ireland) or England, with the latter term meaning the whole UK, the island of Britain, England and Wales, England or even only the southern part of England, depending on context.

The terms for the peoples composing the state, or United Kingdom, were just as varied and confusing: British, Britons, English, Scotch, Welsh, Irish, Northerners, Southerners, Celts, Gaels and Anglo-Saxons. This chapter focuses on such collective discourse, or terminology, in order to reveal the patterns of usage and of perceiving national identity among Victorian travellers. The use of 'patterns' here is significant – national identity discourse suggests ambiguous, sometimes contradictory perceptions, but not whimsical or random ones. A given term of collective identity was more likely to be elicited in certain contexts than in others.

One pattern of collective imagining was an overarching British one, indicated by travellers' use of terms such as 'British', 'Britain' and 'Britons'. This British identity emphasized the unity rather than diversity of peoples in Britain, at times inclusive of peoples in Ireland as well. Travellers did not typically use such terminology, tending to reserve it for specific contexts. When imagining the state in its political, military, commercial and imperial capacities, travellers most often thought in terms of 'Britain' and the 'British'. They also used these terms when speaking of the island as a geographic place. The usage suggests that British identity was primarily a formal, impersonal one linked to a state and a certain geographic location rather than to a nation in the sense of a people unified by a shared culture. When imagining themselves in a cultural sense, travellers were much more likely to identify themselves as English, Scottish or Welsh.

Travellers were certainly aware of being part of a single British political entity, using kingdom and realm to include all of Britain and sometimes Ireland. Stipulations regarding such political matters as the Crown's and Parliament's respective powers were part of the 'British Constitution'. Although the acerbic travel writer Frances Trollope always used 'English' when speaking of her people collectively, she dined with the 'British Minister' and mentioned the 'British Consul'. Similarly, the author of the Toynbee Travellers' Club journal always used 'England' and 'English', except when encountering several war vessels in the Gulf of Spezzia flying the 'British Flag'.[2] Queen Victoria usually was termed the 'British Monarch' who ruled 'British subjects' – never English, Scottish or Welsh subjects – as certified by their passports. On the passport, political officials were linked with Great Britain, but bearers (in their unofficial status as one of the people as opposed to their official subject status in relation to the monarch) were likely to be associated with Scotland or England. Thus one passport was issued by the Lord Provost 'of the City of Glasgow, Great Britain', and another issued to a 'Mary Armstrong of Edinburgh, Scotland, a British Subject'.[3]

The terms 'British' and 'Britain' appeared most frequently in travellers' journals when they discussed the military dimension of the state or kingdom. For example, tools of war such as troops and vessels tended to be described as 'British'. Thus Henry Clark Barlow alluded to 'natives of European nations, English, French, German' but in the same sentence spoke of 'the British troops at Malta'.[4] Other travellers talked of 'British officers', 'British soldiers', 'British arms' and 'British expeditions'. Battlefields, particularly Waterloo, prompted comments about British patriotism and British power. Despite Waterloo's having become a tawdry tourist mecca by the time T.N. Talfourd visited there in 1845, the site made him think of the British forces and 'the adamantine part of British nature'. Nearly 20 years later, Robert Burn made a pilgrimage to the same field. Throughout his journal he referred to 'brave old England', 'the dear old lands of merrie England' and 'we English'. But on making his way to Waterloo, he admitted, 'The visit or pilgrimage to Waterloo is one which every true Briton, finding himself in Brussels, is bound to make.'[5] This is the only time the term 'Briton' appears in Burn's journal, and he was not the only traveller to adopt this rarely used term when speaking of Waterloo.

The Crimean War elicited a feeling of unity among the Welsh and English, although the term 'Briton' was not used as above. When a Welshman told Borrow of the assumed taking of Sebastopol from Russia, they clinked glasses saying proudly, 'May Britain's glory last as long as the world!' But even this relatively intense and emotional identification with Britain had its limits. As news from the Crimea first broke in Llangollen, there was much celebration and fellow-feeling between the Welsh and the English. Borrow revealed:

> O, great was the rejoicing for a few days at Llangollen for the reported triumph; and the share of the Welsh in that triumph reconciled for a time the descendants of the Ancient Britons to the seed of the coiling serpent. 'Welsh and Saxons together will conquer the world!' shouted brats as they stood barefooted in the kennel.[6]

Note that the Welsh and the Saxons are reconciled, but only temporarily in the revelry of military victory. Furthermore, they are referred to collectively as 'Welsh and Saxons' – not as 'Britons'. The most frequent use of the term 'Briton' in travel journals is, as above, in the sense of 'ancient Britons'.

Travellers frequently identified with Britain as an economic entity, especially a commercial one. Journals make reference to 'British' shipping, goods, commerce, prosperity and manufactures. One journal writer even thought of Britain as a commercial nation. Thus the commercial traveller Throne Crick used 'Britain' when talking of 'our nation, in a commercial point of view'.[7] This is one of the two or three travel diaries among the nearly 100 I have looked at that ever directly referred to Britain or the British as a nation. When referring to nations, travellers typically used the terms English, Scotch, and Welsh, as will become clearer below.

When speaking directly of the empire or adopting an imperial frame of reference, travellers most often used 'British' instead of 'English'. Thus the colonies were British colonies or 'Greater Britain societies'. In his four journals of tours on the Continent in the mid-nineteenth century, Henry Campbell-Bannerman never referred to someone from Britain as British. But of a guide he hired in Malaga named Emanuel Bensaken he said, 'He is Moorish by descent & British (Gibraltar) by birth.'[8] Similarly, the prolific travel writer Matilda Betham Edwards used English almost to the exclusion of British. But when she encountered a retired Anglo-Indian in an out-of-the-way spot in the pastoral, Pyrenean area where she expected to find no foreigners, she exclaimed, 'But the ubiquitous British, where are they not?'[9] In explaining what England was fighting for in World War I, Thomas F.A. Smith listed 'English ideals of justice, English homes, and the existence of the British Empire ... let England rely now on herself and not on another nation's steamroller.'[10] The implication here is that England is a nation; Britain an empire.

It is fashionable among current scholars to argue that, in Britain's case, nation and empire cannot be separated.[11] They insist that collective identity among Britons must be understood within the single context, or 'integrated framework', of empire. For these scholars, empire was the central, core ideology of national culture and taste in Britain. When trying to understand aspects of British national character such as a passion for tea drinking, these scholars note that power relations in the empire were paramount. Underlying this stance is a challenge to the centrality, both of Britain's 'Island Story' and of Europe as a whole, that has traditionally dominated studies of national identity and historical scholarship in general. Antoinette Burton forcefully makes the point that Europe's key tropes and values were not generated primarily within the Continent, but rather in the context of constant interaction with non-European peoples.

In that British historians have tended to ignore the empire or to study it separately from Britain itself, this new trend is exciting and promising. But taken to extremes, it is as problematic as the island-centred approach. What this study suggests is that there was no single frame of reference – imperial or otherwise – for national imagining in Victorian Britain. Depending on context, Britain could be a single state or nation, a multinational state or an empire. It was all these things simultaneously. Empire simply does not explain all. It may have enabled Britons to be avid tea drinkers, but it does not explain why they identified themselves so strongly with that imperial item. After all, tobacco, cotton and cocoa were also imported from overseas, but there is no evidence that the peoples of Britain identified themselves with these imperial products. Furthermore, in shifting our focus to Britons' interactions with non-European peoples, we should not forget that the peoples of Britain first experienced empire within Britain itself – an English empire. Nations and empires existed inside the United Kingdom. It is also true that the discourse known as 'colonial' first emerged in Europe to describe other Europeans. We have already discussed the application of this discourse by Protestants to Catholics. The discourse was thus a European phenomenon that was exported to non-European territories.

The use of 'Britain' and 'British' discussed so far was linked directly to the state. These terms were also resorted to when speaking of a geographic place. Thinking of Britain as a geographic location distinct from the Continent, travellers spoke of 'British rivers', 'British mountains', thunder of 'British mildness', a sun that seldom rises on the 'British Isles', 'British seaports', and so forth. Murray's Handbook for France was typical in referring to people as 'English' – in part due to the assumed English audience – but to the island territory as 'Britain'. When discussing inland steamers, for example, the guide noted, 'In almost all cases the engineers employed on these vessels are Englishmen, and the French do not seem to have aptitude for this duty. The rivers of France, however, are more liable than those of Britain to rise and fall.'[12] Like rivers, flora and fauna elicited associations with Britain. One traveller spoke of a particular plant as 'a curious shrub that in Britain grows only on a single limestone ledge of the Great Ormes Head.'[13] Travellers frequently referred to things 'in Britain' or 'of Britain', meaning throughout the entire island or parts familiar to them. Thus Miller talked of 'the mineral springs of Great Britain'. He also used the term 'British' as with 'British intellect', but not in the sense of a kind of intellect different from English or Scottish. His 'British intellect' was a Britain-wide one – a geographic phenomenon again – that included two very different sorts of intellect, which he repeatedly termed 'English' and 'Scotch'.[14]

In addition to these state-related and geographic contexts, 'British' appears in travel journals as a modifier of nouns referring impersonally to people in the mass or abstract. When speaking of the public, for example, travellers typically made reference to the 'British public'. It is interesting that the less abstract term 'people' usually inspired the use of 'English', 'Scotch' or 'Welsh' rather than 'British'. On occasions when travellers spoke collectively of a group to which they did not belong, such as mechanics, workers or farmers, they tended to write of 'British mechanics' but of themselves as Englishmen or Scotchmen. Henry Mayhew commenting on German life and manners in the 1860s was typical in this respect. Observing the German middle class, he was struck by their squalor and lack of comfort compared to the English middle class. Imagining how his English readers would react to descriptions of his middle-class accommodations in Eisenach, Mayhew admitted he 'knew in an instant how they were wondering within themselves that an Englishman, like ourselves, could consent to put up with fare and shelter which were hardly so good as those of a British mechanic.'[15]

As mentioned previously, travellers very rarely referred to themselves collectively as 'Britons'. They were much more likely to use this term to refer to ancient Britons rather than to themselves. Those who did refer to themselves as 'Britons' tended to be Scots or else English, but of mixed family background. For example, John Macgregor (nicknamed Rob Roy) paddled his canoe 1,000 miles around Europe. He often had to coax accommodation out of cosy households nestled by river banks. Late one night he knocked and called until 'a fat farmer cautiously took the light upstairs, and, opening a window, thrust the candle forward, and gazed out upon me standing erect as a true Briton.' Mrs Dinah Craik was the only traveller who repeatedly spoke of 'we Britons', but it should be noted that, although she was from England, her father was Irish and her husband/travelling companion was Scottish.[16]

The rare appearance of 'Britons' and 'British' in reference to people does not mean that the peoples of Britain never imagined themselves as a people unified by certain values and sensitivities. We have already seen how encounters with Europeans sparked a sense of shared identity among peoples from Britain with respect to religion (Protestantism), landscape (accessible, human scale), taste buds (meat eating and sincere), manners (reserved), liberty, and so forth, even though the term 'British' was not necessarily associated with these things. Furthermore, there is linguistic evidence of Britishness besides nationality terminology. The use of 'our', 'we' and 'us', for example, is sometimes indicative of a shared British identity. Even though Nona Bellairs was from England, she could still imagine villages in Wales as *hers*. As she travelled from Boulogne to Paris she noted, 'The villages have a very comfortless look (like *our* Welsh ones).'[17] Similarly, Dorothy Quillinan spoke of 'our Cambrian heights' as if Welsh mountains and landscape scale were hers too. Betham-Edwards felt the same while travelling in eastern France when she said, 'We have just such bits of wood, waterfalls, and mountains in North Wales.'[18] It was the Italian natural world, particularly the vines, lizards and hot rocks, that made an Englishman from Stockton feel kin to all peoples from the British Isles. While touring Italy he declared, '[A]ll nature seemed to bespeak a fresh state of things to us northmen coming from the misty isles of Britain.'[19]

These expressions of solidarity and common possession were sparked by thoughts of Britain's landscape and climate. The same sort of linguistic evidence exists, sparse though it is, for a shared cultural identity. Yorkshire woman Mary Eyre wrote in her journal about how countries and peoples had their particular poets. In describing a well-known Pyrenean poet she said he 'is as much a true poet, and as popular among them as Burns with us'.[20] Her comment suggests that Scotland's national poet also belonged, in her mind, to the English. Churches were sometimes imagined as British cultural shrines, rather than as the property of a specific religion or part of Britain. After touring the Church of Our Lady in Paris, the Scotsman John Dunlop proclaimed it as 'not so fine as *our* Westminster Abbey'.[21] Henry Richard, a fervent Congregationalist, compared Italian churches to 'our own churches', especially St. Paul's.[22] A big difference between churches in Britain and those in Italy, according to Richard, was the absence in the latter of monuments to warriors. He thought of all the marble men struggling, heaving and stabbing each other that decorated British churches and did not feel proud. John Forbes spoke more positively about crosses and kings in Britain. Forbes was born and raised in Scotland but eventually settled as a physician in England. He talked of 'our ancient Gothic crosses, like the monument of Walter Scott in Edinburgh, and the Martyr Monument in Oxford'. While inspecting a castle along the Danube, he even alluded to 'our King Richard' who was once a prisoner there.[23] Forbes admitted to a touch of romantic feeling as he passed the spot where Richard was detained.

Several travellers spoke more directly of the British as being a single people, nation or race. In discussing French fortitude and resignation in adverse circumstances the Scotsman Thomas Brown hoped that these qualities would eventually combine with more favourable feelings towards 'the people of Great Britain'. He wanted the favourable feeling to become mutual, so that the animosity that had 'disturbed the harmony of the two nations' (France and Britain) would cease.[24] The historiographer-royal of Scotland heaped pages of praise on the union between Scotland and England for its making 'British power and progress' possible. He talked of Scotland and England as two nations, but two kindred nations whose union was 'as natural a national adjustment as the restoration of an exiled child is a natural family adjustment'.[25] In other words, the Scots and the English were, to his way of imagining, part of the same family. They were also part of the same country, according to Reverend Francis Trench, who was from England but had Irish ancestry. Trench described himself as a resident of 'the south of Great Britain' who was determined to explore 'parts of our country' that he had not been to before – Scotland and the North of England.[26] Some travellers, like Miss S. Taylor from the Birmingham area, referred to Scotland as 'North Britain', but this was not a very common usage in the nineteenth century.

Other evidence suggests that some Britons thought of themselves as a homogeneous people because of their physical characteristics and surnames. During her trip to the Pyrenees, Mrs Ellis fulminated against English dandies' attempts to look French. She thought it ridiculous to encounter 'the light complexion, fair hair, rosy cheeks, and long upper lip, of a native Briton' under a fashionable French disguise.[27] The European context may have encouraged Ellis to focus on physical similarities, or perhaps she was using 'Briton' here to mean English. For as we will see below, the English often spoke disparagingly of the way Celts and Gaels looked, pointing out their small stature, coarse features, lack of beauty, and so forth. Perspectives on similarities and differences between the peoples of Britain were not consistent, and could change very quickly, as Borrow discovered in Wales when talking with a man who called himself an Anglesey bard. The two shared a passion for poetry, and the bard thus spoke of their kindred spirit. When he did, he referred to Borrow as a fellow 'Briton'. Shortly thereafter, the bard invited Borrow for a drink, but was enraged when Borrow paid for the drinks. In lashing out at Borrow for being insensitive to others' feelings, the bard suddenly resorted to calling him an 'Englishman' and a 'Saxon', emphasizing the differences between the two men.[28]

When it came to surnames, the British thought of themselves as a distinct, unified people in relation to the rest of the world. This assumption of Britishness affected official policy in the Foreign Office, as correspondence from a Mr H.J. Leppoc reveals. Leppoc sent passport certification on an official form for a Mr Arthur Henriques, stating that he was a 'British born subject'. Refusing to accept the form, the Foreign Office asked Henriques to produce certification of his birth. Leppoc sent a letter of protest claiming that this request was an insult, especially given Henriques' position in the Commission of the Peace for the County of Lancaster and also for Manchester. The response from the FO official read, 'I am to explain to you that this precaution is very generally adopted when the name of the applicant is not of British origin.'[29]

There was another form of collective imagining in Britain that was overarching in scope, and that form is reflected linguistically in the use of 'England' either for England and Wales or for Britian as a whole. There is an imperialist assumption underlying this usage, in that things English are simply assumed to be applicable to Wales and Scotland. These two parts of the island appear to make no contribution to Britain and the British. This English arrogance is expressed clearly by a traveller in Wales who was frustrated by his Welsh-speaking guide and complained, 'Why will leaders of opinion persist in encouraging the use of worn out languages in Great Britain when English laws and English equality rules everywhere. It simply festers old antipathies which are better at rest.'[30] No doubt he was not aware or did not think it worth mentioning that laws in Scotland were different from those in England. Nor did he recognize that his sense of English superiority rather than 'equality' was very likely a continuing cause of antipathies in Britain.

Given the imperial relations suggested by this usage, one might expect that it was only the English who used England for England and Wales or used England and Britain interchangeably. But Welsh and Scottish travellers did the same. Henry Richard was a Welsh patriot who worked hard to interpret things Welsh for the English. In discussing 'the opinion and judgement of the great bulk of the English public' on the subject of Mr de Lamartine, Richard explained that he knew that opinion very well because he had 'traversed the whole country, holding public meetings which were attended by crowded audiences, in all the principal towns of England and Scotland.'[31] Given that he travelled the whole country and learned about English public opinion in England and Scotland, it seems clear that Richard is using 'English' here to mean British, which suggests he must have been using 'England' to mean England and Wales.

Others were more obvious about considering Wales to be a part of England. A tourist from Brighton was at Hobbs Point in Pembroke (in southwest Wales) where he and a companion walked to a dockyard that they 'were informed has the largest building sheds in England'.[32] Postal addresses implied as well that Wales was part of England – not Britain. D. Morgan Lewis wrote his address at the beginning of his journal as:

D. Morgan Lewis
Velindre RS6
Pembrokeshire
Wales. England[33]

Some travellers even thought of the North Welsh mountains as England's mountains. Touring the Snowdonia area, a Liverpool merchant thought what a great privilege it was to visit a 'mountain land'. He chastised the Englishman who ignored his own country's mountains in favour of the Alps or Appenines. To his way of thinking, the most picturesque mountains were those that allowed for easy comparison of height and depth as well as rugged barrenness and lush fertility. Based on these critera he claimed proudly, '[T]he mountain scenery of our own land, whether of England, Scotland, or Ireland is almost unrivalled.'[34] Since the merchant was in Wales and it was Wales and not England that was considered the 'mountain land', one assumes he was thinking of Wales as a region of England.

Travellers also used England when Britain would have been the more accurate term, or they used England and Britain interchangeably, often in the same sentence. In talking of churches in Amsterdam, for example, Charles Wood exclaimed, 'There are always two English churches in Amsterdam: the Established Church of England, and the Presbyterian Church of Scotland.'[35] Wood may have used 'English' in this case because of the European context in which all things to do with the British Isles were referred to as English. But even Mrs Craik, who typically used 'Britain' and we 'Britons' when in Europe, was capable of referring to the whole British Isles as England. In France she wrote, 'We are prone to judge France solely by Paris, which is about as just as if we were to judge England, that is to say, the whole of the British Islands, by London.' On one occasion Craik reversed the usage (an uncommon phenomenon), mentioning Britain when England would have been the more appropriate term. Thus when admiring the Bayeux Tapestry she noted, 'Throughout, William is put forward as Britain's rightful heir.'[36]

In some travel handbooks and journals 'English' and 'British' were interchangeable terms of collective identity used as if they were synonyms from a Thesaurus to combat monotonous writing. A classic example is the 1852 edition of Murray's guide to France that advised, 'An English passport may now be obtained at the Foreign Office...by British subjects...and is the best certificate of nationality which an Englishman can carry abroad.' Another Murray handbook contained a section entitled 'British Secretary of State's Passport' but its first sentence read, 'Those who do not grudge the considerable...price of an English Secretary of State's Passport.'[37] Travellers from all parts of Britain at times displayed this casualness and whimsicality regarding nationality terminology, without exhibiting any sense of guilt about betraying their own or anyone else's sense of collective identity. In the late twentieth century people continued to interchange English and British, but tended to do so more cautiously and apologetically. The historian Russell Chamberlin, for example, in his study *The Idea of England*, felt it necessary to include the following dedication:

> To my Scottish, Irish and Welsh compatriots
> with relative apologies for use of the
> universal adjective 'English'.[38]

I never found any such sensitivity expressed by nineteenth-century travellers.

Travellers did not typically use 'England' and 'English' in a universal sense or usually betray the sort of whimsicality about their identity evident in Murray's guide. As the above evidence suggests, an impersonal political or geographic context very often prompted travellers to use the terms 'Britain', 'British' and sometimes even 'Britons' when identifying themselves collectively. If travelling on the Continent, people from Britain sometimes expressed a shared cultural identity as well, even if they did not refer to themselves as 'British' or 'Britons'. But the typical pattern of collective imagining when the context was personal, cultural or involved expressions of emotion, affection or pride was one that emphasized the differences between the English, Scots and Welsh. In this context, whether travellers were on the Continent or touring around Britain, they tended to imagine themselves as 'English', 'Scotch' and 'Welsh' rather than as 'British'.

When travellers from Britain encountered and referred to each other, they usually did not use the terms 'British' and 'Britons', but rather 'English', 'Scotch' and 'Welsh' (the latter term used mostly in Britain, as the Welsh did not often travel to the Continent). In other words, they remained conscious of the distinctions between themselves as *peoples* of Britain, even in Europe where the things they shared were highlighted in their minds. Thus when James Smith described all the company occupying his coach bound for Waterloo, he spoke of them as 'English or Scotch' – not British. Similarly, A. Cunningham made reference to 'the English and Scotch residents' in a French town, and C. Ingleby listed his fellow steamer passengers as 'a majority of Englishmen, two Germans, one Frenchman, and several Scotchmen'.[39] Scotsman William Chambers talked of the 'much respected British consul' at Rotterdam, but was keen to point out that he was a 'Scotsman, an elder of the Scottish church in the town'.[40] Chambers said this with much pride, and seemed intent on reinforcing the worthiness and respected reputations of Scotsmen – not Englishmen or Britons – in Holland.

When travellers referred to themselves collectively as a nation, they almost never used the term 'British'. I found only two or three references to a 'British nation' in all the travel books I examined. Fortunately for my study, travellers in Europe were often asked directly to state their national identity. The year before he toured Scotland, the Reverend Trench crossed the Channel for a holiday on the Continent. In Spain some soldiers inquired of him, 'What nation are you of?' He responded, 'English'.[41] No traveller ever answered 'Britain' or 'British' in response to that question. Trench and others may have been deferring to Europeans' use of 'English' as a universal term. But travellers' own imaginings as reflected in their journals reveal that they thought in terms of separate English, Scottish and Welsh nations. Thus one traveller was amused on a boat bound for Antwerp by watching the passengers and 'seeing the variety of nations represented by them, English, French, Swedes, Scotch, Germans'.[42] Jane Carlyle imagined that her failure to keep her promise to write to her friend Eliza in London had compromised the friend's opinion of the entire Scottish nation. She confessed to Eliza, 'I could wager you now think the Scotch a less amiable Nation than you had supposed.'[43] The Scots were anything but amiable in Eliza Salvin's estimation. She clearly was relieved to be part of the very separate English nation. She and her family attended the English church in Interlaken where they heard a most monotonous sermon. In speaking of certain members of the congregation she noted, 'The vulgar people who so horrified us turn out to be Scotch, which is a satisfaction to one's national pride – they at least are not English.'[44]

The Welsh also thought of themselves and were thought of as a distinct nation. In defending Wales's Eisteddfod, its president talked of how each nation had specific pleasures and amusements. The French revered dancing, the English horseracing and the Welsh poetry and music as performed at the Eisteddfod, according to his way of thinking. He claimed to respect other nations' amusements and wanted 'a reciprocal feeling on their part towards our national passion for the Eisteddfod. We Welsh are an impulsive, impassioned people, proud of our country and all that belongs to it.'[45] English travellers thought of the Welsh as a separate people with their own 'national instrument' (the harp) and 'national costume' (worn mostly by rural women).

Expressions infused with affection, emotion or patriotism almost always inspired the use of 'England' and 'English' if the travellers were from England.[46] In comparing the Continent with things at home, many journals speak of 'dear old England' – never dear old Britain. Fanny Kemble's stay at Marseilles was marred by the filthy water she attributed to a political system too centralized to be effective at the local level. The foul-smelling water had her praising her home-grown political freedoms and declaring, 'How much coming abroad makes us love England!' Declarations of love for England and pride in being English were elicited on the Continent by everything from rancid water to factories. Kemble was gushingly patriotic about a factory in Marseilles set up by an Englishman. According to her, the factory elicited amazement from Frenchmen because of its remarkable success and harmonious employee relations. As she listened to the locals' descriptions, she thought, 'Oh! my dear, dear countrymen, how truly I believe that you, and you alone, could have achieved such a noble triumph. My heart melted and my eyes filled with tears... I could not repress a feeling of patriotic pride in the belief that none but Englishmen could thus have undertaken and thus accomplished.'[47] Borrow felt a similar pride along the Birmingham-to-Tipton stretch of his route to Wales as the belching cathedral-high chimneys, sinister furnaces and steam-driven hammers inspired a rhapsody on the glories of English industry and made him feel 'proud of being a modern Englishman'.[48]

Travellers from Scotland were equally adamant about and proud of their Scottish identity. Jane Carlyle, for example, moved south to London as a new wife and wrote many letters home conveying the sentiments of an exile. English ladies seemed so wasteful and impractical to her, and all of London artificial. She thought of Scotland as fresh and clean, and referred to it as her own land and to the Scotch as 'my... Nation'. She at times could not contain her national pride, as when she admitted to Mrs Carlyle, 'I never cease to be glad that I was born on the other side of the Tweed, and that those who are nearest and dearest to me are Scotch.'[49] Robert Louis Stevenson felt equally patriotic towards Scotland, especially when he was outside the country. In his essay 'The Scot Abroad', Stevenson noted that Scotland was diverse enough to make him feel, when in Scotland, that a Glaswegian was a rival and a man from Barra almost a foreigner. But in thinking of meeting a Glaswegian or any other Scotsman outside of Scotland, he spoke of the shared Scottishness they would feel because 'some ready-made affection joins us on the instant'. He thought the affection between countrymen in Scotland was much more intense than among countrymen in England. In his view, 'An Englishman may meet an Englishman tomorrow, upon Chimborazo, and neither of them care; but when the Scotch winegrower told me of Mons Meg, it was like magic.... And, Highland and Lowland, all our hearts are Scotch.' These thoughts prompted him to exclaim, 'The happiest lot on earth is to be born a Scotchman.' He apparently wanted to die one as well. Although he could imagine dying anywhere in the world, he stated with conviction, 'I long to be buried among good Scots clods.'[50] His nurse was as stongly attached to Scotland as he, thinking of it as her much-loved home. When on the Continent, she frequently felt homesick for 'bonnie Scotland', and scanned the papers to glean news of her native land. Her journal is full of statements such as, 'Scotland is my home, and I yearn to be there.'[51]

The experience of travelling, particularly around Britain, worked to enhance awareness of the differences between her countries and peoples, and thus to intensify identification with England, Scotland, or

Wales. Publishers of guidebooks reinforced these identities and differences by never producing a volume on Britain as a whole. They conditioned travellers to think in terms of smaller geographical frames of reference when describing cities and sites. Thus the bridges over the Menai Straits are 'those modern wonders of Wales' – not of Britain. The *Picturesque Tourist of Scotland* described rivers, lakes, mineral products, and so forth as being features of Scotland. And the guide typically compared things Scottish to those in England, as when it referred to 'the inferiority of the climate and soil, as compared to England'.[52] One handbook for Scotland linked the Scots more to peoples on the Continent than to those in Britain. In discussing ecclesiastical remains in Scotland and England the handbook quoted an authority who maintained:

> Though so near a neighbour, and so mixed up with England in all the relations of war and peace, the Scotch never borrowed willingly from the English, but, owing probably to the Celtic element in the population, all their affinities and predilections were for continental nations and especially for France. So completely is this the case that there is scarcely a single building in the country that would not look anomalous and out of place in England.[53]

Whether this quote is accurate or not, it predisposed travellers to think of the Scots and the English as two distinct peoples whose differences would be immediately apparent upon crossing the border.

We have already seen how travellers' writings about tours around Britain emphasized the differences between the island's peoples, particularly in the area of religion, but also with respect to attitudes about landscape, education, house design, food, language, history, and so forth. Some journals suggest, as does the above quote, that such differences would have been apparent immediately upon crossing the border between England and Scotland. Unlike on the Continent, there were no customs officials or passport checks at borders within Britain signalling the boundaries of different political or national entities. For Reverend Trench, passing from his native England into Scotland was simply a matter of crossing a stream at Gretna Green, and the Tweed near Kelso on his way back south. But almost instantly, in both cases, he was acutely aware of having passed a border between different peoples and environments, making him feel more self-consciously English. On re-entering England he remarked:

> We stopped at a pleasant inn, about a mile on the English side of the border. The character of the old village church told us, in a moment, where we were. I had seen nothing of a similar appearance throughout all Scotland.[54]

The Tweed loomed equally large in Hugh Miller's mind as a dividing line between his native Scotland and England. Writing his *First Impressions* as he travelled through England, Miller felt more Scotish than ever and made no effort to hide his partiality, as his preface reveals:

> It does matter considerably in some things that a man's cradle should have been rocked to the north of the Tweed; and as I have been at less pains to suppress in my writings the peculiarities of the Scot and Presbyterian than is perhaps common with my countryfolk... the Englishman will detect much in these pages to remind him that mine was rocked to the north of the Tweed very decidedly. I trust, however, that he may forgive me my partialities to my own poor country.[55]

This sense of difference frequently produced hostile rather than forgiving feelings between people from opposite sides of the border, making a common British identity problematic. Borrow, one of the more tolerant travellers, repeatedly experienced hostile treatment from Welsh speakers averse to an Englishman speaking their language. He interpreted this as an expression of suspicion, noting that all conquered peoples are suspicious of their conquerors. He spoke 'of the Saxon race, against which every Welshman entertains a grudge' – a grudge responsible for the discomfort felt by many English people he met in Wales. One couple spoke of Wales as a 'strange land' and longed every day to be back in England. When Borrow inquired why they did not befriend their Welsh neighbours, the homesick wife responded, 'The English cannot make friends amongst the Welsh. The Welsh won't neighbour them, or have anything to do with them, except now and then in the way of business.'[56]

Although Borrow himself did not feel Wales to be uncomfortably strange, he did think of Scotland as a particularly foreign country. Of its inhabitants he said, 'A queerer set of people than the Scotch you would scarcely see in a summer's day.'[57] Regular holidays north of the Tweed rendered Beatrix Potter no more tolerant of the Scots. What gentility and intelligence they displayed was, in her mind, only a thin veneer disguising but not hiding the fact that 'they are all savages'.[58] Her critical remarks were mild compared to Edmund Gosse's denunciations. When in Stirling he recorded, 'I was disgusted with the extreme Scottishness of the people. Like Dr Johnson, I could smell them in the dark. The vices of a Lowlander are unseemly, there is no shame in being very drunk before breakfast. We English are not wild till nightfall.... Be it here recorded that I hate the Scotch.'[59] Potter's and Gosse's comments were unusually harsh and derogatory, perhaps because their writings were not intended for publication.

Extremely derogatory remarks and hostile attitudes were more likely to accompany racial terms of collective identity rather than national ones. Victorians sometimes used 'nation', 'race' and 'people' interchangeably as they did 'English' and 'British'. At the same time, anthropologists were using anthropometry, or anatomical measurement, to link the races and 'stocks' within racial groups more methodically and scientifically to physical characteristics such as skull size and shape, facial angle, skin colour, hair texture, and so forth.[60] Over the course of the nineteenth century, people increasingly came to use 'race' when they had in mind biological/physical characteristics and 'nation' when referring to cultural and political qualities, though the two were very closely related in people's minds. That is, physical characteristics were thought to have implications for cultural and political values, and nations were assumed to be characterized by a 'true national type' displaying certain physical qualities. When talking of physical traits and their cultural implications travellers often used 'race' as in 'English race' or 'Scotch race', or they used such terms as 'Anglo-Saxon', 'Celt', 'Cambrian', 'Gael' or 'Norsemen'. These terms suggest origins and identities that pre-date nations in the British Isles, and were used by travellers to emphasize differences *and* hierarchies between the peoples of Britain – even to exclude, at least perceptually, certain people from a national group.

When travel handbooks and journals talked of Celts, for example, they typically noted physical attributes and implied inferior status. The Bretons of Brittany had the same Celtic roots as the Welsh and Cornish, and travel books noted their similarities. Murray's Handbooks for France depicted Brittany as a very inferior place compared to Normandy with respect to scenery and level of civilization. In fact, the books maintained that Brittany was less civilized than nearly every other part of France, and old-fashioned in all things, as were Wales and Cornwall. Travellers read that Bretons were as wild as their countryside, being 'usually mean and small in their persons; coarse-featured in face; squalidly filthy in their habitations'.[61] Their journals reflect a similar view. On crossing from Normandy into Brittany, Campbell-Bannerman observed a decline in the richness of the land and a people who were 'a rough, uncivilized, dirty race, of a much lower type than the Normans'.[62]

Travellers from England and lowland Scotland used the same language of race and inferiority to depict the Celts in Britain. Murray guides once again predisposed them to do so. The guide to Cornwall made reference to the untidy look of Cornish cottages, arguing that the 'utter absence of method in work or business, proclaim the Welsh "Cymry" and the "Cerniwaith" of Cornwall to be of the same blood and race.'[63] It was a physically unattractive race, according to many travellers. On his walking tour of Wales, Charles Lucey, a Londoner, kept a watchful eye on the local women concluding, '[T]he Cambrians are not celebrated for their charms... in general they are short, coarse, and stout as though cased in double folds of Welsh flannel.' Lucey and other English travellers distanced themselves from the Welsh and other Celtic peoples by emphasizing 'racial' origins. A religious service at a Mechanics Institute in Swansea made Lucey feel very foreign and disgusted. Not only did he find the Welsh language sounds 'unearthly' and 'excruciatingly discordant', he also portrayed the minister as 'a coarse dirty Welshman' whose first action at the conclusion of the service was to 'blow his nose with his fingers!'. Lucey found the whole scene so repugnant that he declared, 'I immediately left these descendants of the Druids to worship in their unknown tongue.'[64] The reference to ancient ancestry here was a way for Lucey to reinforce the separateness rather than common bonds between himself and the Welsh.

The Scotsman George Combe was less overwhelmingly negative than Lucey in his evaluation of the Welsh. He thought them to be 'the best race of Celts'. As a phrenologist, Combe was steeped in the sciences of anthropometry and craniometry – the linking of brain size and weight to intelligence and character traits. His relatively high opinion of the Welsh stemmed from their being, in his view, industrious, as evident by their written works in Welsh as well as their chapels and schools. But even these enterprising Celts displayed, to his way of thinking, clear evidence of a common 'Celtic character'. That is, they were 'dirty', their cottages were 'destitute of all beauty or taste... like the same edifices in Celtic Scotland', and their fields were messy with the crops 'choked by weeds'. Combe attributed these negative characteristics to the Celtic brain with its 'narrowness in the anterior lower region'. He did admit, however, that the population was much mixed so that one sees many 'finely organised and some very pretty auburn haired children with blue eyes whose brains are of Saxon forms'.[65] Combe's and others' comments suggest a perceived hierarchy of races in which Saxon and Norman were much superior to Celtic.

The Welshman Henry Richard never spoke ill of his Celtic countryfolk, but he appeared to hold the Scottish Celts in low esteem. Interestingly, he referred to them as 'Gaels' rather than Celts, perhaps in part to separate them from the Welsh. In 1879 he was visiting the Ramsays at Kildalton House not far from Glasgow. They strolled around the estate looking at the cottages Ramsay had built on the premises. Richard admired the cottages but noted how the surroundings and interiors were dirty. Mrs Ramsay complained repeatedly about how difficult it was to persuade the occupants to adopt clean and orderly habits, a dilemma Richard explained simply by saying, 'Most of the inhabitants are Gaels.' He later met a Gaelic-speaker on board a ferry boat and described him as 'a little Baptist Minister...not much to look at and very poorly and thinly clad.'[66] Travellers often postured themselves as being superior to another by using the term 'little'.

Edmund Gosse also focused on physical traits and movements when imagining and conveying the 'inferior' position of Gaels. We have already seen the low regard and hatred he had for the Scots in general. But the lowland Scots were not so exotic, in his view, as to make him feel that he was no longer in Britain when in their presence. This was not the case in Skye where a completely foreign feel enveloped him and his companion. They had just bathed in a refreshing loch and were driving back across a barren moor when 'two mother-naked imps of children' suddenly appeared on a heathery ridge and exhibited 'the wildest gymnastics on heads and hands. It seemed so truly barbaric to see these ruddy little Gaels dancing like little devils in a country peculiarly their own counterpart in savagery, that we had to think twice to persuade ourselves that this was Britain.'[67] Gosse used 'Britain' here for the first time. He certainly did not identify with the Scots or Welsh, or imagine himself as British, but rather as English and a Londoner. Yet, he recognized that England was a part of Britain, and he could not believe that his country and these children were connected in any way, even in the sense of residing on the same island. We might say that Gosse's collective imagining could be mapped by concentric circles, the innermost encompassing London and the outermost cutting through the northernmost Highlands and islands, with the area beyond considered as foreign as a distant continent.

For English travellers, the Anglo-Saxons were as clearly at the top of the racial hierarchy within Britain as the Celts were at the bottom.

Journals and handbooks alluded to how all the best qualities of England and the English – particularly manly power and freedom – stemmed from their Saxon heritage. Henry Mayhew believed that the English owed their creative and productive genius to Saxon roots. He admitted that the 'Norman race' bequeathed to England a fine aristocracy, but went on to wonder and exclaim 'was Newton, was Shakespeare, was Milton, was Watt, was Arkwright, was Bacon, was Locke, of Norman extraction?...they could never have sprung from any other than a Saxon type.'[68] Echoing his pride in Saxon roots, Mary Shelley drew parallels between Germany and England, noting how the former was the 'parent of a race in which women are respected – a race that loves justice and truth'.[69] Victorian travellers repeatedly referred to the kinship between England and Germany, speaking of the two nations as populated by cousins (Murray guides termed the Germans 'first cousins'). They heaped praise on Germany, noting how her people were the source of peace in Europe, unlike the vain French who were so fond of martial glory and dominance. During the Franco-Prussian War (1870–71), English travellers tended to sympathize with Germany and to see France as the main threat to peace in Europe. Samuel Capper, instrumental in administering the War Victims Fund for relief of distress caused by the war, suggested that 'every good man should with his whole soul abominate what is characteristically French civilisation.' He thought the French idolized the senses and were thus more militaristic than other Europeans. By contrast, the Germans were, in his view, 'too well educated and too homeloving to allow themselves to be made instruments of offensive warfare.'[70]

Not surprisingly, this kindred feeling and favouring of Germany had changed markedly by the end of the nineteenth century with the increase of Anglo-German naval rivalry and diplomatic tensions in Europe. English travellers tended by this time to play down differences between the French and the English, and to distance themselves from all things German. Henry Blackburn, for example, emphasized the various likenesses between the English and the Normans. Walking in the fields and along the banks of the Risle, he recorded how English the scene felt in every respect. Even the local peasants looked and sounded to him like kin. Blackburn confessed, '[W]e seem hardly amongst foreigners – both in features and in voice there is a strong family likeness.'[71] A year after the Entente Cordiale (signed 1904) between Britain and France, Betham-Edwards lauded the agreement. Although she admitted to there being many differences between the French and the English, she maintained that their traditional hostilities stemmed from a failure to understand each other. She called for improvement in mutual understanding and concluded by linking France and England as 'the two great democracies of the West' and by urging the two peoples to 'bridge the Channel for ever and a day!'[72] Even I.A.R. Wylie, who lived in Germany prior to the outbreak of the First World War and had been a Germanophile, noted in his *Eight Years in Germany* (1914), '[B]etween the Englishman and the German there is no real affinity whatever. The outward resemblances are superficial and misleading. There is not an idea, or ideal, or ambition which the German shares with us.'[73]

Most of this chapter and book has focused on collective identities that are national in scope, whether British, English, Scottish or Welsh. In the form they were imagined, however, these identities did not necessarily include the entire area of Britain, England, Scotland or Wales and all their peoples. England could be imagined as all of Britain, but in someone like Gosse's mind, it could mean the southern part of England itself, and London in particular. In using Saxon to describe England's heritage, travellers obviously were privileging one people who influenced England and ignoring others including the Normans and Scandinavians. When writing about Cornwall, Murray's guide authors located the region, at least perceptually, more in Wales than in England. Those imagining a Scottish identity did similar things, as in the case of Combe, whose own notion of Scottishness, rooted as it was in an Edinburgh upbringing, excluded the Celtic Scots. The Ramsays of Kildalton did the same. In other words, national imagining often privileged a particular region or people of the nation.

It is also true in travel journals that regional and local identities at times seem more strongly felt or perceived than national ones, though this was not often the case. These identities were highlighted more by travel in Britain than in Europe. For example, long before reaching Scotland, the Reverend Trench recognized that his trek north had taken him into a world different from his familiar one of southern England. In Lancashire, he suddenly felt more southern than English, noting, 'The language of the people... was to me, as a southern, almost like that heard in a foreign clime.'[74] Another traveller was particularly partisan to his county, Gloucestershire, than to a larger English region. While touring the Highlands he met a man from the same county and noted how 'a magnetic attraction sprung up between us, directly we discovered ourselves to belong to the same county – and such a county! We agreed prodigiously with regard to its merits.'[75] Even a European context could inspire a sense of strong identification with a region of England. Elizabeth Carne was surprised to find that this was true, and noted, 'What a strange thing local attachment is!' An invalid and her family staying at Pau prompted the remark. As Carne explained it, the family was from the West of England. Another family unknown to them but from a neighbourhood near to theirs arrived at Pau, but unfortunately the invalid was too ill to see them. When she was told that the visitors came from the West, Carne said her face suddenly brightened up and she emphasized how glad she would be to see them when she was better. '"It is like being with relations," she said.' Carne found the woman's reaction to these strangers very unusual and old-fashioned, given that steamers and railroads were 'gradually stunting and rooting out this instinct of local attachment'.[76] It was hard for her to imagine how anyone could prefer their neighbours to the rest of the world. She explained the preference as expressed here by pointing out that local ties were much stronger in the West of England than elsewhere.

Carne might have been surprised in Wales as well where strong attachments to and hostilities between regions were often very evident. On his travels through Wales, Borrow discovered that the Welsh could hurl venomous outbursts at each other as energetically as at the English. A Bala resident insisted that Llangollen was a town of drunkards set in scenery much inferior to that around Bala, and two men from North Wales told him that South Wales was a 'bad country' full of bad people.

Most collective imagining in travel journals did not focus on the local or regional realms, but rather on the national, though the nations imagined did not always include all regions and inhabitants, as we have seen. National terminology suggests that there were patterns with respect to how people imagined nations, but not precision or consistency. When thinking of the state in a political, military, commercial or imperial context, travellers tended to use the term 'Britain' and to think in terms of an overarching British identity. They also used 'Britain' and 'British' when speaking impersonally about a geographic place or group to which they did not belong. If the context was more personal such that travellers were referring to their cultural identity or to their affectionate and loyal feelings for country, they were more apt to think in terms of Englishness, Scottishness, or Welshness. Just as national imagining could be exclusive by not including certain groups and regions in the nation, it could also be imperialistic by incorporating groups in a way that erased identities, such as when England was used for England and Wales, or for all of Britain. These various usages thus suggest that Britain was simultaneously a single nation, a multinational entity, an English empire and a British Empire, depending on context.

Conclusion

A number of scholars have argued that the nation is the ultimate source of people's loyalty in the modern world. Benedict Anderson has emphasized that people are expected and willing to make the ultimate sacrifice for their national community – that of life itself.[1] People have died in greater numbers for nations over the centuries than for any other type of community. Why? Anderson explained this phenomenon by noting that national identity has been imagined as unchosen and natural, much like familial identity. We have even used words such as 'motherland' and 'fatherland' to describe the nation, and we speak of becoming 'naturalized' when we adopt another nationality. His point is that a community imagined as natural and unchosen possesses the quality of disinterestedness. There is thus a greater moral grandeur in dying for the nation than for some special interest group, whether it be a political party or a professional organization.

We might assume that such extreme loyalty would have been accompanied by certainty with respect to national identity. People in the nineteenth century might reasonably be expected to have been at least as certain and precise as were their passports about their national identity. This book has shown, however, that no such precision existed. In Victorian Britain, there was an ambiguity and elusiveness about national identity. Middle-class men and women exhibited a flexible repertoire of national identities rather than a single one as marked on their passports. To be more specific, there were at least four strongly felt national identities in nineteenth-century Britain, including British, English, Scots and Welsh identities. Geographic context was a key determinant of which one of the four an individual identified with at a given moment. That is, people were more apt to imagine themselves as British when they were on the Continent, and English, Scots or Welsh when in

Britain itself. It is also true that the latter three identities tended to be imagined when the context was cultural or personal, and the British one when the context was political or impersonal.

Focusing only on Britain and Europe as geographic contexts made this book manageable, but very limited in scope. It would have been better to produce a book that included Ireland and parts of the Empire. But what is most important, in my view, is to recognize the contextual nature of national identity, and thus to refrain from making claims for a single such identity or a single framework for understanding national identity in Victorian Britain. Such claims do not seem to coincide with how ordinary people actually conceived of themselves collectively.

This study has implications not only for how people in the past imagined their nations, but also for how we should conceive of our task as historians. Raphael Samuel noted that studies of nations and national identity in the British Isles have not yet answered the question of what the study of history should be mainly about – high politics and government, the state, religion, field systems, family rituals, dining behaviour, landscape, and so forth.[2] Does high politics lend the necessary coherence to our view of the past, or landscape imagery? This book certainly casts doubt on the high politics/government model. It suggests that national identity should be understood in terms of everyday images and rituals to do with landscape, religion, food and drink, recreation, manners, liberty, language and history. These everyday images and experiences were more important in generating a sense of national belonging than the state-sponsored institutions, pageantry and propaganda on which historians of national identity have tended to focus.

Shifting the focus from politics and the State calls into question a current trend in nation studies. Scholars privileging these realms see the state as a constructor of national identity, and thus the emphasis in their analysis has been on invention and newness. This emphasis has greatly enriched national identity studies, making us more aware of how creative and ever-changing the nation-making process is. But we must be careful that this new view does not lead us to ignore the continuities underlying nations. I have argued here for a blending of old and new, by showing that certain aspects of national identity in Victorian Britain incorporated very traditional outlooks that gradually got invested with new meanings.

Although the field of nation studies is burgeoning, there is still scope for future research. We need more studies that explore how ordinary people imagined the nation, in order to balance the many existing ones focused on the construction of national identity by the state and elite institutions. Better yet, future scholars might pay more attention to the relationship between 'official nationalism', or that created by the state, and the sense of national belonging imagined by middle- and working-class people. Such studies will help us better understand the multiple and sometimes competing nationalisms coexisting in a single state. In addition, the relationship between local and national identity is an area of study that has been largely ignored by British historians. Alon Confino has done a superb job of showing how, in Germany, the nation was internalized by means of local images and identities. A similar study based on several counties in Britain might enhance our awareness of what thinking the nation really means.

Appendix: Biographical Information on Travellers

BAILY, Walker – identified himself as being from London. In 1853 he took a short walking tour through North Wales and was most fascinated with engineering feats, including viaducts and roads. Baily was very proud of travelling for ten days on only £6.

BARKER, Edward Harrison (b. 1851, d. 1919) – a journalist/editor educated at Bath Grammar School. He was appointed British Vice Consul for Treport in 1904. Both his father and grandfather (Thomas Barker who painted 'The Woodman') were painters based in Bath. In 1890, Barker travelled by foot in Gascony with only a knapsack.

BARLOW, Henry Clark (b. 1806, d. 1876) – an only child born in Surrey. His father was a revenue officer at Gravesend. He studied medicine in Edinburgh and became a medical doctor. His other main interests were geology and the fine arts. He wrote histories of Italian sculpture and painting. He travelled extensively around Europe and in Scotland between 1841 and 1857.

BARROW, Sir John (b. 1764, d. 1848) – an English explorer born in Lancashire. The *Dictionary of National Biography* (*DNB*) indicates that when asked whether he was a Scotchman, Barrow responded, '"No, my lord, I am only a borderer, I am North Lancashire."' In the 1790s, he became private secretary to Lord McCartney, then ambassador to China, and later (1804) Secretary of the Admiralty. He was founder and vice-president of the Geographical Society (1830).

BAXTER, William Edward (b. 1825, d. 1890) – traveller, author, merchant, and politician born in Dundee, the eldest son of a Dundee merchant. His mother was also from Dundee. Baxter was educated at Edinburgh, returned as a liberal MP for Montrose in 1855, and eventually became Secretary to the Admiralty in Gladstone's first administration (1868). Baxter continued to carry on business as a Dundee merchant until he died. He travelled through Europe in 1849.

BELLAIRS, Nona – identified in her travel journal with England and Protestantism. She travelled for six months through France and Italy with her brother and sister.

BLACKBURN, Henry (b. 1830, d. 1897) – an art editor, author and journalist born in Portsea and educated at King's College, London. He became a Census Officer at Somerset House in 1851. Blackburn travelled around Europe in search of the picturesque.

BORROW, George (b. 1803, d. 1881) – Cornish on his father's side and of Norman stock on his mother's, he was born in Norfolk, though his family moved residences several times. He described himself and his wife as country people of a corner of East Anglia. The *DNB* described him as a great champion of English manliness. Borrow was a communicant of the Church of England. He travelled widely on the Continent and in Britain, taking pride in his linguistic abilities.

BRAITHWAITE, Catherine (b. 1864, d. 1957) – was the youngest daughter of John Bevan and Martha Braithwaite, both Quakers. She spent most of her life in London and Banbury. Braithwaite travelled extensively in Europe for the first time in the 1890s.

BREWSTER, Margaret Maria – daughter of a Scottish physicist. She shared the simple piety of her father, himself licensed as a preacher by the Edinburgh presbytery. She spent time in Cannes and Nice in the mid-nineteenth century.

BROWN, Thomas – appears to have spent most of his life in Scotland. During his school years, he was a friend of Sir Walter Scott.

CAMPBELL-BANNERMAN, Sir Henry (b. 1836, d. 1908) – born in Glasgow and educated at Glasgow University and Trinity College, Cambridge. His father was a Scottish draper, and his mother was from Manchester, though her family was part-Scots as well. Her brother was a well-known Scottish poet. Campbell-Bannerman was the Liberal Prime Minister from 1905 to 1908. His travel diaries detail trips to the Continent in the 1850s and 1860s.

CAPPER, Samuel James – an English Quaker who spent time in France and Germany in 1870/71. He was a representative and member of the Executive Committee of the International Association of Peace and Arbitration and also a sometime Commissioner for the Administration of the War Victims Fund.

CARLYLE, Jane – a Scotswomen who, with her husband Thomas Carlyle, moved to London in the 1830s. Her letters home are full of comments comparing Scotland and England.

CARNE, Elizabeth Catherine Thomas (pseud. John Altrayd Wittitterly) – identified herself with England and the English, considering the 'Scotch' another people. She was a Bible-toting Protestant who travelled in France with three companions in the late 1850s.

CHAMBERS, William (b. 1800, d. 1883) – an Edinburgh publisher born at Peebles in 1800. The *DNB* does not mention his religion, but he was largely responsible for restoring St. Giles Church, Edinburgh so one assumes he was Presbyterian. He travelled to Holland and the Rhineland in the late 1830s, primarily to observe the Dutch system of public primary education.

CHURCHILL, Charles J.F. (b. 1823, d. 1905) – born in Weybridge, Surrey. He and his father ran a wood brokers firm in London. He travelled to the Continent in the 1860s, keeping a journal that is now housed in the Guildhall Library.

222 Appendix: Biographical Information

COMBE, Cecilia – daughter of the actress Sarah Siddons, who married Scotsman George Combe.

COMBE, George (b. 1788, d. 1858) – a phrenologist who was born and raised in Edinburgh. He had a strict religious upbringing and consequently had a poor view of religion once he became an adult. Combe produced many writings on phrenology and the relationship between science and religion. In politics he favoured Richard Cobden, who advocated free trade, and was a great proponent of secular education for all. Combe kept a continuous diary of his travels from 1841 to 1858.

CRAIK, Dinah Maria Mulock (b. 1826, d. 1887) – born in Staffordshire where her father was minister of a small nonconformist congregation. Although she spent most of her life in England, her father was Irish and she married a Scot, George Lillie Craik, in 1864. They had no children. Craik was a successful authoress by the mid-1850s. She went to the Continent for the first time in 1870, touring in Paris, Normandy and Brittany.

CUNNINGHAM, Alison (b. 1822, d. 1913) – born in Fife, she was a Scots Presbyterian who was nurse to Robert Louis Stevenson during a family tour on the Continent in 1863.

DALGAIRNS, Father Bernard (b. 1818, d. 1876) – born on Guernsey of Scots descent on his father's side and of an old Norman family of Guernsey on his mother's. He was educated at Oxford and became a Catholic in 1845.

DICKENS, Charles (b. 1812, d. 1870) – born in Portsea and lived most of his life in southern England. His father was a clerk in the Navy Pay Office, who lived a careless, irresponsible lifestyle that ultimately brought poverty on the family. Dickens's first article appeared in 1833 and by 1836 he was a successful author. Many children and needy family relations placed Dickens under constant financial strain, and so he decided to re-energize himself in Italy in the mid-1840s. He made many trips to the Continent in the 1850s as well.

DONALDSON, Agnes Twining – youngest daughter of tea merchant Richard Twining. She married Andrew Donaldson in 1872, and they kept a joint journal from their wedding day until Agnes's death in 1918. Agnes had also kept journals of family trips to Europe before she married. Andrew Donaldson studied art at both the Royal Academy School and in Rome. He worked mainly in London, but went on frequent painting trips to Europe, often accompanied by his wife and children.

DUNDAS, Mary Winifred – daughter of Robert Dundas, rector of Albury. She called Chilworth in Southwest Hampshire home. Dundas went to the Continent for the first time in 1894.

EDWARDS, Matilda Betham (b. 1836, d. 1919) – the fourth daughter of Suffolk farmer, Edward Edwards, and Barbara Betham, and cousin to the Egyptologist

Amelia B. Edwards. Her travel writing focuses mainly on late nineteenth-century France. She was a socialist at heart, proud of her ability to travel in unfrequented areas without the aid of guidebooks or the comfort of hotels, choosing to stay with friends or locals. Edwards was strongly anti-clerical.

ELLIS, Mrs Sarah Stickney (b. 1799, d. 1872) – born in Yorkshire to a farming family. Although raised a Quaker, she later became a member of the Congregational Church. She married William Ellis, a missionary, in 1837. They had no children. Stickney Ellis shared her husband's missionary zeal, and both promoted the cause of temperance and the moral training of the young. Ellis wrote popular advice books for women, but also composed a journal about her 15-month stay in the Pyrenees.

EYRE, Mary – a Yorkshire woman who walked through the south of France in the 1860s. She travelled alone, and very humbly, carrying only a small waterproof stuff bag.

FABER, Frederick William (b. 1814, d. 1863) – grew up in the North of England and was educated at Oxford. His family was of Huguenot origin, and in his youth he shared their Calvinist beliefs. At Oxford, however, he came under the spell of J.H. Newman. Though he was ordained a deacon in Ripon Cathedral in 1837, he renounced Protestantism eight years later and was received into the Catholic Church. He made many trips to the Continent.

FISHER, T.W. – set off in 1865 from London for a walking tour through North Wales. A fiercely independent traveller who shunned guidebooks and companionship, Fisher walked 200 miles, was away for twelve days, and spent £7 6s.

FORBES, Sir John (b. 1787, d. 1861) – a physician born in Banffshire. He was educated in Scotland, but then settled as a physician first in Penzance, then was very successful in Chichester, and in 1840 settled in London. He travelled to Germany and the Tyrol in the 1850s.

FOUNTAINE, Margaret (b. 1862, d. 1940) – a country Anglican clergyman's daughter born near Norwich in 1862. She had a very conventional upbringing, but eventually fell in love with and pursued unsuccessfully an Irish alcoholic. With a private income of about £400 per year, she decided to travel to study butterflies. She ended up on the road for 28 years, spending most of the time with a Syrian man married with children. Fountaine kept diaries from 1878 until she died. These diaries remained sealed up in a box in Norwich's Castle Museum until 1978, exactly 100 years after the first diary entry and the date Fountaine's will stipulated they be opened to the public for the first time.

FRANCIS, Horace – embarked from London on his first visit to Wales in 1837, travelling 800 miles in three weeks. Although he comments on all sorts of sights, he admits that churches are the first thing he and his party visit in a town.

FREEMAN, Edward (b. 1823, d. 1892) – born in Staffordshire, he was orphaned in infancy. He grew up with his paternal grandmother in Northampton and was eventually educated at Oxford. He characterized himself as an historical inquirer, and was most interested in uncovering the history of central France's smaller cities. He wrote an account of his travels around France in the 1890s.

FRYER, Frederick (b. 1824, d. 1872) – a Yorkshire Quaker who set up as a tea dealer in Leeds and married Elizabeth Longdon, a Manchester woman, in 1850. He travelled for eight months on the Continent with his brother-in-law in 1844.

GISSING, George (b. 1857, d. 1903) – the eldest son of a pharmaceutical chemist, Gissing was a kind of social outcast who spent much of his life living hand to mouth. He published novels from the 1880s on. His imagination was always fired by the classics, and his travels to classical sites, particularly in southern Italy, were most important to him. He was a real English patriot.

GREEN, John Richard (b. 1837, d. 1883) – a clergyman/historian who was educated at Oxford where he came under the influence of Tory, High Church views. He was ordained deacon in 1860, but had to abandon clerical work in 1869 due to ill health. His *Short History of the English People* was very popular.

GRIFFITH, W. Tyndal – was born in 1835 in Bangor, Wales and went to London in 1854 to study medicine. A devout Dissenter, his 3–volume diary deals with mostly spiritual matters.

HOLWORTHY, Sophia Matilda – she identified herself as English and Protestant, but I could find no biographical information on her. On her trip to Switzerland, France and Italy, she travelled alone largely on foot.

HOWITT, Anna Maria – daughter of William and Mary Howitt, both raised as Quakers. They became spiritualists at some point, and Mary Howitt converted to Catholicism later in life. Anna studied art in Munich in the early 1850s, and had lived in Heidelberg with her family during the previous decade.

HOWITT, William – see Anna Howitt.

HUGHES, Rev. Hugh Price (b. 1847, d. 1902) – born in Wales he went to England in 1865 to study at Richmond College and spent most of his adult life there. Hughes was a Methodist minister, who started the *Methodist Times* in 1885.

JERNINGHAM, Hubert E.H. (b. 1842, d. 1914) – entered diplomatic service in the 1860s. Jerningham was a Fellow of the Zoological and Geological Societies, a fellow of the Society of Antiquaries, and an English Knight Commander of the Order of St. Michael and St. George. In the 1860s, he was invited to stay at a château in Normandy, and he wrote a book about his visit.

KEMBLE, Frances (Fanny) – her father Charles Kemble had an English Catholic father and an Irish Protestant mother. They decided to bring the boys up Catholic and the girls Protestant. Charles went to Catholic school in England at Douay. He married Maria Theresa who was born in Vienna and of German descent. Fanny Kemble was born in London and educated in France. She married an American and spent some time in the US where she said she was accosted as a Papist 'because of the little iron crucifix, that badge of the universal religion of sorrow, which I wear round my neck'. See Mrs. Butler (Fanny Kemble). *A Year of Consolation* (London: Edward Moxon, 1847), vol. 1, p. 13.

LAMONT, Martha – raised an Anglican in Lancashire. She speaks of herself as 'des trois nations', which presumably means she has English, Scottish and Irish ancestors – her middle name was MacDonald. In the 1840s, she left home to attend a boarding school in Paris.

LEWIS, David Morgan (b. 1851, d. 1937) – born in Pembrokeshire and educated in Cardigan and Presbyterian College, Carmarthen. In 1872 he went to Trinity College, Cambridge and eventually became a lecturer in physics at Bangor (1884) and at Aberystwyth (1891). Lewis was also a Congregational minister.

LEWIS, Sir John Herbert (b. 1858, d. 1933) – a Welsh Evangelical Protestant born in Flintshire and educated in Denbigh, Montreal and Oxford. He was a founder of the intermediate school system in Wales. Lewis displayed an intense love of Wales and became a Liberal MP in 1892 and president of the National Library of Wales in 1926.

LEWIS, Sir Thomas Frankland (b. 1780, d. 1855) – born into a distinguished family of Radnorshire. Lewis became an MP and was involved with the Poor Law Commission. He also chaired a commission to inquire into the Rebecca Riots in 1843.

LINCOLNE, Lucilla – She and her sisters left many letters and did a lot of global travelling. Born and raised in Suffolk, her father was a shopkeeper and deacon in the Independent Church. The journal about her trip up the Rhine in 1855 is in the Thomas Cook Archive, London.

LINDER, Samuel – identifies himself with London and the English Congregational Church.

LUCAS, E.V. – an essayist and biographer from Kent. His travel journal about Holland focuses more on artists, history and philosophy than on the people and sites Lucas sees on his trips.

LUCEY, Charles – a Londoner from Clapham. He went to Wales in the mid-nineteenth century to abandon the demands of business. Lucey took great pride in being an independent traveller who departed from beaten tracks and trekked mostly on foot.

MACGREGOR, J. – a Scottish philanthropist who travelled the rivers and lakes of Europe alone in a small canoe in the mid-nineteenth century. The canoe was a covered one 15 ft long and weighing 80 lb. MacGregor's luggage for his three-month trip fitted in a black bag 1 foot square and 5 inches deep, and stayed nestled between his knees as he paddled.

MARSH, John (b. 1789, d. 1872) – born in Guilford, Marsh was a Quaker who spent most of his life in the corn business. When he retired in 1848, he and his wife moved to Dorking. He travelled in Europe during the 1840s to speak about the slave trade.

MATTHEWS, John – from Birmingham, he travelled to the Continent in the 1840s.

MAYHEW, Henry (b. 1812, d. 1887) – son of a London lawyer, he was educated at Westminster School but ran away to sea, ending up for a time in Calcutta. He was articled to his father for three years, but eventually abandoned law for literature. In 1862 he lived in Germany – mainly in Eisenach and Jena – and wrote a study of German social life and manners.

MILLER, Hugh – His mother was a Highland Gael and his father a Lowland Scot. Miller himself was a Scottish Nationalist and fervent Presbyterian, though he supported the Union with England. Although he started his adult life as a stonemason, Miller became a self-taught palaeontologist and popular intellectual. In 1845 he travelled around England for the first time, intent on observing people and geological formations. He was particularly interested in seeing 'humble' folk, and often stayed in cottages or second-class coffee houses and inns.

MORRELL, Jemima – a spinster from Selby, Yorkshire who travelled on and wrote about Cook's first conducted tour to Switzerland in 1863. She went with her brother, cousin, two friends and nearly 60 others, spending three weeks touring Switzerland by rail, diligence, foot and mule. Morrell was commissioned by the Junior United Alpine Club to write a record of the journey.

MORRIS, Sir Lewis (b. 1833, d. 1907) – born and educated in Carmarthen, though eventually went to Sherborne and Oxford. Morris was called to the bar in 1861. He eventually became vice-president of University College of Wales, Aberystwyth.

PARDOE, Julia – born and raised in Yorkshire, she travelled alone to the South of France in the late 1830s.

POTTER, Beatrix (b. 1866, d. 1943) – born in London of well-to-do parents who took the family on annual trips to Scotland and the Lake District. She eventually settled in the Lake District and married an Ambleside solicitor. Potter became famous as an author of children's books, and is best known for *The Tale of Peter Rabbit* (1901).

QUILLINAN, Dorothy (b. 1804, d. 1847) – her father was William Wordsworth, and her husband, Edward, was of Irish descent but born in Oporto. Edward attended Catholic schools in England. Dorothy married Edward in 1841, and four years later they took a trip to Spain and Portugal for Dorothy's health.

RAWLINS, Charles Edward – a Liverpool merchant who travelled in North Wales with two friends in 1866.

RICHARD, Henry (b. 1812, d. 1888) – born in Tregaron and educated at Llangeitho and Highbury College, London. In 1835 he was ordained Minister of Marlborough Congregational Chapel, London, but retired from this position in 1850. Richard became Secretary of the Peace Society and was elected MP for the Merthyr boroughs in 1868. A firm upholder of Welsh and nonconformist rights, Richard sought to explain Wales to the English in numerous letters and articles.

ROBERTSON, Janet – a Scottish woman who travelled to Italy and France in the late 1840s. She was in Paris during the revolution of 1848.

SALVIN, Eliza – daughter of Anthony Salvin, member of an old Durham family who became a well-known architect and authority on medieval architecture. From 1833 to 1857 the family lived in Finchley, London, attending the Anglican Church. At 14, Salvin went to the Continent for the first time (1851), and recorded this trip and others in several journals now housed in the Barnet Local Studies and Archive Centre, London.

SEWELL, Elizabeth – she referred to herself as 'English' and identified with the Anglican Church. In 1851 she travelled to the Continent and wrote a journal for the children of a village school. The journal provides lots of details and comparisons with things English.

SHELLEY, Mary (b. 1797, d. 1851) – born and raised in London, she was the daughter of William Godwin and Mary Wollstonecraft. In 1816 she married the poet Percy Bysshe Shelley. Mary Shelley was an avid reader and an accomplished linguist, having mastered Latin, French and Italian. She was also a writer most famous for *Frankenstein*. In the 1840s she travelled with her son to Germany and Italy and published her impressions in 1844.

SKETCHLEY, Arthur (b. 1817, d. 1882) – his real name was George Rose. He was an English clergyman who belonged to the Church of England until 1855 when he converted to Catholicism. At that point, he turned to writing and entertaining. A proponent of Continental travel, he urged those of moderate means to take advantage of Thomas Cook's travel services. His travel writing offers nothing but positive comments on the Catholic churches and services he visited.

STEVENSON, Robert Louis (b. 1850, d.1894) – a writer born and educated in Edinburgh. In 1876 he took a trip through France by canoe and wrote about the journey in his first travel book *An Inland Voyage*. Stevenson went on this trip with a friend, and they travelled in two sail-powered canoes or skiffs – *Cigarette* and *Arethusa*. Several years later Stevenson trekked with a donkey through the French countryside of the Cévennes. They travelled 120 miles in twelve days. This trip Stevenson chronicled in *Travels with a Donkey*.

SYMONDS, John Addington (b. 1840, d.1893) – born in Bristol and educated at Harrow and Oxford. Symonds was a poet, critic and travel writer most famous for his 7-volume work *Renaissance in Italy*. He spent considerable time in Italy and Switzerland in the hope of combating his tuberculosis. Although he eventually married, he was not shy about acknowledging his homosexuality, especially in his *Memoirs*.

TALFOURD, Sir Thomas Noon (b. 1795, d.1854) – an English Dissenter born in Reading. His father was a brewer and his mother the daughter of an Independent minister in Reading. Talfourd was a barrister, judge and author, especially of tragedies. In 1835 he became an MP.

TOYL, William – took a month's trip in 1857 to see the scenery of North Wales. He was from Liverpool.

TRENCH, the Reverend Francis (b. 1805, d. 1886) – although his family on both sides was of Huguenot origin and settled initially in Ireland, he was an Anglican clergyman born and raised in England. His father was a barrister and his mother was raised by her grandfather, an Anglican bishop. His wife, Mary Caroline, was the daughter of a Worcester canon. In the 1840s, Trench travelled to France and Spain, as well as to Scotland.

TROLLOPE, Mrs Frances (b. 1780, d. 1863) – raised in Bristol, Trollope spent most of her adult life in London as well as abroad in Belgium and the US. Her son, Anthony, is the more famous writer, but Frances wrote 34 novels, mostly of the social reform type. She is most famous, however, for *Domestic Manners of the Americans* (1832). Trollope also wrote a travel book on Belgium and western Germany.

TUPPER, Martin Farquhar (b. 1810, d. 1889) – an English Protestant educated at Charterhouse and Oxford. His family was of Huguenot descent who came to England in the sixteenth century. Although he studied law, he never practised, preferring to write. He took a family tour to the Continent in the 1850s.

TWINING, Agnes – daughter of the tea merchant Richard Twining. She kept detailed journals of family trips to the Continent during the five years prior to her marriage in 1872 to Andrew Donaldson. She and her husband then kept a joint journal from their wedding day until Agnes's death in 1918.

WALKER, Saunderson – a Quaker who considered Newcastle to be home. He travelled to the Mediterranean in winter of 1837 mainly for the healthier climate. Taking detailed notes while travelling, he later copied them neatly into a journal complete with contents and dedication to his father.

WILBERFORCE, Edward – an Englishman who lived in Munich and wrote about it as a foreign resident. He was the nephew of Samuel Wilberforce, Bishop of Oxford.

WOOD, Charles – although both his parents were English, Charles was born in France and educated both abroad and privately in England. His father was head of a banking and shipping firm and was for a time canon of Worcester Cathedral. Charles was, for a short time, editor of *The Argosy* and a publisher on the Strand. He took two trips with a friend to Holland in the late 1870s and one to the Black Forest area in the early 1880s.

Notes

Introduction

1. This certainly is no longer the case. Studies about travel and travel writing have flooded the market since 1990, suggesting that many besides myself were drawn to the field in the early and mid-1980s. With the rise of postcolonial, feminist and cultural studies, scholars now focus on the culture of travel itself, and even more frequently on the language and ideology of travel writing as vehicles for exploring identity, particularly the imperial mentality. See, for example, P. Brendon, *Thomas Cook: 150 Years of Popular Tourism* (London: Secker & Warburg, 1991); J. Buzard, *The Beaten Track: European Tourism, Literature, and the Ways to Culture* (Oxford: Oxford University Press, 1993); C. Endy, 'Travel and World Power: Americans in Europe, 1890–1917', *Diplomatic History*, 22, no. 4 (Fall 1998) 565–94; S. Foster, *Across New Worlds: Nineteenth-Century Women Travellers and Their Writings* (New York: Harvester Wheatsheaf, 1990); J. and M. Gold, *Imagining Scotland: Tradition, Representation and Promotion in Scottish Tourism Since 1750* (Aldershot, Hants.: Scolar Press, 1995); I. Grewal, *Home and Harem: Nation, Gender, Empire, and the Cultures of Travel* (Durham, NC: Duke University Press, 1996); E. Leed, *The Mind of the Traveler: From Gilgamesh to Global Tourism* (New York: Basic Books, 1991); B. Melman, *Women's Orients: English Women and the Middle East, 1718–1918* (Ann Arbor: University of Michigan Press, 1992); S. Morgan, *Place Matters: Gendered Geography in Victorian Women's Travel Books about Southeast Asia* (New Brunswick, N.J.: Rutgers University Press, 1996); M. O'Connor, *The Romance of Italy and the English Imagination* (New York: St. Martin's Press, 1998); I. Ousby, *The Englishman's England: Taste, Travel and the Rise of Tourism* (Cambridge: Cambridge University Press, 1990); J. Pemble, *The Mediterranean Passion* (Oxford: Oxford University Press, 1988); M.L. Pratt, *Imperial Eyes: Travel Writing and Transculturation* (London: Routledge, 1992); E. Said, *Orientalism* (New York: Vintage Books, 1979); J. Urry, *The Tourist Gaze: Leisure and Travel in Contemporary Societies* (London: Sage Publications, 1990); L. Withey, *Grand Tours and Cook's Tours: A History of Leisure Travel, 1750–1915* (New York: W. Morrow and Co., 1997); A. Woollacott, '"All This is the Empire I Told Myself": Australian Women's Voyages "Home" and the Articulation of Colonial Whiteness', *American Historical Review*, 102, no. 4 (October 1997) 1003–29.
2. For some of the more traditional approaches to the study of nations, see E. Gellner, *Nations and Nationalism* (Oxford: Basil Blackwell, 1983); C.J.H. Hayes, *Nationalism: A Religion* (New York: Macmillan, 1960); and H. Kohn, *The Idea of Nationalism* (New York: Macmillan, 1944).
3. A good introduction to this newer approach to the study of nations and nationhood would include: B. Anderson, *Imagined Communities: Reflections on the Origin and Spread of Nationalism* (London: Verso, 1991, rev. edn; first pub. 1983); P. Brass, *Ethnicity and Nationalism* (New Delhi: Sage Publications, 1991); L. Colley, *Britons: Forging the Nation, 1707–1837* (New Haven: Yale

University Press, 1992); A. Confino, *The Nation as a Local Metaphor: Wurttemberg, Imperial Germany, and National Memory, 1871–1918* (Chapel Hill: University of North Carolina Press, 1997); A. Coombes, *Reinventing Africa: Museums, Material Culture and Popular Imagination in Late Victorian and Edwardian England* (New Haven: Yale University Press, 1994); W. Donaldson, *The Jacobite Song: Political Myth and National Identity* (Aberdeen: Aberdeen University Press, 1988); R. Helgerson, *Forms of Nationhood* (Chicago: University of Chicago Press, 1992); J.R. Gillis, ed., *Commemorations: The Politics of National Identity* (Princeton: Princeton University Press, 1994); E.J. Hobsbawm, *Nations and Nationalism since 1780* (Cambridge: Cambridge University Press, 1990); Hobsbawm and T. Ranger, eds, *The Invention of Tradition* (London: Cambridge University Press, 1983); R. Samuel, ed., *Patriotism: The Making and Unmaking of British National Identity*, 3 vols. (London: Routledge, 1989); Samuel, *Island Stories: Unravelling Britain*, vol. 2 of *Theatres of Memory* edited by A. Light (London: Verso, 1998); P. Womack, *Improvement and Romance: Constructing the Myth of the Highlands* (London: Macmillan, 1989).
4. For several pioneering works on national identity in Britain, see R. Colls and P. Dodd, eds, *Englishness: Politics and Culture, 1880–1920* (London: Croom Helm, 1986); Hobsbawm and Ranger, *Invention of Tradition*; G. Newman, *The Rise of English Nationalism, 1740–1830* (London: Weidenfeld and Nicolson, 1987); and K. Robbins, *Nineteenth-Century Britain: England, Scotland and Wales, The Making of a Nation* (Oxford: Oxford University Press, 1989).
5. A most recent example of this view can be seen in C. Kinealy's *A Disunited Kingdom?: England, Ireland, Scotland and Wales, 1800–1949* (Cambridge: Cambridge University Press, 1999). The chapter on 'Nationalism and Cultural Identity' discusses Ireland, Wales and Scotland, but ignores England.
6. Two important articles by J.G.A. Pocock were very influential in moving scholars to a less English-centred approach to the history of Britain. See J.G.A. Pocock, 'British History: A Plea for a New Subject', *Journal of Modern History*, 47, no. 4 (December 1975) 601–28; and Pocock, 'The Limits and Divisions of British History: In Search of the Unknown Subject', *American Historical Review*, 87, no. 2 (April 1982) 311–36. A classic example of a study focusing on the interaction of cultures in the British Isles is H. Kearney, *The British Isles: A History of Four Nations* (Cambridge: Cambridge University Press, 1989).
7. In addition to the five early studies noted above, see L. Brockliss and D. Eastwood, eds, *A Union of Multiple Identities: The British Isles, c. 1750–1850* (Manchester: Manchester University Press, 1997); Colley, *Britons*; J. Ellis, ' "The Methods of Barbarism" and the "Rights of Small Nations": War Propaganda and British Pluralism', *Albion*, 30, no. 1 (Spring 1998) 49–79; A. Grant and K. Stringer, eds, *Uniting the Kingdom?: The Making of British History* (London: Routledge, 1995); R.M. Jones, 'Beyond Identity? The Reconstruction of the Welsh', *Journal of British Studies*, 31 (October 1992) 330–57; D. Lowenthal, 'European and English Landscapes as National Symbols', in D. Hooson, ed., *Geography and National Identity* (Oxford: Blackwell, 1994) 15–38; R. Porter, ed., *Myths of the English* (Cambridge: Polity Press, 1992); K. Robbins, *Great Britain: Identities, Institutions and the Idea of Britishness* (London: Longman, 1998); Robbins, *History, Religion and Identity in Modern Britain* (London: Hambledon Press, 1993); Samuel, *Patriotism*; Samuel, *Island Stories*.

8. See B. Porter, 'The Victorians and Europe', *History Today*, 42 (January 1992) 16–22.
9. Less attention is given to Welsh travellers simply because I was not able to find many travel journals written by men and women from Wales.
10. O'Connor, *The Romance of Italy and the English Political Imagination*, p. 9.
11. Linda Colley has been criticized for ignoring Ireland in her study of the emergence of a British national identity during the eighteenth century. There is, perhaps, even more cause for criticism of a study of national identity in the nineteenth century that ignores Ireland. Such a study might also be criticized for ignoring the Empire. I accept these criticisms as valid, but offer the following response. My study suggests that there can be no single model or framework for understanding national identity, because the form national imagining took shifted depending on context. One of my primary aims was to document this very point. It would have been ideal to include Ireland and the Empire as contexts, but not necessary. What was important was to include multiple contexts, which I did do. Had time permitted, I would have included Irish travellers as well as Ireland and the Empire as travel destinations.
12. Gerald Newman warned me several years ago about placing too much emphasis on invention and ignoring continuities when it came to studying nations. More recently, R. Samuel has reminded us about how persistent national stereotypes are in people's imagination. See *Island Stories*, chapter 1.
13. For a superb exception in the area of German history, see Confino, *The Nation as a Local Metaphor* (1997).
14. E. Evans, 'Englishness and Britishness-National Identities, c. 1790–1870', in Grant and Stringer, eds, *Uniting the Kingdom?*, chapter 13. In addition to Evans and Colley, scholars emphasizing Britishness include: J.S. Ellis, '"Methods of Barbarism" and the "Rights of Small Nations"', *Albion* and Ellis, 'Reconciling the Celt: British National Identity, Empire, and the 1911 Investiture of the Prince of Wales', *Journal of British Studies*, 37, no. 4 (October 1998) 391–418; Robbins, *Nineteenth-Century Britain*; and J. Wolffe, *God and Greater Britain: Religion and National Life in Britain and Ireland, 1843–1945* (New York: Routledge, 1994). For studies that stress the survival of traditional identities rather than Britishness see: Brockliss and Eastwood, eds, *A Union of Multiple Identities*; Colls and Dodd, eds, *Englishness*; W. Donaldson, *The Jacobite Song*; M. Hechter, *Internal Colonialism: The Celtic Fringe in British National Development, 1536–1966* (Berkeley: University of California Press, 1975); Kearney, *The British Isles*; Newman, *The Rise of English Nationalism*.
15. D.W. Bebbington, 'Religion and National Feeling in Nineteenth-Century Wales and Scotland', in S. Mews, ed., *Religion and National Identity* (Oxford: Blackwell, 1982) 489–503.
16. For studies of travel and the imperial mentality, see Grewal, *Home and Harem*; Melman, *Women's Orients*; Morgan, *Place Matters*; Pratt, *Imperial Eyes*; Said, *Orientalism*; Woollacott, '"All this is the Empire, I Told Myself"'.
17. See A. Burton, 'Who Needs the Nation? Interrogating "British" History', *Journal of Historical Sociology*, 10, no. 3 (September 1997) 227–48 and S. Marks, 'History, Nation and Empire: Sniping from the Periphery', *History Workshop Journal*, 29 (Spring 1990) 111–19.

Chapter 1 The Meaning and Mechanics of Travel

1. E. Gosse, 'Journal in Scotland', (1870) f. 17v, MS.2562, National Library of Scotland (NLS). Edward Lear had a similar experience in Calabria when he encountered locals who had never travelled outside their southern Italy community. With no larger frame of reference, they could not understand that their locale might be unique, or at least different, and therefore of interest to others. They could do nothing but stare in amazement at the traveller as if to say, ' "Have you *no* rocks, *no* towns, *no* trees in your own country? Are you not rich? Then what *can* you wish *here*? – *here*, in this place of poverty and incommodo? What *are* you doing?" ' E. Lear, *Edward Lear in Southern Italy* (London: W. Kimber, 1964) p. 59.
2. Leed, *Mind of the Traveller*, p. 264. Other scholars who emphasize the importance of the 'other' for framing identity are: J. Bailey-Goldschmidt and M. Kalfatovic, 'Sex, Lies and European Hegemony', *Journal of Popular Culture*, vol. 26, no. 4 (Spring 1993) 141–53; Colley, *Britons*; Pemble, *The Mediterranean Passion*; J. Taylor, *A Dream of England: Landscape, Photography and the Tourist's Imagination* (Manchester: Manchester University Press, 1994); and Urry, *The Tourist Gaze*.
3. On the significance of departure as a stage in the travel experience, see Leed, pp. 25–52.
4. On Boswell's passion for role playing, see Leed, pp. 265–8.
5. S.M. Holworthy, *Alpine Scrambles and Classic Rambles* (London: J. Nisbet, [1885]), page before dedication.
6. A.G. Dunlop, 'Journals' (1838–39), f. 91v, MS. 9265, NLS.
7. C. Lucey, 'Journal of an Excursion to Wales and Ireland' (1848) p. 2, MS. 23064Di, NLW.
8. Gosse, 'Journal', f. 23r.
9. J. Morrell, *Miss Jemima's Swiss Journal* (London: Putnam, 1963; written 1863) p. 67.
10. W. Kitchener, *The Traveller's Oracle*, 2 vols. (London: H. Colburn, 1827).
11. F.C. Selous, 'Travel', in *The Illustrated London News Record of the Glorious Reign of Queen Victoria, 1837–1901*.
12. On the growth of travel and tourism in the nineteenth century, see Brendon, *Thomas Cook: 150 Years of Popular Tourism*; Buzard, *The Beaten Track*; Ousby, *The Englishman's England*; Pemble, *The Mediterranean Passion*; J. Simmons, 'Railways, Hotels, and Tourism in Great Britain, 1839–1914', *Journal of Contemporary History*, 19 (1984) 201–22; L. Tissot, 'How Did the British Conquer Switzerland?', *Journal of Transport History*, 16, no. 1 (March 1995) 21–54.
13. G. Gissing, *The Letters of George Gissing to Edvard Bertz, 1887–1903*, edited by A.C. Young (Westport, CT: Greenwood Press, 1980) p. 33.
14. 'Modern Tourism', *Blackwood's Edinburgh Magazine*, 64 (August 1848) p. 185.
15. G. Stratton, 'Diary of Chester and North Wales' (1865) f. 18r, MS. 21992A, NLW. Some of those ferns can be found today stuck to the pages of journals housed in the National Library of Wales. I once spent considerable time brushing crumbly fern matter from my clothes. It had fallen from a journal containing 20 pages of pressed ferns from Snowdon.
16. G.J. Elliot, 4th Earl of Minto, 'Trip to Northern Italy' (1894) f. 5v, MS. 12508, NLS.

17. It is also true that local people often acted on the basis of their expectations about tourists' tastes, making 'authentic' experiences hard to come by. See the account, at the opening of this chapter, of Edmund Gosse's encounters with locals in Stornoway.
18. *The Logbook of the Expedition to Florence* (1888) p. 126, A/TOY/12/1, Toynbee Hall Collection, Greater London Record Office (GLRO).
19. Holworthy, *Alpine Scrambles and Classic Rambles*, p. 76.
20. W.A. Stephenson, 'A Trip to Edinburgh and Glasgow' (1890) p. 31, MS. 9234, NLS.
21. *Handbook for Travellers in France*, 13th edn, vol. 2 (London: J. Murray, 1875).
22. G. Combe, 'Continuous Diary' (30 August 1841) f. 51r, MS. 7421, NLS.
23. *Bradshaw's Handbook for Tourists in Great Britain and Ireland* (London: W.J. Adams, 1867), advertisements, section 4.
24. M.W. Dundas, 'Journal in Switzerland', (July 1894) f. 59r, MS. 14199, NLS.
25. *Bradshaw's Handbook for Tourists in Great Britain and Ireland*, advertisements, section 4.
26. H. Richard, 'Journal of Tours in France', (1849) New MS. 10200A, NLS.
27. For photos, see in particular 'Toynbee Travellers' Club Log of the Expedition to Siena, Perugia, Assisi', compiled by J.C. Scargill (1890) A/TOY/12/2, Toynbee Collection, GLRO.
28. A.J.C. Hare, *The Years with Mother*, edited by M. Barnes (London: Century, 1984) p. 138.
29. Tissot, 'How Did the British Conquer Switzerland?', p. 25.
30. H. Francis, 'Notes of a Three Weeks Tour Through Monmouthshire and Wales', vol. 2 (1837) p. 339, MS. 11597b, NLW. Francis had to wait until the 1860s to have his question answered by Murray guides. The first guide to South Wales appeared in 1860, and one for North Wales a year later.
31. Sir J. Forbes, *Sight-Seeing in Germany and the Tyrol* (London: Smith, Elder & Co., 1856) p. 378, and Morrell, *Miss Jemima's Swiss Journal*, p. 23.
32. N. Bellairs, *Going Abroad* (London: C.J. Skeet, 1857) p. 215 and E.V. Lucas, *A Wanderer in Holland*, 6th edn. (London: Methuen & Co., 1906) p. 65.
33. F.W. Faber, *Life and Letters of Frederick William Faber* by J.E. Bowden, 3rd edn (London: Burns and Oates, Ltd., 1869) p. 122; C.M. Ingleby, 'Journal of a Tour to Scotland' (1 September 1842) f. 28r, MS. 8926, NLS; and E.C.T. Carne (John Wittitterly, pseud.) *Three Months' Rest at Pau* (London: Bell and Daldy, 1860) p. 171.
34. J.B. Greenshields, 'Journal in Italy' (1847–48) f. 26r, MS. 19768, NLS. Not everyone found this transformation in journal writing a desirable one. A writer for *Fraser's Magazine* complained about the lack of instruction to be found in mid-nineteenth-century travel books. The writer explained the lack by noting, '[T]he majority of travellers who have no specific object in view merely skim the surface, and bring back what are popularly called impressions...': 'Recent Travellers', *Fraser's Magazine*, 42 (July 1850) 44.
35. S. Linder, 'Tour in North Wales' (1859) f. 41r, MS. 23065c, NLW.
36. Tissot, 'How Did the British Conquer Switzerland?', p. 23.
37. This paragraph is based on J. Böröcz, 'Travel-Capitalism: The Structure of Europe and the Advent of the Tourist', *Comparative Studies in Society and History*, 34, no. 4 (October 1992) 708–41. Böröcz bases his conclusions on

the two popular guides *Appleton's European Guide Book Illustrated* and *A Satchel Guide for the Vacation Tourist in Europe*.
38. This section on Thomas Cook draws on Brendon, *Thomas Cook: 150 Years of Popular Tourism* and Buzard, *The Beaten Track*, pp. 48–65.
39. Brendon, *Thomas Cook*, chapter 5.
40. *A Handbook for Travellers in Switzerland*, 16th edn (London: J. Murray, 1879) p. xv.
41. J.C. Burdon, 'Cook's Tour 1871', volume b, Mss.Add. 179/83 b, University College London Library.
42. Foreign Office Correspondence on Passports, 1870–73, FO 612 36, Public Record Office (PRO), Kew, London.
43. House of Commons Sessional Papers, XXVIII.545, 1852.
44. *A Handbook for Travellers in France*, 5th edn (London, 1854) p. xvi and *Hansard's Parliamentary Debates* CXV (20 March 1851) p. 229.
45. Foreign Office Correspondence (24 May 1855) FO 612 11, PRO Kew, London.
46. Travellers from Britain tended to associate passports with despotism, and to take great pride in their absence in the British Isles. One writer for *Fraser's Magazine*, however, complained bitterly of an English hindrance to free travel as vexatious, in his mind, as the passport – the turnpike. Turnpikes contained periodic roadside cottages housing a staff of officials whose business it was to collect road rates, or taxes, from travellers. *Fraser's* professed 'Grumbler' complained of such an obstacle to travel in a 'locomotive century' and suggested replacing it with a tax on horses, carriages or counties that would not hinder the flow of traffic on the roads. See *Fraser's Magazine*, 57 (May 1858) 614–15.
47. A.E. Twining, 'Tours Around Europe, 1866–71' (3 September 1867) F/DON/28, GLRO.
48. E.A. Salvin, 'A Fortnight in Paris and Normandy, 1851' in 'Journals of Foreign Tours' (6 September 1851, copied 1860) MS. 6787/5, Barnet Local Studies and Archive Centre, London; and Lt.Col. E.H. Legge, 'Journal to Europe, 1862', F/LEG/902, GLRO.
49. Lucey, 'Journal of an Excursion to Wales and Ireland' (1848) p. 62.
50. J. Smith, 'Trip to Switzerland' (21 August 1855) Acc. 8736, NLS.
51. Most journal writers complained of Continental customs officers and revelled in the freedom from such 'creatures' afforded by travel around the British Isles. While it was true that one could travel through the United Kingdom without encountering customs officials, they were stationed at ports of entry into Britain. Unlike most British travellers, George Combe found the officials at home even more taxing than their counterparts on the Continent. Upon arriving at the north English port of Hull, he had to endure what seemed an interminable delay because of a new customs regulation and an inaccessible key. Noting that several of his fellow passengers were from the Continent, he confessed, 'I was ashamed of the slow proceedings of the English officials when compared with the activity of their brethren on the continent. They were, however, all very civil', a compliment rarely paid by Combe or any other traveller to Continental officials. See Combe, 'Continuous Diary' (21 September 1845) f. 44r, MS. 7425, NLS.
52. W. Merry, 'Through Europe in 1829', edited by Father M. Crowdy, *Oratory Parish Magazine* (August 1969) p. 8.

53. F. Fryer, 'Travels in Europe, 1844' (26 October 1844) MS. Vol. s. 50, Friends Library, London.
54. Legge, 'Journal', p. 63. Some travellers explained these sort of travel delays as 'the miserable custom-house espionage'. The phrase referred to a partnership existing between some customs officials and innkeepers. As Henry Richard explained it, customs officials were sometimes in league with innkeepers, and thus attempted to delay passengers so long at customs that they would miss their travel connections and have to stay in the nearby inn for the night. See Richard, 'Journal...France', p. 224.
55. Two other things were perplexing to Victorian travellers because they were less standardized than they are today – time and distance measurements. Swiss time, for example, was 27 minutes ahead of Paris, and 35 minutes in advance of Greenwich time. Railway times were no more standardized. An end-of-the-century handbook for northern France explained that railway time in France was Paris time, except that station clocks by which trains started were purposely kept five minutes slow. Greenwich railway time was 4 minutes behind French, and mid-Europe time (for Germany, Switzerland, and Italy) 56 minutes ahead of French time. It was not until 1884 that an international conference on time standards held in Washington, DC divided the world into time zones.

    Murray's handbooks alerted travellers to different ways of measuring distance as well. Instead of using miles, for example, the Swiss reckoned distance by *stunden* or leagues, which indicated hours' walking. According to the handbook, the length of the *stunde* had been calculated at approximately 3 English miles (different from other countries' miles – Scots mile = 2,446 yards, English mile = 1,760 yards; German mile = 4.816 English miles). But the Swiss *stunde* also varied depending on the terrain, being only 2 English miles in very steep ascents and 2 1/2 over lesser rises. See *A Handbook for Travellers*, 3rd edn (London: J. Murray, 1846) pp. xvi and xvii.
56. Sir J. Barrow, *Excursions in the North of Europe* (London: J. Murray, 1835).
57. Merry, 'Through Europe' (October 1969) p. 9.
58. Bellairs, *Going Abroad* (1857) p. 40.
59. Mrs. Ellis, *Summer and Winter in the Pyrenees* (London: Fisher, Son & Co., 1847) p. 4.
60. Dunlop, 'Journal', pp. 12–14.
61. *Handbook...Switzerland*, 16th edn, p. xvii.
62. Forbes, *Sight-Seeing* (1856) p. 120.
63. Boxall MSS, quoted in Pemble, *The Mediterranean Passion*, p. 22.
64. For a map of the Scottish rail networks in 1852 and 1914, see Gold, *Imagining Scotland*, p. 95.
65. Simmons, 'Railways, Hotels, and Tourism in Great Britain 1839–1914', p. 201. For information on the extent of railways in Britain and the Continent at mid-century, see *Bradshaw's Continental Railway, Steam Navigation and Conveyance Guide* (Paris: Gallignani & Co., 1847) and D. Lardner, *Railway Economy* (New York: A.M. Kelley, 1968; reprint of London 1850 edn).
66. Reverend F. Trench, *Scotland, Its Faith and Its Features*, vol. 1 (London: R. Bentley, 1846) p. 34. This availability of rail travel did not extend to all parts of Britain equally. In the mid-nineteenth century, a railway passenger

in the western part of Scotland could have gone no further north than Glasgow, and in the eastern part no further north than Aberdeen. In other words, there was no rail service at this time in the Highlands and Western Isles of Scotland. By 1914, there was an east/west rail route running as far north as Inverness and one could travel by rail as far as Thurso. Nevertheless, the rail network in the Highlands was still very sparse compared with that in the central and southern parts of Scotland.

Similarly, rail lines in Cornwall and Wales were not nearly as dense as in England outside of Cornwall. At mid-century, the main western line stopped at Plymouth, and in Wales there was track only in the south and across the northern boundary to Holyhead. By the late 1870s, the more remote parts of Cornwall could nearly be reached by rail and several lines cut through central Wales, with one or two cross lines penetrating the Welsh mountains. For maps of railway development, see Gold, *Imagining Scotland*, p. 95; W.T. Jackman, *The Development of Transportation in Modern England* (London: F. Cass & Co., 1962; and H. Pollins, *Britain's Railways: An Industrial History* (Totowa, N.J.: Rowman & Littlefield, 1971).

67. Smith, 'Trip...Switzerland', Thursday, 23 August 1855.
68. B. Potter, *The Journal of Beatrix Potter, 1881–1897*, transcribed by L. Linder (London: Frederick Warne & Co., 1966) p. 267.
69. Bellairs, *Going Abroad*, p. 260.
70. Bellairs, *Going Abroad*, p. 246.
71. K. Harris, 'Travel Diary in North Italy, 1847–50', p. 24, BM Add.MS 52503 and 'Logbook' (1888) p. 14. Lady C. Duff Gordon did come to the conclusion that nothing – not even trains – could rob Venice of its romance and uniqueness. In her travel journal she stated, 'We got to the Rail Road Station at Venice...it is a strange bustling way of getting into Venice – a queer way of joining the past to the present – and trying to make Venice an *everyday* place – but even steam can not do it!' See Lady C. Duff Gordon, 'Journal', vol. 3 (1846) f. 85v, MS. 15590B, NLW.
72. T. Crick, *Sketches From the Diary of a Commercial Traveller* (London: J. Masters, 1847) p. 147.
73. H. Miller, *First Impressions of England and its People* (London: J. Johnstone, 1847) pp. 51 and v.
74. M.M. Brewster, *Letters From Cannes and Nice* (Edinburgh: T. Constable, 1857) p. 41.
75. Salvin, 'Germany and Switzerland', in 'Journals of Foreign Tours' (1856) p. 386.
76. J. Marsh, 'Diary of John Marsh' (8 September 1849) Box Q4/2, Friends House, London.
77. Quoted in Pemble, *The Mediterranean Passion*, p. 37. See A. Dunlop, 'Journals', f. 7v.
78. 'Logbook...to Florence', (1888) p. 100.
79. Salvin MSS, 'Germany and Switzerland, 1856', p. 340.
80. Combe, 'Continuous Diary' (10 September 1845) f. 75r.
81. 'A Journal of a Few Days from Home' (1856) f. 21v, MS. 9233, NLS.
82. Father A. Hutchison, 'Letters From the Holy Land and Egypt' (1857–8) vol. 27, Brompton Oratory.

83. The information in this paragraph on train wrecks is taken from Lardner, *Railway Economy* (1850), pp. 321–2. He investigated 100 accidents and found that their causes occurred in the following proportion:

    Accidents from – collision 56
    broken wheel or axle 18
    defective rail 14
    by switches 5
    impediments on road 3
    cattle 3
    bursting boiler 1

84. This paragraph draws on W. Schivelbusch's *The Railway Journey: The Industrialization of Time and Space in the Nineteenth Century* (New York: Berg Publishers, 1986; first published in German, 1977).

Chapter 2 Landscape and Climate

1. K. Ishiguro, *The Remains of the Day* (New York: Vintage Books, 1993) p. 44. See pp. 23–44 for Stevens's guesthouse musings in Salisbury.
2. D. Lowenthal, 'European and English Landscapes as National Symbols', pp. 15–38.
3. On the subject of landscape and identity, see N. Everett, *The Tory View of Landscape* (New Haven: Yale University Press, 1994); A. Janowitz, *England's Ruins: Poetic Purpose and the National Landscape* (Oxford: Basil Blackwell, 1990); D. Lowenthal, 'European and English Landscapes'; S. Schama, *Landscape and Memory* (New York: Alfred Knopf, 1995); and Taylor, *A Dream of England*.
4. C.W. Wood, *In the Black Forest* (London: R. Bentley & Son, 1882) p. 8.
5. See K.M. Elisabeth Murray, *Caught in the Web of Words* (New Haven: Yale University Press, 1977) p. 12.
6. Quoted in C. Corner, *Rhineland* (London: J. Burns, [1884]) p. 68.
7. Miller, *First Impressions*, p. 26.
8. G.G. Ramsay, 'The President's Address', *The Scottish Mountaineering Club Journal*, 1 (1891) p. 2.
9. M. Law, 'Journal of Lisbon' (1845) f. 19v, MS. 10340, NLS.
10. J. MacGregor, *A Thousand Miles in the Rob Roy Canoe*, 2nd edn (London: Sampson, Low, Son, and Marston, 1866) p. 269.
11. J.R. Green, *Stray Studies from England and Italy* (London: Macmillan, 1876) p. 49.
12. D. Quillinan, *Journal of a Few Months' Residence in Portugal, and Glimpses of the South of Spain*, vol. 1 (London: E. Moxon, 1847) p. 33.
13. A.M. Howitt, *An Art Student in Munich*, vol. 1, p. 148 and J.C.B. Sanderson, 'Cook's Tour 1871', p. 59, Mss.Add. 179/83, vol. c, University College London Library.
14. Sir L. Morris, 'Journal of a Tour Through Belgium, Holland and the Rhine', (1863) 6938a, NLW.
15. J. Dunlop, 'Journal 1845–46', p. 43, MS. 9269, NLS.
16. 'Logbook of the Expedition to Florence', p. 69.
17. Bellairs, *Going Abroad*, p. 82.

18. MacGregor, *A Thousand Miles*, p. 256.
19. *A Hand-book for Travellers on the Continent* (London: J. Murray, 1836) p. xiii.
20. M. Tupper, *Paterfamilias: Diary of Everybody's Tour* (London: T. Hatchard, 1856) p. 99.
21. Wood, *Black Forest*, p. 238. This preference for summit viewing contrasts with the late eighteenth-century picturesque taste explained so vividly by M. Andrews in *The Search for the Picturesque* (Aldershot, Hants.: Scolar Press, 1989). According to Andrews, the picturesque tourist shunned top-down, survey-all-I-see prospects in favour of views from a low-down position making the viewer feel enveloped by the landscape. Such an enclosed vantage-point humbled the viewer in the face of wild, untamed nature. Andrews suggested that this taste for humbling is indicative of a failure of confidence in the late 18th century that made people wary of the long, see-ahead view. The Victorian period, especially the middle segment, was a more confident time, and perhaps this fact helps explain the attraction of peak viewing.
22. Salvin, 'Germany and Switzerland', pp. 321 and 342.
23. T. Letts, 'Tour in the Lake District and Scotland' (Saturday, 31 July 1847) MS. 21691b, NLW.
24. A. Cunningham, *Cummy's Diary* (London: Chatto & Windus) p. 52.
25. R.L. Stevenson, *Travels with a Donkey* (London: J.M. Dent, 1992; first pub. 1879) p. 163.
26. C.L. Smith, *Journal of a Ramble in Scotland* (Cheltenham: J.J. Hadley, 1835) p. 87.
27. G. Borrow, *Wild Wales*, vol. 1 (London: J. Murray, 1862) p. 172.
28. 'Access to Mountains Bill', *The Scotsman* (11 April 1888) in 'Summer Holiday in Sutherland', (1888) MS. 10975, NLS.
29. *Handbook ... Continent* (1836), p. 189, and E. Sewell, *A Journal Kept During a Summer Tour*, vol. 1 (London: Longman, Brown, Green, and Longmans, 1852) p. 52.
30. C. Struthers, 'Notebooks' (1873) f. 31v, MS. 8901, NLS.
31. Dundas, 'Journal in Switzerland', f. 12r.
32. T.W. Fisher, 'Tour Through North Wales' (1865) p. 20, MS. 899D, NLW.
33. T.N. Talfourd, *Vacation Rambles and Thoughts; 1841, 1842, 1843*, vol. 2 (London: E. Moxon, 1845) p. 250.
34. Carne, *Three Months' Rest at Pau*, p. 184.
35. E.A. Freeman, *Sketches From French Travel* (Leipzig: Tauchnitz, 1891) p. 18.
36. M. Eyre, *A Lady's Walks in the South of France* (1864) p. 23.
37. Talfourd, *Vacation Rambles*, pp. 251 and 247.
38. M.M. Lamont, *Impressions, Thoughts, and Sketches, During Two Years in France and Switzerland* (London: Edward Moxon, 1844) p. 276.
39. Wood, *In the Black Forest* (1882) p. 263.
40. Linder, 'Tour in North Wales', f. 44r.
41. Sewell, *Journal ... Summer Tour*, vol. 2, p. 170.
42. *A Handbook for Travellers in North Wales*, 5th edn (London: J. Murray, 1885) p. 116 and *Handbook for Travellers in Scotland*, 5th edn (London: J. Murray, 1883) p. 16.
43. See P.H. Hansen, 'Albert Smith, the Alpine Club, and the Invention of Mountaineering in Mid-Victorian Britain', *Journal of British Studies*, 34 (July 1995) 300–24.

44. Ramsay, 'The President's Address', p. 2.
45. For discussions of mountaineering, see R.W. Clark, *The Victorian Mountaineers* (London: B.T. Batsford, 1953); Hansen, 'Albert Smith, the Alpine Club, and the Invention of Mountaineering in Mid-Victorian Britain'; A. Lunn, *A Century of Mountaineering, 1857–1957* (London: Allen & Unwin, 1957); and W. Unsworth, *Hold the Heights: The Foundations of Mountaineering* (Seattle: The Mountaineers, 1994).
46. See S. Schama, *Landscape and Memory*; and Andrews, *Search for the Picturesque*.
47. 'Among the Alps', by an Englishman, mid-nineteenth century, MS. 10259, NLS.
48. On the role Scotland played in the world of nineteenth-century British tourism, see K.J. Haldane, '"No human foot comes here": Victorian Tourists and the Isle of Skye', *Nineteenth Century Studies*, 10 (1996) 69–91.

    John and Margaret Gold argued that Sir Walter Scott was more responsible than any other single individual for drawing tourists to Scotland in the nineteenth century. He set his stories in real Scottish landscapes such as the Trossachs and Loch Katrine, and people would visit with his prose or verse in hand. A late nineteenth-century Cook's guide referred to Scotland as 'the land of the mountain and the flood' – a line from Scott's *Lay of the Last Minstrel*. See Gold, *Imagining Scotland*, chapter 4 and p. 104.
49. S. Taylor, 'Journal of a Tour to Scotland' (1842) f. 167v, MS. 8927, NLS.
50. Gosse, 'Journal', f. 12v, MS. 2562.
51. 'Tour in Scotland', by a Lady (1836) f. 35r, NLS MS. 2729. The rest of this paragraph is based on f. 35r and the next two on fs. 19r, 19v, and 20r of this same source.
52. See Haldane, '"No human foot comes here"'.
53. 'Journal of a few days from Home', f. 36v.
54. W. Chambers, *A Tour in Holland, the Countries on the Rhine, and Belgium* (Edinburgh: W. and R. Chambers, 1839) p. 58.
55. 'Summer Holiday in Sutherland', f. 5r.
56. 'Access to Mountains Bill' (11 April 1888).
57. W.E. Baxter, *Impressions of Central and Southern Europe* (London: Longman, Brown, Green, and Longmans, 1850) p. 32
58. Struthers, 'Notebooks', f. 36v.
59. Combe, 'Continuous Diary', fs. 34r and v, MS. 7422; C. Combe, 'Diary of a Continental Tour' (1837) f. 16v, MS. 7463, NLS.
60. H. Richard, 'Tour in Scotland' (Thursday, 4 September 1879) MS. 10208A, NLW.
61. Linder, 'Tour in North Wales', f. 63r.
62. W.T. Griffith, 'Diary', NLW MS. 10211 B, 21 August 1860.
63. Richard, 'Journals of Tours to France, Belgium, and Germany' (1850) p. 152, MS. 10205B, NLW.
64. J.A. Symonds, *New Italian Sketches* (Leipzig: B. Tauchnitz, 1884) pp. 32 and 85.
65. This discussion of the history of linking trees with liberty is based on Schama, *Landscape and Memory*, ch. 3.
66. H. Blackburn, *Artistic Travel in Normandy, Brittany, the Pyrenees, Spain and Algeria* (London: Sampson Low, Marston & Co., 1895) p. 41.
67. M. Betham Edwards, *A Year in Western France* (London: Longmans, Green, and Co., 1877) p. 76.

68. Rev. F. Trench, *Diary of Travels in France and Spain*, vol. 2 (London: R. Bentley, 1845) p. 270, and Tupper, *Paterfamilias* p. 66.
69. Howitt, *Art Student*, vol. 1, p. 19, and E. Price, *May in Anjou, With Other Sketches and Studies* (Edinburgh: D. Douglas, 1889) p. 40.
70. Mrs. Ellis, *Summer and Winter in the Pyrenees* (London: Fisher, Son & Co.) p. 23.
71. Sewell, *A Journal*, vol. 2, p. 45.
72. Sewell, vol. 2, p. 45.
73. Talfourd, *Vacation Rambles*, p. 54.
74. *A Handbook for Travellers in North Wales*, 5th edn, p. x.
75. 'Journal of a Tour in Wales' (1836) p. 26, MS. 12392b, NLW.
76. Francis, 'Notes...Wales', vol. 1, pp. 305 and 327; W. Toyl, 'Rambles in Wales', (1857) p. 33, MS. 23178b, NLW.
77. Ingleby, 'Journal...Scotland', f. 18r, MS. 8296.
78. Lucey, 'Journal...Wales and Ireland', p. 35.
79. Lucey, p. 64.
80. Francis, 'Notes', vol. 2, p. 226.
81. *Handbook...Continent* (1836) p. 7.
82. *Hand-book For Travellers in France* (London: J. Murray, 1843) p. 430.
83. See in particular M.J. Wiener, *English Culture and the Decline of the Industrial Spirit, 1850–1980* (Cambridge: Cambridge University Press, 1981).
84. R.W. Long, 'Notes of a Tour of Ten Days Among Some of the Beauties of North Wales' (1847) p. 69, MS. 5912b, NLW.
85. Alon Corfino has said the same of Germans in the late nineteenth and early twentieth centuries in his masterful study *The Nation as a Local Metaphor*.
86. E.H. Barker, *Wayfaring in France* (London: R. Bentley, 1890) p. 128.
87. Faber, *Life and Letters*, ed. by J.E. Bowden, 'Extract from Journal', p. 95.
88. Sewell, *Journal*, vol. 2, p. 37.
89. Revd. Trench, *Scotland*, vol. 1, p. 74.
90. W. Howitt, *The Rural and Domestic Life of Germany* (London: Longman, Brown, Green and Longmans, 1842) p. 6.
91. Carne, *Three Months' Rest*, p. 2.
92. Smith, 'Trip to Switzerland', Wednesday, 22 August 1855.
93. Miller, *First Impressions*, p.26.
94. Miller, *First Impressions*, p. 26.
95. C. Dickens, *Pictures From Italy* (London: Bradbury & Evans, 1846) p. 157.
96. Faber, *Life and Letters*, quoted on p. 109.
97. J. Cobbett, *Journal of a Tour in Italy* (London: Bolt-Court, Fleet St., 1830) p. 205.
98. *Handbook...Continent*, p. 189.
99. Cobbett, *Journal...Italy*, p. 128, and Howitt, *Rural and Domestic...Germany*, p. 6.
100. Howitt, *Rural and Domestic*, p. 6.
101. E.A. Freeman, *Sketches From French Travel*, p. 92.
102. See Everett, *The Tory View of Landscape*.
103. Cobbett, *Journal...Italy*, p. 89.
104. E. Wilberforce, *Social Life in Munich* (London: W.H. Allen, 1863) p. 287.
105. Bellairs, *Going Abroad*, p. 279.
106. A.G. Dunlop, 'Journals', f. 89v.

107. Quillinan, *Journal...Portugal*, vol. 2, p. 111.
108. Talfourd, *Vacation Rambles*, p. 61.
109. *Handbook...France*, p. 2.
110. Bellairs, *Going Abroad*, p. 279.
111. Talfourd, *Vacation Rambles*, p. 44.
112. S. Walker, 'Memoranda of an Excursion in the Mediterranean' (29 May 1837) Ms vols. 84 & 85, Friends Library, London.

Chapter 3   Religion

1. This paragraph draws on D. Cressy, 'The Fifth of November Remembered', in Porter, ed., *Myths of the English*, pp. 68–90.
2. On the relationship between Mary's reign and English national consciousness, see E.H. Harbison, *Rival Ambassadors at the Court of Queen Mary* (Princeton: Princeton University Press, 1940). For a discussion of the link forged between Protestantism and national identity in England from 1558 to 1642, see A.J. Fletcher, 'The Origins of English Protestantism and the Growth of National Identity', in Mews, ed., *Religion and National Identity*, pp. 309–17.
3. This discussion of the Tudor/Stuart calendar is based on D. Cressy, *Bonfires and Bells* (London: Weidenfeld & Nicolson, 1989) and Cressy, 'National Memory in Early Modern England', in Gillis, ed., *Commemorations: The Politics of National Identity*. See also A.J. Fletcher, 'The Origins of English Protestantism and the Growth of National Identity', on the growing link between English national identity and Protestantism between 1558 and 1642.
4. C. Haydon, *Anti-Catholicism in Eighteenth-Century England, c. 1714–80* (Manchester: Manchester University Press, 1993) p. 18. This paragraph is based on Haydon's study.
5. It should be pointed out that the law discriminated against Protestant Dissenters as well. Technically, they could not hold public office, nor could they attend Oxford and Cambridge Universities.
6. See Colley, *Britons*, 1992.
7. Protestant Dissenters received full political rights in law with the Repeal of the Test and Corporation Acts the previous year.
8. Colin Haydon makes this point as well for the seventeenth and eighteenth centuries. He notes that Protestant Dissenters, like Catholics, were often the victims of hostile stereotyping. In addition, violent outbursts were sometimes directed at Dissenters such as during the Sacheverell and Priestly Riots.

    The scholar who has argued most forcefully for religion as a force for both unity and diversity in Britain is Keith Robbins. See in particular Robbins, 'Religion and Identity in Modern British History', in S. Mews, ed., *Religion and National Identity* (Oxford: Blackwell, 1982) pp. 465–87; and Robbins, *Great Britain: Identities, Institutions and the Idea of Britishness*.
9. This discussion of religious background is based on Robbins, *History, Religion and Identity in Modern Britain*; E. Royle, *Modern Britain: A Social History, 1750–1985* (London: E. Arnold, 1987); and J. Wolffe, *God and Greater*

Britain: *Religion and National Life in Britain and Ireland, 1843–1945* (New York: Routledge, 1994). All statistics in this section on religious geography are taken from chapter 6 of Royle, *Modern Britain*.
10. *A Hand-Book for Travellers on the Continent* (1836) p. 77.
11. 'Among the Alps', by an Englishman, f. 60r; Richard, 'Journals of Tours to France, Belgium, and Germany' (1850) pp. 68 and 70.
12. Tupper, *Paterfamilias*, p. 80.
13. MacGregor, *A Thousand Miles* (1866) p. 256.
14. M. Betham-Edwards, *Holidays in Eastern France* (London: Hurst and Blackett, 1879) pp. 108 and 106.
15. Edwards, *A Year in Western France*, p. 41.
16. Morrell, *Miss Jemima's Swiss Journal*, p. 56 and Tupper, *Paterfamilias*, p. 118.
17. Trench, *Diary*, vol. 1 (1845) p. 315.
18. Edwards, *Holiday...Eastern France*, p. 205.
19. See J.W. Cunningham, *Cautions to Continental Travellers* (London: Ellerton & Henderson, 1818) and *Handbook...France* (1843) pp. xxxviii.
20. On colonial discourse in travel writing, see especially Grewal, *Home and Harem*; Morgan, *Place Matters*; and Pratt, *Imperial Eyes*.
21. A good example is when Englishman Charles Lucey passed by a Swansea Mechanics Institute where a religious service was being conducted. Upon entering, he found the sounds so 'unearthly' that he felt compelled to bury his face in his hat to hide his laughter. He described the minister as a 'coarse dirty Welshman' who insisted on blowing his nose with his fingers at the end of the service. Lucey noted, 'This so disgusted me that I immediately left these descendants of the Druids to worship in their unknown tongue.' Lucey, 'Journal of an Excursion to Wales and Ireland', p. 8.
22. Father B. Dalgairns, 'Letters to J.H. Newman', #41 (29 December 1847) vol. 6, Brompton Oratory.
23. W. Gladstone, 'Letter from Calais', 25 September 1845, in *Gladstone to His Wife*, edited by A.T. Bassett (1936) p. 56.
24. Marsh, 'Diary of John Marsh', 29 August 1849.
25. Bellairs, *Going Abroad* (1857) pp. 53 and 60.
26. Chambers, *A Tour in Holland, the Countries on the Rhine, and Belgium*, p. 49.
27. S.J. Capper, *Wanderings in War Time* (London: R. Bentley and Son, 1871) p. 314.
28. 'Logbook...Expedition...Florence' (1888) p. 126.
29. Combe, 'Continuous Journals' (1843) f. 14r, MS. 7423.
30. Cunningham, *Cummy's Diary*, p. 19 and R.L. Stevenson, *An Inland Voyage* (London: J.M. Dent, 1992; first pub. 1878) p. 79.
31. H.C. Barlow, 'First Part of my Tour from May 1841 to 1845', in 'Diaries and Journals, 1841–57', Barlow Papers, University College Library, London.
32. Griffith, 'Diary' (24 December 1859).
33. Quillinan, *Journal...Portugal...Spain*, vol. 1, p. 236.
34. Dickens, *Pictures from Italy*, p. 170.
35. Rev. H.P. Hughes, *The Morning Lands of History: A Visit to Greece, Palestine and Egypt* (London: Horace Marshall & Son, 1901) p. 6.
36. Dickens, *Pictures*, p. 195.
37. Howitt, *An Art-Student in Munich* vol. 1, p. 62 and Hughes, *Morning Lands*, p. 324.

38. Cunningham, *Cummy's*, p. 152.
39. Smith, 'Trip... Switzerland' (Thursday, 23 August 1855).
40. Howitt, *The Rural and Domestic Life of Germany*, p. 293.
41. In discussing differences among Protestants, travellers often noted such things as style of music, manner of preaching or whether the congregation stood or sat when singing – things that may seem trivial compared to the theological beliefs and principles shared by Protestants (though there are differences here as well). But matters concerning rituals and aesthetics were not trivial, especially in the eyes of those not part of the clergy. Comments about Catholicism show that church settings, music and displays often drew more hostility from Protestant travellers than theological matters.
42. H. Mayhew, *German Life and Manners* (London: W.H. Allen & Co., 1864) p. 497. Mayhew is exaggerating here. Public Registrar's Offices only became legal in England in 1838. Tolerance towards those dissenting from the Established Church had its limits in England as well. Oxford and Cambridge did not admit non-Anglicans until 1871.
43. Lucas, *A Wanderer in Holland*, 6th edn, p. 134.
44. E.G.E. Ward, *Outside Paris* (London, 1871) p. 22.
45. Brewster, *Letters* (1857) p. 238.
46. D.M. Craik, *Fair France: Impressions of a Traveller* (London: Hurst & Blackett, 1871) p. 137.
47. J. Dunlop, 'Journal', pp. 61 and 36. Instrumental music and hymns did not become accepted by the Presbyterian Churches in Scotland until the late nineteenth century.
48. Richard, 'Journal of Tours to France, Belgium, and Germany', p. 151 and Richard, 'Journal of Tours in France', p. 50.
49. Baxter, *Impressions of Central and Southern Europe*, p. 47.
50. Mrs Craik, *Fair France* (1871) p. 134. Once again, the importance of context is clear with respect to religious identity. When the context was pulpits and pastors, the similarities between French Protestantism and Scots Presbyterianism seemed striking to Mrs Craik. Earlier in the chapter when the context was hymns, the differences between the two types of Protestantism seemed paramount.
51. Trench, *Scotland, its Faith and its Features*, vol. 1, p. 273.
52. Borrow, *Wild Wales*, vol. 2, p. 356.
53. Trench, *Scotland*, vol. 1, p. 70.
54. Mr Sydow, quoted in Trench, *Scotland*, vol. 1 (1846) p. 249.
55. Trench, *Scotland*, vol. 1, p. 300. The Kirk and Free Church remained separate institutions until their union in 1929, by which time patronage had been abolished in the Kirk (1878) and Parliament no longer had the right to interfere in the spiritual freedom of Scotland's Established Church.
56. Ingleby, 'Journal of a Tour to Scotland', f. 42v.
57. Smith, *Journal of a Ramble in Scotland*, p. 70.
58. Miller, *First Impressions* (1847) p. 405.
59. Miller, *First Impressions*, p. 395.
60. Miller, *First Impressions*, pp. 10 and 376.
61. F.M. MacKenzie, 'Travel Journals' (1839–44) p. 30, MS. 2542, NLS.
62. C.E. Rawlins, 'Rambles in Snowdonia', (1866) f. 93r, MS. 23066c, NLW.

Notes 245

63. Legge, 'Journal' (1862) p. 268 and C. Braithwaite, 'First Journey on the Continent' (1892) p. 69, MS vol. S, 298, Friends House, London.
64. A. and A. Donaldson, 'Journey to Rome, 1880–81' (18 May 1881) F/DON/29, GLRO.
65. B.R. Mitchell, *International Historical Statistics: Europe 1750–1993*, 4th edn (London: Macmillan, 1998).
66. Trench, *Scotland*, vol. 1, p. 14
67. F.W. Faber, Letter #38 from Cologne, 25 August 1839 in 'Letters to Revd. J.B. Morris, 1833–63', vol. 17, Brompton Oratory.
68. F.W. Faber, Letter to Brother John Strickson from Florence, 27 February 1846 in *Selected Letters By Frederick William Faber*, edited by R. Addington (Glamorgan: D. Brown & Sons, 1974).
69. F. Faber, *Growth in Holiness; or the Progress of the Spiritual Life* (London, 1854), p. viii, quoted in M. Heimann, *Catholic Devotion in Victorian England* (Oxford: Oxford University Press, 1995) p. 27.
70. A.E. Twining, 'Tours Around Europe, 1866–71' (16 August 1868).
71. Howitt, *Art Student*, vol. 1 (1853) pp. 54, 3 and 6.
72. A.G. Dunlop, 'Journals', fs. 61v and 61r.
73. C.J.F. Churchill, 'Diary of Tours to the Continent' (18 May 1873) MS.17943, Guildhall Library, London.
74. This paragraph is based on R.J. Grace, 'Macaulay, Mummery, and Mystery: Christmas, 1838 at Rome', *Catholic Historical Review*, 74, no. 4 (October 1988) 558–70.
75. J.B. Greenshields, 'Journal in Italy' (1847–48) f. 15v.
76. Lamont, *Impressions, Thoughts, and Sketches, During Two Years in France and Switzerland*, p. 34.
77. Law, 'Journal of Lisbon' (1845) fs. 17v, 18r, and 18v.
78. Bowden, *Life and Letters of Frederick William Faber*, 3rd edn, p. 126.
79. Barlow Papers, #145, p. 12.
80. Mrs. F. Trollope, *Belgium and Western Germany in 1833*, 2nd edn, vol. 1 (London: J. Murray, 1835) p. 5.
81. J. Dunlop, 'Journal', MS. 9269, pp. 28–9.
82. Combe, 'Continuous Diaries', MS. 7426, 7429, and 7423 (13 May 1844, 11 July 1853, and 27 September 1843).
83. F.W. Faber, 'Letters From Abroad', #2 (Paris, 12 February 1846) and 'Letters From Abroad', #6 (Florence, 11 March 1846) vol. 16, Brompton Oratory.
84. This paragraph is based on Heimann, *Catholic Devotion in Victorian England*.
85. *Hand-book...Continent* (1836) p. 185.
86. Morrell, *Swiss Journal*, p. 13.
87. Fryer, 'Travels', 1 December 1844.
88. Richard, 'Journals...Belgium, and Germany' (1850) p. 123.
89. Faber, extract from 1841 journal, quoted in *Life and Letters*, p. 140.
90. M. Fountaine, *Love Among the Butterflies*, edited by W.F. Cater (London: Penguin, 1980; written in the 1890s), p. 35.
91. 'A Journal ...from Home', f. 63r, MS. 9233.
92. Trench, *Scotland*, vol. 1, p. 77.
93. Chambers, *Tour in Holland*, p. 11.
94. Smith, 'Trip to Switzerland' (26 August 1855).

Chapter 4 Customs, Comfort and Class

1. Blackburn, *Artistic Travels*, p. 167.
2. S. Smiles, *Self-Help* (London: J. Murray, 1859) p. 323.
3. Though meat seemed to be an important part of the diet throughout Britain, English travellers did identify with it more strongly than did Scots or Welsh travellers. And, one English traveller thought the Scots, at least those in Glasgow, to be indifferent to meat at meals. In Gosse's view, 'Shops entirely consecrated to sweets are in full display everywhere, and form a novel feature to an Englishman, but meat and potatoes Glasgow bodies seem supposed to never need.' 'Journal', f. 6r.
4. Lamont, *Impressions... France and Switzerland*, p. 33.
5. Mayhew, *German Life and Manners*, p. 313.
6. J. Matthews, 'Journal of a Tour in France, Switzerland, Germany' (1842) MS 23063c, NLW.
7. R. Perren, *The Meat Trade in Britain, 1840–1914* (London: Routledge & Kegan Paul, 1978) p. 1. The following paragraph is based on this study.
8. Perren, *Meat Trade*, p. 160.
9. Lear, *Edward Lear in Southern Italy*, p. 31.
10. Sir J.H. Lewis, 'Diary of Journey to Brittany and the Channel Islands' (5 June 1900) J.H. Lewis Collection, B86, NLW.
11. Smith, 'Trip... Switzerland', 22 August 1855.
12. Combe, 'Diaries', f. 131v, MS. 7421, NLS.
13. Edwards, *Year in Western France*, p. 99.
14. Linder, 'Tour', p. 29.
15. Faber, *Life and Letters*, Letter to Revd. F.A. Faber, 1843.
16. Barlow, 'Diaries and Journals' (1849) p. 49.
17. V. Verax, *Continental Excursions: Cautions for the First Tour* (London: J. Ridgway, 1863) p. 34.
18. Sir L. Morris, 'Journal', and Sir J.H. Lewis, 'Diary of Journey to Brittany and the Channel Islands' (1 June 1900).
19. Law, 'Journal of Lisbon', f. 29v.
20. Taylor, 'Journal', f. 15r.
21. H.E.H. Jerningham, *Life in a French Château* (London: Hurst and Blackett, 1867) p. 174 and Ellis, *Summer... Pyrenees*, p. 389. For a discussion of the significance of sincerity for Englishness by the early nineteenth century, see Newman, *The Rise of English Nationalism*, Ch. 6.
22. Tupper, *Paterfamilias*, p. 59.
23. Verax, *Continental Excursions*, p. 60.
24. C.W. Wood, *Through Holland* (London: R. Bentley & Son, 1877) pp. 160 and 29.
25. 'Day-Book on the Continent' (September 1862) f. 6v, MS. 8928, NLS.
26. J. Dunlop, 'Journal', p. 15.
27. 'An Excursion to the English Lakes and Scotland' (1857) p. 6, Acc. 8139, NLS.
28. See R. Sheppard and E. Newton, *The Story of Bread* (London: Routledge & Kegan Paul, 1957).
29. Price, *May in Anjou*, p. 16.
30. Lady S.C. Campbell-Bannerman, 'Travel Diaries' (1862) BM Add.Mss 41250 A.
31. Lamont, *Impressions... France, Switzerland*, pp. 47 and 7.

32. Morrell, *Swiss Journal*, p. 12.
33. The account in this paragraph is taken from Combe, 'Continuous Diary', pp. 15–17, MS. 7421, NLS.
34. Ellis, *Summer...Pyrenees*, p. 58.
35. Craik, *Fair France*, p. 67.
36. This comparison of house names is made by E.V. Lucas, *A Wanderer*, p. 75.
37. M. Betham Edwards, *Scenes and Stories of the Rhine* (London: Griffith and Farran, 1863) p. 109.
38. Holworthy, *Alpine Scrambles*, p. 27.
39. Jerningham, *Life in a French Chateau*, p. 36.
40. Fountaine, *Love Among the Butterflies*, p. 78.
41. For a discussion of the sincere behaviour code, see M. Morgan, *Manners, Morals and Class, 1774–1858* (London: Macmillan, 1994).
42. Wood, *Through Holland*, p. 128.
43. Eyre, *A Lady's Walks*, p. 193.
44. See J. Robertson, *Lights and Shades on a Traveller's Path* (London: Hope and Co., 1851) and Carne, *Three Months...Pau*, p. 67.
45. Mrs. Butler (F. Kemble), *A Year of Consolation*, vol. 1, p. 81.
46. Capper, *Wanderings*, p. 309 and R.S. Burn, *Notes of an Agricultural Tour in Belgium, Holland and the Rhine* (London: Longman, Green, Longman, Roberts & Green, 1862) p. 176.
47. Gissing, *Letters...to Edvard Bertz*, p. 38.
48. J.R. Green, *Stray Studies*, p. 53.
49. Wood, *In the Black Forest*, p. 19.
50. Taylor, 'Journal...Scotland', f. 165v.
51. Miller, *First Impressions*, p. 372.
52. MacKenzie, 'Travel Journals', f. 42v.
53. This paragraph on education is drawn from R.D. Anderson, *Education and Opportunity in Victorian Scotland* (Oxford: Clarendon Press, 1983; E. Begley, *Of Scottish Ways* (New York: Harper & Row, 1977); R. Bell and N. Grant, *Patterns of Education in the British Isles* (London: G. Allen & Unwin, 1977); and P. and F. Somerset Fry, *The History of Scotland* (London: Routledge, 1995; first published, 1982)
54. See Anderson, *Education and Opportunity in Victorian Scotland*, p. 8.
55. Somerset Fry, p. 217.
56. See Baxter, *Impressions of Central and Southern Europe*, pp. 22–6.
57. J. Holland, 'Letters From Llangollen' (1863) f. 62r, MS. 16722D, NLW.
58. This paragraph draws on *Handbook for Travellers in South Wales* (London: J. Murray, 1870) pp. 25–6.
59. Edwards, *Year in Western France*, p. 57.
60. Law, 'Journal of Lisbon', f. 28v.
61. I.A.R. Wylie, *Eight Years in Germany* (London: Mills & Boon, 1914) p. 173.
62. M. Browne, *Chats About Germany* (London: Cassell & Co., [1884]) p. 11.
63. Wylie argued that nature had become a background for sport to the English, with even mountains considered as things only to be climbed. He contrasted the German love of living outdoors and enjoying beautiful scenery with the English obsession with taking outdoor exercise, saying 'the Englishman plays games out of doors and the German lives.' See Wylie, *Eight Years*, p. 157.

64. G.C. Davies and Mrs M. Broughall, *Our Home in Aveyron* (Edinburgh: W. Blackwood & Sons, 1890) p. 207.
65. E.A. Salvin, 'Paris in 1855', in 'Journals of Foreign Tours' (copied 1860) p. 177, Ms. 6787/5, Barnet Local Studies and Archive Centre, London.
66. T.F.A. Smith, *The Soul of Germany, 1902–1914* (London: Hutchinson & Co., 1915) p. 1. In emphasizing the importance of home and domestic life for British national identity in the Victorian period, Smith and other travellers mentioned in this section challenge several scholars' view. Jane Mackay, Pat Thane, Chris Waters and John Taylor see Englishness and Britishness in the nineteenth century as mainly public and masculine. They argue that these national identities were not feminized and made more domestic until the interwar period. See J. MacKay and P. Thane, 'The Englishwoman', in Colls and Dodd, eds, *Englishness*, 191–229; Taylor, *A Dream of England*; and C. Waters, '"Dark Strangers" in Our Midst: Discourses of Race and Nation in Britain, 1947–1963', *Journal of British Studies*, 36, no. 2 (April 1997) 207–38.
67. Mrs Ellis, *Summer...Pyrenees*, p. 88.
68. Mayhew, *German Life and Manners*, 309.
69. Smith, 'Trip...Switzerland', 26 August 1855.
70. Griffith, 'Diary', 16 August 1860.
71. Davies and Broughall, *Our Home*, p. 211. Betham-Edwards speculated on the reasons for the different attitudes in France and England regarding emigration. She suggested that a typical French woman was very much a companion to her husband – more so than an English woman – but averse to leaving France to set up home with him elsewhere. English couples were more apt to stay together, in her view, even when faced with the disorientation of emigration. According to Edwards, 'the secret of English colonization lies not so much in national energy as in the tremendous strength of the marriage tie. A celibate bureaucracy...cannot compete with the family life characterizing Greater Britain societies.' M. Betham Edwards, *Home Life in France* (London: Methuen & Co.) p. 94.

Emigration Societies also helped to promote family life in 'Greater Britain'. A large number of unmarried men staffed the civil bureaucracies throughout the Empire in the second half of the nineteenth century. At the same time, there were more women than men in Britain itself, resulting in a growing population of single, or 'redundant' women. One purpose of the Emigration Societies was to facilitate the movement of unmarried women from Britain to distant imperial lands to satisfy the male population desiring wives.
72. Mrs Butler (F. Kemble), *A Year*, 11.
73. 'Logbook...to Florence', pp. 134 and 135.
74. Eyre, *A Lady's Walks*, p. 44.
75. For a discussion of how cities were transformed in the nineteenth century see M. Girouard, *Cities and People: A Social and Architectural History* (New Haven: Yale University Press, 1985).
76. V. Tissot, *Vienne et la vie Viennoise*, 2nd edn (Paris, 1881), p. 197 quoted in Girouard, *Cities and People*, p. 328.
77. Carne, *Three Months'...Pau*, p. 38.
78. Letts, 'Tour...Scotland', Monday, 16 August 1847.
79. Richard, 'Tour...Scotland', Thursday, 11 September 1879. On other occasions, Richard adopted a condescending tone when writing of Gaelic men

and women. When travellers wrote about someone they perceived to be inferior to themselves in terms of rank, wealth, culture, and so forth, they often used the adjective 'little'. Thus Richard wrote, 'Met a little Baptist Minister on board, not much to look at and very poorly and thinly clad, but a man of great intelligence, who was well acquainted with the Gaelic language in which he preached.' Richard, 'Tour... Scotland', Monday, 22 October 1879.
80. 'Tour in Scotland', by a Lady (1836) fs. 33v and 34r.
81. *Handbook... Continent* (1836) p. 18.
82. Carne, *Three Months'... Pau*, p. 1.
83. Tupper, *Paterfamilias*, p. 37.
84. *A Handbook For Travellers in Holland and Belgium*, 21st edn (London: J. Murray, 1889) p. 18.
85. M. Shelley, *Rambles in Germany and Italy* (London: E. Moxon, 1844) p. 8.
86. Wilberforce, *Social Life in Munich*, p. 215.
87. Morris, 'Journal', (1863) section about Ostend.
88. Smith, 'Trip to Switzerland', Wednesday, 22 August 1855.
89. Edwards, *Home Life*, p. 107.
90. Edwards, *Year in Western France*, p. 134.
91. Eyre, *A Lady's Walks*, p. 62.
92. Edwards, *Holidays... Eastern France*, p. 125.
93. Combe, 'Continuous Diaries', fs. 76v, 77r, and 77v, MS. 7421, NLS.
94. Edwards, *Year in Western France*, p. 114.
95. Chambers, *A Tour in Holland...*, p. 66.
96. Lamont, *Impressions... France and Switzerland*, p. 27.
97. On class relations in train station waiting-rooms, see J. Richards and J. M. MacKenzie, *The Railway Station* (Oxford, 1988; first pub. 1986) ch. 6.
98. Lucas, *A Wanderer*, p. 239.
99. *Handbook... Continent* (1836) p. 186.
100. This paragraph and the next is based on 'Tour in Scotland' (1836) fs. 41v and 50r, MS. 2729, NLS.

Chapter 5   Liberty, Language and History

1. See D. Cannadine, 'The Context, Performance and Meaning of Ritual: The British Monarchy and the Invention of Tradition, c. 1820–1977', in *The Invention of Tradition*, chapter 1.
2. See Colley, *Britons: Forging the Nation*; and Hugh Trevor-Roper, 'The Invention of Tradition: The Highland Tradition of Scotland', in Hobsbawm and Ranger, *The Invention of Tradition*, pp. 15–41.
3. See M. Duffy, *The Englishman and the Foreigner* (Cambridge: Chadwyck-Healy, 1986).
4. See J. Surel, 'John Bull', in R. Samuel, ed., *Patriotism: The Making and Unmaking of British National Identity*, vol. 3, pp. 3–25.
5. Sewell, *Journal... Summer Tour*, vol. 2, 179.
6. E.C.T. Carne, *Three Months... Pau*, p. 263.
7. Ibid., p. 42. A bit of mythmaking clearly had been applied to hedges by Carne's time. In fact, hedges emerged in former times as entrepreneurial

250 *Notes*

   landlords bought up freeholds and enclosed lands, making those working the land more, rather than less, dependent on the aristocracy.
8. Brewster, *Letters*, p. 193.
9. Trollope, *Visit... Italy*, vol. 1, p. 167.
10. 'Memo' (30 September 1850), in Foreign Office Correspondence – Passports (1870–73), FO 612 36, PRO, Kew.
11. Shelley, *Rambles*, p. xi.
12. Smith, 'Trip to Switzerland', pp. 12 and 13.
13. Baxter, *Impressions*, p.160.
14. *Handbook... France* (1843) p. viii.
15. J. Pardoe, *The River and the Desart: or, Recollections of the Rhone & the Chartreuse*, vol. 1 (London: H. Colburn, 1838) p. 14.
16. Burn, *Notes... Agricultural Tour*, p. 3.
17. A.G. Dunlop, 'Journals', f. 72v.
18. Smith, 'Trip to Switzerland' (1855).
19. Talfourd, *Vacation Rambles*, p. 4.
20. Sessional Papers, LXX (1872) p. 489.
21. 'Memo', Foreign Office Correspondence (28 September 1871), FO 612 40, PRO, Kew.
22. Chambers, *Tour*, p. 17.
23. Wilberforce, *Social Habits*, p. 306.
24. Barker, *Wayfaring*, p. 151.
25. Salvin, 'Paris in 1855', p. 216.
26. This paragraph is based on J. Dunlop, 'Journal', pp. 71–4.
27. Freeman, *Sketches*, p. 247.
28. Butler (Kemble), *A Year of Consolation*, vol. 1, p. 99.
29. Carne, *Three Months'... Pau*, p. 124. Compared to the Continent, Britain may have had fewer government regulations. But to say in 1860 that the British government forsook regulation in favour of free competition of interests obscures changes that were in fact taking place in the area of government behaviour at mid-century. Although 'free trade' and 'laissez-faire government' were popular in theory at the time Carne wrote, in practice the government was increasing its regulatory role, as the Anatomy Act (1832), Factory Act (1833), Poor Law Act (1834), Mines Act (1842) and establishment of central inspectorates for prisons and lunatic asylums (1830s and 1840s) suggest.
30. Chambers, *Tour*, p. 63.
31. Baxter, *Impressions*, pp. 141 and 143. Prussian officials turned serious attention to the state of elementary education as early as 1806 following their military defeat. The goal was to provide elementary education for all. In 1861, when the Newcastle Commission offered recommendations for improving elementary education in England and Wales, no mention was made of compulsory attendance which had been implemented in Prussia years before. Elementary education did not become compulsory in England and Wales until 1880; in Scotland in 1872.
32. Smith, *Soul of Germany*, p. 12.
33. Lucas, *A Wanderer*, p. 94.
34. Trollope, *Visit... Italy*, vol. 1, p. 168.
35. Lamont, *Impressions... France and Switzerland*, p. 324.
36. Tupper, *Paterfamilias*, p. 67.

37. *Westminster Review* (1854) quoted in R. Corson, *Fashions in Hair* (London: P. Owen, 1965), p. 410. According to Corson, *The Habits of Good Society: A Handbook of Etiquette for Ladies and Gentlemen* (1859) was the first etiquette book to condone beards.
38. Wilberforce, *Social Life*, p. 184.
39. I.A.R. Wylie, *Eight Years in Germany*, p. 33.
40. Wylie, p. 86.
41. Holland, 'Letters From Llangollen', f. 22r.
42. Long, 'Notes of a Tour of Ten Days Among Some of the Beauties of North Wales', p. 213.
43. H. Richard, 'Journal of a Journey to Switzerland', in 'Journal of a Short Tour in Switzerland and Italy' (1880) p. 69, MS. 10204B, NLW.
44. Wood, *Through Holland*, p. 231.
45. Fountaine, *Love...Butterflies*, pp. 53 and 54.
46. Fountaine, pp. 92 and 60.
47. Salvin, 'Journals of Foreign Tours', p. 219.
48. Holworthy, *Alpine Scrambles*, preface.
49. Eyre, *A Lady's Walks*, p. 7.
50. Pardoe, *The River and the Desart*, vol. 1, p. 80.
51. Pardoe, vol. 2, p. 218.
52. Pardoe, vol. 1, pp. 80 and 76.
53. See 'Regulations Respecting Passports', FO 612/40, 59, and 68. It should be noted that the reverse was true as well. That is, a foreign woman who married a British subject legally assumed her husband's status as a British subject – a status she retained after divorce or becoming a widow.
54. Jerningham, *Life...French Chateau*, p. 196.
55. Edwards, *Home Life*, p. 99.
56. M. Lucas, *Two Englishwomen in Rome, 1871–1900* (London: Methuen & Co., 1938) p. 101.
57. *Home Life*, p. 102.
58. To this day, there is some suspicion in Britain of written speeches. A factsheet published by the House of Commons's information office states forcefully, 'To maintain the spontaneity of debate, reading a prepared speech is not allowed (Members will call *"Reading"* loudly if they suspect a set-piece oration is being read out): not every Member, however, is a good extempore speaker, so copious notes are allowed.' 'Some Traditions and Customs of the House of Commons', no. 52 (London: Public Information Office, House of Commons, 1989) p. 4.
59. Bellairs, *Going Abroad*, p. 261.
60. Lamont, *Impressions*, p. 196.
61. Forbes, *Sightseeing...the Tyrol*, p. 205.
62. Sewell, *A Journal*, vol. 1, p. 15.
63. Dundas, 'Journal in Switzerland', fs. 3v and 4r.
64. Salvin, 'Journals of Foreign Tours', p. 296.
65. Smith, 'Trip to Switzerland', 27 August 1855. Though Smith's remarks suggest otherwise, one English traveller's comments indicate that this division of rural labour according to gender was not as marked in Scotland as in England. When in Jedburgh, Scotland Miss Taylor noted, 'Groupes of 50 & 60 men & women with their sickles were working together in one field – women

work in the fields as men do with us & are called bond women.' Taylor, 'Journal', f. 16v.
66. Howitt, *Rural and Domestic Life*, p. 45.
67. J. Cobbett, 'Journal...Italy', p. 118.
68. Tupper, *Paterfamilias*, p. 241.
69. Mrs Trollope, *Belgium and Western Germany*, pp. 310 and 312.
70. Lamont, *Impressions*,
71. Eyre, *A Lady's Walks*, p. 311.
72. Eyre, p. 161.
73. Eyre, p. 115.
74. Richard, 'Journal...France', p. 184.
75. Lamont, *Impressions*, pp. 5 and 224.
76. Marsh, 'Diary' (13 November 1849).
77. Lamont, *Impressions*, p. 297.
78. On this emergence, see R. McCrum, W. Cran and R. MacNeil, *The Story of English* (New York: Penguin, 1987) pp. 21–6.
79. Miss Taylor, 'Journal', f. 8r and Stephenson, 'A Trip', f. 64v.
80. Robbins, *Nineteenth-Century Britain*, pp. 31 and 32.
81. Gissing, *Letters...to Edvard Bertz*, p. 217.
82. C. New, 'Journal of North Wales' (1871) f. 6r, MS. 22021, NLW.
83. A carefully folded copy of the card can be seen in F. Sissons, 'Typescript of a Journal in North Wales' (1905), MS 23079E, NLW.
84. Combe, 'Continuous Diary', MS. 7428, p. 45.
85. Borrow, *Wild Wales*, vol. 1, p. 151 and New, 'Journal', f. 8r.
86. See McCrum, Cran, and MacNeil, *The Story of English*, pp. 60–1 for a discussion of this mutual antipathy.
87. Lewis, 'Diary', 1 June 1900.
88. See 'The Guid Scots Tongue', in *The Story of English* pp. 127–61 for a discussion of the Scots language.
89. Stevenson, *An Inland Voyage*, p. 28.
90. Smith, 'Trip', 23 August 1855.
91. 'Diary of Edinburgh and Perthshire' (12 and 14 September 1848) Acc. 8442, NLS.
92. Gosse, 'Journal', p. 4.
93. 'An Excursion to the English Lakes and Scotland', p. 21.

Chapter 6   The Discourse of National Identity

1. Cunningham, *Cummy's Diary*, pp. 94 and 145.
2. Trollope, *Belgium and Western Germany in 1833* and 'Logbook...Florence', (1888) p. 99.
3. Passport, FO 655/383, 1900 and Passport, FO 655/360 (1914).
4. Barlow, '1st Voyage Pisa, Genova etc. 1844', p. 36, Barlow Papers, #145.
5. Talfourd, *Vacation Rambles*, vol: 2, p. 237 and Burn, *Notes of An Agricultural Tour*, p. 197.
6. Borrow, *Wild Wales*, vol. 2, pp. 274 and 276.
7. Crick, *Sketches From the Diary of a Commercial Traveller*, p. 10.
8. Sir H. Campbell-Bannerman, 'Travel Diaries', vol. D, p. 46, BM Add.Mss 41248.
9. Edwards, *Home Life in France*, p. 143.

Notes 253

10. Smith, *The Soul of Germany, 1902–1914*, p. 342.
11. See in particular Burton, 'Who Needs the Nation? Interrogating "British" History', and Marks, 'History, Nation and Empire: Sniping from the Periphery'.
12. *Hand-book For Travellers in France* (1843) p. xxviii.
13. Lees, 'Notes of a Tour Among the Scenery of North Wales' (1849) chapter 3, MS. 1250D, NLW.
14. Miller, *First Impressions*, pp. 209 and 369.
15. Mayhew, *German Life and Manners*, p. 120.
16. MacGregor, *A Thousand Miles*, p. 93 and Craik, *Fair France*, pp. 32 and 211.
17. Bellairs, *Going Abroad*, p. 10. Emphasis is mine.
18. Quillinan, *Journal...Portugal*, vol. 2, p. 41 and Betham-Edwards, *Holidays in Eastern France*, p. 160.
19. 'Alpine Log' (1860) f. 79v., MS. 6343, NLS.
20. Eyre, *A Lady's Walks*, p. ix.
21. J. Dunlop, 'Journal', p. 28. Emphasis is mine.
22. Richard, 'Journal...Italy', p. 129.
23. Forbes, *Sight-seeing*, pp. 39 and 122.
24. T. Brown, *The Reminiscences of an Old Traveller* (Edinburgh: J. Anderson, 1840) p. 147.
25. J.H. Burton, *The Scot Abroad* (Edinburgh: W. Blackwood and Sons, 1881) pp. 153–4.
26. Trench, *Scotland*, vol. 1, p. 1.
27. Ellis, *Pyrenees*, p. 32.
28. Borrow, *Wild Wales*, vol. 2, pp. 41 and 43.
29. Passport Correspondence, 10 October 1871, FO 612 40.
30. 'Diary of a Tour of the English Lakes and North Wales' (1870) f. 105r, 12523, NLW.
31. Richard, 'Journal...Tours...France', p. 107.
32. 'Tour of Wales and Cambridge' (1860) p. 7, MS. 6266, NLW.
33. D.M. Lewis, 'Journals of Tours to Germany, Switzerland and Scotland' (1895 and 1899) 11638A, NLW.
34. Rawlins, 'Rambles in Snowdonia' (1866) f. 102r, NLW MS. 23066c.
35. Wood, *Through Holland*, p. 66.
36. Craik, *Fair France*, pp. 136 and 207.
37. *Handbook for Travellers in France*, 4th edn (London: J. Murray, 1852) p. xvi and *Handbook...Continent* (1836) p. xvii.
38. R. Chamberlin, *The Idea of England* (London: Thames and Hudson, 1986).
39. Smith, 'Switzerland', Wednesday, 22 August 1855; Cunningham, *Cummy's*, p. 76; and Ingleby, 'Journal', f. 3v.
40. Chambers, *Tour*, p. 19.
41. Trench, *Diary*, vol. 2, p. 151.
42. L.S. Lincolne, 'Visit to Holland, Belgium and the Rhine' (1855) p. 1, Thomas Cook Archive, London.
43. J. Carlyle, *New Letters and Memorials of Jane Welsh Carlyle*, edited by A. Carlyle, vol. 1 (London: J. Lane, 1903) p. 41.
44. Salvin, 'Germany and Switzerland', p. 337
45. Quoted in Holland, 'Letters From Llangollen', f. 62r, MS. 16722D, NLW.
46. Eric Evans argues that it is difficult to find evidence of an English identity during the period 1790 to 1870. According to Evans, 'British' was the term

used for patriotic identification, and when people from England identified with anything smaller than Britain it was with their local area. Travel journals suggest just the opposite, though local and regional identifications co-existed with English, Scots, Welsh and British ones. See Evans, 'Englishness and Britishness-National Identities, c. 1790–c. 1870', chapter 13.
47. Butler (Kemble), *A Year*, vol. 1, pp. 99 and 92.
48. Borrow, *Wild Wales*, vol. 1, p. 15.
49. J.W. Carlyle, 'Letter to Mrs Carlyle', (Scotsbrig, 1834) in *Letters and Memorials of Jane Welsh Carlyle*, edited by J.A. Froude, vol. 1 (London: Longmans, Green & Co., 1883) p. 6.
50. R.L. Stevenson, *The Silverado Squatters* (1883), Everyman edition with an introduction by T. Royle (1992) pp. 216–17.
51. Cunningham, *Cummy's Diary*, p. 94.
52. *Picturesque Tourist of Scotland*, 3rd edn (Edinburgh: A. & C. Black, 1844) p. 8.
53. *Handbook For Scotland*, reprint of 1894 edn (Newton Abbot, Devon: David and Charles Pubs, 1971) p. xxv.
54. Trench, *Scotland*, vol. 2, p. 273.
55. Miller, *First Impressions*, p. xi.
56. Borrow, *Wild Wales*, vol. 2, p. 232 and vol. 3, p. 79.
57. Borrow, *Wild Wales*, vol. 3, p. 160.
58. Potter, *The Journal of Beatrix Potter, 1881–1897*, transcribed by L. Linder (1966) p. 268.
59. Gosse, 'Journal', f. 34v.
60. For a discussion of nineteenth-century anthropometry, see J.S. Haller, *Outcasts from Evolution: Scientific Attitudes of Racial Inferiority, 1859–1900* (Carbondale: Southern Illinois University Press, new edn, 1995) pp. 3–39.
61. *Handbook... France* (1843) p. 105.
62. H. Campbell-Bannerman, 'Travel Diaries', p. 26.
63. *A Handbook for Travellers in Cornwall*, 9th edn (London: J. Murray, 1879) p. 13.
64. Lucey, 'Journal', pp. 21 and 8.
65. Combe, 'Continuous Diary' (4 and 5 September 1852).
66. Richard, 'Tour... Scotland' (11 September and 22 October 1879).
67. Gosse, 'Journal', f. 23r.
68. Mayhew, *German Life*, p. 325.
69. Shelley, *Rambles*, p. 174.
70. Capper, *Wanderings*, p. 37.
71. Blackburn, *Artistic Travel*, p. 3.
72. Edwards, *Home Life*, p. 300.
73. Wylie, *Eight Years*, p. 5.
74. Trench, *Scotland*, vol. 1, p. 35.
75. C.L. Smith, *Journal*, p. 15.
76. Carne, *Pau*, pp. 30–1.

Conclusion

1. See Anderson, *Imagined Communities*.
2. See Samuel, *Island Stories*, chapter 2.

Bibliography

Unpublished primary sources

'Alpine Log' (1860) MS. 6343, National Library of Scotland (NLS).
'Among the Alps', by an Englishman, mid-nineteenth century, MS. 10259, NLS.
Barlow, H.C. 'Diaries and Journals' (1841–1857) Barlow Papers, University College Library, London.
Braithwaite, C. 'First Journey on the Continent' (1892) MS. vol. s. 298, Friends House, London.
Burdon, J.C. 'Cook's Tour 1871', vol. b, Mss.Add. 179/83b, University College London Library.
Campbell-Bannerman, Sir H. 'Travel Diaries' (1855–64) BM Add.Mss. 41248, A-D, British Museum.
Campbell-Bannerman, Lady S.C. 'Travel Diaries' (1855–64) BM Add.Mss. 41250 A, British Museum.
Churchill, C.J.F. 'Diary of Tours to the Continent' (1868, 1869) MS. 17943, Guildhall Library, London.
Combe, C. 'Diary of a Continental Tour' (1837) MS. 7463, NLS.
Combe, G. 'Continuous Diary' (1841–1858) MS. 7421–7432, NLS.
Dalgairns, Father B. 'Letters to J.H. Newman', vol. 6, Brompton Oratory.
'Day-Book on the Continent' (September 1862) MS. 8928, NLS.
'Diary of a Tour of the English Lakes and North Wales' (1870) MS. 12523, National Library of Wales (NLW).
'Diary of Edinburgh and Perthshire' (1848) ACC.8442, NLS.
Donaldson, A. and A. 'Journey to Rome' (1880–81) F/DON/29, Greater London Record Office (GLRO).
Dundas, M.W. 'Journal in Switzerland' (July 1894) MS. 14199, NLS.
Dunlop, A.G. 'Journals' (1838–39) MS. 9265, NLS.
Dunlop, J. 'Journal 1845–46', MS. 9269, NLS.
Elliot, G.J., 4th Earl of Minto. 'Trip to Northern Italy' (1894) MS. 12508, NLS.
'Excursion to the English Lakes and Scotland, An' (1857) Acc. 8139, NLS.
Faber, F.W. 'Letters from Abroad', vol. 16 (1846, 1851) Brompton Oratory.
Faber, F.W. 'Letters to Revd. John Brande Morris, 1833–1863', vol. 17, Brompton Oratory.
Fisher, T.W. 'Tour Through North Wales' (1865) MS. 899D, NLW.
Foreign Office Correspondence. (24 May 1855) FO 612 11, Public Record Office (PRO) Kew, London.
Foreign Office Correspondence on Passports. (1870–73) FO 612 36, PRO, Kew, London.
Francis, H. 'Notes of a Three Weeks Tour Through Monmouthshire and Wales', 2 vols. (1837) MS. 11596B and 11597B, NLW.
Fryer, F. 'Travels in Europe, 1844', Ms. vol.s. 50, Friends Library, London.
Gordon, Lady C.D. 'Journal', 3 vols. (1842, 1844, 1846) MS. 15588–90B, NLW.
Gosse, E. 'Journal in Scotland' (1870) MS. 2562, NLS.

Greenshields, J.B. 'Journal in Italy' (1847–48) MS. 19768, NLS.
Griffith, W.T. 'Diary' (1859–61) MS. 10211 B, NLW.
Harris, K. 'Travel Diary in North Italy, 1847–50', BM Add.Ms. 52503, British Museum.
Holland, J. 'Letters From Llangollen' (1863) MS. 16722D, NLW.
Hutchison, Father A. 'Letters from the Holy Land and Egypt', vol. 27 (1857–58) Brompton Oratory.
Ingleby, C.M. 'Journal of a Tour to Scotland' (1842) MS. 8926, NLS.
'Journal of a Few Days from Home, A', author born nr. Dover. (1856) MS. 9233, NLS.
'Journal of a Tour in Wales' (1836) MS. 12392B, NLW.
Law, M. 'Journal of Lisbon' (1845) MS. 10340, NLS.
Lees, E., FLS. 'Notes of a Tour Among the Scenery of North Wales' (1849) MS. 1250D, NLW.
Legge, Lt.Col. E.H. 'Journal During Travels to Europe, 1862' F/SEG/902, GLRO.
Letts, T. 'Tour in the Lake District and Scotland' (1847) MS. 21691B, NLW.
Lewis, D.M. 'Journals of Tours to Germany, Switzerland and Scotland' (1895 & 1899) MS. 11638A, NLW.
Lewis, Sir J.H. 'Diary of Journey to Brittany and the Channel Islands' (1900) J. Herbert Lewis Collection, B86, NLW.
Lincolne, L.S. 'Visit to Holland, Belgium and the Rhine' (1855) Thomas Cook Archive, London.
Linder, S. 'Tour in North Wales' (1859) MS. 23065C, NLW.
'Logbook of the Expedition to Florence, The' (1888) Toynbee Hall Collection, A/TOY/12/1 GLRO.
Long, R.W. 'Notes of a Tour of Ten Days Among Some of the Beauties of North Wales' (1847) MS. 5912B, NLW.
Lucey, C. 'Journal of an Excursion to Wales and Ireland' (1848) MS. 23064Di, NLW.
Mackenzie, F.M. 'Travel Journals' (1839, 41, 44) #2542, NLS.
Marsh, J. 'Diary of John Marsh' (1849) Box Q4/2, Friends House, London.
Matthews, J. 'Journal of a Tour in France, Switzerland, Germany' (1842) MS. 23063c, NLW.
'Memo' (30 September 1850) FO Correspondence on Passports (1870–73) FO 612 36, PRO, Kew.
'Memo' (28 September 1871) FO Correspondence on Passports (1870–73) FO 612 40, PRO, Kew.
Morris, Sir L. 'Journal of a Tour Through Belgium, Holland and the Rhine', (1863) MS. 6938A, NLW.
New, C. 'Journal of North Wales' (1871) MS. 22021A, NLW.
Passport Correspondence. (10 October 1871) FO 612 40, PRO, Kew.
Rawlins, C.E. 'Rambles in Snowdonia' (1866) MS. 23066C, NLW.
'Regulations Respecting Passports', FO 612/40, 59, and 68, PRO, Kew.
Richard, H. 'Journal of a Short Tour in Switzerland and Italy' (1880) MS. 10204B, NLW.
—— 'Journal of Tours in France' (1849, 1856) MS. 10200A, NLW.
—— 'Journals of Tours to France, Belgium, and Germany' (1850) MS. 10205B, NLW.
—— 'Tour in Scotland' (1879) MS. 10208A, NLW.

Salvin, E.A. 'Journals of Foreign Tours' (copied 1860) Ms. 6787/5, Barnet Local Studies and Archive Centre, London.
—— 'Journals to Scotland and the Continent', 3 vols. (1851–60) MS. 6787/2,3 and 5, Barnet Local Studies and Archive Centre, London.
Sanderson, J.C.B. 'Cook's Tour 1871', 3 vols. Mss.Add. 179/83 a–c, University College London Library.
Sissons, F. 'Typescript of a Journal in North Wales' (1905) MS. 23079E, NLW.
Smith, J. 'Trip to Switzerland' (1855) Acc. 8736, NLS.
Stephenson, W.A. 'A Trip to Edinburgh and Glasgow' (1890) MS. 9234, NLS.
Stratton, G. 'Diary of Chester and North Wales' (1865) MS. 21992A, NLW.
Struthers, C. 'Notebooks' (1873) MS. 8901, NLS.
'Summer Holiday in Sutherland' (1888) MS. 10975, NLS.
Taylor, S. 'Journal of a Tour to Scotland' (1842) MS. 8927, NLS.
'Tour of Wales and Cambridge' (1860) MS. 6266, NLW.
'Tour in Scotland', by a Lady (1836) MS. 2729, NLS.
Toyl, W. 'Rambles in Wales' (1857) MS. 23178B, NLW.
'Toynbee Travellers' Club Log of the Expedition to Siena, Perugia, Assisi' (1890) A/TOY/12/2, Toynbee Collection, GLRO.
Twining, A.E. 'Tours Around Europe' (1866–71) F/DON/28, GLRO.
Walker, S. 'Memoranda of an Excursion in the Mediterranean', 2 vols. (1837) Ms. vols. 84 and 85, Friends Library, London.

Published primary sources

Barker, E.H. *Wayfaring in France*. London: R. Bentley & Son, 1890.
Barrow, Sir J. *Excursions in the North of Europe*. London: J. Murray, 1835.
Bassett, A.T., ed. *Gladstone to His Wife*. London: Methuen, 1936.
Baxter, W.E. *Impressions of Central and Southern Europe*. London: Longman, Brown, Green, and Longmans, 1850.
Bellairs, N. *Going Abroad*. London: C.J. Skeet, 1857.
Blackburn, H. *Artistic Travel in Normandy, Brittany, the Pyrenees, Spain and Algeria*. London: Sampson Low, Marston & Co., 1895.
Borrow, G. *Wild Wales: Its People, Language, and Scenery*. 3 vols. London: J. Murray, 1862.
Bradshaw's Continental Railway, Steam Navigation and Conveyance Guide. Paris: Gallignani & Co., 1847.
Bradshaw's Handbook for Tourists in Great Britain and Ireland. London: W.J. Adams, 1867, advertisements.
Brewster, M.M. *Letters From Cannes and Nice*. Edinburgh: T. Constable, 1857.
Brown, T. *The Reminiscences of an Old Traveller*. Edinburgh: J. Anderson, 1840.
Browne, M. *Chats About Germany*. London: Cassell & Co. [1884].
Burn, R.S. *Notes of an Agricultural Tour in Belgium, Holland and the Rhine*. London: Longman, Green, Longman, Roberts & Green, 1862.
Burton, J.H. *The Scot Abroad*. Edinburgh: W. Blackwood and Sons, 1881.
Butler, Mrs (Fanny Kemble). *A Year of Consolation*. 2 vols. London: E. Moxon, 1847.
Capper, S.J. *Wanderings in War Time*. London: R. Bentley and Son, 1871.

Carlyle, J.W. *Letters and Memorials of Jane Welsh Carlyle*, ed. by J.A. Froude. 3 vols. London: Longmans, Green, & Co., 1883.

Carlyle, J. *New Letters and Memorials of Jane Welsh Carlyle*, ed. by A. Carlyle. 2 vols. London: J. Lane, 1903.

Carne, E.C.T. *Three Months' Rest at Pau*. London: Bell and Daldy, 1860.

Chambers, W. *A Tour in Holland, the Countries on the Rhine, and Belgium*. Edinburgh: W. and R. Chambers, 1839.

Cobbett, J.P. *Journal of a Tour in Italy*. London: Bolt- Court, Fleet St., 1830.

Corner, C. *Rhineland*. London: J. Burns [1884].

Craik (Muloch), D. *Fair France: Impressions of a Traveller*. London: Hurst and Blackett, 1871.

Crick, T. *Sketches From the Diary of a Commercial Traveller*. London: J. Masters, 1847.

Cunningham, A. *Cummy's Diary*. London: Chatto & Windus, 1926.

Cunningham, J.W. *Cautions to Continental Travellers*. London: Ellerton & Henderson, 1818.

Davies, G.C. and Broughall, M. *Our Home in Aveyron*. Edinburgh: W. Blackwood & Sons, 1890.

Dickens, C. *Pictures from Italy*. London: Bradbury & Evans, 1846.

Edwards, M.B. *Holidays in Eastern France*. London: Hurst and Blackett, 1879.

—— *Home Life in France*. London: Methuen & Co., 1905.

—— *Scenes and Stories of the Rhine*. London: Griffith & Farran, 1863.

—— *A Year in Western France*. London: Longmans, Green, and Co., 1877.

Ellis, S. *Summer and Winter in the Pyrenees*. London: Fisher, Son & Co., 1847.

Eyre, M. *A Lady's Walks in the South of France*. 1864.

Faber, F.W. *Life and Letters of Frederick William Faber*. edited by J.E. Bowden. 3rd edn. London: Burns and Oates, Ltd, 1869.

Faber, F.W. *Selected Letters by Frederick William Faber*. edited by R. Addington. Cowbridge, Glamorgan: D. Brown & Sons, 1974.

Forbes, Sir J. *Sight-Seeing in Germany and the Tyrol*. London: Smith, Elder & Co., 1856.

Fountaine, M. *Love Among the Butterflies*. edited by W.F. Cater. London: Penguin, 1980; written 1890s.

Fraser's Magazine. vol. 57 (May 1858) 614–15.

Freeman, E.A. *Sketches from French Travel*. Leipzig: Tauchnitz, 1891.

Gissing, G. *The Letters of George Gissing to Edvard Bertz, 1887–1903*, edited by A.C. Young. Westport, CT: Greenwood Press, 1980.

Green, J.R. *Stray Stories From England and Italy*. London: Macmillan, 1876.

Handbook For Scotland, reprint of 1894 edn. Newton Abbot, Devon: David and Charles, 1971.

A Handbook for Travellers in Cornwall, 9th edn. London: J. Murray, 1879.

Handbook for Travellers in France. London: J. Murray, 1843.

Handbook for Travellers in France. 4th edn. London: J. Murray, 1852.

A Handbook for Travellers in France. 5th edn. London: J. Murray, 1854.

A Handbook for Travellers in France. 13th edn. 2 vols. London: J. Murray, 1875.

A Handbook for Travellers in Holland and Belgium. 21st edn. London: J. Murray, 1889.

A Handbook for Travellers in North Wales. 5th edn. London: J. Murray, 1885.

Handbook For Travellers in Scotland. 5th edn. London: J. Murray, 1883.

Handbook for Travellers in South Wales. London: J. Murray, 1870.
A Handbook for Travellers in Switzerland. 16th edn. London: J. Murray, 1879.
A Hand-Book for Travellers on the Continent. London: J. Murray, 1836.
Hansard's Parliamentary Debates CXV (20 March 1851).
Hare, A.J.C. *The Years With Mother*, edited by M. Barnes. London: Century, 1984; first pub., 1896.
Holworthy, S.M. *Alpine Scrambles and Classic Rambles*. London: J. Nisbet, [1885].
House of Commons Sessional Papers. XXVIII 545, 1852 and LXX (1872) 489.
Howitt, A.M. *An Art-Student in Munich*. 2 vols. London: Longman, Brown, Green, and Longmans, 1853.
Howitt, W. *The Rural and Domestic Life of Germany*. London: Longman, Brown, Green and Longmans, 1842.
Hughes, Rev. H.P. *The Morning Lands of History: A Visit to Greece, Palestine and Egypt*. London: H. Marshall & Son, 1901.
Jerningham, H.E.H. *Life in a French Chateau*. London: Hurst and Blackett, 1867.
Kitchiner, W. *The Traveller's Oracle*. 2 vols. London: H. Colburn, 1827.
Lamont, M.M. *Impressions, Thoughts, and Sketches During Two Years in France and Switzerland*. London: E. Moxon, 1844.
Lardner, D. *Railway Economy*. New York: A.M. Kelley, 1968; reprint, 1850 edn.
Lear, E. *Edward Lear in Southern Italy*. London: W. Kimber, 1964.
Lucas, E.V. *A Wanderer in Holland*. 6th edn. London: Methuen & Co., 1906.
Lucas, M. *Two Englishwomen in Rome, 1871–1900*. London: Methuen & Co., 1938.
MacGregor, J. *A Thousand Miles in the Rob Roy Canoe*. 2nd edn. London: Sampson Low, Son and Marston, 1866.
Mayhew, H. *German Life and Manners*. 2 vols. London: W.H. Allen & Co., 1864.
Merry, W. 'Through Europe in 1829', edited by Father M. Crowdy, *Oratory Parish Magazine* (August 1969).
Miller, H. *First Impressions of England and Its People*. London: J. Johnstone, 1847.
'Modern Tourism', *Blackwood's Edinburgh Magazine* 64 (August 1848) 185–9.
Morrell, J. *Miss Jemima's Swiss Journal*. London: Putnam, 1963; written 1863.
Pardoe, J. *The River and the Desert: or, Recollections of the Rhone and the Chartreuse*. 2 vols. London: H. Colburn, 1838.
Picturesque Tourist of Scotland, 3rd edn. Edinburgh: A. and C. Black, 1844.
Potter, B. *The Journal of Beatrix Potter, 1881–1897*. London: F. Warne & Co., 1966.
Price, E. *May in Anjou. With Other Sketches and Studies*. Edinburgh: D. Douglas, 1889.
Quillinan, D. *Journal of a Few Months' Residence in Portugal, and Glimpses of the South of Spain*. 2 vols. London: E. Moxon, 1847.
Ramsay, G.G. 'The President's Address', *The Scottish Mountaineering Club Journal* 1 (1891) 1–11.
'Recent Travellers', *Fraser's Magazine* 42 (July 1850).
Robertson, J. *Lights and Shades on a Traveller's Path*. London: Hope and Co., 1851.
Selous, F.C. *The Illustrated London News Record of the Glorious Reign of Queen Victoria, 1837–1901*.
Sewell, E. *A Journal Kept During a Summer Tour*. 3 vols. London: Longman, Brown, Green, and Longmans, 1852.
Shelley, M. *Rambles in Germany and Italy*. 2 vols. London: E. Moxon, 1844.
Smith, C.L. *Journal of a Ramble in Scotland*. Cheltenham: J.J. Hadley, 1835.
Smith, T.F.A. *The Soul of Germany, 1902–1914*. London: Hutchinson & Co., 1915.

Stevenson, R.L. *An Inland Voyage*. London: J.M. Dent, 1992; first pub., 1878.
—— *Travels with a Donkey*. London: J.M. Dent, 1992; first pub., 1879.
Symonds, J.A. *New Italian Sketches*. Leipzig: B. Tauchnitz, 1884.
Talfourd, T.N. *Vacation Rambles and Thoughts; 1841, 1842, 1843*. 2 vols. London: E. Moxon, 1845.
Trench, Rev. F. *Diary of Travels in France and Spain*. 2 vols. London: R. Bentley, 1845.
—— *Scotland, Its Faith and Its Features*. 2 vols. London: R. Bentley, 1846.
Trollope, F. *Belgium and Western Germany in 1833*. 2nd edn. 2 vols. London: J. Murray, 1835.
Tupper, M. *Paterfamilias: Diary of Everybody's Tour*. London: T. Hatchard, 1856.
Verax, V. *Continental Excursions: Cautions For the First Tour*. London: J. Ridgway, 1863.
Wilberforce, E. *Social Life in Munich*. London: W.H. Allen, 1863.
Wood, C.W. *In the Black Forest*. London: R. Bentley & Son, 1882.
Wood, C.W. *Through Holland*. London: R. Bentley & Son, 1877.
Wylie, I.A.R. *Eight Years in Germany*. London: Mills & Boon, 1914.

Secondary sources

Anderson, B. *Imagined Communities: Reflections on the Origin and Spread of Nationalism*. London: Verso, 1991, revised edn; first pub., 1983.
Anderson, R.D. *Education and Opportunity in Victorian Scotland*. Oxford: Clarendon Press, 1983.
Andrews, M. *The Search for the Picturesque*. Aldershot, Hants.: Scolar Press, 1989.
Bailey-Goldschmidt, J. and Kalfatovic, M. 'Sex, Lies and European Hegemony: Travel Literature and Ideology', *Journal of Popular Culture* 26, no. 4 (Spring 1993) 141–53.
Bebbington, D.W. 'Religion and National Feeling in Nineteenth- Century Wales and Scotland', in Mews, S., ed. *Religion and National Identity*. Oxford: Blackwell, 1982, pp. 489–503.
Begley, E. *Of Scottish Ways*. New York: Harper & Row, 1977.
Bell, R. and Grant, N. *Patterns of Education in the British Isles*. London: Allen & Unwin, 1977.
Böröcz, J. 'Travel Capitalism: The Structure of Europe and the Advent of the Tourist', *Comparative Studies in Society and History* 34, no. 4 (October 1992) 708–41.
Brass, P. *Ethnicity and Nationalism*. New Delhi: Sage Publications, 1991
Brendon, P. *Thomas Cook: 150 Years of Popular Tourism*. London: Secker & Warburg, 1991
Brockliss, L. and Eastwood, D, eds. *A Union of Multiple Identities: The British Isles, c. 1750–1850*. Manchester: Manchester University Press, 1997.
Burton, A. 'Who Needs the Nation? Interrogating "British" History', *Journal of Historical Sociology* 10, no. 3 (September 1997) 227–48.
Buzard, J. *The Beaten Track: European Tourism, Literature, and the Ways to Culture*. Oxford: Oxford University Press, 1993.
Chamberlin, R. *The Idea of England*. London: Thames & Hudson, 1986.

Clark, J.C.D. 'English History's Forgotten Context: Scotland, Ireland and Wales', *Historical Journal* 32 (1989) 211–28.
Clark, R.W. *The Victorian Mountaineers.* London: B.T. Batsford, 1953.
Colley, L. *Britons: Forging the Nation, 1707–1837.* New Haven: Yale University Press, 1992
Colls, R. Dodd, P., eds. *Englishness: Politics and Culture, 1880–1920.* London: Croom Helm, 1986.
Confino, A. *The Nation as a Local Metaphor: Wurttemberg, Imperial Germany, and National Memory, 1871–1918.* Chapel Hill: University of North Carolina Press, 1977.
Coombes, A. *Reinventing Africa: Museums, Material Culture and Popular Imagination in Late Victorian and Edwardian England.* New Haven: Yale University Press, 1994.
Corson, R. *Fashions in Hair.* London: P. Owen, 1965.
Cressy, D. *Bonfires and Bells.* London: Weidenfeld & Nicolson, 1989.
Cressy, D. 'The Fifth of November Remembered', in Porter, R. *Myths of the English.* Cambridge: Polity Press, 1992.
Donaldson, W. *The Jacobite Song: Political Myth and National Identity.* Aberdeen: Aberdeen University Press, 1988
Duffy, M. *The Englishman and the Foreigner.* Cambridge: Chadwyck-Healy, 1986.
Ellis, J.S. ' "The Methods of Barbarism" and the "Rights of Small Nations": War Propaganda and British Pluralism', *Albion* 30, no. 1 (Spring 1998) 49–79.
Ellis, J.S. 'Reconciling the Celt: British National Identity, Empire, and the 1911 Investiture of the Prince of Wales', *Journal of British Studies* 37, no. 4 (October 1998) 391–418.
Endy, C. 'Travel and World Power: Americans in Europe, 1890–1917', *Diplomatic History* 22, no. 4 (Fall 1998) 565–94.
Evans, E. 'Englishness and Britishness: National Identities, c. 1790–c. 1870', in Grant, A. and Stringer, K., eds. *Uniting the Kingdom?: The Making of British History.* London: Routledge, 1995.
Everett, N. *The Tory View of Landscape.* New Haven: Yale University Press, 1994.
Fletcher, A.J. 'The Origins of English Protestantism and the Growth of National Identity', in Mews, S., ed. *Religion and National Identity.* Oxford: Blackwell, 1982.
Foster, S. *Across New Worlds: Nineteenth-Century Women Travellers and Their Writings.* New York: Harvester Wheatsheaf, 1990.
Gellner, E. *Nations and Nationalism.* Oxford: Basil Blackwell, 1983.
Ghose, I. *Women Travellers in Colonial India: The Power of the Female Gaze.* Delhi: Oxford University Press, 1998.
Gillis, J.R., ed. *Commemorations: The Politics of National Identity* Princeton: Princeton University Press, 1994.
Girouard, M. *Cities and People: A Social and Architectural History.* New Haven: Yale University Press, 1985.
Gold, J.R. and M. *Imagining Scotland: Tradition, Representation and Promotion in Scottish Tourism since 1750.* Aldershot, Hants.: Scolar Press, 1995.
Grace, R.J. 'Macaulay, Mummery, and Mystery: Christmas, 1838, at Rome', *Catholic Historical Review* LXXIV, no. 4 (October 1988) 558–70.
Grant, A. and Stringer, K., eds. *Uniting the Kingdom? The Making of British History* London: Routledge, 1995.

Grewal, I. *Home and Harem: Nation, Gender, Empire and the Cultures of Travel.* Durham, NG.: Duke University Press, 1996.

Haldane, K.J. '"No Human Foot Comes Here": Victorian Tourists and the Isle of Skye', *Nineteenth Century Studies* 10 (1996) 69–91.

Haller, J. *Outcasts from Evolution: Scientific Attitudes of Racial Inferiority, 1859–1900.* Carbondale: Southern Illinois University Press, new edn, 1995.

Hansen, P.H. 'Albert Smith, the Alpine Club, and the Invention of Mountaineering in Mid-Victorian Britain', *Journal of British Studies* 34 (July 1995) 300–24.

Harbison, E.H. *Rival Ambassadors at the Court of Queen Mary.* Princeton: Princeton University Press, 1940.

Haydon, C. *Anti-Catholicism in Eighteenth-Century England, c.1714–80.* Manchester: Manchester University Press, 1993.

Hayes, C.J.J. *Nationalism: A Religion.* New York: Macmillan, 1960.

Hechter, M. *Internal Colonialism: The Celtic Fringe in British National Development, 1536–1966.* Berkeley: University of California Press, 1975.

Heimann, M. *Catholic Devotion in Victorian England.* Oxford: Oxford University Press, 1995.

Helgerson, R. *Forms of Nationhood.* Chicago: University of Chicago Press, 1992.

Hobsbawm, E. and Ranger, T., eds. *The Invention of Tradition.* London: Cambridge University Press, 1983.

Hobsbawm, E. *Nations and Nationalism since 1780.* Cambridge: Cambridge University Press, 1990.

Ishiguro, K. *The Remains of the Day.* New York: Vintage Books, 1993.

Jackman, W.T. *The Development of Transportation in Modern England.* London: F. Cass & Co., 1962.

Janowitz, A. *England's Ruins: Poetic Purpose and the National Landscape.* Oxford: Basil Blackwell, 1990.

Jones, R.M. 'Beyond Identity? The Reconstruction of the Welsh', *Journal of British Studies* 31 (October 1992) 330–57.

Kearney, H. *The British Isles: A History of Four Nations.* Cambridge: Cambridge University Press, 1989.

Kinealy, C. *A Disunited Kingdom?: England, Ireland, Scotland and Wales, 1800–1949.* Cambridge: Cambridge University Press, 1999.

Kohn, H. *The Idea of Nationalism.* New York: Macmillan, 1944.

Leed, E.J. *The Mind of the Traveler: From Gilgamesh to Global Tourism.* New York: Basic Books, 1991.

Lowenthal, D. 'British National Identity and the English Landscape', *Rural History* 2, no. 2 (1991) 105–30.

—— 'European and English Landscapes as National Symbols', in D. Hoosen, ed. *Geography and National Identity.* Oxford: Blackwell, 1994, pp. 15–38.

Lunn, A. *A Century of Mountaineering, 1857–1957.* London: Allen & Unwin, 1957.

Marks, S. 'History, Nation and Empire: Sniping from the Periphery', *History Workshop Journal* 29 (Spring 1990) 111–19.

Melman, B. *Women's Orients: English Women and the Middle East, 1718–1918.* Ann Arbor: University of Michigan Press, 1992.

Mews, S., ed. *Religion and National Identity.* Oxford: Blackwell, 1982

Mitchell, B.R. *International Historical Statistics: Europe 1750–1993.* 4th edn. London: Macmillan, 1998.

Morgan, S. *Place Matters: Gendered Geography in Victorian Women's Travel Books about Southeast Asia*. New Brunswick, N.J.: Rutgers University Press, 1996.
Murray, K.M.E. *Caught in the Web of Words*. New Haven: Yale University Press, 1977.
Newman, G. *The Rise of English Nationalism, 1740–1830*. London: Weidenfeld and Nicolson, 1987.
O'Connor, M. *The Romance of Italy and the English Imagination*. New York, London: Macmillan Press, St. Martin's Press, 1998.
Ousby, I. *The Englishman's England: Taste, Travel and the Rise of Tourism*. Cambridge: Cambridge University Press, 1990.
Pemble, J. *The Mediterranean Passion*. Oxford: Oxford University Press, 1988.
Perren, R. *The Meat Trade in Britain, 1840–1914*. London: Routledge & Kegan Paul, 1978.
Pocock, J.G.A. 'British History: A Plea for a New Subject', *Journal of Modern History* 47, no. 4 (December 1975) 601–28.
—— 'The Limits and Divisions of British History: In Search of an Unknown Subject', *American Historical Review* 87 no. 2 (April 1982) 311–36.
Pollins, H. *Britain's Railways: An Industrial History*. Totowa, N.J.: Rowman & Littlefield, 1971.
Porter, B. 'The Victorians and Europe', *History Today* 42 (January 1992) 16– 22.
Porter, R., ed. *Myths of the English*. Cambridge: Polity Press, 1992.
Pratt, M.L. *Imperial Eyes: Travel Writing and Transculturation*. London: Routledge, 1992.
Richards, J. and MacKenzie, J.M. *The Railway Station*. Oxford: Oxford University Press, 1988; first pub., 1986.
Robbins, K. *Great Britain: Identities, Institutions and the Idea of Britishness*. London: Longman, 1998.
—— *History, Religion and Identity in Modern Britain*. London: Hambledon Press, 1993.
—— *Nineteenth-Century Britain*. Oxford: Oxford University Press, 1989.
—— 'Religion and Identity in Modern British History', in Mews, ed. *Religion and National Identity*. Oxford: Blackwell, 1982, pp. 465–87.
Royle, E. *Modern Britain: A Social History, 1750–1985*. London: E. Arnold, 1987.
Said, E. *Orientalism*. New York: Vintage Books, 1979.
Samuel, R. *Island Stories: Unravelling Britain*. vol. 2 of *Theatres of Memory* edited by A. Light. London: Verso, 1998.
Samuel, R., ed. *Patriotism: The Making and Unmaking of British National Identity*. 3 vols. London: Routledge, 1989.
Schama, S. *Landscape and Memory*. New York: A. Knopf, 1995.
Schivelbusch, W. *The Railway Journey: The Industrialization of Time and Space in the Nineteenth Century*. New York: Berg, 1986; first published in Germany, 1977. '
Sheppard, R. and Newton, E. *The Story of Bread*. London: Routledge & Kegan Paul, 1957.
Simmons, J. 'Railways, Hotels, and Tourism in Great Britain, 1839–1914', *Journal of Contemporary History* 19 (1984) 201–22.
Smiles, S. *Self-Help*. London: J. Murray, 1859.
Somerset Fry, P. and F. *The History of Scotland*. London: Routledge, 1995; first pub., 1982.

Taylor, J. *A Dream of England: Landscape, Photography and the Tourists' Imagination*. Manchester: Manchester University Press, 1994.

Tissot, L. 'How Did the British Conquer Switzerland?' *Journal of Transport History*, 16 no. 1 (March 1995) 21–54.

Unsworth, W. *Hold the Heights: The Foundations of Mountaineering*. Seattle: The Mountaineers, 1994.

Urry, J. *The Tourist Gaze: Leisure and Travel in Contemporary Societies*. London: Sage, 1990.

Waters, C. ' "Dark Strangers" in Our Midst: Discourses of Race and Nation in Britain, 1947–1963', *Journal of British Studies* 36 no. 2 (April 1997) 207–38.

Withey, L. *Grand Tours and Cook's Tours: A History of Leisure Travel, 1750–1915*. New York: W. Morrow and Co., 1997.

Wolffe, J. *God and Greater Britain: Religion and National Life in Britain and Ireland, 1843–1945*. New York: Routledge, 1994.

Womack, Peter. *Improvement and Romance: Constructing the Myth of the Highlands*. London: Macmillan, 1989.

Woolacott, A. ' "All This is the Empire I Told Myself": Australian Women's Voyages "Home" and the Articulation of Colonial Whiteness', *American Historical Review* 102 no. 4 (October 1997) 1003–29.

Index

Access to Mountains Bill, 64
accidents, *see also* railway accidents; railways; road conveyances
   causes of, 44
   and illness, 44–5
   railway, 43–5
   road, 42–3
Act of Union (1707), 85, 104
Alexander III (of Scotland), 193
Alpine Club (English), 58
Anatomy Act (1832), 250 n. 29
Anglican Church, 86, *see also* Church of England
   in Wales, 87–8, 102, 107, 154
Anglo-Saxon
   view of Celts, 62–3
Anne I, Queen, 84
Anniversary Days Observance Act, 83
Arminianism, 107
atmospheric conditions, *see also* climate
   coal, 51–2
   and tolerance for colour, 51–2

Baedeker guides, 20, 21, 174
Baptists, 87
Barker, Edward Harrison, 164
Barlow, Henry Clark, 96, 112, 124, 197
Barrow, Sir John, 32
Baxter, William Edward, 64, 103, 137, 167
Bellairs, Nona, 20, 33, 38, 52, 79, 81, 95, 128, 147, 178, 201
Ben Nevis, 54, 64
Betham-Edwards, Matilda, *see* Edwards, Matilda Betham
Blackburn, Henry, 75, 119–20, 214
Blue Book Report (1847), 187
boats, 34–5, *see also* transport

Bonfire Night, 83, *see also* Gunpowder Treason Day
Borrow, George, 54, 70, 76, 103, 133, 188, 198, 203, 208, 210, 216
Boswell, James, 10
Boxall, William, 35
Bradshaw's *Railway Timetables*, 36
Braithwaite, Catherine, 41, 108
Brewster, Margaret, 41, 101, 159, 164
bribery
   effects of, 30
bridges, *see also individual bridges*
   as symbols of moderation, 72
britzska, 32
Brown, Thomas, 202
Browne, Maggie, 139
Burn, Robert, 163, 197
Burns, Robert, 185, 189
Butler, Lady Eleanor, 172

Cader Idris, 54, 70
calash, 32
cameras, 19, 22
Campbell-Bannerman, Sir Henry, 21, 198, 211
Campbell-Bannerman, Lady Sarah Charlotte, 129
Capper, Samuel J., 95, 214
Carlyle, Jane, 207, 208
Carne, Elizabeth, 21, 56, 74, 133, 145, 147, 158–9, 167, 170, 215–16
carriole, 32
Catholic Emancipation, 85
Catholicism
   diversity within, 107–9
   in England, 108–9, 114–15
   hostility towards, 84–6
   and national identity, 114–15
   perceived characteristics of, 93–100

Catholicism (*cont*)
  relaxed attitude towards, 85–6, 94, 109–14
Chambers, William, 63, 95, 117, 151, 164, 167, 206
Channel crossings, *see also* travel, vexatious aspects of
  discomforts, 28
  history and routes, 28
char à banc, 32
Chartism, 139
Chesterfield, Lord (Philip Stanhope), 130, 132
Church of England, 86, *see also* Anglican Church
circular notes, 31
cityscapes, *compare* ruralness and Englishness, 79–82
climate, 50–1, 71, *see also* atmospheric conditions
  effect on social and cultural life, 50–1
  and religion, 52, 90
Cobbett, James, 76, 77, 133, 181
colonial discourse, 93–4, 199, *see also* Orientalism
Combe, George, 17–18, 21, 43, 65, 113–14, 123, 129–30, 150, 187, 212, 215
comfort, 50, 120, 174–5
  cleanliness and, 143–6
  perceptions of, 143–9
  usefulness and, 211–12
commercialization
  and quantification, 16–17
  of travel, 16–25, *see also* Cook's Tours; Murray's guides; packaged tours; travel
Congregationalists, 87
Cook, John, 24
Cook, Thomas, 13, 14, 21, 31, 163
Cook's Tours, 23–5, 159 *see also* commercialization; packaged tours; travel

cost, 31
dissatisfaction with, 24–5
first foreign, 24
first world, 24
ticket, 24
Corner, Caroline, 48
cottages, 78–9, 81, 92
Craik, Dinah, 101, 103, 130, 179, 201, 205
Crick, Throne, 39, 198
Crimean War, 198
Cuillins, 64
Cunningham, Alison, 53, 98, 195, 206
Cunningham, J.W., 92
currency, 30–1
  exchange rates, 31
customs, 28–30, 162–3, 235 n. 51, *see also* travel, vexatious aspects of
  delays and, 30

Dalgairns, Father, 94
Defoe, Daniel, 47
Dickens, Charles, 75, 97, 98
diligences, 33–4, 36, 43, *compare* posting; *vetturino*; *voiturin*
  and national character, 34
Donaldson, Andrew and Agnes (née Twining), 108, 165, *see also* Twining, Agnes
Dundas, Mary, 18, 55, 179
Dunlop, Alexander Graham, 11, 12, 42, 110, 163
Dunlop, John, 34, 52, 101–2, 113, 126, 166, 202

education, 136–7
Education Act (1870), England and Wales, 137
Education Act (1872), Scotland, 137
Edwards, Matilda Betham, 68, 91, 92, 123, 131, 139, 149, 150, 177, 178, 198, 201, 214
Eisteddfodau, 138, 207
Elizabeth I, Queen, 84

Ellis, Sarah, 34, 125, 130, 141, 202
empire
    and landscape, 55
    and national identity, 199
English Church, *see* Anglican Church;
    Church of England
Entente Cordiale, 214
Episcopalian Church of Scotland, 87,
    105
Etnas, 42
Excursionist, the, 24
Eyre, Mary, 57, 77, 133, 144, 149, 174,
    181–2, 201

Faber, Frederick William, 21, 73, 76,
    108–9, 112, 114, 116, 123
Factory Act (1833), 250 n. 29
Fawkes, Guy, 83
Fisher, T.W., 55
Forbes, Sir John, 35, 179, 202
Forth Railway Bridge, 16–17, 72
Fountaine, Margaret, 116–17, 132, 173
Free Church of Scotland, 87, 104
Freeman, Edward A., 56, 166
Fryer, Frederick, 30, 116, 179

gendarmes, 29, 162, 163, 164–5
gender spheres, 178–84
George I, King, 84
George III, King, 85
Gissing, George, 15, 128, 134, 186–7
Gladstone, William, 94
Gosse, Edward, 9–10, 11, 12, 61, 193,
    210, 213, 215
government
    and liberty, 160–7
Green, John Richard, 50, 134
Greenshields, J.B., 111
Griffith, W. Tyndal, 66, 96–7, 142
guidebooks, 17, 19–23, 69, 88–9,
    92–3, 101, 162, 208–9, *see also*
    Baedeker guides; Murray's
    Handbooks
    affect on travel literature, 22

and national identity, 22–3
Gunpowder Plot (1605), 190
Gunpowder Treason Day, 83, *see also*
    Bonfire Night

Hare, Augustus, 19
Harris, Katharine, 38
Haussmann, Baron Georges E., 144
hedgerows, 73–4, 75, 77, 78, 81,
    158–9, 249–50 n.7
    Scottish hostility towards, 49
hierarchy
    obsession with, 130, 149–54, 170
    and recreation, 151
history
    and national identity, 190–4
Hogarth, William, 121, 127
Holworthy, Sophia, 16, 131, 174
home
    importance of, 141–2, 248 n. 66
    ties to, 183
Howitt, Anna, 51, 68, 74, 77, 78, 98
Howitt, William, 99, 110, 150, 170,
    180
Hughes, Reverend Hugh Price, 97,
    98
Hutchison, Father Anthony, 43–4

Ingleby, Clement, 70, 105, 206
insects, 41, 55
    remedies for, 55

Jacobite Rebellions (1715 and 1745),
    85
James I, King, 189
James II, King, 84
James IV, King, 193
Jerningham, Hugh, 131, 177
John Bull, 123

Keating's Powder, 18
Kemble, Fanny, 36, 37, 40, 134, 143,
    166–7, 207
Kodak, 19, *see also* cameras

Lamont, Martha, 57, 111, 121, 126, 129, 151, 170, 179, 181, 183, 184–5
landscape
  definition of, 47–8
  and empire, 55
  and liberty, 67–8, 74, 75–6, 78, 80–1, 157–9
  majestic, attitudes towards, 54–65
  and order, 68–74
  preferred viewing position of, 52–4
  and productivity, 81–2
  Tory and Whig views of, 78
language, 184–90
  and liberty, 185
  and national identity, 188–90
  perceptions of Welsh, 186–8
  Scots, 189
law
  women's rights in, 176–7
Law, Margaret, 49, 51, 111, 125, 135, 139
lazarettos, 41–2
Lear, Edward, 122
Legge, Lt-Col. Edward H., 28, 30, 107
Letts, Thomas, 53, 145
Lewis, Sir John Herbert, 122, 124, 188
liberty
  government and, 157, 160–7
  landscape and, 74–8, 80–1, 157–9
  language and, 185
  mountains and, 57–8
  passports and, 162–4
  Protestantism and, 100, 103, 156–7, 159–60
  restrictions on in Britain, 169–84
  trees and, 67–8
libraries, 147–8
Lincolne, Lucilla, 159
Linder, Samuel, 22, 58, 65–6, 123
Llanberis Pass, 22
Long, R.W., 172
Lucas, E.V., 20, 100, 140, 168
Lucey, Charles, 11, 28, 70, 212

Macaulay, Thomas, 110–11
MacGregor, John, 12, 50, 90, 169, 170, 201
MacKenzie, Frances, 107, 136
manners, 149
  national identity and, 128–34
Manning, Cardinal H.E., 114
Marsh, John, 42, 94, 184
Mary, Queen of Scots, 193
Mary I, Queen, 83–4
Mary II, Queen, 84
Mayhew, Henry, 100, 121, 141, 200, 213
medicinal products, 18–19
Merry, William, 30, 32
Methodism, 86
Miller, Hugh, 39, 49, 74–5, 106–7, 135, 200, 210
Mines Act (1842), 250 n. 29
Mont Blanc, 54, 65
Mont Cenis Pass, 31: Tunnel, 36, 39
Morrell, Jemima, 12, 20, 50, 91, 116, 129
Morris, Sir Lewis, 51, 124, 148
mountaineering, attractions of, 59–62
mountains, *see also individual mountains*
  attitudes towards, 57–67, 76
  liberty and, 57–8
Murray, James, 48
Murray, John, 19
Murray's Handbooks, 14, 19–23, 25, 40, 53, 54, 58, 63, 69, 71, 73, 76, 81, 88–9, 93, 100–1, 115, 117, 127, 138–9, 143, 147, 152, 162, 185, 200, 205, 211–12, 215, *see also* guidebooks
  adverts in, 17
  origins, 19
  authors, 19–20
  deference to, 20–2
  mistakes in, 21

Napoleon, 31

Napoleon III, Emperor, 144
national identity, study of, 2–3, 5–7
national identity discourse
  British, 196–203
  English imperial, 203–5
  English, Scots, and Welsh, 206–11
  racial, 211–15
New, Charles, 188
Newcastle Commission, 250n. 31
Nonconformity, *see individual sects*
  in Wales, 88, 102

octroi, 29
Orientalism, 7, *see also* colonial discourse

packaged tours, 23–5, *see also* commercialization; Cook's Tours; travel
Palmerston, Viscount, 26
Papists, 85, 90
Pardoe, Julia, 99, 162, 175
passports, 25–8, 40, 160–1
  definition and format, 27
  liberty and, 233–6
  national identity and, 195, 197, 233–6
  reform of British, 25
  rules regarding, 25–6
  value of British, 26–7
  women's, 176–7
patronage, 104
phaeton, 32
Philip II, King of Spain, 83
picturesque, 59–62, 72, 239 n. 21
Ponsonby, Sarah, 172
Pont d'Enfer, 21
Poor Law Act (1834), 250 n. 29
Popery, 108
port-a-loos, 17–18
posting, 32, 33, 36, *compare* diligences; *vetturino*; *voiturin*
Potter, Beatrix, 37, 145, 210
Presbyterian Church (Scotland), 87

split in, 104
Price, Eleanor, 68, 128
Protestantism
  beliefs and perceived characteristics, 90–2
  divisions within, 143–54, 244 n. 41
  liberty and, 100, 103, 156–7, 159–60
  national identity and, 83–6, 89–92, 100–7

quarantining rituals, 41–2
Quillinan, Dorothy, 51, 80, 97, 168, 201

railway accidents, causes of, 44, *see also* railways
'Railway Spine', 44
railways, 35–40, *see also* transport
  accidents, 43–5, 238 n. 83
  attitudes towards, 37–9
  journey times, 39–40
  origins, 35–6
  spread of, 36, 236–7 n. 66
  as symbol, 44–5
Ramsay, G.A., 49, 59
recreation
  domestic, 141–2
  drinking, 134–5
  hierarchy and, 151
  intellectual, 135–6
  music, Wales, 137–8
  national identity and, 134–42
  sport, 139–41, 247 n. 63
restaurants, 15, 140
Richard I, King, 202
Richard, Henry, 65, 66, 89, 102, 116, 145–6, 165, 172–3, 178, 183, 202, 204, 212
road conveyances, 32–4, *see also individual conveyances*
  accidents, 42–3
roads, 31–2, *see also* transport
roast beef, English, 121–2
Robertson, Janet, 133, 176

roulage, 32
Rowland's Kalydor, 18
ruralness, 76–9, *compare* cityscapes

Sabbath, the
  national identity and, 115–18
Salvin, Eliza Anne, 28, 29, 37, 41, 53, 141, 165, 174
Sanderson, Jane, 51
Scott, Sir Walter, 193, 224, 240 n. 48
Scottish Mountaineering Club, 49, 59
Sewell, Elizabeth, 54, 58, 73, 158, 179
Shelley, Mary, 130, 147, 161, 171, 177, 214
Simplon Pass, 31: Tunnel, 39
sincerity, 125, 132, 139
sketching, British passion for, 29
Smiles, Samuel, 120
Smith, C. Lesingham, 54, 105
Smith, James, 29, 36, 37, 41, 74, 99, 118, 123, 141–2, 148, 161, 180, 191–2, 206
Smith, Thomas F.A., 141, 168, 199
smoking carriages, 41
Snowdon, 15, 54, 55, 58, 233 n. 15
Spanish Armada, 84
St. Paul's Cathedral, 202
St. Peter's Cathedral, 16, 97, 111
steamers, 35
Stephenson, W.A., 16, 186
Stevenson, Robert Louis, 53, 96, 133, 190, 195, 208
Stornoway, 9–10
Struthers, Christina, 55, 65
Suspension Bridge, 72
Symonds, John Addington, 67

table d'hôte, 37, 118, 120, 125, 129, 134, 147, 151, 173, 184, 195
Talfourd, T.N., 55, 57, 69, 80, 82, 141, 163, 197
Taylor, Miss S., 125, 135, 186, 202
ticket tours, 24
Tissot, Victor, 144

tourism, 14, 16
Toynbee Travellers Club, 183
traditions, invention of, 5, 155–7
transport, 45–53, *see also* boats, railways, road conveyances, steamers
'traumatic neurosis', 44–5
travel, *see also* Cook's Tours; Murray's Handbooks; packaged tours
  annoyances and hazards, 41–4
  burgeoning of, 14–15
  commercialization of, 16–25
  delays in, 40–1, 43, 236 n. 54
  democratization of, 13
  identity and, 9–10, 12–13, 45
  meaning of, 9–13
  paraphernalia, 17–19
  vexatious aspects of, 24–31
travel literature
  changes in, 22
  identity and, 2, 3–4
  study of, 2
trees, and liberty, 67–8
trekschuit, 35
Trench, Reverend Francis, 29, 36, 73, 92, 103, 104–5, 108, 117, 135, 202, 206, 209, 215
Trollope, Frances, 112–13, 160, 169, 181, 197
Tubular Bridge, 72
Tupper, M.F., 53, 90, 92, 125, 147, 170, 181
Twining, Agnes, 28, 109, 183, *see also* Donaldson, Andrew and Agnes

United Presbyterian Church of Scotland, 87

vetturino, 32, 33, 75, *compare* diligences; posting
Victoria I, Queen, 144, 197
voiturin, 32, 35, *compare* diligences; posting

Walker, Sanderson, 40, 82
Ward, Emma, 101
Waterloo, 161, 197, 190–2
Westminster Abbey, 202
Wilberforce, Edward, 79, 147–8, 164, 171

William III, King, 84
William of Orange, 84
Wood, Charles, 48, 53, 57–8, 126, 133, 135, 173, 205
Wylie, I.A.R., 139, 171–2, 214